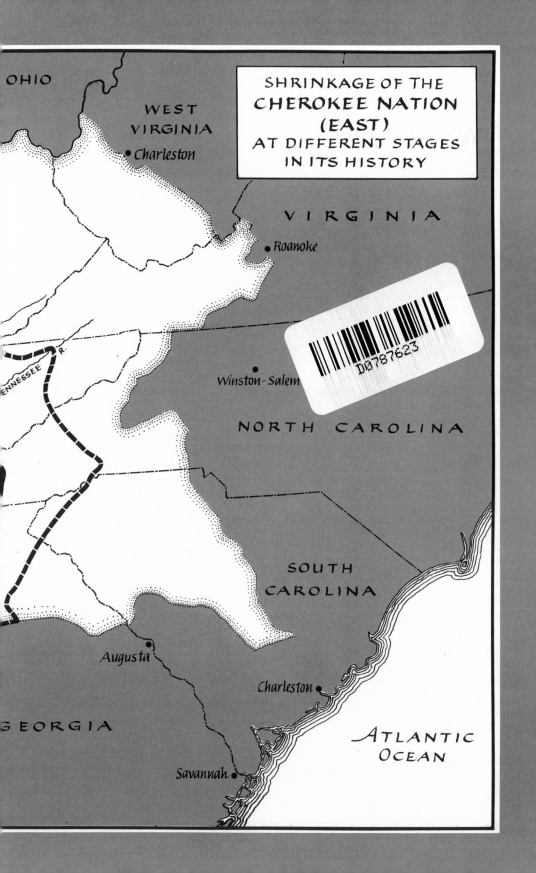

SHRINKAGE OF THE
**CHEROKEE NATION
(EAST)**
AT DIFFERENT STAGES
IN ITS HISTORY

OHIO

WEST
VIRGINIA

• Charleston

VIRGINIA

• Roanoke

TENNESSEE R.

• Winston-Salem

NORTH CAROLINA

SOUTH
CAROLINA

Augusta •

Charleston •

GEORGIA

ATLANTIC
OCEAN

Savannah •

Samuel Carter III attended Princeton, Oxford, and the Sorbonne. Since the 1930s he has been a prolific writer in several fields. His short stories have appeared in *Collier's* and *Woman's Home Companion,* as well as other magazines, and he has worked as a radio and TV script writer in Hollywood and elsewhere. Among his twelve previous books is his 1960 biography of Cyrus Field. He lives in Ridgefield, Connecticut.

CHEROKEE SUNSET
A Nation Betrayed

A Narrative of Travail and Triumph,
Persecution and Exile

by Samuel Carter III

DOUBLEDAY & COMPANY, INC., GARDEN CITY, NEW YORK
1976

LIBRARY OF CONGRESS CATALOGING IN PUBLICATION DATA

CARTER, SAMUEL, 1904–
   CHEROKEE SUNSET.

   BIBLIOGRAPHY: P. 300.
   INCLUDES INDEX.
   I. CHEROKEE INDIANS—HISTORY. 2. CHEROKEE REMOVAL,
1838. I. TITLE.
E99.C5C24   970'.004'97
ISBN: 0-385-06735-6
LIBRARY OF CONGRESS CATALOG CARD NUMBER 74-33634

For Barbara and Caleb

ᎣᏏᏲ ᎠᏂᎦᎣᏢᏗᏁᏏ ᎦᎮᏙᎿᏗᎢ ᎤᎣᎾ ᎠᏂᏃᏉ

(*Kind hearts are more than coronets.*)

CONTENTS

Illustrations

PREFACE

OF THE MANY civilized achievements of the Cherokees in the early nineteenth century, none outshines the development of their own written language, a feat unparalleled in American Indian history. Linked with that was their nearly simultaneous publication of the *Cherokee Phoenix,* the first Indian-language newspaper. Much of the material for this narrative is drawn from the columns of the *Phoenix,* often quoted verbatim—for it is time the Cherokees had a chance, as much of a chance as possible, to tell their story in their own words.

While the *Phoenix* published contemporary news, it undertook also to record Cherokee history, customs, legends, and philosophy, which up to that time had had no printed outlet for expression. There were the writings and official documents of white Americans, of course. But how often did these reflect the Indian truths, or the Cherokees' way of looking at things? Not that the *Phoenix* was always accurate or free of bias; but the Indians' role in American history has so often been presented by the white man from the white man's point of view that it is fair to present the Cherokees' side with whatever bias they are tempted to inject.

The *Phoenix,* however, had a relatively short life: only six years beginning with February 1828. Its columns, as noted, covered much previous Cherokee history, but after 1834 one must look elsewhere for the records. By that time, fortunately, literacy was well advanced among the Cherokees. Many had mastered their own tongue and could also write in English, so that, where the *Phoenix* leaves off, the correspondence of numerous Cherokee leaders, their recorded laws, speeches, memorials, and recollections, offer much insight into what occurred in the later years.

In the Houghton Library of Harvard University are the Papers of the American Board of Commissioners for Foreign Missions, which provide abundant material on the formative days of the Cherokee Nation, when its people struggled for preeminence and national identity through education and religious training. Nowhere in time or geography has the American missionary played a more courageous and enlightened role. The Mission Papers, mostly unpublished, cover the important period of 1820 to 1839 (including some subsequent years), and the writer is much indebted to the library's staff for help and guidance in reviewing this material.

For documents covering the Cherokees' prolonged dispute with Georgia, much was obtained from the Georgia Department of Archives and History in Atlanta, particularly from its massive collection of *Cherokee Indian Letters,*

Talks, and Treaties, covering the period from 1786 to 1838, and the Georgia Governors' Letter Books dating from 1831 to 1838. Together these give a comprehensive picture of both sides of the Cherokee-Georgia controversy and of important events and developments following the suppression of the *Phoenix*.

Western sources provide abundant material on Cherokee affairs both before and after their enforced removal via "the Trail of Tears" to Oklahoma. Of particular value to this presentation were the John Ross Papers in the archives of the Thomas Gilcrease Institute in suburban Tulsa. Since Ross saved, alike, copies of the letters he wrote and those that he received during his four decades as Principal Chief of the Cherokee Nation, his correspondence gives a two-dimensional picture of his own participation in Cherokee affairs as well as portraits of his enemies and his associates.

Visits to Cherokee historical locations East and West, while adding limited factual data to the record, provide an enlightening background to the story. The Qualla Reservation of North Carolina and the adjoining Cherokee Museum and re-created eighteenth-century Oconaluftee Village offer a glimpse of Cherokee occupations, craftsmanship, and mode of life. The Cherokee National Forest in Tennessee, one of the most striking landscapes in America, inspires an understanding of the Cherokees' devotion to their homeland. And to walk through the partial restoration of their capital at New Echota, or to visit the Ridge's mansion outside Rome, gives an idea of how they graced, with taste and sometimes elegance, this corner of their cherished world.

In the West, in Oklahoma, many Cherokee landmarks—especially the fine old homes that best expressed the Cherokees' continued quest for civilization— were destroyed in the Civil War. Only plaques mark the sites of mission schools and public buildings; graveyards such as the Ross Family Cemetery at Park Hill record on their headstones only dates and names of those who shaped the Western Nation. But Sequoyah's cabin still stands not far from Sallisaw; and at the traditional capital of Tahlequah, with its Cherokee Museum, the tragic pageant "The Trail of Tears" is still presented each summer.

There is a contradiction in the term "selective history." History is not selective. But in this narrative an atempt has been made to compress the Cherokee story into its essentials. There has been a deliberate omission of much statistical data that might be called for in a book of reference. And certain side issues, such as the Cherokee Nation's affairs with the neighboring Creeks, are not elaborated, to keep the focus on the Cherokees themselves.

Liberties have been taken, at times, with quoted material. Wording remains unchanged, but spelling and punctuation have occasionally been corrected for the sake of clarity, except in instances where confusion is a key to character. The spelling of towns and personal names is often a matter of arbitrary choice. Map makers, government officials, contemporary writers, and the Cherokees themselves applied different spellings to local villages and tribal leaders. One can only select a likely usage and abide by it.

More important to note is the fact that eyewitness accounts of Cherokee events may vary widely, a human trap that applies to history in general. Did Chief Junaluska save Andrew Jackson's life at the Battle of Horseshoe Bend—

or during an unrelated scuffle months before? You can take your pick of the varying accounts. But Jackson's indebtedness to Junaluska and his Cherokee allies remains unaffected by the choice.

Similarly there are numerous versions of the Tsali legend; of the shooting of James Vann; of the murder of Doublehead by The Ridge. Even on-the-spot reports of Cherokee Council meetings, at which historical issues were debated and decided, may vary according to the witness. Again, one can only accept the version that seems best to fit the circumstances, knowing that others may not agree with the selection or interpretation.

Thus any faults on the following pages are attributable only to the writer, and not to those who contributed so greatly and so generously to this work. Of the latter, there are many. My unmeasured thanks are due to the following for indispensable assistance and direction: Miss Ruth Corry of the Georgia Department of Archives and History; Franklin Garrett and Richard T. Eltzroth of the Atlanta Historical Society; David B. Estes of Emory University; Miss Paula Jean Richardson of the National Anthropological Archives of the Smithsonian Institution; Elmer O. Parker of the National Archives' General Services Administration; Dr. Thurman Wilkins of Queens College, Long Island; Miss Martha E. Shaw of Houghton Library, Harvard University; and Frederick E. Bauer, Jr., of the American Antiquarian Society.

Also to: Miss Marie E. Keene and Curator D. M. Pike of the Thomas Gilcrease Institute in Tulsa, Oklahoma; Librarian Jack Haley of the University of Oklahoma; Mrs. Martha R. Blaine of the Oklahoma Historical Society; Miss Lucinda Simmons of the Woolaroc Museum in Bartlesville; James Manford Carseloway of Adair, Oklahoma; Librarian Monteray Nelson of the Oklahoma Publishing Company; Mrs. Mavis Yoachum of the University of Oklahoma Press; Mrs. Helen Wheat, Special Collections Librarian at Northeastern State College in Tahlequah, Oklahoma; and Miss Agness Cowen, Co-director of the Cherokee Bilingual Education Program at Tahlequah.

And to: Mrs. Hildreth Daniel of the Cornwall (Conn.) Library Association and Mrs. Gunnar K. Holmes of the Cornwall Historical Society; Mrs. Carl Camp of the New Hampshire Historical Society; Mrs. Margie Douthit and Mr. Carol White of the Cherokee Historical Association in Cherokee, North Carolina; and Messrs. David J. Kaminsky and Kenneth H. Thomas, Jr., of the Historic Preservation Section, Georgia Department of Natural Resources.

The writer is much indebted to Dr. Henry T. Malone, Dean of the School of General Studies and Professor of History at Georgia State University, for his time and patience in checking the completed maunscript and for his invaluable corrections and editorial suggestions.

Finally, my thanks to Thomas O'Conor Sloane III of Doubleday for his encouragement and guidance throughout the preparation of this work; to Mrs. Virginia Canfield for her expert typing of the manuscript; to Alison Carter for her diligent correcting of the proofs; and to Mona Brady of New Echota, who showed me around the restoration of this ancient capital with an eloquent sympathy for her fellow Cherokees and an even more eloquent admiration for the writings of F. Scott Fitzgerald.

CHEROKEE SUNSET

1

The Glory and the Dream

IT WAS A DAY to remember, and their memories were long. Some historians would call it the greatest Indian battle ever waged on American soil. But to the Cherokees—proudest and most valiant of the southeast Indian tribes—the occasion had a deeper meaning. It was the day, March 27, 1814, when they fought beside their friend and brother Andrew Jackson, and turned the tide of the Creek campaign in favor of their ally, the United States.

If, indeed, it should work out that way.

But now it was noon, and so far, in the hours since daybreak, nothing had evolved but sound and fury. A blood-red Alabama sun bored through the smoke to highlight the crimson war clubs of a thousand Creeks, entrenched on the Horseshoe Bend of the Tallapoosa River. Across the narrow neck of the peninsula the "Red Sticks" had raised a seemingly impregnable barrier of logs and earth. Since dawn General Jackson's field artillery had pounded the barricade without effect. United States regulars, unable to advance against the murderous Creek fire, could only waste their bullets on an unseen enemy.

And on the east bank of the river, where the general had dispatched them, six hundred Cherokees chafed at the inaction. If Sharp Knife Jackson could not take that stronghold, they would have to take it for him—somehow.

Many of these braves had been with Jackson since the start of the campaign. It was a direct reversal of the course the Cherokees had followed faithfully for almost thirty years. Once warlike, and siding with the British in the Revolution, they had "buried the hatchet forever" by signing a treaty of peace with the Americans in 1785—a treaty which established their "inviolable boundaries" and their independence as a sovereign Nation.

From that point on, with only slight divergences, they had largely turned from hunting game to the civilized pursuits of industry and agriculture, as both Washington and Jefferson had counseled. They had engaged in trade and simple manufactures; had built homes and villages, roads and ferries, mills and trading posts; had supported schools in which to educate their young—toward the day when they might take their place among the white man's family of nations.

Then came the War of 1812. The Cherokees had every right to remain neutral. They were not committed by the treaty of 1785 to take up arms for the United States. But to the Cherokees the spirit of a treaty was as sacred as the words. They had pledged allegiance to their northern brothers; they could not forsake them in a time of crisis. First as individuals, then in organized groups, they dropped what they were doing to come to the aid of the United States.

In this they were the opposite of the Creeks, who were divided in their loyalties. While many Creeks were friendly to the United States, a large portion, known as "Red Sticks," partially prompted by Tecumseh, saw in this second war with England a chance to renew hostilities against the white Americans. The Creek War, or Creek Insurrection, call it what you will, flamed into action with the massacre of five hundred white civilians at Fort Mims, Alabama, in late August 1813. Five weeks later Andrew Jackson launched his counter-campaign against the Red Sticks, handicapped at first by lack of troops, provisions, and knowledge of the Indian terrain. Indian Agent Jonathan Meigs, acting in behalf of the United States Government, appealed for Cherokee support. The Cherokees responded almost to a man, while those who remained at home, including the women, worked on their farms to furnish food and provisions for the troops.

Chief Pathkiller of the Cherokees, too old for action himself, instructed a full-blood warrior, The Ridge, to call for volunteers. He chose well when he chose The Ridge. The name itself was magic among the Cherokees, signifying one who walked on mountain ridges and saw farther than his fellows. The Ridge donned battle dress, mounted his favorite horse, and rode through the Cherokee Nation to collect recruits. Some six to eight hundred braves responded; there would have been more if he had asked for them.

They were the cream of the Cherokee Nation who joined Jackson's forces in the winter of 1813-14, wearing feathers and deer tails on their heads to distinguish them from the enemy. Many bore English names inherited from white forebears or adopted for convenience. Jackson gave them appropriate military titles: Colonel Gideon Morgan in top command; Lieutenant Colonels John Lowrey and Richard Brown; Majors John Walker, Alexander Saunders, and The Ridge, who cherished the title of Major Ridge for years to come; and a one-eighth Cherokee named Guwisguwi, or John Ross, whom Jackson selected as his adjutant and who scouted the site of the general's first great victory at Talladega.

Others also bore proud English-rendered names that history might little note but the Cherokees would long remember: Captain Richard Taylor, who would talk with American Presidents in Washington; Charles Hicks, who would someday be Principal Chief of the Cherokee Nation; a slightly lame mixed-breed named George Guess or Gist, whom the English-speaking world would honor as Sequoyah; and an "invincible" warrior named Dasigiyagi, or Shoe Boots, who knew the magic Indian formulas for blunting an adversary's sword or stopping a bullet in midair. Jackson affectionately dubbed him "the Rooster," for the cock's crow he used as a private war cry, and half believed his claim of immortality.

As Jackson's forces reached the Tallapoosa before dawn on the day of battle, General John Coffee, second in command, led the Cherokees across the river to a position opposite the Creek encampment. Here they blocked the enemy's only possible escape route, should the Creeks try to withdraw by means of the fleet canoes they kept in readiness on their side of the river.

Jackson, meanwhile, marshaled his remaining troops, which included the crack 39th U. S. Infantry, before the Creek fortifications across the neck of the peninsula. Since the river could not be forded at this point, he was committed to a frontal assault against the ramparts. Coffee had told him that nothing could breach those earthworks but artillery fire, and the general had produced two puny six-pound field guns that shelled the target from eighty yards away. The shot buried itself harmlessly in the soft earth of the barricades while the Creek sharpshooters picked off the gunners as fast as Jackson could replace them.

So it went, hour after hour, through the morning. Ensign Sam Houston had replaced John Ross as Jackson's adjutant when Ross had joined his fellow Cherokees across the river. He had vowed that the public would "hear of me" before this campaign was over, and he, too, chafed at the inaction. Was there a chance that Jackson would withdraw? Seemingly impregnable in their river-girt, hundred-acre stronghold, the Creeks continued to taunt the Americans with derisive whoops and stinging rifle fire, challenging the paleface general to bring his men a little closer.

On the opposite bank John Coffee with a thousand legionaries, most of them Cherokees, was as helpless as his commanding officer. He could do nothing but observe the stalemate, and later recorded his impression. Of the Cherokees he noted that

. . . they could no longer remain silent spectators. While some kept up a fire across the river to prevent the enemy's approach to the bank, others plunged into the water and swam the river for canoes that lay at the other shore in considerable numbers and brought them over, in which crafts a number of them embarked and landed on the bend within the enemy.[1]

Precisely which of the Cherokees first thought of seizing the canoes, crossing the river, and attacking the enemy's rear is open to dispute. Some said it was Major Ridge, and others, The Ridge's nephew by marriage, Charles Reese. One contemporary chronicler gave the credit to Chief Junaluska, despite the fact that his name meant "One Who Tries but Fails." Twenty years later, however, the United States Congress heard from Representative Henry Wise that John Ross was first to risk his life by swimming across the river to capture the Creek canoes.

There was enough glory in the act for all to share. It took the enemy by surprise. As fast as the captured canoes could bring them over, all six hundred Cherokees stormed up the bank of the peninsula and fell upon the rear-guard Creeks. Disposing of these, they fought their way across the hundred acres to come on the main body of defenders from behind. Creek forces turned from the ramparts to meet the new threat, and in that diversion Jackson saw his chance. He ordered his infantry to charge the breastworks.

Major Lemuel P. Montgomery led the assault and fell dead atop the barricade. Close behind came Ensign Houston, clawing his way up the steep face of the parapet and down into the midst of howling Creeks. The Americans who followed saw him flailing away with his sword at the surrounding Creeks, with an arrow protruding from his thigh. He yelled at a private to yank the arrow out while he held off his attackers. Later a bullet smashed his shoulder, another shattered his arm, but he kept on fighting till he dropped from loss of blood. As he had vowed, the people would hear of young Sam Houston.

There was no longer any form or order to the struggle. Three thousand screaming men fought twenty different battles in that small enclosure, using knives, swords, tomahawks, and bare hands when they got too close for rifles. The Creeks asked and gave no quarter. "Not a warrior offered to surrender," recalled Ensign Houston, "even while the sword was at his breast." They battled for every foot of ground, slipping back into a natural ravine and fighting from this shelter, then withdrawing to a thicket in the center of their demi-island. Jackson ordered the thicket set afire and gave them the choice of being burned alive or shot as they emerged. Some two hundred plunged into the river and were massacred by Cherokee sharpshooters as they tried to swim across. "Few ever reached the bank," wrote General Coffee, "and that few was killed the instant they landed."

In Jackson's official report of the engagement, the general wrote:

The enemy, although many of them fought to the last with that kind of bravery which desperation inspires, were at last entirely routed and cut to pieces. The battle may be said to have continued with severity for about five hours, but the firing and slaughter continued until it was suspended by the darkness of night.[2]

To his wife Rachel at the Hermitage in Nashville the general gave an even more succinct report. "The *carnage,*" he wrote, "was *dreadfull.*" For one who held Indian life of little value, it sounded almost like the outcry of a stricken conscience.

By nightfall the battle had subsided. Almost a thousand dead and dying Red Sticks cluttered the bloody hundred acres or lay half buried on the muddy banks. By contrast, though the figures would vary according to the source, Jackson lost only forty-four killed, of whom eighteen, or almost half, were Cherokees. Shoe Boots, despite his knowledge of protective magic, was among the missing. "Poor old cock," said Jackson, "he has crowed his last." Then a shrill whoop sounded from the smoldering thicket and the grinning Shoe Boots trotted out, smoke-grimed and bloodied, with a Creek scalp in his hand.

The Creek campaign was over, and the Cherokees' decisive part in that campaign was history. But history was about to take some unexpected turns.

With the Creeks subdued, never to rise in force again, the Cherokees returned home to their Nation—then occupying sizable portions of Georgia, Alabama, Tennessee, and the Carolinas—where many had productive farms and prosperous plantations. During the early months of the War of 1812, before they had left to fight the Creeks, these farmers and planters had helped alleviate the famine threatening American troops by supplying the soldiers with beef, corn, and pork, along with fodder for their horses.

They came back to find their charity shabbily rewarded. During their absence, these same American troops, or others like them, had ravaged their lands as the regiments moved north and south in military operations. In fact, the Cherokees had suffered more from United States soldiers than from their enemies, the Creeks. Among the marauding troops, young Davy Crockett, who would one day be an influential champion of Cherokee ambitions, confessed to the slaughter of "a large gang of hogs" to feed his itinerant campmates.

Sadly the Cherokees began repairing fences, barns, and corncribs torn down for firewood, and protested to Indian Agent Meigs the loss of their cattle, horses, hogs, and chickens. Meigs carried their protest to the Secretary of War, writing in part:

These depredations may at first sight seem incredible: but I have no doubt of the justice of the statements: they are well known to thousands. I received a letter from an officer of high rank in the army, in which he says, "The return of the Horse [cavalry] thro' their country has been marked by plunder & prodigal, unnecessary and wanton destruction of property: their stocks of cattle & hogs have been shot & suffered to rot untouched—their horses in some instances shared the same fate; their clothing intended to defend them from the wet & cold in the present campaign has been stolen and in some instances where they remonstrated their lives have been threatened.[3]

Though many Cherokees filed claims for their losses with Agent Meigs, who passed them on to the War Department, there was no promise that these claims would be acknowledged. One of the chief obstructionists to justice for the victimized Cherokees was Andrew Jackson, who called their charges "one complete tissue of groundless falsehood, exceeding all corruption." He, for one, would delay the payment of compensation to the Cherokees as long as possible.

There was more disillusionment to come, essentially from the same direction. In the treaty of peace which Jackson forced upon the vanquished Creeks in August 1814, the general demanded the cession of twenty-three million acres of land to the United States, approximately half the later state of Alabama. The terms were severe, but perhaps no more than a victor might rightfully exact from a defeated enemy.

The flaw in this treaty was that four million acres of the ceded lands were claimed by the Cherokee Nation. Again the Cherokees protested—to Meigs, to Madison, to the War Department. Again their former ally Jackson branded these claims as "Cherokee intrigue," even suggesting to the War Department that, with United States troops already in the field, this might be an opportune time to drive the Cherokees, as well as the Creeks, from all their landholdings in the state of Tennessee.

One could say that thus began the great betrayal. But broken treaties, broken promises, had marked the history of Cherokee-American relations since the last days of the Revolution. More to the point, this marked the drawing of new battle lines, in which allegiances were redefined and ancient allies became future foes.

Ten months later, Andrew Jackson went on to glory at the Battle of New Orleans, to become not only a national hero but in time the President of the United States.

John Ross, his onetime adjutant, rose in the ranks of Cherokee leaders to become, almost on the day of Jackson's inauguration, Principal Chief of the independent, sovereign Cherokee Nation.

When the smoke had cleared at Horseshoe Bend, they had thought of themselves, perhaps, as lifetime allies. Before that memory appreciably faded, they were lifetime enemies, dedicated to a quarter century of battle that was just beginning.

Perhaps the conflict was purely a matter of the color of one's skin, aggravated and accentuated by the greatest catalyst of all mankind's destructive impulse: human greed. Curiously, none of this seemed evident when Hernando de Soto arrived among the Cherokees in 1540, coming via the Winding Stair Trail across the southern Alleghenies. The Cherokees were neither envious nor fearful of these velvet-clad, steel-armored strangers with skull-colored faces. They welcomed them with a minimum of courtesy, spread food before them, but disdained to eat with the barbarians.

When de Soto and his men departed, the Cherokees forgot them, not even recording the occasion on their wampum belts—in itself an extraordinary footnote in the history of the Spanish conquistadors, who generally made sure, by wholesale slaughter of the natives, that they would not be forgotten.

But if de Soto brought the Cherokees nothing and taught them nothing, they acquired two priceless possessions from the Spanish colonists who followed in de Soto's wake: guns and horses—generally stolen in swift raids on Spanish settlements. It was these which helped create their warrior image among the later, eighteenth-century English colonists who settled in neighboring Virginia and the Carolinas. Wrote one of these, a Charleston planter named William Fyffe:

War is their principal study & their greatest ambition is to distinguish themselves by military actions . . . Their young men are not regarded till they kill an enemy or take a prisoner. Those houses in which there is the greatest number of scalps are most honoured. A scalp is as great a Trophy among them as a pair of colours among us.[4]

This martial posture made the Cherokees potentially useful allies in the European struggle for supremacy in North America, and also presented a problem to the English settlers of the early eighteenth century. The detailing of the irritating minor skirmishes between the Indians and whites makes repetitious reading. They became important only in relation to the larger conflict between the British and the French in North America. The Cherokees cared little for either—though leaning toward the florid Gallic courtesy of the French—but both European powers courted an alliance with the Indians, beginning as early as 1730.

Early on the scene of rivalry was a quixotic Scot named Sir Alexander Cuming, who engineered the first diplomatic contact between Cherokees and Europeans. Sent by the Crown in 1730 to wean the Indians from the French, Sir Alexander arranged for seven outstanding members of the tribe—Chief Attacullaculla, or "the Little Carpenter," among them—to accompany him back to England for an audience with King George II.

The visit was a landmark in Cherokee affairs. Housed in the basement of a Covent Garden mortuary, the chiefs were coached in manners of court and two weeks later appeared before the King at Windsor Castle, mostly naked except for a horse-tail breechclout and feathered headdress. Presenting His Majesty with a symbolic crown of eagle tails and human scalps, they received in return gifts obviously suggested by their mode of dress: voluminous garments of silk and satin trimmed with gold.

Thus clad, they were paraded around London in a coach-and-four, flanked by mounted grenadiers, and lionized by society wherever they appeared. They attended the theater, where they stole the show; sat for their portraits for His Grace the Duke of Montague; and dined on a saddle of mutton at Shakespeare's Mermaid Tavern.

Then came the animus of their visit. Meeting with the Lords Commissioners of the Crown, they discussed and signed papers labeled Articles of Agreement. The essence of this agreement was expressed by Chief Attacullaculla:

We look upon the Great King George as the Sun, and as our father, and upon ourselves as his children. For though we are red, and you are white yet our hands and hearts are joined together. What we have seen, our children from generation to generation will always remember it. In war we shall always be with you.[5]

It was an extraordinarily submissive speech for a proud and warlike people. And the pact was also the Cherokees' introduction to the white man's subtle use of treaties as a substitute for conquest. What they had signed committed the Cherokees to trade exclusively with England (red clay from Cherokee territory started Britain's first porcelain factories) and to fight exclusively for England. The cession of lands in payment for these privileges would come later.

The seven chiefs returned to the Nation with further gifts of guns, rum, and red war paint; and guns and rum would be the white man's principal contributions to the Indians throughout the balance of the century.

This diplomatic coup of England's did not go unchallenged by the French.

Six years later a Jesuit priest named Christian Gottlieb Priber infiltrated the Nation, learned the language, adopted the native dress and customs, and by boldness and enterprise acquired an extraordinary influence among the Cherokees. He sought to mold the Nation into a communist republic with Cherokee Chief Moytoy as its emperor and himself as "His Majesty's Principal Secretary of State"—both dedicated to alliance with the French.

Priber's surrogate reign was brief. The English sent troops to arrest him, a move that was stoutly repelled by the Cherokees themselves. But the Imperial Secretary made the mistake of leaving the safety of the Nation to visit the French Fort Toulouse in Alabama. He was captured on the way by British traders, and turned over to English authorities, and he languished in a Georgia jail until his death. This ended any tangible French hold on the Cherokees, and parenthetically introduced the jails of Georgia as persuasive elements in history to come.

Along with these two European contacts in the first half of the century came the thrust of a third and greater power: epidemic. Priber's supporters would claim that it was the English who introduced smallpox into the Nation by injecting the germs of the disease into the rum they sold the Indians. Highly unlikely but highly effective as propaganda. The Cherokee medicine men could find no charm against the plague which wiped out nearly half the tribe in 1738–39. Hundreds of braves committed suicide at sight of their disfigured faces reflected in the streams. Recorded the Irish-born trader James Adair:

> Some shot themselves, other cut their throats, some stabbed themselves with knives and others with sharp-pointed canes; many threw themselves with sullen madness into the fire and there slowly expired, as if they had been utterly divested of the native power of feeling pain.[6]

Generally diminished and debilitated, with their fighting power by midcentury cut in half, the Cherokees entered the era of the French and Indian War, 1754–63, at a disadvantage, to say the least. Though divided in sympathy, they honored the compact signed in London and sided with the English. In fact, Colonel George Washington of Virginia believed that the war could not have been won for England without Indian support. It was Washington who sent fellow Virginian Nathaniel Gist to seek volunteers among the Cherokees ("They will be of particular service—more so than twice their number of white men"), and it was later believed to be Gist who became the father of Sequoyah, a name long venerated among Cherokees.

But the shaky alliance between Cherokees and English was a sad and tragic one. Washington had urged that Cherokee warriors be treated with respect ("One false step might . . . turn them against us"). But Anglo-Saxon distrust of Indians—and to the colonists, apparently, all Indians looked alike—led to the massacre of twenty-four Cherokees who were merely foraging for fodder on Virginia soil. The Cherokees retaliated by taking a number of Virginian scalps and burning homesteads—and a local border war broke out between the Indians and their colonial allies.

Retaliation bred retaliation. The Cherokees took possession of the British-garrisoned Fort Loudon on the Tennessee, despite an attempted intervention by four companies of Royal Scots.

Surrender of the fort was a bitter blow to British pride. "I must own I am ashamed," confessed the later Lord Jeffrey Amherst, "for I believe it is the first instance of His Majesty's troops having yielded to the Indians." Two of the garrison, however, were granted their freedom by Chief Attacullaculla, a minor incident of some importance. One of the two, Captain John Stuart, remained in the Nation to take an active part in Cherokee affairs under the Indian sobriquet of "Bushyhead." The other, William Shorey, a Scotsman like Stuart, married a full-blood Cherokee related to John Ross.

In late September 1760, the Virginia massacre avenged, the Cherokees sued for peace. But British pride had been too sorely stung. Peace was postponed until a punitive expedition could be launched against the Nation, during which the Cherokees were so thoroughly chastised, their towns destroyed, their crops laid waste, their warrior battalions shattered, that the terms which were finally agreed to a year later were distinctly to the English enemy's advantage. The Cherokees gained one significant concession. They asked that Captain John Stuart be appointed British ambassador, or agent, to the Nation. For, as Chief Attacullaculla stated simply, "All the Indians love him."

Stuart's subsequent appointment as British superintendent of Indian affairs was of questionable value to the Cherokees. In one sense, at any rate. Under his aegis three more treaties, signed between 1768 and 1775, stripped the Cherokees of much of their remaining territory. Almost all their lands north of Georgia and east of the Blue Ridge Mountains were surrendered, along with their rich Kentucky hunting grounds and much of Tennessee.

East and west their boundaries were compressed accordion-fashion. "The truth is," remarked Old Tassel, Chief of the Cherokee Nation after Attacullaculla's death, "if we had no lands, we should have fewer enemies." It was perhaps the most astute ten-word analysis of the Indians' position that had yet been broached. He and the Cherokees could only be thankful that these sacrifices promised an era of peace and a chance to reconstruct their stricken Nation.

In these fitful years of Cherokee-English relations one social revolution was accomplished. Many British officers—a disproportionate number of them Scots and Irish—married Cherokee women and generated mixed-blood families of importance to the future of the Nation. In every instance, though bearing the English names of their progenitors, the descendants remained unequivocally Cherokee—for such was the law of the tribe, which, almost without exception, those who intermarried with the Indians accepted.

Thus one of Stuart's deputies, John McDonald, married Anne Shorey, mixed-blood daughter of William Shorey, whom Chief Attacullaculla had released with Stuart from Fort Loudon. In turn, the daughter of this union, Molly McDonald, married Daniel Ross, later successful trader among the Cherokees and father of John Ross, who would guide the Nation's destiny for half a century. It would be futile to list, and try to stamp upon the memory, these in-

numerable marriages. But if this period accomplished nothing else, it inter-
mingled Cherokee blood with English blood to form an almost magic, vital po-
tion.

The outbreak of the American Revolution in 1776 found the Cherokees,
along with virtually all Indian tribes and federations, ranged on the side of the
British. It was a pragmatic choice. With the French defeated in North
America, the English loomed as the Cherokees' sole protectors against white
encroachment on their lands. They had lost much territory to their British
overlords, but this alliance might afford an opportunity to get some back from
the American colonials. Their allegiance was further cemented by gifts of
hatchets, rifles, and ammunition, and bounties offered for rebel scalps.

A British naval assault on Charleston in June 1776 signaled a multi-pronged
Cherokee attack on border settlements of North and South Carolina and outlying villages of Georgia. Supported by bands of Tories, whites dressed as Indians, the raiders sacked and burned the unprotected towns, destroyed crops
and cattle, slaughtered men, women, and children indiscriminately, and forced
the survivors to flee in panic to protective forts.

The raids brought quick retaliation. In August and September punitive expeditions from the Carolinas and Virginia and some parts of Georgia, numbering some 6,500 men in all, struck the Nation from four directions simultaneously—laying waste more than fifty Cherokee towns, killing horses and
livestock, and destroying fields and orchards. The avenging forces showed little
mercy. Adopting Indian war practices, they scalped their victims, tortured captives to death, made slaves of Cherokee women and children.

At year's end, most of the Cherokee Nation lay ravaged and helpless. The
following spring of 1777 a peace of sorts was arranged with the separate American states, which cost the Cherokees another five million acres of land on their
northern and eastern borders. And the peace itself was an uneasy one. Along
Chickamauga Creek near present-day Chattanooga, a belligerent band of die-
hard Cherokees held out against the enemy. Known as "Chickamaugans" and
led by Chief Dragging Canoe, they continued to launch lightninglike guerrilla
raids on neighboring white communities, leaving a trail of scalped and murdered victims, ravaged fields, and burned or looted homesteads. It took Colonel
John Sevier and his backwoods Tennesseans to pry them from their mountain
base and drive them into the northwestern corner of the Nation, where their
nuisance value was diminished but not, for years, suppressed.

The Cherokees' alliance with the British Crown had brought them to the
edge of extinction as a Nation, with most of their villages destroyed, their warrior force reduced to a few scattered hundreds, their population largely in hid-
ing, living in wilderness areas on roots and acorns. A second smallpox epidemic, which struck in 1783, taking a toll of 2,500 dead, compounded their near
annihilation. The final Treaty of Paris signed by Great Britain and the United
States in September of that year had no more meaning for them than the
tolling of a distant bell. There was little to hope for when, two years later, rep-

resentatives of the Cherokee Nation were summoned to Hopewell, South Carolina, to sign a treaty of peace with the United States.

Surprisingly, the American commissioners made no demands for territory. Taken at face value, the Treaty of Hopewell, signed in November 1785, was an enlightened document. Declaring that the Cherokees were now under "the favor and protection of the United States," it confirmed the existing boundaries of the Nation and forbade any American citizen from trespassing within those boundaries. Trade with the Indians would be regulated by the Congress subject to Cherokee approval; justice within the Nation would be administered according to tribal law; and any United States citizen settling or trespassing unlawfully on Cherokee soil would be subject to that law.

The document closed with two reassuring paragraphs:

ARTICLE XII

That the Indians may have full confidence in the justice of the United States, respecting their interests, they shall have the right to send a deputy of their choice whenever they think fit, to Congress.

ARTICLE XIII

The hatchet shall be forever buried, and the peace given by the United States, and friendship reestablished between the said states on the one part, and all the Cherokees on the other, shall be universal; and the contracting parties shall use their utmost endeavors to maintain the peace given as aforesaid, and friendship reestablished.[7]

With a thousand Cherokees as witnesses, the treaty was signed for the Indians by thirty-seven chiefs, including Old Tassel, successor to Oconostota; and for the United States by four commissioners, including Colonel Benjamin Hawkins, an able and close associate of General Washington. At the close of the ceremonies a remarkable half-breed Cherokee named Nancy Ward, niece of Chief Attacullaculla, rose to speak:

I have a pipe and a little tobacco to give to the commissioners to smoke in friendship . . . You having determined on peace is most pleasing to me, for I have seen much trouble during the late war. I am old, but I hope yet to bear children, who will grow up and people our Nation, as we are now to be under the protection of Congress and shall have no more disturbance. I speak for the young warriors I have raised in my town, as well as for myself. They rejoice that we have peace, and we hope the chain of friendship will never more be broken.[8]

A pipe and some tobacco were then passed around to consecrate her words.

But peace was not that easily attained. The Treaty of Hopewell left unsettled the fate of legions of white Americans already settled within the borders of the Nation, notably between the French Broad and Holston rivers in eastern Tennessee. This was a matter, it was felt, to be adjusted later—by an overworked, indifferent Congress. The renegade Chickamaugans continued their raids on surrounding white communities, while land-hungry Americans, flushed with their new independence, encroached by the thousands on Cherokee soil. The peaceful majority among the Cherokees did no more than verbally protest, sending their first delegation to the new United States seat of government in Philadelphia.

Here was a seed of hope. With the inauguration of President Washington in April 1789 the Cherokees had an ally in the new administration. A friend, too, in Secretary Henry Knox, who formulated the first Indian policy for the United States, by which "a noble, liberal, and disinterested administration of Indian affairs" should fall under the aegis of the War Department. It was one thing, however, to adopt a policy and another to apply it to two juxtaposed races with little in common but a love of land.

Say this for Secretary Knox. He listened to those Cherokees who came to Philadelphia to protest the white invasions of their territory. And he carried their protest by letter directly to the President, declaring:

The disgraceful violation of the Treaty of Hopewell with the Cherokees requires the serious consideration of Congress. If so direct and manifest contempt of the authority of the United States be suffered with impunity, it will be vain to extend the arm of government to the frontiers. Indian tribes can have no faith in such imbecile promises, and the lawless whites will ridicule a government which shall, on paper only, make Indian treaties and regulate Indian boundaries.[9]

How right he was. And how many generations away from the acceptance of this truth.

In the wake of Knox's letter, the federal government issued a proclamation forbidding any further encroachment on Cherokee lands. But the transgressions continued, aggravated by Governor John ("Nolichucky Jack") Sevier's ambitions for his short-lived state of Franklin on the northern border of the Nation. Friction between whites and Indians increased and, with a new white government since 1789, it seemed obligatory to conclude another pact to supplement the Hopewell treaty. In July 1791, on the banks of the Holston River near the mouth of the French Broad, a new Treaty of Holston was signed by the United States commissioners and forty-one principal men among the Cherokees.

As the Cherokees had long since learned, the signing of treaties was usually consecrated by cession of more lands. The matter of unlawful settlers within the Nation was settled by the Cherokees yielding claim to the Cumberland Valley and other sections in the Carolinas. This did, however, increase to $8,500 the annuity owed to them for all lands ceded to the United States. Up to now the Cherokees had relied on barter in their dealing with white traders, or on script or paper drawn on the banks of the surrounding border states. But with their boundaries shrinking, and their people forced into an agricultural economy, money was taking on a new importance.

The Treaty of Holston was intended as the final settlement of differences between the Cherokee Nation and the United States. It differed from the

Hopewell pact principally in strength and amplification—reaffirming "perpetual peace" between the two nations, redefining Cherokee boundaries "for all time," forbidding inhabitants of the United States from trespassing on Cherokee lands without a passport, and giving the Cherokee Councils authority to try and sentence white offenders on their soil.[10]

The most important provisions were contained in just two paragraphs, one stating that "the United States solemnly guarantee to the Cherokee Nation, all their lands not hereby ceded." A final Article XIV was wholly new in concept. In a sense it made the United States partners with the Cherokees in promoting "a greater degree of civilization" among the Indians. With their hunting grounds diminished, they would turn their attention to animal husbandry and agriculture. To this end, the federal government would supply, gratuitously, needed supplies and implements "from time to time," and would send to the Nation certain qualified agents, or superintendents, to direct them and advise them.

"These persons," the article concluded, "shall have lands assigned by the Cherokees for cultivation for themselves and their successors in office; but they shall be precluded from exercising any kind of traffic [trade]."

Thus was born the office of Indian Agent, appointed by the War Department, and later by the Bureau of Indian Affairs, to live more or less permanently within the Nation, counsel and guide the Indians when called upon to do so, and serve as a liaison between the Cherokee Nation and the federal government. It was a key position; and the Cherokees were lucky to have it generally occupied by men who were sympathetic and who understood their problems, the first of these being Benjamin Hawkins, who established his agency at Tellico in eastern Tennessee. At about the same time, Governor William Blount of Tennessee was appointed by President Washington to the post of Superintendent of the Southern Indians.

One who could not be expected to be pleased with these developments was Andrew Jackson. Old Hickory, as he was now affectionately known, not only disliked Washington's Indian policy but, after reaching Congress as representative from Tennessee, suggested the President's impeachment! His reasons were personal. Either by himself or jointly with associates, Jackson claimed nearly 100,000 acres of Cherokee land, which he put up for sale in Philadelphia, asserting that the Treaty of Holston did not apply to his particular case.

No more pleased with the treaties of Hopewell and Holston were the Chickamaugans, even though their chiefs had duly signed these documents, including Dragging Canoe's successor, Doublehead. Disregarding the treaties, the Chickamaugans kept the frontier in a state of terror with continued raids on bordering communities. On one of these, Doublehead not only killed and scalped two white men, one of them an army officer, but allegedly chopped them into steak-size bits and ate them. If true, it was another reason why the Cherokees in general took a dim view of the Chickamaugans and in time would take a dimmer view of Doublehead.

Washington and Knox tried nobly to come to terms with Doublehead, sending a warship to Georgia to bring him and his associates to a conference in Philadelphia. Here the Chickamaugans asked, as the price of their good behavior, that the Cherokees' annuity be increased by $3,500 in goods and materials to be paid to Doublehead in person. The Cherokee Nation was little benefited by the settlement. When Doublehead later received the goods he distributed them among his friends, keeping the better portion for himself.

Plainly, only brute force would bring the Chickamaugans to heel. In the summer of 1794 the United States launched its last—hopefully, at any rate, the last—military thrust against Cherokees. General James Robertson and Governor William Blount organized an expedition of 550 volunteers from Kentucky and Tennessee to invade and devastate the Chickamaugan territory. The Indians themselves were hard to corner; only some fifty were killed and scalped—scalping now being a practice adopted by the frontier whites—but the total destruction of their towns in northwestern Georgia broke the Chickamaugans' heart for war. A conference at Tellico in early November 1794 brought "satisfactory results."

"Peace with the Indians," declared Governor Blount, "exists now not only in name or upon paper in form of treaty but in fact . . ." A half century of conflict, marked by mutual distrust and bitterness, had ended. Little Turkey, Old Tassel's successor as chief of the Cherokees, hailed the achievement of a great wish for his people: "To live so that we might have gray hairs on our heads." Even the roisterous Chickamaugans echoed these sentiments with the statement of their chief: "Our tears are wiped away, and we rejoice in the prospect of our future welfare, under the protection of Congress."[11]

Thus the Cherokees, at the turn of the century, faced the future with renewed hope. The hatchet was "forever buried," as declared by the Treaty of Hopewell. Their boundaries and sovereign independence had been guaranteed for all time. With this security and with the promised help of their white brothers in the North, there were no hills too steep to climb, no heights to which they might not rise.

2

"The Principal People"

LITTLE JAY BIRD, the son of Humming Bird, who mined the red hills of Georgia in the early 1800s, knew precisely where the Cherokees had come from. And what their past had been:

Our history went back over twelve thousand years—back to a period when according to our wise chiefs our ancestors were a race of gods who came to the earth from the sky. They came from the East in flying craft that gathered its power from the sky. They also knew from which great constellation of our stars in the heavens our immortal ancestors had come.[1]

Other, less fanciful beliefs still gave the Cherokees an ancient origin. James Adair, an Irish trader who lived among the Cherokees for forty years, believed they were one of the ten Lost Tribes of Israel; and Daniel Butrick, a volatile New England missionary to the Nation, stretched Biblical data to prove this to his satisfaction.

Later scholars might have come closer to the mark. As was believed of other Indian tribes, the Cherokees were thought to have crossed Bering Strait from Asia and drifted eastward like blown leaves, to collect against the nearer slopes of the southern Appalachians. Others surmised, by a comparison of artifacts, that they were linked to the South American Indians of the Amazon and Orinoco valleys. Still others, by similar clues, related them to the Caribs of the West Indies.

There was no written history, of course, to solve this riddle; only the oral sagas and the hieroglyphic wampum belts. These indicated that at some time in their past had occurred a great migration from the north, which suggested an early link with the Iroquois Confederacy. Perhaps from the Great Lakes region they had moved or been driven south of the Ohio River to settle finally in the vast domain they occupied before de Soto's time.

It was an immense area of 43,000 square miles bounded on the north by the Ohio River and on the south by a line just short of Georgia's Chattahoochee River. Its western region included most of Kentucky and Tennessee; its eastern boundary reached beyond the Blue Ridge Mountains to claim portions of Virginia, West Virginia, and the Carolinas.

Other tribes—principally Choctaws, Chickasaws, and Creeks—might and did dispute those boundaries. But it hardly mattered. The perimeters of their Nation were their hunting grounds, chiefly Kentucky and western Tennessee. The people themselves chose to live in the rugged, generally mountainous sections of northern Georgia, central Tennessee, and the Smoky Mountain regions of the Carolinas. Over this area they built some sixty towns or villages with dwellings for a population estimated at from 20,000 to 25,000 in de Soto's time. Though they had no official seat of government, having no formal government as such, they recognized Chota on the Little Tennessee as their principal "Mother Town" or capital.

The country itself was eminently suited to their nature and their way of life. It was a lovely, lyrical land of craggy peaks and fertile valleys, of gently flowing rivers fed by chattering streams. Deer, elk, and buffalo were plentiful, as were song and game birds, larks and thrashers, pheasant, partridge, and wild turkey. Tall stands of hardwood ranged along the lower slopes, changing to hemlock, pine, and balsam as the land rose higher. In the spring the air was scented by the blossoming azaleas, laurels, rhododendrons, and magnolias; in the fall the mountains flamed with the scarlet of the maples and the gold of oaks and cottonwood, colors the Cherokees loved and wove into their shawls and blankets.

"It was an amiable country," as one said, "designed to harbor an amiable people."

There were at least forty different names or versions of the names that they were known by, most of them invented by outsiders. The word Cherokee itself had no meaning in their language, and was difficult to trace. They were known at times, and for no clear reason, by such Indian labels as "Red Fire Men" or "Children of the Sun," but themselves expressed a preference for Ani-Yun Wiya, meaning "The Real, or Principal, People." That at least had some foundation in their standing among Eastern Indians. Of all Five Civilized Tribes they seemed, in character and conduct, to stand a little taller, walk more proudly than their neighbors.[2]

In physical appearance, too, they were distinctive. William Bartram, American botanist and explorer, whose observations inspired such poets as William Wordsworth and Samuel Taylor Coleridge, toured the Nation in the late eighteenth century. He found the Cherokee braves taller and more robust than the neighboring tribes, and "by far the largest race of men I have ever seen; their complexions brighter and somewhat of the olive cast, especially the adults; and some of their younger women are nearly as fair and blooming as European women."

Bartram's descriptions sometimes seem so flattering as to need a grain of salt. Still, he was coming cold upon the scene, with no bias or preconceptions. He attributed to the adult Cherokees "a perfect human figure, their features regular . . . the forehead and brow so formed, as to strike you instantly with heroism and bravery; the eye . . . full of fire; the pupil always black, and the nose commonly inclining to the aquiline." Cherokee women he found "tall, slender, erect and of delicate frame, their features formed with perfect symmetry," their movements marked by "becoming grace and dignity."

Plumbing their character through this surface, Bartram noted traits of "magnanimity and independence," and added further:

The Cherokees in their disposition and manner are grave and steady; dignified and circumspect in their deportment; rather slow and reserved in conversation; yet frank, cheerful and humane; tenacious of their liberties and natural rights of men; secret, deliberate and determined in their councils; honest, just and liberal, and are ready always to sacrifice every pleasure and gratification, even their blood, and life itself, to defend their territory and maintain their rights.[3]

As to clothing, de Soto found them "naked," and Bartram, coming upon a group of Cherokee maidens picking berries, described them as "disclosing their beauties to the fluttering breeze, and bathing their limbs in the cool, flitting streams." In general, however, the men in early times wore deerskin breechclouts, and the women short vests, fringed skirts, and sometimes leggings of the same material, with leather moccasins the universal footwear. The braves might dye or tattoo their skins, were naturally beardless, and often kept their heads shorn of all but a decorative crown piece. The women kept their hair long, plaited in wreaths, and tied in a tight knot behind.

Their manner of dress would change, of course, as contact with Europeans introduced more sophisticated customs. In any event, their clothing was suited to the occasion. The ceremonial garments of a chieftain might include "a gold-dyed buckskin shirt and leggings with matching feather headdress," while women would favor a long skirt woven of feathers with a fringe of down. They had the Indian's proverbial fondness for ornaments of every sort, silver jewelry, bracelets, beads, porcupine quills, shells, and feathers.

Their life style, while geared to the simple tasks of daily survival, was not uncomfortable or primitive. Their tidy homes were cabins of solid logs caulked with clay and roofed with bark and branches. Their towns were connected by wagon roads and well-blazed trails. Their diet was varied according to the hunt, with game fowl and venison predominating. They had wild berries, chestnuts, and potatoes, and corn to be pounded into meal; they cooked over an open fire and ate from earthenware plates and bowls.

Their society was oriented toward seven clans whose Indian names might be loosely translated as Bird, Wolf, Deer, Paint, Blue, Long Hair, and Wild Potato. Marriages were permitted only outside the clan. Polygamy, while allowed, was far from universal, and divorce was a matter of mutual consent. Since there were no courts or magistrates and no police force, the clan enforced the unwritten laws on the basis of an eye for an eye and a life for a life; and if a culprit fled from justice, a kinsman was executed in his stead.

Their government, in de Soto's time and into the early eighteenth century, was merely a loose confederation of towns, each with its elected chief and local Council. There was no central government, no principal chief. The Cherokees' love of liberty and independence would have rejected any such despotism. But after Cuming and Priber's efforts to weld them into political unity, the local chiefs began to meet in General Council at their Mother Town of Chota. Thereafter a principal chief was elected as at least a figurehead authority.

Women occupied a high position in the tribal Councils, especially when these became concerned with war. Their advice was heeded not only on matters of policy but on targets and strategy as well. Nancy Ward was one such *Ghighau,* or "Beloved Woman," whose "queenly and commanding" presence carried more than ordinary weight. When, during the Revolution, Nancy warned the Americans of a sneak attack upon them by the Cherokees, her seeming treachery was not denounced. Clairvoyant, she had seen wisdom in avoiding a battle that might have been disastrous to both parties.[4]

Still, matters of government had little appeal for the early Cherokees. The political process was foreign to their nature. Social behavior was a matter for personal or family discipline, and if these broke down, the clan or Council was the final arbiter. Yet the strong-willed Cherokee seemed never without some inner control. Perhaps it was a matter of a well-developed conscience; perhaps it was something more, for his god or gods were everywhere he looked.

The early religion of the Cherokees was pantheistic, undemanding, unencumbered with claptrap or ceremony. If there were a supreme being it was the Great Spirit who had granted them the land they dwelt on (strictly as a loan, however; no Cherokee owned land, but only the man-made improvements, the houses, barns, or tilled fields he impressed upon that land). There were also the Little People, who lodged in caves in the mountain slopes and were friendly to travelers and hunters; and there were the Immortals on the mountain peaks, who tended to more serious matters beyond human comprehension. There were early references to a Sun God and a Red Fire God to whom some Cherokees prayed, but they prayed seldom and they worshiped very little.

All nature was animate or humanized—rivers, rocks, trees, birds, and animals. The stars in the heavens were creatures, too, who sometimes fell to earth as snowy owls. Long Man the River was a beneficent being whose waters, in the rite of "going to the river," cleansed the flesh of sin and sickness. The bears were people, like anyone else, who could talk if they had a mind to, but chose wisely to keep silent. If one were obliged to kill an animal for food, it was obligatory first to ask for its forgiveness.[5]

Thus religion and myth were intertwined, and all of such common knowledge as never to require much attention. There were no priests in the religious sense, but the medicine men or conjurors were indispensable when illness struck or one was faced with a difficult decision. To the conjurors one went for rain when the corn or tobacco asked for rain; or for a magic lotion or incantation that would make a warrior invulnerable in battle; or for herbs that would cure one of the fits or fever when "going to the river" failed. Next to the chiefs, in fact, the conjurors wielded formidable influence—sometimes greater than that of the chiefs themselves.

But even the conjurors were no match for the Raven Mockers, who swooped through the air "in fiery shape, with arms outstretched like wings" to rob the dying man of life. What happened after death was never satisfactorily figured out, except that there was no heaven or Valhalla. Little Jay Bird believed the souls of the dead were carried on a three-day journey back to the stars from which they came. More commonly it was thought that they went somewhere west—and it is hauntingly significant that to the Cherokees the East was a land of light and sun; the West was the "Darkening Land" where lost souls found extinction.

Their festivals which were also their principal diversions, were a combination of religious and pagan rites. Chief among these was the Green Corn Dance in the August harvest season. While this might include some giving of thanks for the fruition of the crop, it might also involve a vigorous session of ball-play—a murderous version of lacrosse—and was always accompanied by feasting, music, and all-night dancing on the turf.

Their principal occupation, as William Fyffe had noted in the eighteenth century, was making war—against the Creeks to the south, or the Choctaws to the west, or any tribe handy to their borders. Fyffe was struck by the Cherokees' method of fanning a militant spirit among the young, teaching them not only combat skills but courage, endurance, and indifference to pain. If courage was sometimes confused with barbarity, there were other consequences of this schooling. Like the early Vikings of Scandinavia, the Cherokees learned to honor their warrior forebears. No Indian tribe in North America became more dedicated to the land which held their fathers' graves. Sacred soil. Inviolable earth.

Another trait: they listened to the past. William Fyffe recorded their devout attention to the reciting of their sagas, and observed that "these recitations of war deeds encouraged their youths to become orators who even surpassed those of Greece and Rome." He later added that a diplomatic Cherokee could outwit both Richelieu and Horace Walpole. (Eloquence hardly fitted the popular image of the taciturn Indian who expressed himself, if at all, in no more than primeval grunts.)

The musical tonality of the Cherokee language was something which caught the ear of later visitors. The Cherokees spoke as if chanting, in measured cadences, with syllables as resonant as bells. Without at first a written language, they stored the sounds in the chambers of their minds to be played back like recorded music. A man's word was a precious thing, to be remembered. And above all, honored. James Adair noted that they despised a liar and were apt to tell him so, embarrassingly, to his face.

So it was, until the closing years of the eighteenth century, when the treaties of Hopewell and Holston opened gateways on new vistas for the Cherokees and they stepped from the past into future.

Benjamin Hawkins, Indian Agent to the Cherokees in Washington's admin-istration, was gratified by the swift and visible progress of the Indians. It was part of his job to see to the implementation of Article XIV of the Treaty of Hol-ston, which had promised the Indians tools of farming and animal husbandry so that, in Secretary Knox's words, "our knowledge of cultivation and the arts might be imparted to the red men."

Hawkins had helped to see that the promise was kept; and while there were not sufficient supplies of hoes, plows, spinning wheels, and such to work an overnight reversal of the Cherokee pursuits, the change was on its way. Hawkins was able to report that "in the Cherokee agency, the wheel, the loom, and the plough is in pretty general use, farming, manufactures, and stock rais-ing the topic of conversation among men and women."[6]

Touring the country in 1796, the agent saw evidence of the transformation. There was "a general air of prosperity throughout the Nation." He observed substantial herds of cattle in the pastures, flocks of poultry in the farmyards. He passed streams of hogs being driven to the Georgia markets, "the Indian pork being esteemed better than that raised in the white settlements on account of the chestnut diet." The Cherokees' natural love of horses had led to the rais-ing and breeding of excellent stocks of both draft animals and saddle ponies.

Peach trees and potatoes were prevalent in the fields as well as abundant crops of the native corn and beans. Some farmers kept bees and did a consid-erable trade in beeswax and honey. While pottery and basket making had al-ways been practiced by the women, they were now eager to make their own clothing. A group of housewives (the term "squaw" was never used) at the In-dian town of Etowah—later corrupted to Hightower—told Hawkins "they would follow the advice of their great father General Washington, they would plant cotton and be prepared for spinning as soon as they could make it, and they hoped they might get some wheels and cards as soon as they should be ready for them . . ."

The Cherokees had always clung closely to the land. Their Council Houses seemed to be a natural extension of the soil, dome-shaped and rising like earth-colored mounds from the center of their villages. But now their habits were becoming more domestic, focusing more on the table and the hearth than on the hunt. Of a visit to one of their comfortable dwellings Hawkins wrote:

They gave me good bread, pork, and potatoes for supper, and ground peas and dry peaches. I had corn for my horses. The hut in which I lodged was clean and neat. In the morning I breakfasted on corn cakes and pork. They had a number of fowls, hogs and some cattle, the field of 4 acres for corn fenced, and half an acre for potatoes.[7]

Everywhere Hawkins stopped he was told that the Cherokees were eager to "follow the instruction of the agent and the advice of the President," and was asked when they would receive more hoes, more plows, more spinning wheels, more looms. There was a certain intersectional rivalry in this race for progress, with the North Carolina mountaineers complaining that the Chickamaugans "had received more than their share of spinning wheels and cards, and were consequently more advanced in making their own clothing as well as in farming."

Beneath the rich red soil of Tennessee and Georgia, so arduously being furrowed by the plows from Yankee foundries, lay a secret natural resource not yet tapped or fully realized. Though gold had already been discovered in North Carolina, only a trained geologist could have detected the direction of the vein—straight as an arrow into the heart of northern Georgia. There were legends which hinted that the Cherokees had always known of its existence. If so, they kept quiet about it. They mined some silver in the hills for ornaments and jewelry; Little Jay Bird's father, Humming Bird, was able to dig ten feet down and find where the vagrant white prospectors unearthed enough of the precious metal to counterfeit silver dollars. And there were rubies in the hills as well. But the Cherokees were superstitious about precious stones and metals; they were not to be used as articles of trade.

Trade was of growing importance to the Cherokees. Becoming more productive, they wanted to be more than self-sufficient; they wanted to share in the traffic that appeared to be a tool of white supremacy, a term they only half acknowledged. The Cherokees, wrote Hawkins, "were willing to labor if they could profit by it," would grow more corn if they could sell it. Even the women asked the agent, if they made cotton fabrics could they find a market for them?

By the Treaty of Hopewell the United States Congress retained the "sole and exclusive right" of regulating trade with the Cherokees "in such manner as they think proper." After seven years of nothing being done, a Cherokee chief reminded Knox of this responsibility. "We wish you to attend to this matter," he said bluntly. Knox did, promoting an act which required traders to post bond and be licensed before doing business with the Indians, the license being subject to cancellation if the trader's conduct warranted.

A trading house, or "factory," was established at Tellico in which Hawkins himself had no commercial interest. It was described by a visitor as "a kind of warehouse where the Cherokees carry ginseng and furs, consisting of bear, stag, and otter skins. They give them in exchange for coarse stuffs, knives, hatchets, and other articles that they stand in need of." In a short time their demands and needs would become far more sophisticated. For the Cherokees learned quickly from their contact with the whites. What they learned would not always be to their advantage. But they were on the way up the ladder to the white man's level in agriculture, domestic arts, and simple industrial skills. They would take the good with the bad—until, in years to come, the cost became too great.

Along with the shift from dependence on the chase to a domestic, agricultural economy went a subtle change in the composition of the Cherokees—from predominantly pure-blood Indians to a mixture of Indian and white. It had started during colonial days when European traders found desirable wives among the adaptable Cherokee women, and was furthered during the Revolution, when British officers and agents married into the clans and remained in the Nation to raise mixed-blood families.

The compression of the Nation's boundaries, by pressure from the border states, ironically contributed to this development. The mixed-bloods tended to desert the mountains and settle in the flatlands and the valleys, where they could raise crops and engage more readily in frontier trade. "With the beginning of the present century," wrote James Mooney of the Bureau of American Ethnology in the late 1800s, "we find influential mixed bloods in every town, and the civilized idea dominated even the national councils." They were a minority but a strong minority which helped to shape the Nation's destiny.[8]

A notable exception was The Ridge. His was as close to a pure-blood royal family as one could find among the Cherokees. Born about 1771 on the north bank of the Hiwassee River in eastern Tennessee—mountainous country that remained a stronghold of tradition-minded Cherokees—he was the brother of Chief Oowatie, "the Ancient One," both members of the Deer Clan and according to legend, if not demonstrable fact, descendants of Chief Attacullaculla. Schooled in the warrior tradition, The Ridge took his first scalp at seventeen in one of Doublehead's raids against the Unakas, or whites, in the trouble following the Hopewell Treaty.

To escape James Robertson's retaliatory expedition, the family moved down to Georgia to settle between the Etowah and Oostanaula rivers near the southern border of the Nation. Here The Ridge took as wife the Princess Sehoya, about whom little was known beyond that she was "industrious and persevering" and schooled "in the domestic arts."

Marriage tempered The Ridge's warlike inclinations. In fact, the barbarity of Doublehead's tactics had so repelled him that, elected to the Council at twenty-one, he caused the repeal of the Blood Law demanding a life for a life. He accomplished this by the expedient of threatening to kill any who tried to enforce the law, and elicited from Benjamin Hawkins the tribute that "the Cherokees are giving proof of their approximation to the customs of well-regulated societies . . ."

Perhaps it was Sehoya's influence, or perhaps his new responsibilities as councilman, that convinced The Ridge that the Cherokees should adopt the white man's culture. Before long he cleared land for a substantial plantation manor with a board roof and "the luxury of a chimney," planted peach and apple orchards, raised cattle and horses, cotton and tobacco, and purchased a band of slaves to work the fields.* In time he would become an exemplary

---

* Black slaves were owned by the Cherokees as early as the eighteenth century, possibly before. They were often runaways captured in Cherokee territory, or were obtained as war booty in raids on white settlements before and during the Revolution. But they were few in number; in the days of hunting as a means of livelihood, slave labor was of scant importance. In the early nineteenth century, however, slavery became regarded as one of the "civilized" contributions of the white economy, along with the plow, the spinning wheel, and other tools of productivity and trade. When an official census was taken in 1835, the proportion of black slaves to Cherokees was almost 10 percent—1,600 out of a total population of less than 17,000. Most of these were owned by only the wealthier families, such as Vanns and Ridges. There was considerable equality and intermingling.

Cherokee planter-merchant, as well as diplomat, sage, and counselor—high qualifications that ultimately spelled his doom.

Four children were born to The Ridge and Sehoya (whose name the English-speaking natives changed to Susanna), including a son John and a daughter Sarah. The Ridge's brother Oowatie had also married and settled on an adjoining plot of land. His half-breed wife Susannah Reese bore two sons who would leave their mark on the Indian wampum belts. Dropping the double-O prefix to the name, they were Stand Watie and Galagina, or "the Buck." The latter was later known, at his request, as Elias Boudinot. Four of these would qualify the Ridge-Watie connection as one of the great families among the Cherokees: The Ridge himself, his son John, Stand Watie, and Elias Boudinot—names as illustrious in history as John Ross.

Ross, the grandson of John McDonald and son of Anne Shorey and Daniel Ross, was born in 1790 on the Coosa River not far west of the Ridge family compound. By lineal descent he was only one-eighth Cherokee, fair-skinned and blue-eyed. Strangely, and in contrast to the bronze-colored Ridges and Waties who sought to emulate the whites, Ross regarded his light complexion as the mark of a pariah. When his parents sent him off to school in an American-tailored suit, and his classmates greeted him with the epithet Unaka (white man), John tore off his clothes in a fury and reverted to the buckskin garments of the Cherokees.

It was more than a gesture. It was a dedication. John Ross would, for the rest of his life, personify Cherokee culture and aspirations as devoutly as the Ridge-Watie family would seek some form of compromise, or coexistence, between Indians and whites.

After the Treaty of Holston had made things relatively quiet in the north, Daniel Ross moved his family to what became known as Rossville, on the Tennessee, not far from present-day Chattanooga. John and his older brother Lewis were sent to Kingston Academy, also attended at the time by young Sam Houston. Kingston itself was a busy commercial river town, where both learned American twists of speech, trade, and behavior. The knowledge served them well in later managing the family's commercial ventures, a trading post and ferry at Ross's Landing. It served them better as a weapon.

Of equal influence among the mixed-breeds at the turn of the century were the families of Hicks and Vann and Lowrey, all three descended from eighteenth-century traders in the Nation. Charles Hicks, a contemporary of The Ridge, was born near the Hiwassee River in 1767, the son of a Scotsman, Nathan Hicks, and a full-blood Cherokee chieftain's daughter. The mixture produced a lad of sensitive perception and an extraordinary knowledge of both English writing and philosophy. At the turn of the century he was hailed by Indian Agent Meigs, for whom he acted as interpreter, as "a man of as much information as anyone in the Nation." He was biding his time at that point.

Blacks worked side by side with their masters, were allowed to plant their own crops, sent their children to the same schools, often intermarried with the Indians. The offspring of Cherokee-Negro parents were born free.

Settling down as a farmer near Red Clay, Tennessee, he married a full-blood Cherokee—in a sense reversing his white inheritance—sired an offspring named Elijah, and began to study a strange subject for a Cherokee, religion.

The Lowrey name went back to 1730, when the first George Lowrey married a Cherokee maiden of the Long Hair Clan. Of his two sons, John and George, the older John was first to gain fame as a colonel in the Battle of Horseshoe Bend. But it was George Lowrey, born about 1770 and a contemporary of The Ridge, who was destined to play the larger role in Cherokee affairs. He started out by calling on Washington after the latter's inauguration and hearing at firsthand the President's hope that the Cherokees would follow in the white man's footsteps. These words he took home and pondered; he would never be quite certain of their wisdom.

Among the mixed-breeds, James Vann was a legend in his time, and one that the Cherokees had trouble living down. Seemingly schizophrenic, he was both drunken renegade and Christian benefactor, the despair and hope of his neighbors at Spring Place in Georgia. In the early 1800s he was rich by any standard—with a two-story manor of solid brick, a tavern used to trap the victims of his sadistic urges, hundreds of acres of cotton and tobacco worked by scores of slaves, whom he either whipped or shot for any infraction of his whims.

But even James Vann had a role to play. Sooner or later he would have to be shot—that, no one doubted. But meanwhile his Spring Place mansion was like a spider's web, where terrified wives were held in captivity, where chance visitors had their throats cut or their pockets picked, and where at any hour of the night Vann's bullhorn voice would shatter the Cherokee calm with drunken song. The tune might change, but not James Vann—not even when a meek Moravian missionary, already making plans, came gently tapping at his door. . . .

Then there was George Gist or Guess, allegedly the half-breed son of Nathaniel Gist dispatched by General Washington to negotiate with the Indians during the Revolution. Partially lame, possibly from a childhood wound or illness, he was a skillful silversmith, and there was plenty of silver in the Georgia mountains for him to work with. At some stage in his early life he became intrigued with the white man's writing and the "talking leaves" that formed his books. Gist, named Sequoyah by the Cherokees, became absorbed in trying to fathom the mystery of writing, seeking to create some signs or characters that would capture the musical Indian language.

There could be no such thing as an all-white Cherokee, of course. But there was an anomalous exception. The aristocratic Houston family of Virginia, falling on hard times in the early 1800s, moved to a Tennessee farm on the Nation's border. Their fifth son, sixteen-year-old Sam, envying the freedom of the Indians, ran away from home to live among the Cherokees, adopting their mode of dress and language, learning to track deer and hunt with bow and arrow. Chief Oolooteka, admiring his skill and courage, adopted the lad and christened him Kalanu, or "the Raven." When Houston returned to white society, to enlist as a private under Jackson in the Creek campaign, he vowed he would always remain one of "the children of the forest." To a large degree he kept that vow.[9]

There were, of course, countless others, mixed-breeds and pure-bloods, among the Principal People of the Nation in its early years: Walter Adair, descended from the Irish trader James Adair; John Martin, who, though national treasurer, was hard to pin down when it came to money; names like Rogers, Brown, McCoy, and Hilderbrand, which, with all the rest, would highlight the Cherokee story that was only just beginning.

And among Americans one name in particular would punctuate that story: Andrew Jackson, who had been their inspiring leader at the Battle of Horseshoe Bend, and who at this turn-of-the-century point was mounting the bench of the Tennessee Supreme Court, dedicated to the cause of justice.

The important role of the agent in Cherokee affairs was enhanced when Benjamin Hawkins was replaced in 1801 by Return Jonathan Meigs. ("Return, Jonathan!" his mother had commanded her reluctant husband when he sought to leave the marriage bed, and the offspring of his compliance had a ready name.) Meigs's reputation among the Indians—true friend or crafty diplomat? —might vary according to his critics, but from experience he knew the people and their problems and was sympathetic.

A Connecticut Yankee, Meigs had served in the Continental Army and accompanied Benedict Arnold on his disastrous expedition against Quebec. He later ingeniously captured Sag Harbor from the British with a fleet of whale boats and harpoons, for which achievement he was presented with a sword by Congress. After the war he became surveyor for the Ohio Company, a wilderness occupation which made him familiar with Indian lore and customs. He was sixty-two and supposedly retired when he accepted from President Adams the agency post at Tellico.

One of the agent's duties was the distribution of annuities due to the Cherokees in return for land cessions to the government. These were often paid in goods instead of cash, on the same equation of values that purchased Manhattan Island for a string of beads. Significantly, under Meigs the goods supplied to Cherokee wives changed character—from "silk stockings, ostrich feathers, damask tablecloths and earrings" to kettles, blankets, needles, thread, and scissors. Meigs meant what he said when he told War Secretary Henry Dearborn that he meant "to keep an eye on the community."

He had more arduous duties and fulfilled them well. One of these was control of unprincipled white intruders in the Nation—land-hungry settlers who had no business being there, traders who took advantage of their license to take advantage of the Cherokees, itinerant artisans such as carpenters and blacksmiths who appropriated Indian property in return for services, not to mention criminal fugitives from the border states. "The conduct of these intruders," Meigs complained forbearingly, "disturbs the peace & quiet of the Indians . . ."

Meigs investigated each complaint and, if the circumstances warranted, called on the nearest military garrison to expel the culprits. "From the moment of his arrival," writes Dr. Henry T. Malone, "the sixty-year-old Indian agent was an active guiding force on Cherokee development, serving his Indian wards as parent, adviser, doctor, lawyer, and home demonstration agent." He might later sponsor questionable treaties that would gain him Cherokee distrust, but after the confusions and conflicts of the last years of the eighteenth century Meigs was "a stabilizing force in a crucial period of Cherokee history."

Of more importance than Meigs's arrival was Thomas Jefferson's first term as President. Parenthetically, in earlier years, Jefferson's interest in the Indians had been aroused by what he called "their eminence in oratory," which he compared with that of Demosthenes and Cicero. He was prepared to believe that, unimpeded and given the chance, they could rise above their savage state and win a high position among the family of nations. How this could be accomplished while the President's first obligation was to citizens of the United States was a problem neither he nor his successors could resolve.

Jefferson committed himself, however, to the enlightened policies of Washington and Adams. He confirmed his belief in this approach to Cherokee chiefs who called on him in Washington:

You are becoming farmers, learning the use of the plough and hoe, enclosing your grounds and employing that labor in their cultivation which you formerly employed in hunting and in war; and I see handsome specimens of cotton cloth raised, spun and wove by yourselves. You are also raising cattle and hogs for your food, and horses to assist your labors. Go on, my children, in the same way and be assured the further you advance in it the happier and more respectable you will be . . .

You will find your next want to be mills to grind your corn, which by relieving your women from the loss of time in beating it into meal, will enable them to spin and weave more. When a man has enclosed and improved his farm, builds a good house on it and raised plentiful stocks of animals, he will wish when he dies that these things shall go to his wife and children . . .[10]

One thing that would puzzle the Cherokees who heeded this advice—people like The Ridge, who thought of their homes as the equivalent of Monticello—was why, having counseled that they improve their hold upon the land, as a heritage for the future, Jefferson would later suggest that they abandon it. Perhaps American oratory had shades of meaning unfamiliar to their form of speech. A supposition that they found, as time went on, was true.

3

This Last Little

W HEN, in 1733, James Edward Oglethorpe arrived with his English colonists to settle in Georgia, the territory granted him by charter from the King stretched in a wide band from the Atlantic seacoast clear to the Pacific—an area greater than western Europe, barring the Italian and Iberian peninsulas. This immensity was, of course, a parchment dream. Oglethorpe himself never got much beyond the sandy dunes at the mouth of the Savannah River, though he did establish the fort of Augusta as a buffer against marauding Carolinians. West of the Mississippi was alternately claimed by France and Spain, and the Pacific was light-years away.

Even by 1800 western Georgia, now accepted as stretching to the Mississippi, was occupied solely by Indians—Choctaws, Chickasaws, and Creeks—abandoned by their Spanish allies when Spain ceded most of its eastern claims to the United States. Not much thought had been given to that stretch of wilderness. But by the turn of the century, Georgia's population had grown to roughly 163,000 (it would double and triple in the next three decades), and bonus-minded veterans particularly looked to those unsettled reaches. The post-Revolutionary land rush had begun.

Land speculation invited wholesale chicanery. If surveys were made at all, they often created fictitious boundaries, until the point was reached where warrants were issued for more than three times as much land as existed. But the Yazoo Fraud surpassed them all. While it rocked the state of Georgia, which would never be the same again, it indirectly had more dire consequences for the Cherokees. In a certain manner the Cherokee Nation, both its present and its promise, would never be the same again.

The Yazoo Fraud, named for the Yazoo River running through the area, involved some fifty million acres of western Georgia sold to four companies of speculators for $500,000. Outraged citizens not benefiting from the sale demanded that the contract be annulled. The legislature, intimidated by a sense of guilt, complied. But by that time much of the land had been sold to individual buyers, who either refused to turn it back or sued for damages. The suits dragged on for many years, even reaching John Marshall of the Supreme Court, who was destined to play an important role in the drama of the Cherokees.

It was a mess that Georgia wanted to be rid of. The state solved its dilemma by selling the whole area west of the Chattahoochee River to the United States for $1,250,000 (the Yazoo speculators went to court and later collected $4,300,000 from the federal government). Buried in the terms of that 1802 transaction were provisions for the Cherokees' ultimate annihilation, if those provisions were to be observed. In addition to the cash payment the United States guaranteed to "extinguish, for the use of Georgia, as early as the same can be peaceably obtained upon reasonable terms . . . the Indian title to all [their] lands lying within the limits of the state."

It was a backhanded mortal blow, potentially at least—the seeds of conflict yet to come. There was no immediate demand from Georgia that the federal government implement this clause. But henceforth it hung over the Nation like a Damoclean sword.

The Cherokees at this point kept their mouths shut, ignoring the Georgia compact as something illegal and improbable. They would deal with the matter when and if it became a threat. But the question of Indian removal gained renewed attention two years later when Jefferson concluded the greatest real-estate venture in history, buying the Louisiana territory from Napoleon for fifteen million dollars. Here was a made-to-order repository for the Eastern Indians. Not that Jefferson had that idea in mind, though he shortly proposed that the Eastern tribes consider the opportunities in the West, and Secretary Dearborn wrote to Meigs suggesting that he direct Cherokee thinking in this direction. Let them consider that

. . . the money & goods which they will receive for the lands, more especially that part which will be paid annually will be of more real benefit to the Nation under their improved state than the lands can be: that they will be enabled to make still greater progress in the useful arts, & will more & more rely on agriculture & domestic manufactories for their support & of course become a happy people.[1]

There would always be a naïve rationalization in the United States approach to Indian affairs. A principle of this approach was the dubious parental edict: We are only doing this for your own good—words that hide a multitude of sins against humanity. The process called for some verbal sleight of hand. The Indians were exhorted to improve and farm the land and in the same breath told that they would be better off—and happier!—somewhere else.

The Cherokees were not deceived. Anxious to receive and cooperate with American help in their advancement, they were simply puzzled by this tactic. As a Chickamaugan later told a group of missionaries:

The Indians say they don't know how to understand their Father the President. A few years ago he sent them a plough and a hoe—said it was not good for his red children to hunt—they must cultivate the earth. Now he tells them there is good hunting at the Arkansas; if they will go there he will give them rifles.[2]

Jonathan Meigs was caught in the middle of these contradictions. Perhaps a victim of them. In any event, he complied with Dearborn's recommendations to the extent of squeezing a number of quick land cessions from the Cherokees: the Long Island in the Holston River; a tract known as the Wafford Settlement in northeastern Georgia; and in 1805 and 1806 two large areas in Tennessee and southern Kentucky and a part of Alabama. For these the Cherokees received $20,600 in cash and $4,000 in annuities.

The transactions were tarnished by what Meigs referred to as "silent considerations," such as cash and rifles paid to reluctant chiefs who signed the treaties. In the case of Doublehead, Speaker of the Council, and his brother-in-law Tahlonteskee, two tracts of land in the ceded territory were reserved for their personal use in return for their compliance. These bribes, of course, were secret, but the Indian grapevine spread word of Doublehead's complicity. To the conservative pure-bloods, personified by The Ridge, it was bad enough to endorse a sale of Cherokee land—infinitely worse to profit from it.

To The Ridge, by popular consensus, fell "the honor of destroying Doublehead." James Vann, adept at murder, was to assist him but reneged on the assignment—not from a fastidious conscience. The Ridge found another assistant and waylaid Doublehead at his favorite tavern at Hiwassee, where a ball-play was in progress. A lighted candle in the tavern signaled the arrival of his victim.

Doublehead proved as hard to kill as a later-day Rasputin. The Ridge first shot him through the head below the ear. Doublehead fled to a nearby house and hid beneath blankets. The Ridge pursued him, fired his rifle into the bundle, then emptied his pistol into Doublehead's body. Doublehead struggled to his feet and grappled with his attacker. For a while they rocked back and forth in a mortal embrace, until The Ridge managed to extract his tomahawk and bury it deep in his opponent's skull.

No explanation was needed to justify the execution. The Ridge was more than ever honored for the act, as one who would tolerate no compromise on the sanctity of Indian territory. Jonathan Meigs and the War Department, and even Thomas Jefferson, had been served fair warning that the days of surrendering Cherokee lands were over. If they would only heed it. . . .

There was another significant consequence of Doublehead's murder. Fearing the same fate, Tahlonteskee and a band of followers fled the Nation and made their way through the wilderness by secret paths, to cross the Mississippi and settle in the upper regions of the Arkansas. Known in time as the "Old Settlers," they formed the nucleus of what would become the Cherokee Nation in the West.

Up to the nineteenth century the tribe had generally resisted education and religion. These were white men's institutions, and hence suspect. But the Cherokees were a people of natural curiosity and quick perception. Deeply embedded in their character was a respect for knowledge, a hunger to know, and an unusual capacity for learning. And after 1800 their distrust of formal education underwent a major change.

The treaties of Hopewell and Holston provided funds for the "civilizing" of the Indians, a word that was happily open to interpretation, and Jonathan Meigs had been authorized to import carpenters, blacksmiths, wheelwrights, and weavers to instruct the Cherokees in their trades. But this was training for the hand and not the mind. They wanted more, especially for their children; they wanted books and teachers and, above all, schools.

Gideon Blackburn, a Presbyterian minister from Tennessee, was among the first fully to recognize the potentialities for education in the Nation. He felt, as did the Cherokees, that the hope for their future was in the young, in the bright eyes and the quick minds of their children. Being a theologian, he was suspect; but he appeared before the General Council at Ustanali and not only obtained permission to open a school in the Overhills near Tellico, but was given the title of Superintendent of Education among the Cherokee Indians.

Encouraged perhaps by Blackburn's success, a more enduring start was made by the United Moravian Brethren of Salem, North Carolina, who had had their evangelical eye on the Nation for some time. Appearing before the Council in 1799, their agent proposed establishing a mission and school at Spring Place, near the home of James Vann. "Their desire appears to be good," Little Turkey told the Council, "to instruct us and our children and improve our and their minds and Nation. These gentlemen, I hope, will make the experiment; we will be the judge from their conduct and their attention to us and our children, this will enable us to judge properly."[3]

Little Turkey made no mention of religion; religious instruction was not considered germane to the project; the Moravians were to teach and not to preach. In fact, the Cherokees were so anxious that the school be started that they threatened to expel the missionaries when they seemed to move too slowly.

Support came to the Moravians from an unlikely source. James Vann seemed beyond redemption in the missionaries' eyes; beyond redemption in Cherokee eyes as well. His conduct was considered "outrageous in the Extreme and he threatens the Life of any persons who dare to call him to account." Yet Vann welcomed the Moravians, possibly thinking of the future of his young son Joseph. He gave them land on which to build the mission school and fields on which to plant their crops and offered the service of his slaves to get things started.

If Vann was hoping by these charities to obtain atonement for his sins, or at least postpone the day of judgment, it failed to work. In January 1809 the Moravians were relieved of both his benevolence and his pernicious influence. Telling his wife at a whiskey breakfast, "I have already killed one man this morning, and when I finish this quart I'm going to kill another," he was hailed to the door by his brother-in-law, who shot him dead. The estate, including the house, mill, ferry, tavern, store, and slaves, went to his son, who thereafter was known as "Rich Joe" Vann.[4]

By this time Gideon Blackburn's school at Tellico had fulfilled its promise. There were not many students; he had deliberately chosen a location he considered "difficult to civilize"; but he made scholastic prodigies of the twenty-five boys and girls who lived and boarded there.

A tribute to their training and scholarly progress came from the Indian fighter "Nolichucky Jack" Sevier, now governor of Tennessee, who had once called Cherokee children "nits that make lice" and had instructed his troops to shoot them on sight. In July 1805, Governor Sevier attended an exhibition given by Blackburn's students in which the little "nits," neatly dressed and in disciplined file, sang hymns, recited poetry, and demonstrated their skill at reading, spelling, and arithmetic. At the end of the performance the governor wiped the tears from his eyes and warmly shook the principal's hand.

"I have often stood unmoved amidst showers of bullets from Indian rifles," Sevier told the educator, "but this effectively unmans me. I see civilization taking the ground of barbarism, and the praises of Jesus succeeding the war whoops of the savages."[5]

The Moravian school at Spring Place had been equally successful, after some money problems that delayed the opening till October 1804. In the following year a remarkable couple came down from Salem to run the mission, the Reverend John Gambold and his wife, Anna Rosel. They seemed more like parents than teachers to the little Cherokees who scurried about on domestic tasks that kept the school clean and tidy, the crops cut, and the chickens fed. With their help, Mrs. Gambold planted an herb garden behind the mission that became to foreign visitors one of the more remarkable projects of its kind in the United States.

Along with the teaching of the three R's, the Gambolds turned their pupils' minds to the meaning of religion. Christmas was celebrated by the singing of carols and of Christmas hymns in English, the story of the Nativity was recited and explained to them, and the Gambolds found their charges "very attentive and happy." But their acceptance of Christianity was slow in coming; there was too much conflict with their own more comfortable beliefs. The first major breakthrough came when Charles Hicks consented to be baptized in 1813—the second adult conversion in the Nation—and was given the middle name of Renatus, or "Reborn."

Few men among the Cherokees were more respected, and Hicks's conversion broke the ice that blocked the Indians' acceptance of the new religion. The Ridge's wife Susanna followed Hicks's example, though The Ridge himself would hold out for a while. Perhaps the most startling convert was James Vann's mother, Wawli Vann, who may have sought comfort for her son's untimely end. "I let you know that God has changed my heart," she informed her many relatives. "I am so happy as I have never been all my life. Formerly, for many years, I thought as you do and lived as you live. God has had mercy on me. May you all make the same experience."[6]

For a Vann to introduce the name of God, with such passionate reverence, was indeed an apocalyptic tribute to the white man's deity. Perhaps this thing called Christianity bore looking into.

One of the consequences of Doublehead's execution, however much condoned, was a revision of the Cherokees' unwritten laws. Like their children at the Tellico and Spring Place schools, the adults were learning—and absorbing some of the white man's ideas of government and principles of justice. In 1810 the Blood Law assigning vengeance to the clans was abolished by a General Council meeting at Ustanali. The judicial power was vested in the Council, and sentence would be passed on those accused of crimes only after adequate testimony had been offered.

"The period has at last arrived," wrote Gideon Blackburn, "on which I have long fixed my eager eye. The Cherokee Nation has at length determined to become men and citizens."[7]

As a token of their undiminished confidence in The Ridge, the Council appointed him head of the Nation's first police force. Called the Light Horse Guard or simply the Light Horse, it consisted of two mounted "regulating companies" of six men each, assigned to patrol the territory and, among other things, to curb just such arbitrary acts of vengeance as The Ridge himself had perpetrated. The chief bent over backward to adhere to the new code of justice, showing no partiality. If a Cherokee abused or mistreated a white man within the boundaries of the Nation, he was hauled before the Council to be duly tried.

Judge John W. H. Underwood of Georgia, who later would play a role in Cherokee affairs, noted to what degree The Ridge's Light Horse leadership enhanced his reputation with the white community. It gave the chieftain, wrote Underwood, "an honorable name among the pale faces, who ever after looked to him to redress wrongs committed by members of his tribe; and when he fought so bravely at the Battle of the Horseshoe, several years later, under Gen. Jackson, all felt that his laurels were lightly worn."

It goes without saying that Cherokee progress was fostered by white competition. One thing, however, still was lacking: a strong central government with a stable constitution. They could debate matters of the common good at General Council, called where and as required. But they had no solid precedents or written laws to guide them. They were still a loose confederation of communities searching for a national identity. They could have no national policy, of course, until they created that identity.

The same might be said of the American Indians in general. Their strong sense of independence rejected a central Indian authority. The idea of an Indian league of nations would have struck them as preposterous. They looked up to their tribal chiefs and leading warriors. They formed alliances in time of intertribal war. But they never thought to marshal their forces in one combined defense against their greatest enemy, the white man who was stripping them of their inheritance. They would fight the invader separately but not together.

Until Tecumseh came along. Son of a Shawnee chief, he and his half-blind brother, Tenskwatawa, or "the Prophet," were a formidable team, a combination of warrior and messiah. Like the Cherokees, they believed that the Indian lands were sacred grants from the Great Spirit, and there could be no compromise with white intrusion. Tecumseh sought to weld the Northwestern tribes into a tight confederation, bound by Indian traditions. He banned the use of liquor, proscribed trade and intermarriage with the whites, advocated a return to ancient Indian ways.

Techumseh's proposed pan-Indian alliance was a defensive measure, not a call for war. The Ohio River was to be a boundary, not a front line of attack. But William Henry Harrison, territorial governor of Indiana, did not see it that way, branding Tecumseh "one of those uncommon geniuses which spring up occasionally, to produce revolutions and overturn the established order of things." It was this hostile American attitude that led Tecumseh to side with the British in Canada in the coming war with England, and sent him south in the summer of 1811 to secure the allegiance of the Choctaws, Chickasaws, Cherokees, and Creeks.

The Ridge and forty-eight other Cherokee chiefs attended a Council to hear what the "Flying Panther" had to say. Tecumseh apparently had some of The Ridge's gift of oratory. According to Lewis Cass, later Secretary of War, his address to the assembly was "the utterance of a great mind":

When he spoke to his brethren on the glorious theme that animated all his actions, his fine countenance lighted up, his firm and erect frame swelled with deep emotions, which his own stern dignity could scarcely repress; every feature and gesture had its meaning, and language flowed tumultuously and swiftly, from the fountains of his soul.[8]

But the words were alien to the Cherokees' goal of civilization and coexistence with the whites—calling upon them to renounce their schools and books and English alphabet, abandon their farms and mills, their plows and spinning wheels, and "put on paint and buckskin, and be Indians again." To imitate the white man would only bring destruction by his hand.

It was a message that appealed to the more backward Cherokees, especially those of the mountain regions, where the old traditions lingered and antagonism to the white man was implacable. But not to The Ridge, who saw it as a regressive, anti-American policy. "We turned away our ears," he later told President Madison, "and never listened a moment to the orations of the enemies of our father."[9]

But many Cherokees listened, and when the matter came up for discussion in the General Council, one of their conjurors or prophets—speaking, he said, for the Great Spirit—called upon the assembly to accept Tecumseh's plan. The Cherokees must "discard all the fashions of the whites, abandon the use of any communication with each other except by word of mouth, and give up their mills, their houses, and all the arts learned from the white people." Those who failed to follow this counsel, the Great Spirit had decreed, must die.

For once The Ridge had trouble getting attention. The conjuror's speech had raised a frenzy of applause. But The Ridge stood and waited until his presence had restored some order in the crowd. Then he told them:

My friends, the talk you have heard is not good. It would lead us to war with the United States, and we should suffer; it is false; it is not a talk from the Great Spirit.

I stand here and defy the threat that he who disbelieves shall die. Let the death come upon me. I offer to test this scheme of imposters![10]

He had barely stopped speaking when the onslaught came. From all sides the Cherokees attacked, pounding him with their fists, striking him with the bone handles of their knives. But The Ridge was as hard as the mahogany that matched his skin. He beat them back until one of the fighting Vanns came to his rescue, followed by others who formed a flailing ring around their chief.

The defeated conjuror made a last move to regain control. There were obviously disbelievers, he admitted. But they were about to perish in a mighty hailstorm that The Ridge's heresy would bring upon their heads. He urged the Cherokees to follow him to a mountaintop in the Smokies where they could escape destruction. Hundreds did; and waited for the awesome blast. When nothing happened, they walked down again—humiliated. Ridicule was traumatic to the Cherokees. Never again would the role of conjuror play a significant part in their affairs.

Among the Southeastern tribes only the Creeks really listened to Tecumseh, and they listened poorly. Mistaking his message as calling for immediate war on white Americans, they responded with the Fort Mims massacre, which led to Jackson's punitive campaign and the Creeks' annihilation as a Nation.

At the time, the Cherokees seemed to have chosen wisely in supporting Jackson. They had always had trouble with Creeks themselves. But almost as soon as the Battle of Horseshoe Bend was over they began to doubt that wisdom.

To young John Ross, visiting Washington City for the first time in his life, the American capital was an unimposing place of dismal distances. It looked, as another visitor had written, "as if some giant had scattered a box of child's toys on the ground." And then dropped a lighted match among them. The Capitol building, set afire by the British, was charred and sightless and minus its dome. Pennsylvania Avenue was a sea of mud that floated saloons and gambling halls and brothels. With the miasma seeping up from the city canal it even smelled bad.

The President's House, beginning to be called "the White House," had not been repaired, and Madison was obliged to conduct business in the "queer octagonal house" of a Washington landlord. It was little more elegant than the Daniel Ross home at Rossville, or the manor that John had built for himself and his young bride, Quatie, after returning from the war. Nor was President Madison in this last month in office, February 1816, a formidable figure. Shorter than Ross, a little plumper, and dressed in black with tight knee breeches, the Chief Executive seemed timidly apprehensive, as if looking over his shoulder for a glimpse of the returning British forces bent on wreaking further havoc on his city.

Still, this interview was an event for Ross and one on which he would cut his wisdom teeth. He was here as one of six delegates whose purpose was, politely phrased, "to wait upon the President." More specifically their mission concerned an adjustment of Jackson's error in lumping Cherokee lands with the territory he demanded from the Creeks, and the settlement of damage claims resulting from the depredations of federal troops who had foraged through the Nation in the War of 1812.

Besides John Ross and Agent Meigs as intermediary and adviser, the delegation included The Ridge, George Lowrey's gifted older brother John as spokesman for the group, Richard Taylor, Chief Kummessee or Dragging Canoe, Richard Taylor, and John Walker. All had aided Jackson in the Creek campaign—a fact which should have carried weight with President Madison, who was both impressed and intimidated by the hickory-hard former senator from Tennessee. Before leaving the Nation, Chief Pathkiller had instructed them to "take our Father, the President of the United States, by the hand and express to him the satisfaction we feel in having successfully carried through the late war."

Though no Cherokees had visited the ,capital for seven years, Indians in Washington were not an unfamiliar sight. But this particular delegation did not conform to the popular image of painted and untutored savages. Pathkiller had committed them to "wise and prudent conduct" and they lived up to his counsel. "These are men of cultivation and understanding," noted the *National Intelligencer* of their arrival; "their appearance and deportment are such as to entitle them to respect and attention."

They got both. The Ridge could hardly be denied attention. In frock coat and silk cravat, his now white hair contrasting sharply with his bronze complexion, The Ridge was every inch the statesman, whether striding on boot-shod feet down Pennsylvania Avenue or riding with his black attendant in the team-drawn carriage that he used on such occasions. Approaching fifty, he was the senior delegate. Ross, twenty years his junior, was the youngest. Like the others, he was dressed in American-style clothes and with his fair complexion could have passed for white.

John Lowrey acted as speaker for the delegation, and Ross recorded the dialogue that prefaced their discussion:

COLONEL LOWREY: Father, I have now the pleasure to be in your presence. I am directed by my National Council to take you our Father by the hand. This day was appointed by the Great Spirit for us to see one another. It makes my heart as glad to enter your house as it does when I enter my own house. . . .

HIS EXCELLENCY JA. MADISON: I was apprised of your coming before you arrived at this place. It always gives me great pleasure to receive my friends at my house especially my red Brethren the Cherokees who have fought by the side of their White Brethren and spilt their blood together.[11]

With this auspicious start both sides got down to business. War damage claims were acknowledged with a promised payment of $25,600, which, however, might be slow in coming. The millions of acres Jackson had appropriated in his treaty with the Creeks were reinstated. It was agreed that the federal government would have the right to build and maintain roads and river navigation in the Nation, to facilitate commerce with adjoining states, which would benefit both Indians and whites.

Yet the Cherokees had long since realized that no favors came from the United States without some territorial concessions. Included in the treaty signed on March 22, 1816, was the sale of their remaining lands in South Carolina for $5,000. They got in return, however, a guarantee of all their claims south of the Tennessee River. On the whole, things balanced out to indicate a fruitful mission, as the delegates reported to the people on returning to the Nation.

But they had yet to reckon with Governor Joseph McMinn of Tennessee and the still more outraged Andrew Jackson. The treaty protecting Cherokee lands below the Tennessee was, in Jackson's words, "a wanton, hasty, and useless act." He vowed to "undo it," and intended to accomplish this by appealing "to the predominant and governing passions of all Indian tribes, i.e., their avarice or fear."

As a first step Jackson had himself appointed one of three commissioners—the other two being Governor McMinn, a facsimile of Jackson, and fellow traveler David Meriwether—to make a new deal with the Cherokees that would abrogate the earlier 1816 treaty. Bribery would be the lever, and the more susceptible chiefs, those with the least reputation to lose, would be the targets. Jackson ferreted out a dozen of these and in the summer of 1816 obtained their signatures on a contract ceding 3,500 square miles below the Tennessee for $5,000 in cash and $6,000 in annuities.

As Jackson confessed to War Secretary John Calhoun: "In concluding the treaty with the Cherokees, it was found both well and polite to make a few presents to the chiefs and interpreters." However, to secure the treaty's ratification by the Cherokee General Council was another hurdle to be surmounted. Here again, resentment over the betrayal of the Nation by a dissident minority was overcome by "presents offered to the influential chiefs, amounting to $4,500, to be paid on the success of the negotiations."

United States hunger for Indian lands was an appetite that fed upon itself. Having made this further dent in Cherokee territory, the commissioners went after more, applying a different sort of pressure. Since Tahlonteskee's flight to the West after Doublehead's murder, and even before, isolated groups of Cherokees had drifted across the Mississippi to settle between the White and Arkansas rivers. There were an estimated 2,000 to 3,000 out there now, reportedly having trouble with the neighboring hostile Osages, who regarded the Eastern Indians as interlopers.

Jackson appeared before the Cherokee Council to propose a solution to their problems in the Arkansas. The United States could not protect the Western Cherokees from the surrounding tribes or even from white invaders since they had no title to the territory they had settled on. That land could not be reserved for them unless an equivalent amount of land was ceded in the East. Were the Cherokees going to let their Western brothers down?

With these arguments went a far more pregnant suggestion. Would not the Cherokees as a whole be better off in the West, where, by the cession of their eastern lands, they would enjoy guaranteed security?

"As free men you have now to make your choice," said Jackson. "Those who go West go to a country belonging to the United States. There your father, the President, can never be urged by his white children to ask their red brothers, the Cherokees, for any of the lands laid off at that place for them." The general concluded with the hint that no such promise protected their territory in the East, regardless of what treaties had been formulated in the past.[12]

The Cherokees listened in stunned silence. This made no sense. They considered themselves already an established sovereign Nation over which the United States had no control beyond trade regulations. Why this talk of having to make a choice? The matter of where they should live and maintain their Nation had been settled at Hopewell and Holston twenty years before. If those who had unwisely emigrated to the West were having trouble out there, let them come back to the East where they belonged.

It was hard to fight their case with so loose an organization as the General Council. A less unwieldy "committee of thirteen" was created to protect their interests, and John Ross, now only twenty-six, entered public life as a member of that chosen group. The Ridge had had his eye on Ross for some time. He himself had no education, he could neither read nor write; and though he spoke English he found it better, in dealing with whites, to talk through an interpreter. Ross was well spoken in both Cherokee and English, well read, and well informed on American and Cherokee affairs. In promoting his selection for the new committee, The Ridge, with extraordinary prescience, told the young man, "You are being relegated into purgatory." And in a sense The Ridge was right.

John worked with Elijah Hicks, son of Second Chief Charles Renatus Hicks, in drafting a memorial of protest which was signed by sixty-seven of the chiefs and presented to Andrew Jackson. It stated simply that the Cherokees chose to remain where they were, "in the land of their birth where they were rapidly advancing in civilization." It politely suggested that this matter of emigration be pressed no further. The subject was closed.

But Jackson and the War Department pressed it further. They had some support from Jonathan Meigs, who, to be charitable, may have reached the conclusion that removal was inevitable and possibly in the best interests of the Cherokees. Jackson also urged Sam Houston, now a rising young lawyer in Tennessee, to use his influence as an adopted Cherokee. Houston agreed to do so and joined his foster father Chief Oolooteka, or John Jolly, at the latter's home on the Hiwassee River. As Tahlonteskee's brother, Jolly had already given thought to moving West with his family, relatives, and friends.

The treaty that Jackson advocated did not make removal mandatory. It simply held out inducements. Those willing to move West would receive free transportation plus reimbursement for the "improvements"—homes, barns, crops, and such—that they were forced to leave behind. To those who needed them would be provided blankets, cooking utensils, rifles, and ammunition. With these lures the commissioners secured minority approval of a treaty, signed on July 8, 1817, which ceded two large tracts in Tennessee and Georgia for an equivalent amount of territory in the West.

The annuities now paid the Cherokees for previously ceded lands would be reapportioned between Eastern and Western Cherokees according to their relative numbers. Payment would meanwhile be withheld until a census could be taken to establish this apportionment. Another cunning clause was tucked into the document. Those who chose to remain in the East would receive title to 640 acres provided they qualified as citizens of those states in which these reservations lay.

Had the Cherokees possessed a strong central government they could have outwitted or resisted the commissioners. But they had no control over the minorities in their society; and Jackson and the War Department—and the United States Senate when matters got that far—were willing to recognize any contract properly drawn and signed by any Indians who professed to represent the tribe. The opportunities for bribery and/or coercion were immense.

In vain the Cherokees sent another mission to Washington to protest a treaty that still lacked majority approval. They never got as far as President Monroe or Secretary John Calhoun. Instead, they were confronted with a *fait accompli*. Boats and provisions were being assembled for the journey West, for all those consenting to removal.

At the Tellico agency Jonathan Meigs estimated that some 3,500 Cherokees had enrolled for emigration. These suffered such disdain and persecution from their fellow tribesmen that their numbers shrank as summer blended into autumn. There were no precise records of how many made the journey; and it was not until midwinter that John Jolly led the principal contingent, about 700, aboard the nineteen flatboats waiting for them on the Tennessee.

They started downriver in February 1818 in the first organized emigration in the Nation's history. With Jolly's party was the silversmith Sequoyah, who was leaving partly to escape his Xanthippe-like wife. He had never abandoned his hot pursuit of a written language for the Cherokees, and in recent years had moved from his house to a nearby hut where he could work in peace. Sally agreed with the neighbors that her husband was up to no good; the secretive hut was harboring some sort of hanky-panky. She lured Sequoyah from his refuge long enough for neighbors to set fire to the place, destroying the shelter and all current samples of his work.

Philosophically, Sequoyah resolved to start anew. Flight to the West might change his luck. All down the Tennessee, the Ohio, and the Mississippi he toiled over slabs of bark with a piece of charcoal, trying to master the art of changing sounds to symbols. On the steamboat creeping up the Arkansas he listened to how people talked, to the sounds of birds, to the mysterious voices of spirit folk singing from the banks. He was, without a doubt, a little crazy.

After a journey of over seventy days the party disembarked in the Arkansas River area northwest of Little Rock where the earlier emigrants, the "Old Settlers," had put down roots. But, wrote Chief Jolly to War Secretary John Calhoun, "you must not think that by removing we shall return to the savage life." They had brought with them the Cherokee urge for self-improvement. They intended to become farmers, cattle raisers, ironmongers, weavers. "It is the wish of our people that you will send us . . . teachers. We shall settle more compactly on our new lands than we were [in the East]; and this will be of advantage to teaching our children."[13]

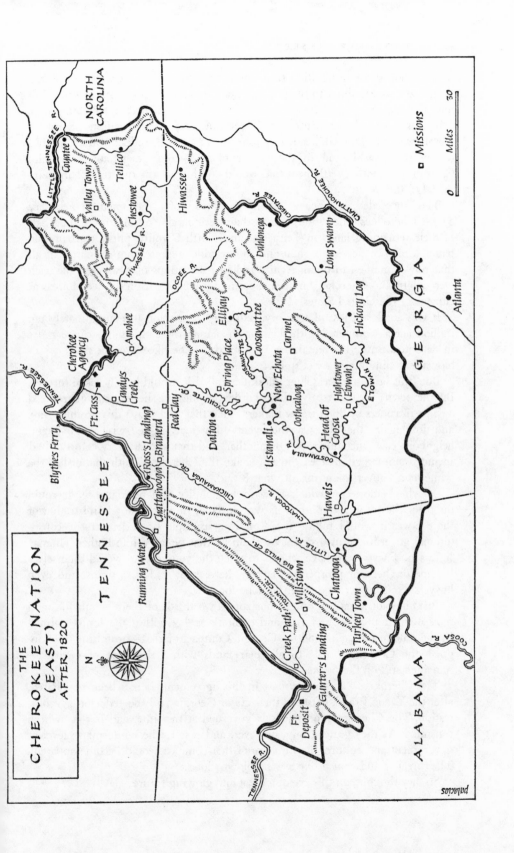

THE
CHEROKEE NATION
(EAST)
AFTER 1820

N

TENNESSEE

NORTH CAROLINA

GEORGIA

ALABAMA

□ Missions

0   Miles   30

LITTLE TENNESSEE R.

Coyatee
Valley Town
Tellico
Chestowee
HIWASSEE R.
Hiwassee
OCOEE R.
Amohee
Cherokee Agency
TENNESSEE R.
Blythes Ferry
Candys Creek
Ft. Cass
Ross's Landing
Brainerd
Chattanooga
Running Water
CHICKAMAUGA CR.

Dahlonega
Long Swamp
CHESTATEE R.
CHATTAHOOCHEE R.
Atlanta

Ellijay
Spring Place
Coosawattee
COOSAWATTEE R.
Carmel
Hickory Log
Hightower
(Etowah)
ETOWAH R.
New Echota
COOSAWATTEE R.
Red Clay
Dalton
Ustanali
Oothcaloga
Head of Coosa
OOSTANAULA R.
CHATOOGA R.
Haweis

Creek Path
Willstown
TOWN CR.
BIG WILLS CR.
LITTLE R.
Chatooga
Turkey Town
Gunter's Landing
Ft. Deposit
TENNESSEE R.
COOSA R.

palacios

They hoped for recognition from the United States as a new Cherokee Nation in the West, allied to the Eastern Nation. That might come in time. But now the Eastern Cherokees chose to regard them as a heretic splinter group, and still resented the drumhead Treaty of 1817. A delegation of twelve members of the Council, headed by John Ross as new President of the Committee, visited Washington in the winter of 1818–19 to negotiate with John Calhoun yet another settlement that would end forever the question of mass removal to the West.

They succeeded, at a heavy cost. By the Treaty of 1819, signed on February 27, the Cherokees ceded thousands of their peripheral acres and more than half of their remaining lands in Tennessee and North Carolina plus a tract in Alabama, a total of nearly six thousand square miles representing a quarter of all that now remained to them. Again, Indian reservations of a square mile each were allotted to Cherokee families choosing to remain within the ceded areas as citizens of the United States.

It was a colossal loss of territory, reducing the Nation to approximately ten million acres. Compared with their original forty-three thousand square miles in de Soto's time, this remainder resembled in Cherokee eyes "a small windblown leaf clinging to a wet stone."

But "this last little," as Chief Pathkiller called it, would be Cherokee forever. By the terms of the treaty, their borders would be henceforth guaranteed against intruders or illicit treaty makers. That they had heard this promise time and time again; that this was the twenty-fifth treaty signed with Anglo-Saxon neighbors, each one superseded by another, and that almost every compact had included similar guarantees, did not shake the Cherokees' faith that at last the white man's government meant what it said.

So—the Nation could look forward to stability and permanence. It could build for the future, strengthen its written laws, improve the administration of those laws. It would follow the American example of a democratic, constitutional government as urged upon them by that Great White Father Thomas Jefferson. They would have schools to teach the young, who would themselves become teachers, or prosperous farmers, herdsmen, traders, artisans, and even lawyers. Nothing was too much to hope for now.

Just one blot remained on the horizon. Two thirds of their population, and most of their prosperous farms and plantations, lay within the limits claimed by the state of Georgia. And the Georgia Compact of 1802—promising to extinguish the Cherokees' title to all their lands within the state of Georgia—remained still on the books.

The Cherokees had had no part in this agreement. It had been negotiated, after the Yazoo Fraud, between the state of Georgia and the Jefferson administration. The Cherokees, only loosely governed at the time, had not even been consulted. As they grew strong, however, and rose to the white man's level of government and culture, the injustice of that compact would become apparent. The threat would vanish like a wind-blown cloud.

So they thought, on this eve of a great and glowing future.

4

The Light of Athens

HE HAD BEEN teaching starry-eyed young Cherokees for only five years. Yet Gideon Blackburn, supervisor of education, was able to conclude his progress report with the paragraph:

Thus far are the Cherokees advanced; further I believe than any other Indians in America . . . This is the most critical period I have ever seen . . . and a time which calls forth all the energy in the minds of the Indians.[1]

He was right on several points. In a few short years the Cherokees as a whole had made extraordinary progress—to outstrip, in the so-called "civilized arts," their principal competitors: Creeks, Seminoles, Chickasaws, and Choctaws. They had reached that critical point when a sudden rise to unfamiliar heights could lead to a loss of balance and a danger of collapse. The stabilizing factor lay in their fertile, energetic minds.

There was something in the Cherokee character that made learning a psychological imperative. It was not merely a drive to match or ape the white man's ways, however much those ways might be to their advantage. It was more a desire for knowledge for its own sake; a curiosity toward the unknown; an eager reaching out for the beyond. Though often self-taught, they were eminently teachable.

The Moravian school at Spring Place had become the central seat of learning, and the gentle Brethren—sticking to their pledge to put teaching first, preaching second—had done much to plumb the Cherokee potential. But though centrally positioned, the school served a limited area. And it did not, at first, accept female students even though woman's role ranked high in Cherokee society.

Spring Place, however, and the whole future pattern of education was given a lift when Charles Hicks had knelt before Brother Gambold to be baptized—putting a stamp of acceptance on the white man's Christianity. The Cherokees would not quickly abandon the old myths, the Immortals and the Little People, or lose faith in the magic of their conjurors. But they were curious at least about this new approach to the Great Spirit, which seemed roughly the same as their ancient and simplistic doctrine: "If you are good, you go up; if bad, down." Following Hicks's example, many conceded it was worth a try.

Blackburn's two schools were forced to close in 1810 because of the principal's failing health, and the educator returned to his native Tennessee. But Blackburn and the Moravians had broken the ice of suspicion and hostility toward the missionary movement, and other evangelical orders saw in the Cherokee Nation a fertile field for their ambitions.

They slipped in quietly and were welcome in a score or more of hamlets in the valleys. The Baptists opened a mission and school on the Hiwassee River, with some religious rituals endearing to the Cherokees; baptism by submersion was close to their rite of "going to the river." The Welsh-born superintendent Evan Jones was prepared, he vowed, to spend his lifetime with the Indians. The Methodists came with an ebullient approach that included lively camp meetings, song fests, and even informal ball-play—the latter considered a pagan, barbaric diversion by the other sects. John Ross became an early convert of the Methodists, though his wife Quatie remained with the Moravians.

But the principal force for education and religious training in the Nation, and one which preceded all but the Moravians, was the American Board of Commissioners for Foreign Missions which had been founded in Boston in 1810 with the audacious goal of evangelizing the entire heathen world within a decade. It was an ambition not incommensurate with the strength of Puritan faith in New England; but the Board sensibly limited its initial campaign to selected areas—Africa, the Pacific islands, and the Indian territories of the Eastern seaboard (leaving the Western tribes to the head-start Methodists). In its annual report for 1816, prepared by its founder and secretary, Jeremiah Evarts, the Board stated its aims regarding the Cherokee Nation: "To make the whole tribe English in their language, civilized in their habits, and Christian in their religion."

A pioneer of this movement was the Congregational minister Cyrus Kingsbury, who first approached the United States government for funds, then sought and obtained permission from the Cherokee Council to build a coeducational school in the Nation on a larger scale than either the Moravians or Gideon Blackburn had conceived. Kingsbury would not stay long, only long enough to record his initial efforts and to institute the keeping of a "Mission Journal," which would ultimately come to rest, in manuscript form, at Harvard University. Two early entries for the winter of 1817:

Saturday Jan. 18. arrived at Chickamauga, for the purpose of making preparations to commence and establish a Lancastrian school at that place. The work is of the highest importance & I feel the need of emploring the divine aid and direction.

Sabbath, Feb. 26 . . . But alas! how little do I feel of the divine ardour . . .[2]

The twin comments suggest some of the mental anguish, the initial doubts and discouragement of the early missionaries. But between the two dates, and from then till summer, Kingsbury made rapid progress. He met Charles Hicks, John Ross, and Ross's nephew William Shorey Coodey, and probably through them was able to purchase the farm of Ross's grandfather, John McDonald. It was located on Chickamauga Creek in Tennessee just north of the Georgia line. With the aid of Jonathan Meigs he converted and enlarged the farm into a cluster of buildings the size of an Indian village, with classrooms and separate dormitories for the boys and girls, naming the complex "Brainerd" for two earlier, kindred missionaries to the Indians. Joined by two other cohorts appointed by the Boston Board, Kingsbury sounded a more positive, clarion note in his next Journal entry:

Sabbath. March 9.   We are now a little band of missionaries, who profess to have renounced the world for the sake of Christ. O! that we may be faithful to our covenant vows.[3]

By early summer the fifty-acre school was operating in full swing with classrooms, dormitories, kitchen, washroom, granary, barns, and stable. The establishment was designed to be self-sustaining: the fields were plowed for corn, hogs and cattle would be raised, and much of the work was done by students as an adjunct to their education—the boys tilling the soil, clearing roads, doing carpentry; the girls tending to the housework, to the kitchen and washroom, to sewing, weaving, candle making.

Like Kingsbury, the initial staff came largely from Massachusetts, some of them graduates of the Andover Theological Seminary, a womb of Puritanism in New England. To their credit and despite their disciplinary background, they adjusted with discernment to the needs and freer thinking of the Cherokees. There was a great deal of give and take, to the point where it was sometimes a question of who was instructing whom; in time the missionaries found they had as much to learn as the Cherokees themselves.

An early arrival from the Mission Rooms in Boston was William Chamberlin, who took Kingsbury's place as teacher and preacher of the gospel, adhering to the Cherokees' rule that education must come first. Dr. Elizur Butler, though less of a scholar than his associate, brought some medical training plus a good deal of dedication and tough durability to the community—enough of these traits to make him a national figure in the years to come.

Daniel S. Butrick, twenty-eight when he arrived, a self-sworn celibate fresh from Andover, had two characteristics that endeared him to the Cherokees: unbounded enthusiasm and a knack of doing everything wrong. They could laugh with and at Butrick, a splendid combination. He was forever falling off horses and ridgepoles in his eagerness to share in their activities; and on expeditions through the forest he would end up, mystifyingly, on the wrong side of the river and have to be retrieved by exhausting rescue operations.

There was another puzzling side to Butrick. Several of the Brainerd teachers kept daily journals, and Butrick's diary reveals a soul in torment. "O how wicked and foolish I am! . . . I have cause to weep day and night over the depravity of my heart & life . . . I am always exercising myself in great matters & in things too high for me . . . O thou dear Saviour, Farewell . . . I sink beneath the flood."[4]

Butrick's self-castigation would, perhaps, explain a later, greater personal quandary. But his immediate problem was the vice of smoking, a ritual among the Indians but an addiction in the case of Butrick. He threw his pipe in a thicket, but awoke the next morning with "phlegm on the stomach," and thought it advisable to resume the habit. After another period of swearing off, he found that abstinence damaged his memory, and retrieved the pipe from the customary thicket.

It was the Cherokees who cured him. Seeking to convert, through an interpreter, an unregenerate drunkard to whom he gave the name of Moses, Butrick suggested that they pray together. The two knelt side by side, and Daniel, effluvial pipe in mouth, beseeched his Redeemer to save old Moses' wayward soul. He then suggested through the interpreter that Moses say a prayer. The besotted Indian spoke a few words in Cherokee—with feeling.

"What did he say?" Butrick asked the interpreter.

"He thanks the Great Spirit for the tobacco smoke that drowns his face."[5]

Butrick gave up smoking.

There were women as well as men on the Brainerd staff, though these were often wives or daughters of the missionaries. Some were merely helpmates to begin with, until unforeseen circumstances forced them into larger roles—as would be the case with Elizur Butler's wife Lucy and Isaac Proctor's sister Elizabeth. A few who heard the call came unattached, evangelists in their own right, such as Catherine Fuller of Fitchburg, Massachusetts, and Sophia Sawyer of Rindge, New Hampshire.

Sophia Sawyer—ah, there was a woman! From the first, the Brainerd community was at a loss to explain Sophia. With no existing daguerreotype or portrait of the lady one can only assume, from a description of her as "angular in mind and body," that she was homely, awkward, and most likely difficult. But one trait was inescapable. Temperamental and emotional, she burned with a reckless zest for life that was peculiarly at odds with her instructions.

When the bell sounded at the end of classes, and the Cherokee children tumbled out, to tear off their clothes and race naked as jaybirds to the nearest stream, Miss Sophia did not exactly follow their example, though she may have wished to. But she went with them to the swimming hole, organized berry-picking parties, and took them on picnics to places where the larks made nests or deer were apt to come. She explained what made a cricket chirp, and taught them to see extraordinary creatures in the stars. Like Butrick, Miss Sophia did not fit the missionary mold. And so they loved her.

The Ridge was sorely troubled. Above all, he wanted an education for his son John, fourteen, and his daughter Nancy, sixteen; he had been among the first to favor admitting missionary teachers to the Nation. John and Nancy had started their education with the Gambolds at Spring Place, but the Moravians

offered classes only in the elementary grades. The Ridge had his children transferred to Brainerd almost as soon as the mission opened.

Nancy was attractive, but no brilliant student; John was brilliant but a problem. It was noted in the Brainerd Journal, a daily record kept by the teachers,
that John had complained "in a hasty & petulant manner" of the insufficient
time and attention he was getting at the school. "Little had we expected such
an attitude, least of all from John, a boy of whom he had such great hopes."
When the teachers remonstrated with the boy, "he burst into a flood of tears—
said he meant no harm & was sorry he had given us so much pain—we could
freely forgive him."

But The Ridge could not be so easily appeased. He called at the school, having just heard that "my children are so bad you could not manage them." He
had with him a little Creek girl, captured after the Battle of Horseshoe Bend,
whom he was raising as his own. He suggested the teachers take her as a re-
placement for his children "and see if she will do better." Reassured that the
teachers were generally satisfied with John and Nancy, "he appeared overjoyed,
exclaiming 'Never was I so glad.' "[6]

Among the fifty-odd pupils enrolled by midsummer in the mission school
were others who brought joy and frustration, in sometimes equal doses, to the
Brainerd staff. There was the sirenlike Catherine Brown (none could pro-
nounce her Indian name of Tsaluh Yaunugungyahshi), shapely, ravishingly
beautiful, and queenlike in her manner, who appeared at the school so
bedecked in jewelry and sophisticated clothing that the missionaries doubted
that a child so worldly, so concerned with finery, could be serious in mind and
spirit.

They learned, however, that Catherine in earlier years had battled like a savage to protect her chastity when American troops came through the Nation in
the Creek campaign. So they took a chance and let her in. In a matter of weeks
she was referred to as "the saintly Catherine." She learned to read the Bible in
English in sixty days, was the first student to be baptized at Brainerd, and
shortly became a teacher in her own right. In four years, like a wasted Camille,
she was dead of consumption. Into the mission journal went the entry: "O ye
who enjoy the community of saints, remember Catherine in your prayers!"[7]

In physical contrast to Catherine was the appearance, one morning, of John
Arch, who had walked some seventy miles across the North Carolina mountains to arrive at Brainerd caked with dirt and with his clothes in shreds.
Speaking a few words of English, he offered to trade his rifle, all he had, for a
white man's education. Again the missionaries took a chance. They gave John
clothes in exchange for the rifle, put him to work at arithmetic and grammar—
and waited with apprehension for the consequences. John Arch, or Asti in
Cherokee, would also achieve a degree of sainthood before his premature death
a few years later.[8]

Discipline among the supposedly savage youngsters was rarely a serious
problem. One or two were dismissed for unexplained absences; and there were
a few infractions based on a different set of morals. One girl was found to be
keeping amatory trysts with a visiting Cherokee lad in a nearby cabin. The out-

raged missionaries burned the cabin to the ground, as a sample of God's wrath and a warning to the others. Thereafter, the Cherokee maiden, apparently cleansed of sin by fire, appeared more discreet and more content. Her conscience, the teachers felt, had been relieved of its unholy burden. They were right, in a way. She and her partner had found a safer, more isolated cabin.

There was no doubt among the Cherokees that the mission schools brought education of tremendous value to their young. Like The Ridge, they had never felt so glad for anything. Parents insisted that their children be accepted whether there was room for them or not. Brainerd, conceived for fifty pupils, found itself with eighty at the end of the first year. When a boy was dismissed for truancy or misbehavior, the family brought another to replace him. If a child was, for some reason, not up to performing physical chores, the father offered to send a slave to do the work.

The missionaries' goal, however, was not only to educate, civilize, and evangelize the Cherokees. It was also to train them as disciples of the gospel, prepared to spread the word and serve as teachers in an expanding network of mission schools. William Chamberlin was sent to help open a school at Willstown in Alabama; Daniel Butrick and Isaac Proctor established missions at Carmel and Hightower in north central Georgia. Other posts opened, as adjuncts to Brainerd, at Candy's Creek in Tennessee, Creek Path in Alabama, and Haweiss on the lower Oostanaula River.

The American Board of Commissioners for Foreign Missions, Presbyterian and Congregational, had no monopoly on education; the Methodists, Baptists, and Moravians helped expand the school network to twenty-six in number by 1825. The different sects as a rule got on well together, though some Brainerd missionaries looked with skepticism on the Methodists. "It is said when the Cherokees once join the Methodists, they have done with us," wrote Daniel Butrick in the undated journal he was keeping. The Methodists, he charged, encroached on Brainerd territory and, hearing of any dissatisfaction among the Indians there, would "fly with comfort on their wings and steal the hearts of all around us."

In general, however, there was more harmony than competition among the various denominations. But the American Board exerted the greater influence, mixing enterprise with a bit of daring and imagination. Unwilling to settle for carrying religion to the countries of the "heathen," such as the Cherokee Nation, the Board evolved a plan to bring the heathen to New England—to be trained in theology and returned to their respective lands to spread the faith among their compatriots.

The quiet little New England town of Cornwall, in the northwestern corner of Connecticut, was supremely blessed. Piously content beneath the shadow of Coltsfoot Mountain, it was an ideal place for religious contemplation. The Reverend Timothy Stone, from the pulpit of the Cornwall church, had instilled strict Puritan principles in the community. Deacon Benjamin Gold and his elder son, Ruggles Gold, among the town's foremost citizens, had been active supporters of New England missionary work. No less a divine than Lyman

Beecher—father of Henry Ward Beecher and Harriet Beecher Stowe—had helped to consecrate the site as an "outpost on the frontier of God's Kingdom."

Here the American Board of Foreign Missions decided to conduct a bold experiment, establishing, in 1817-18, the first mission school for the heathen on New England soil.

"The great object of the Foreign Mission School," said ex-governor John Treadwell at its opening, "is to afford a hospitable asylum for such unevangelized youth, of good promise, as are or shall be . . . cast upon us." These would be instructed in English and the sacred scriptures, in agriculture, science, and the classics, to the end that they might be returned to their people "to become preachers of the Gospel, or translators of the Sacred Volume."[9]

The school itself, which opened its doors in 1817, was an unpretentious gable-roofed building on the village green. There was provision for two class-rooms and a makeshift dormitory, whose limitations forced some students to live with families in the town. There must have been difficulties of adjustment between the somewhat narrow-minded but well-meaning townsfolk and these alien students of many races, nationalities, and languages—Polynesians, Melanesians, Sandwich Islanders, and Cherokees. The experiment called for almost incredible tolerance and understanding from all sides. Had the Board in Boston bitten off more than Cornwall citizens could chew?

In another outpost of the Kingdom, Brainerd in Tennessee, eight of the more promising students were selected for four years, more or less, of advanced study in the Cornwall school. The Ridge was quick to seek this advantage for his son John. The winters, he knew, were cold in New England, and John, slight and delicate, suffered from a scrofulous hip condition. But one must risk everything for learning. John had had the necessary training at Brainerd, and The Ridge had the necessary influence to see that John was appointed to the school.

Two other boys of rare ability were among the eight Cherokees attending Cornwall: "saintly Catherine's" brother David Brown, prize student at Brainerd, and Buck Watie, The Ridge's nephew, from the Moravian mission school at Spring Place. Youths entering the white man's world were allowed to adopt the name of mission benefactors. A likely donor was Dr. Elias Boudinot, president of the American Bible Society and a strong supporter of the Board of Foreign Missions. Buck Watie's first letter to the Gambolds at Spring Place expressed gratitude for having heard the voice of God that directed him to Cornwall; he promised to return to the Nation to spread the word among his fellows; and he signed the letter "Elias Boudinot"—a name that would endure and shine more brightly than the reputation of its original owner.

How, at first, the good people of Cornwall regarded these multi-hued heathens in their midst is hard to say. Most of the Cherokees spoke English, and David Brown, John Ridge, and Elias Boudinot were fluent in the language. But there were unpredictable pitfalls in the common ground of human nature. To the young maidens of the Litchfield Hills, so carefully drilled in Puritan behavior, there was something appealing in these handsome, proud, athletic-looking men from a distant, more primitive world.

As Ellen Gibbs, attending a school exercise, observed, "The Indian pupils appeared so graceful and genteel on the stage that the white pupils appeared uncouth beside them." Of The Ridge's son, who seemed to catch her eye, she noted, "John was a noble youth, beautiful in appearance, very graceful, a perfect gentleman everywhere."

So, not unexpectedly, there were innocent meetings on the school grounds between Cornwall girls and Cherokee youths; more intimate walks in the Litchfield Hills in which the mutual attraction made subtle headway. And sometimes circumstances helped to push them toward each other. . . .

When John Ridge fell ill with a hip infection during his second year at Cornwall, he was cared for at the home of John P. Northrup, steward of the school. All was congenial, and Ridge was soon able to get around on crutches. But when Sarah Bird Northrup, the steward's daughter, proclaimed her love for John and her wish to marry him, the Northrups felt that hospitality had gone too far. They sent Sarah to her grandmother's in New Haven for three months to get over the attachment, but it didn't work. Finally, they recommended that John return home until he fully regained his health—at least until he could discard the crutches—and let the matter of love and marriage simmer down.

John went back to his father's plantation in the summer of 1823. The following winter "a magnificent coach drawn by four white horses driven by a black in sumptuous livery" arrived at Cornwall. In it sat The Ridge, "stately in form and of aristocratic bearing." Beside him was his son John, fully restored to health and minus the crutches. John had returned to claim his prospective bride and take her back to the home he had built for them both near his father's mansion.

Perhaps it was The Ridge's commanding presence, his air of royal breeding and obvious wealth, that won the Northrups over. It was easy to entertain visions of Sarah as an Indian princess, dressed in silks and attended by slaves. In any event, the two were married with the family's consent, though without the approval of an outraged town. According to one account, "Ridge came near to being mobbed." Disdaining the commotion and the "excited throngs," The Ridge with his son and white-skinned daughter-in-law remounted the coach and headed back to Georgia.

When Cornwall fully realized what had happened, the reaction was explosive. The editor of *The American Eagle* in nearby Litchfield depicted Cornwall as a hotbed of miscegenation; he bewailed the young woman who had made herself a "squaw" and had "connected her ancestors to a race of Indians." The newspaper blamed the school, its staff, and the missionaries for this particular outrage and for generally aiding the downfall of the maidens of Connecticut.

A group of fair-minded youthful whites, signing themselves the "Bachelors of Cornwall Valley," took a charitable view of the affair. They gallantly wrote to the editor that they would take their chances with the Indians and that all was fair in love and war. They did not consider themselves "eclipsed by the intervention of these tawny rivals . . ." But the Board of Foreign Missions was less tolerant. The Cornwall school was warned against further mixed marriages. These would destroy the good work so far accomplished and would totally disrupt the program.[10]

Then another bombshell fell. Harriet Gold, youngest daughter of Benjamin and Eleanor Gold, "one of the fairest, most cultured young ladies of the place," announced her intention of marrying the handsome Elias Boudinot. Her shocked and troubled parents did their best to dissuade her. It was at last agreed that the matter should be kept a secret while Elias with his classmate David Brown went on to continue their studies at Andover Theological Seminary. The enforced delay and separation caused Harriet to waste away until her parents, fearing for her health, consented to their future marriage.

Looking ahead, it was a black day for Cornwall when Elias Boudinot returned for his bride in March 1826 and the banns were posted outside the Cornwall church. The old witch-hunting days of Salem returned briefly to the Litchfield Hills, bringing the darkness of the Middle Ages to the Puritan community. The white-robed girls of the choir were ordered to wear black armbands in mourning for their fallen sister. Poison-pen letters rained on Harriet and her family, and the Reverend Timothy Stone did all but deck his church in crepe.[11]

The climax came on the night before their marriage, when Harriet, her mother, and her groom were burned in effigy on the village green by a hooting mob that included Sarah's brothers. As the church bells tolled funereally, Harriet watched the bonfire from her bedroom window, and hung her head in sorrow but not in shame. She thought of the New Testament words: "Blessed are ye, when men shall revile you . . . for great is your reward in heaven," and she was sure her heaven was with Elias Boudinot, among the Cherokees.

Lyman Beecher rode into town to derail the "pagan" marriage, and he and Timothy Stone and agents of the Mission School posted a notice condemning "this evil" and "this outrage upon public feeling." So, abandoning their plans for a church wedding, Harriet and Elias were secretly married in the Gold home on March 28. They left immediately for Boudinot's ancestral country in the Etowah River valley, where Elias, now more than qualified, joined the staff of the mission which the Boston Board had opened at Hightower as an adjunct to the work at Brainerd.

The citizens of Cornwall had been cheated. The culprits had escaped unscathed, however shaken by the spleen of Puritan theology. Cornwall vented its wrath on the Foreign Mission School for corrupting, with its foreign students, the morals of Connecticut youth. Throughout New England former patrons withheld their financial support. Reluctantly, the Boston Board of Foreign Missions succumbed to the pressure, and in January 1827, with the dismayed students shipped back to their places of origin, the school was closed.

Despite its lamentable finish the school contributed much to the future of the Cherokees. It sent back from Cornwall many of the Nation's promising young men, prepared for leadership in their respective fields. Among them: John Ridge, Elias Boudinot, and David Brown; James Fields, a relative of the Ridges; Leonard Hicks, son of the Assistant Principal Chief; and John Vann of the notorious Vann family, whose younger generation was striving, with some success, to live down the sins of father James. And Cornwall was also responsible for two New England women who would almost warrant sainthood in their time: Sarah Northrup Ridge and Harriet Gold Boudinot, both of whom showed a more commendable kind of Puritan conscience than that displayed at Cornwall.

John Ross had not attended Cornwall. He and his wife Quatie had moved from Ross's Landing on the Tennessee to the head of the Coosa River in Georgia. Here John built a commodious two-story house as elegant as that of his near neighbor, Major Ridge, with fruit orchards, cotton and tobacco fields, herds of grazing cattle, and decorative peacocks on the lawn.

The Major's son, John Ridge, had ridden about this neighborhood with Elias Boudinot before Elias left for Cornwall, speculating on their future homesites if they ever married. They had passed Sequoyah's hut, before the neighbors had destroyed it, and had seen that secretive Cherokee scratching away on pieces of bark in his relentless pursuit of a written language for the Cherokees. Both agreed that Sequoyah, alas, would never amount to anything.

But they were wrong. Even then, on his way to the West, he was on the brink of an extraordinary feat.

Sequoyah remained in the Arkansas country less than three years. During that time, he continued to search for a method of putting the Cherokee language into written form. If the white man was able to make "talking leaves," or words on paper, why not the Indian? He got no more encouragement from his companions in the West than he had had before he emigrated from his home in Willstown. If he wanted to learn to write, they said, why not learn the white man's way, as the children at the mission schools were doing.

They missed the point. Sequoyah sought to free his countrymen from bondage to the white man's writing. English, the Indian knew, was "the language of deceit." His goal was to create a calligraphy peculiar to the Cherokees, by which they could express their thoughts, record their history, communicate with one another without alien interpretation.

He tried first to develop a form of picture writing—combining drawings of trees and men and horses to convey an idea. But as the pictures multiplied he found their number too great to remember. Having a good tonal ear, he began to think in terms of sounds. Sounds, after all, were the bricks of spoken language; why not the bricks, as well, of written language? He listened to others while they talked, and kept track of the different syllables.[12]

There were not so very many. One character for each basic sound or syllable might add up to a greater number than the English alphabet, but not much greater. He began to see the light at the end of the tunnel—a light that might illuminate the Nation. With homemade pen and ink he began to scratch out magic characters—some shaped like English or Greek letters, others of pure invention—each character representing one of the syllables of his native tongue. They came to only eighty-six in all.

He tried his invention out on some of the Western Cherokees. The results surpassed the dream. Willing students were able to learn the syllabary in two days. Almost immediately half the Western community was writing messages to the other half. Some, at Sequoyah's suggestion, addressed letters to their friends and cousins in the East, and the inventor promised to deliver them in person. For his heart was in the homeland, in the East, and he returned in early 1821 to present his gift of writing to the Nation.

The gift was not, at first, enthusiastically accepted. The chiefs were skeptical of the letters written by the Western Cherokees to their relatives in the East. Except for Sequoyah, who could tell what the letters really said? Sequoyah enlisted his six-year-old daughter's help in convincing the assembled Council. He invited the chiefs to dictate a message in secret to his daughter; she would write it down, and then he would read aloud to them the message she had written. The chiefs were still unconvinced. This was some father-and-daughter trick. They agreed, however, to a further demonstration.

At a General Council called for this purpose, several of the Nation's brighter and more reliable youths were instructed in Sequoyah's alphabet, then asked to transcribe messages dictated to them separately. The messages were then shuffled and redistributed to the youths to be read aloud in the assembly. The successful test convinced the Council. Sequoyah was not a trickster or a pseudo-conjuror. He was like a god arriving from another planet who had brought them the divine gift of a written language.

The effect upon the volatile Cherokees was apocalyptic. Sequoyah's alphabet spread like the winds which swept across the Georgia mountains. Overnight the Nation turned into a vast academy, as it was found that one could learn the new syllabary in a week or less—sometimes even in a single day. One man taught another; passing strangers carried it from town to town. Sequoyah himself instructed as many who cared to come to him, sitting in the center of the circle like a turbaned prophet, smoking his long, slender, curving pipe.

Gone were the stuffy classroom exercises of the missionaries where one learned by rote the white man's language. Every cabin in the wilderness, every public house and fireside, became a place of learning. In leafy groves, on the banks of streams, the old and young practiced and helped one another master the new syllabary—proving, as one New England educator held, that all that was needed to create a university was a log in the woods with a pupil at one end and a teacher at the other.

Instructors were assigned by the Council to spread the written word among the people. New, exciting vistas opened. Young men rode scores of miles to mail a letter in the white man's postbox and have it delivered by the U. S. Postal Service. Urchins rejoiced at being able to scratch obscenities on the bark of trees. The old chiefs sent to Tennessee for supplies of paper and pens. Letters received by mail became the status symbols of a people made literate, it seemed, by a single flash of lightning.

In Boston, where the eminent philologist John Pickering had been trying to work out his own orthography for the Cherokees—and having scant success—the American Board was taken by surprise. They no longer held the reins of education in their hands; the key had passed to the Cherokees themselves.

Wrote one historian of the Board, "the question of a native literature was taken out of the control of the missions, by one of the most remarkable events in the history of mind . . ."[13]

In Washington, Albert Gallatin, American statesman and diplomat, found Sequoyah's feat "incredible." He observed that once a Cherokee had learned the new syllabary, "he can read; he is perfect in his orthography without making it the subject of a distinct study. The boy learns in a few weeks that which occupied two years of the time of our boys."[14]

Once certain of his success, and little concerned with reward or tribute, Sequoyah returned to the Arkansas Territory in 1822, knowing now that the two branches of the Cherokees would be linked by his invention. The extraordinary effect of that invention would continue, as the Cherokee Nation in the East advanced with giant steps toward the future, united by a written language that was theirs exclusively.

"It was to be the truest claim of the Cherokees to distinction," wrote one chronicler of the period, "for no other people in history has ever had anything quite like it." Adding eloquently: "something of the light that once shone on Athens rested for a moment on the Cherokees . . ."

5

"What Hath
God Wrought!"

IT WOULD BE a different and fast-changing world that the
young men of Cornwall would return to.

For John Ross, in their absence, had had a vision. It was one he shared with
many others: The Ridge for one, The Ridge's son John, Charles and Elijah
Hicks, and the venerable Chief Pathkiller. All the omens now were good. By
the Treaty of 1819 the Nation's borders were secure against outside aggression.
The Council's adherence to the law which banned unauthorized land cessions
under penalty of death, would prevent erosion from within. The Nation could
build a future without fear. It could create a true republic along the lines of the
United States.

How much Sequoyah's alphabet contributed to the Cherokees' growing
confidence and high ambition is difficult to say. Certainly it gave them a new
sense of national identity. Laws and proclamations written in their own exclusive language now assumed a new authority. Before, they had had to accept the
white man's word for lack of any other. And the white man's word was suspect. Cherokee writing meant what it said because the Cherokees had never
comfortably learned to lie.

By popular assent the Council voted a silver medal to Sequoyah "as a token
of respect and admiration," and Ross had the medal struck in Philadelphia. But
by the time the award was completed, Sequoyah had returned to the Arkansas
Territory and the Nation was so deeply involved in matters at home that the
presentation was postponed.[1]

A motivating force behind the Cherokees' new drive for self-improvement
was the sharpening hostility of Georgia. The Treaty of 1819 had done nothing

to implement the Pact of 1802. The United States had consistently stalled on its agreement to remove the southern Indians, suggesting that the government was not too certain of its grounds.

But Georgia was certain of its grounds. The Georgians had waited almost a quarter of a century for Washington to make good on its promise; most of the Creeks were gone or going, but the Cherokees remained. Georgia's patience was wearing thin—which the Georgia bloc in Washington made plain to President Monroe. Reluctantly the President requested and obtained congressional funds with which to start negotiations with the Cherokees. It was the opening salvo of a conflict that would shake the Nation and the state of Georgia for another eighteen years.

If the Cherokees were effectively to meet this threat they could do it best by strengthening their national character, political and social. They must rise not only to the white man's level in government, education, and economy; they must if possible surpass that level. If they proved themselves worthy of recognition as an independent nation, the United States and even Georgia would see the justice of their position.

Starting in 1820, they moved with sure steps toward a constitutional republic based on free elections. A permanent national capital was established at New Town near the mouth of the Coosawattee River. Here a new Council House was built, with sheds and log huts to accommodate the delegates. And here at the October Council the government was reconstructed on what the Cherokees considered Jeffersonian principles.

The executive power rested with the Principal Chief assisted by the Second Chief, to be elected every four years. The legislative body or General Council became bicameral: the thirteen-member National Committee representing the upper house or senate, and a thirty-two-member National Council corresponding to the lower branch or house of representatives.

To facilitate elections, the Nation was divided into eight districts, each entitled to send four members to the National Council for a term of two years, the National Committee being chosen by the Council. The districts would have their own Council Houses, courts, and local judges to administer justice; while to maintain order and enforce the laws each district would have its marshal and its company of Regulators or Light Horse consisting of six mounted constables and captain.

Enlarging on the written laws established ten years earlier, additional measures were passed to circumscribe the sale of liquor, discourage polygamy, raise taxes for the maintenance of roads and schools, and prevent irregularities in the biannual elections. The right to punish offenders was given to the district courts. And above all, the sale or cession of Cherokee lands without full Council approval was again declared an act of treason, punishable by death.

In skeleton form the structure of government appeared like this in the early 1820s:

Principal Chief: Pathkiller
Second Chief: Charles R. Hicks

National Committee: John Ross, President
National Council: Major Ridge, Speaker of the House
Districts (8): Coosawattee, Amohee, Hickory Log, Etowee, Tawquohee, Aquohee, Chickamauga, Chatooga (each with a district judge and company of Light Horse)[2]

A weak point in this structure was the matter of a national treasury. Perhaps because the Cherokees were not greatly concerned with money and used the bank notes of neighboring states in trading with those states, they were slipshod when it came to finance. For now, Second Chief Hicks doubled as Treasurer of the Nation, handling the income in annuities from the United States—generally below $10,000—plus a poll tax of fifty cents a family and national taxes listed as "small—not collected."

Scarcely two years passed before the Cherokees were ready for the next step. In 1822 the Council created a National Superior Court corresponding to the United States Supreme Court. It would hold sessions concurrently with the October General Council. Four judges elected from the separate districts were authorized to impanel juries that would hear both criminal and civil cases. Though not scheduled to meet until the following autumn, the high court antedated by twenty years the supreme court established by the state of Georgia.

In Georgia's eyes these giant steps toward the stars were an effrontery. How did these presumptuous savages hope to rise to man's estate? And should they succeed in any degree, it would spell disaster for the whites. The stronger they became, the harder it would be to dislodge the Indians from Georgia's soil.

Governor George Michael Troup—aristocratic, stubborn, and a strong states' righter—took his case to Washington. With a congressional fund to finance efforts to remove the Indians, Secretary of War John C. Calhoun appointed two commissioners, Duncan G. Campbell and James Meriwether, to begin negotiations. The commissioners wrote to the Cherokee chiefs setting a January date and place for their discussion. The Cherokees replied curtly that if the commissioners wanted to talk to them they could come to the October Council at New Town.

Without waiting for the commissioners' arrival the Cherokees made their position clear in a message to President Monroe, saying in part:

Sir . . . we beg leave to observe . . . that the Cherokee are not foreigners but original inhabitants of America, and that they now inhabit and stand on the soil of their own territory and that the limits of this territory are defined by the treaties which they have made with the government of the United States, and the states by which they are now surrounded have been created out of land which was once theirs, and that they cannot recognize the sovereignty of any state within the limits of their territory.[3]

More impudence, cried Georgia, on hearing of this attitude. The Cherokees had it just the wrong way round. It was Georgia's sovereignty that was being violated by these aborigines.

Cherokee agent Jonathan Meigs, for a long time ailing, died that winter after twenty-three years of service. Despite the Cherokees' request for someone of their own choice, Monroe appointed Joseph McMinn, ex-governor of Tennessee, to the post, "apparently on the theory that the more obnoxious an agent was the more effective he would be." McMinn got off on the wrong foot by charging the Cherokees with disrespect in their message to the President and with arrogance in insisting that the United States commissioners come to them at New Town, instead of sending representatives to Washington. The Cherokees replied in a way that fits the present-day vernacular. They told the agent to "get lost."

The October Council of 1823 was a momentous one in Cherokee history. Others might later deserve that adjective, but this was the first assembly in which the Cherokees came face to face with demands for their removal. New Town, normally deserted, was crowded with both delegates and spectators. Large open sheds were constructed near the Council House where thirty cooks prepared the beef, venison, pork, fowl, and baked goods provided by the Council for visitors and deputies. Precisely at dawn of October 6, The Ridge arrived "on a tall white horse" and the conference got under way.

The Cherokees insisted, wisely, that all proposals from the commissioners and all replies should be in writing, to avoid misunderstanding. The two commissioners, Campbell and Meriwether, presented their case from manuscript. It was a proposition to be heard in many forms, at many times to come. The Cherokees were asked, for their own good—again that insidious phrase!—to relinquish their lands in the East for equivalent territory in the West, along with certain financial compensations for their trouble and for the possessions they would have to leave behind. Previous treaties, such as that of Hopewell, were dismissed as having recognized only the Cherokees' "lease," or right to live upon the land but not to own it.

The assembly heard them out with grave attention. Then they drafted their reply. Their answer was based not only on their "love of the soil which gave them birth" and their progress thereon which promised them "prosperity and future happiness." Nor did they wrangle over broken treaties. They were here first; the land had been theirs for centuries before the Europeans came. Why discuss whether or not a white man's treaty gave them the right to live there? There was more, much more, than that. . . .

In preparation for this encounter, Ross had made a trip to the Arkansas Territory and had found that "the unfortunate part of our Nation who have emigrated to the West have suffered severely since their separation from this Nation. . . . Sickness, wars, and other fatalities have visited them . . . and many of them, no doubt, would willingly return to the land of their nativity, if it were practicable for them to do so . . ." No, the Eastern Cherokees had no desire to follow in the path of their unfortunate brothers. They could state their position, and did, in just two concluding sentences:

"We cannot accede to your application for a cession. It is the fixed and unalterable determination of this Nation never again to cede *one foot* more of land."[4]

Stung and defeated, the commissioners made a fatal move. Possibly at the suggestion of Governor Troup, they persuaded the Creek chief William McIntosh to intervene. Apart from the fact that the half-breed McIntosh was a cousin of the governor, was working both sides of the fence, and had treacherously signed a treaty forcing his fellow Creeks from Georgia, the commissioners could not have made a worse choice. A Creek was not a Cherokee; a two-faced man was not an Indian.

McIntosh approached John Ross as one who, like himself, had Scots blood in his veins. Ross demanded that anything he had to say be put in writing—unfortunate for McIntosh, but he complied, saying in part:

My Friend . . . If the chiefs feel disposed to let the United States have the [Cherokee] land . . . I will make the commissioners give you two thousand dollars, McCoy [clerk of the Council] the same, and Charles Hicks $3,000, and nobody shall know about it.[5]

In all, McIntosh stated, he was authorized to offer "as presents, $12,000 you can divide among your friends."

The following day, while McIntosh and the commissioners squirmed red-faced in their chairs, Ross read the message aloud to the assembled Council. The letter, he said, spoke for itself. "Fortunately the author has mistaken my character and my sense of honor."

After a stunned silence, Chief Pathkiller rose and turned his back on the commissioners and their Creek accomplice. "Set him aside," he said of McIntosh.

The Ridge also arose. "As speaker for the Cherokee Nation," he said in a voice charged with emotion, "I cast him behind my back . . . We are not to be purchased with money."

The Council ended abruptly, and McIntosh was last seen riding south at so furious a pace that his horse collapsed on the trail. But while the Cherokees had made their position plain—they would not yield another foot of land—they could not let it go at that. Georgia was on their backs and so was Tennessee's McMinn, though they tried (and failed) to have Commissioner McMinn removed. The insatiable greed of the white man was not erased by getting rid of McIntosh. A four-man delegation consisting of Ross, The Ridge, George Lowrey, and Elijah Hicks was authorized to go to Washington and present their position to the President and John Calhoun.

Flushed with victory over the United States commissioners, confident of the justice of their case, the delegates arrived at Washington in January 1824 and put up at Tennison's Hotel on Pennsylvania Avenue. As on previous visits, they surprised the capital with standards of conduct and appearance matching or exceeding those of European diplomats. It was customary for the War Department, in charge of foreign visitors, to deck arriving Indians in army uniforms or appropriate civilian clothes before presenting them to government officials. In this case, it was far from necessary. Secretary of State John Quincy Adams, himself always nattily attired, observed that the Cherokees "dress like ourselves," with occasional touches of elegance, and that their manners were those of "well-bred country gentlemen." Major Ridge, in satin-collared great-coat, buff vest and silk cravat, with "fine figure and handsome face, made a great impression."

They were guests at the home of John Calhoun, were welcomed at receptions given by the Adamses, and attended the Wednesday-night balls at the White House, where their appearance contrasted favorably with the tobacco-chewing, dirty-collared, and untidy guests among the senators and foreign diplomats.

To the Georgians present at these affairs, the deference shown to the Cherokees was a personal affront, especially when they were addressed as "Gentlemen." One Georgia congressman who had publicly referred to them as "savages who subsisted on roots" was seated at dinner close to George Lowrey, who, on being served sweet potatoes, took great delight in loudly calling to the waiter: "More roots! More roots! We Indians are very fond of roots!"—to the infinite amusement of surrounding guests.[6]

Getting down to serious business with Calhoun and the President, the delegates reaffirmed what they had stated at their Council: they would not cede another foot of land. Their population was growing, they had lost much space by previous treaties. Only their fertile valleys were left them, and on these shrunken acres they had built a progressive, self-sufficient, orderly society. They politely but firmly requested the President to abrogate the Pact of 1802, in which the Cherokees had had no part, and which would have forced them to release their lands in Georgia to the state.

When Calhoun replied in effect that abrogation was impossible, that the Cherokees could not remain as a national entity within the limits of the state of Georgia, they reminded the Secretary of what they had already stated—that Georgia was created out of land that was originally theirs, and not the other way around. And added: "An exchange of territory twice as large, west of the Mississippi, . . . or all the money now in the coffers of your treasury, would be no inducement for the Nation to exchange or sell their country."

Throughout these discussions President Monroe said little; he was a man of few words, poker-faced and glum. But as the Cherokees returned to the social whirl of Washington, awaiting his decision, he thought the matter over, consulted his cabinet, and formulated his reply.

In his Message to Congress on March 30, 1824, the President reviewed with discernment and impartiality all aspects of the argument for Cherokee removal, and concluded: "I have no hesitation . . . to declare it as my opinion, that the Indian title was not affected in the slightest circumstances by the compact with Georgia, and that there is no obligation on the United States to remove the Indians by force."

He did add, however, that the Cherokees might find it wise to emigrate voluntarily across the Mississippi, and thus put that river between themselves and those with whom there was so much friction. But he left it up to them.

Georgia was outraged. Georgia congressmen upbraided the government for "having instructed the Indians in the arts of civilized life and having thereby

The Ridge, who acquired the title of "Major" serving under Andrew Jackson, was a dominant figure in Cherokee society during the Nation's era of greatest progress.
SMITHSONIAN INSTITUTION NATIONAL ANTHROPOLOGICAL ARCHIVES

Bearing his father's proud name, John Ridge played a great but controversial role in Cherokee politics and white-American relations.
SMITHSONIAN INSTITUTION NATIONAL ANTHROPOLOGICAL ARCHIVES

John Ross was elected Principal Chief of the Cherokee Nation in 1828 and held that office, in the East and later in the West, until his death in 1866.

FROM THE ORIGINAL OIL PAINTING BY ROBERT LINDNEUX,
WOOLAROC MUSEUM, BARTLESVILLE, OKLAHOMA

Cherokee Chief Junaluska, with knife, thwarts a Creek assassination attempt on the life of Andrew Jackson during the Creek campaign of 1814; scene from "Unto These Hills," presented annually in Cherokee, North Carolina.

The seven Cherokee chiefs, with Attacullaculla at far left, who visited London to pledge allegiance to King George II in 1730.

Replica of a typical Cherokee cabin of the mid-eighteenth century.

Interior of an early Cherokee council house, circular with log walls and conical roof, hearth in center. Reconstruction at the Oconaluftee Indian Village, Cherokee, North Carolina.

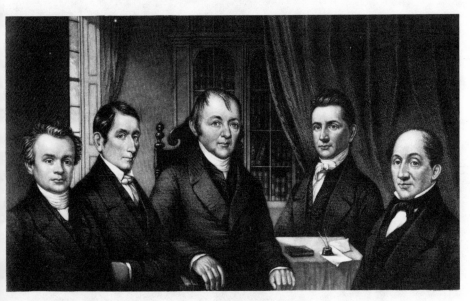

Return Jonathan Meigs, pioneer
government agent to the Cherokee Nation
until his death in 1823. From a
contemporary engraving.

LIBRARY OF CONGRESS

The Joseph Vann house as it stands today
in Spring Place, once one of the finest homes
in northern Georgia.

HISTORIC PRESERVATION SECTION,
GEORGIA DEPARTMENT OF NATURAL RESOURCES

Secretaries of the American Board of Foreign Missions, who provided aid and impetus
to Cherokee education. In center, Dr. Samuel Worcester, uncle of Samuel Austin
Worcester; second from left, Jeremiah Evarts, author of the "William Penn" letters.

HOUGHTON LIBRARY, HARVARD UNIVERSITY

Elias Boudinot, editor of the
Cherokee Phoenix *throughout mos*
of the newspaper's lifetime.
HISTORICAL PRESERVATION SECTION,
GEORGIA DEPARTMENT OF
NATURAL RESOURCES

Harriet Gold Boudinot gave up a
life of comfortable security in
Connecticut to live and work with
her husband, Elias Boudinot,
in the Cherokee Nation.
WESTERN HISTORY COLLECTIONS,
UNIVERSITY OF OKLAHOMA

Samuel Austin Worcester
provided inspired leadership to
the American missionary movement
in the Cherokee Nation.
BY PERMISSION OF THE
HARVARD COLLEGE LIBRARY

Sam Houston, "adopted son" of
Chief Jolly of the Cherokees, later
became governor of Tennessee
and first president of the short-lived
Republic of Texas.
LIBRARY OF CONGRESS

George Gist or Guess, better known as Sequoyah, gave the Cherokees the first and only written language in American Indian history.

FROM THE ORIGINAL OIL PAINTING BY ROBERT LINDNEUX,
WOOLAROC MUSEUM, BARTLESVILLE, OKLAHOMA

imbued them with a sense of property." They accused the Cherokees of hiring white collaborators to write their presentations for them, for no Indian could present his case as eloquently as the newspaper summaries suggested. To this John Ross responded in the Washington *National Intelligencer* that every Cherokee communication "was not only *written* but dictated by an Indian. We are not so fortunate as to have such help. The white man seldom comes forward in our defense. Our rights are in our own keeping."[7]

To the indignant Governor Troup, who reminded the President of the government's promise to remove the Indians, Monroe observed that the Pact of 1802 referred to removal by "peaceable means." Unless the Cherokees chose voluntarily to emigrate, his hands were tied. And on the word "peaceable" the future of the Cherokees appeared secure.

That was the year the boys came home. A few of the Young Men of Cornwall had returned in 1822 and 1823; Elias Boudinot had gone on to the Andover Theological Seminary in Massachusetts for advanced study, as had the scholarly David Brown. Both were back in the Nation now (though Boudinot had yet to return for his marriage to Harriet). David, with a knowledge of languages obtained at Andover, was working on a Cherokee-language translation of the New Testament from the original Greek and was serving wherever needed as an interpreter. Elias, it was hoped, would become a teacher at Brainerd, but was having a little difficulty readjusting to the old ways. He was seen attending a ball-play, much to the distress of the missionaries, who began to wonder if the fruits of Cornwall had been wasted on him.

John Ridge, of course, was back with Sarah Northrup, and it was a proud day for The Ridge when John and David Brown appeared before the October Council at New Town to speak on the Cherokee experience at Cornwall. The Ridge himself addressed the assembly on the blessings of a Christian education, as introduced and promoted by the missionaries, and promised Chamberlin that hereafter Council meetings would be opened with a prayer, possibly even with a reading of the scriptures.

The light of learning shone all the brighter because the year of 1824 had been a year of famine, caused by unprecedented drought. With the widespread failure of crops the mountain and backcountry Indians were forced to live on chestnuts and the roots of trees, briefly confirming the Georgia congressman's remark that the "savage" Cherokees ate roots. But this seemed a minor misfortune compared with the glowing outlook for the future, when the Nation would be run by learned scholars such as Ridge and Boudinot and Brown.

It was the year, too, when The Ridge and his son expanded the family home on the Oostanaula, which John and Sarah at first shared. The ancestral cabin of a quarter century before became a two-story eight-room mansion with porches front and back and balconies supported on Greek columns. Four brick fireplaces, thirty framed windows, elegant paneling on walls and ceilings, showed, according to one contemporary visitor, "the wealth and civilization of the owners." An arched triple window in the front overlooked the ferry and the river, while in back were kitchens, stables, cabins for thirty servants, and eventually fruit orchards, cotton and tobacco fields, and cattle pens. It was the home of a patriarch, wrote Colonel Thomas L. McKenney, Superintendent of Indian Affairs, "the scene of plenty and hospitality."

For himself and Sarah, John built a more modest home six miles upriver, with the musical name of Tantatarara, or "Running Waters." Though not as large and splendid as the Major's, it was, his son would later remember, "a large, two-storied house, on a high hill, crowned with a fine grove of oak and hickory, a large clear spring at the foot of the hill, and an extensive farm stretching away down into the valley, with a fine orchard on the left." John himself liked to feel that his and his father's mansions would "look well in New England."

Despite the temporary famine, prosperity—or a look of prosperity—was coming to the Nation. The families whose offspring had been educated at the mission schools, at Cornwall, or at academies in Tennessee, began to spruce up their homes, their dress, their life style in emulation of the educated whites. One who recalled John Ross's childhood shame at wearing white man's clothes, reported, "Now every boy is proud of a civilized suit, and those feel awkward . . . who are destitute of it. At the last session of the General Council, I scarcely recollect having seen any members who were not clothed in the same manner as the white inhabitants of the neighboring states . . ."[8]

The missionaries had reason to be pleased with what they saw around them. To an increasing degree the Cherokees were aiding them in their work and taking over much of it themselves. Jesse Bushyhead, mixed-breed descendant of John Stuart, having overcome a predilection for strong drink, was teaching and preaching at the Baptist station under Evan Jones. Additional teachers were arriving from New England, including Delight Sargent—like Sophia Sawyer, a spinster from New Hampshire. There were more schools and more churches—though the definition of a church was any available location where a preacher and a congregation met.

This expanding activity brought a shuffling of personnel among the different mission posts around the Nation. Chamberlin went to Willstown, and Isaac Proctor was transferred to Carmel, some miles below Spring Place. Daniel Butrick remained at Brainerd, though the irrepressible Butrick could stay nowhere very long. He was beginning to have doubts about his vows of chastity, and confessed as much by letter to Jeremiah Evarts in Boston. Was not a man entitled to a mate?

Without waiting for an answer Butrick took off on one of his many high-geared evangelizing trips around the Nation. Passing through Carmel, he stopped to call on Isaac Proctor, but found Proctor away and his sister Elizabeth in charge of the pupils and the school. "The sight of their lonely condition disarmed me," he later wrote to Jeremiah Evarts. "Dear loves, said I, how can I leave them alone in this wild desert?"

Fate stepped in to answer Butrick's question. His horse, "a wicked beast," ran away. It was the sort of thing that was always happening to Butrick, but this time the mishap seemed to bear a message. Stuck in Carmel, he could not with discretion stay unchaperoned with sister Proctor. "Considering the situation I enquired whether it were not my duty to propose a connection with her. My mind was soon convinced on this subject." He proposed, Elizabeth accepted, and they were married by Dr. Chamberlin, who by another act of kindly fate was also visiting the mission. "O blessed day!" wrote Butrick in his journal, which thereafter included no further self-deprecating entries.[9]

No romance blessed the life of Miss Sophia Sawyer, however much she might have welcomed it. But she was deeply devoted to her young girl pupils, as were they to her. She strove, as she wrote to Jeremiah Evarts, so to improve their appearance, minds, and characters as to make them "fit companions" in a male society—for Sophia herself yearned to be a part of that society.

She was having, it appeared, personal problems in her relations with the Brainerd staff. She named no names, made no specific charges; but her letters to Evarts were frequently interrupted by such phrases as: "What right have others to judge me? I am what I am." She marked the letters PRIVATE, cautioned often that "these words are for your eyes only," and signed herself "Affectionately." It was Evarts who had approved her appointment as missionary to the Cherokees, and Sophia seemed to be enlisting him as an ally in the struggle to find her niche in life.[10]

The work of the mission schools had been somewhat eclipsed by an unrelated phenomenon. Literacy had taken a tremendous leap forward with Sequoyah's alphabet. The vast majority between the ages of six and sixty could read and write the Cherokee language. "There is no part of the Nation where the new alphabet is not understood," wrote a Brainerd missionary. "They have but to learn their alphabet and they can read at once."

Isaac Proctor wrote to the American Board that the schools no longer were in desperate need of teachers. Provide writing materials—pens, paper, ink—and the Cherokees would teach themselves. "The knowledge of Mr. Guess's alphabet is spreading like fire among the brush," wrote William Chamberlin in October 1824. "If Christians neglect the duty, Satan will no doubt furnish reading for the Cherokees."

The Christians were not neglecting duty. The fact was, however, that the Cherokees outstripped the missionaries in mastering Sequoyah's syllabary. They seemed to learn it overnight—even those who had never written or read a word of any language in their lives. Highly intelligent people like Chamberlin, Proctor, and Elizur Butler were baffled by the gymnastic characters of Sequoyah's alphabet. Many never came near mastering the language.

Thus arose the strange situation in which students and former students acted as interpreters for their instructors, and translations from English into Cherokee were left, in large degree, to the Cherokees themselves. David Brown, along with his work on the New Testament, acted as interpreter for Chamberlin, turning the latter's English sermons into Cherokee. John Arch, who had come over the mountains as a ragged vagabond and traded his rifle for an education, also served as an interpreter while working on his own translation of the Gospel of St. John.

So theology was not neglected; it was in fact advancing in the Nation. There were no mass conversions, but something of a religious revival was in progress

—led by the chiefs who followed the examples of such leaders as John Ross and Charles Renatus Hicks. The Ridge remained a holdout, perhaps because the thought of kneeling was abhorrent to him—he knelt to nobody. But he was heard to speak out for the new religion, and, as The Ridge had recommended, sessions of the General Council now opened with prayers, hymn singing, and a reading of the scriptures.

"When I reflect on the astonishing change that has taken place among this people within a few years," wrote Chamberlin, "I cannot but exclaim, Lo, what hath God wrought!"[11]

The Cherokees were looking less and less to Washington and to the missionaries for help, and taking matters into their own hands. At the 1824 October Council cultural concerns took precedence over even the still hot issue of removal. That problem, it was felt, would fade from exposure to the light of progress. In proportion as a people became civilized, their right to national survival was secure.

The Council proposed the establishment of a National Academy at New Town. This would provide advanced education and serve as a cultural center for the Nation. It would have classrooms and lecture halls, a substantial library and reading rooms. An adjoining museum would house samples of Cherokee achievements in the arts and crafts, natural-history displays and historical exhibits. Just as in the United States people were flooding the new Smithsonian Institution with everything from grandmother's rocker to the skeleton of a Nova Scotia seabird, Cherokees went on a treasure hunt for family heirlooms, wampum belts, forms of headdress, ancient weapons, to give to the museum. The Ridge donated his favorite pipe, and Charles Hicks contributed an Indian headpiece of buffalo horns.

To further these goals an organization was created the following month of November 1824, called the Moral and Literary Society of the Cherokee Nation. The high-sounding name was not mere hyperbole. The society's constitution provided for "the suppression of vice, the encouragement of morality, and the general improvement of the Nation." It would achieve these high-minded goals through the dissemination of knowledge. Its dues of one to five dollars per member would be used for the purchase of books for the National Academy that dealt with "Morality, History, Religion, Jurisprudence, and general Literature."

As secretary of the society, Elias Boudinot undertook to solicit from sympathetic sources in the northern states "Books on travels, Histories, both ancient and modern, Maps, and in fine, books of all descriptions . . ." To this end, he suggested that John Ridge write to American newspapers of the aims and needs of the society. This John did, concluding his presentation with the paragraph:

Civilization has shed the beams of gladness among this people. Religion's lamp is seen to luminate the darkness of ignorance. The Indians know their value, and with fond delight, anticipate a time when liberality will place them on a footing with other nations whose merits have not been sacrificed by prejudice on oblivion's altar.[12]

David Brown, bursting with enthusiasm for the new society and what it represented, composed his own appraisal of Cherokee progress, which he dispatched to the War Department and to *Niles' Weekly Register* in Baltimore. After describing the beauty of the land, the majestic mountains, silver streams, and fertile valleys, he wrote of the herds of cattle grazing on the plains; the flocks of sheep, goats, and swine covering the slopes and valleys; the rich crops of corn, tobacco, cotton, wheat, oats, indigo, and potatoes which were exported via the riverways, by Cherokee boats, to New Orleans. He told of the peach and apple orchards, the well-tended vegetable gardens, and the dairy herds that put fresh fruit and vegetables, butter and cheese on Cherokee dinner tables. And added further:

There are many public roads in the Nation, and houses of entertainment kept by natives. Numerous and flourishing villages are seen in every section of the country. Cotton and woolen goods are manufactured here. Blankets of various dimensions by Cherokee hands, are very common. *Almost every family in the nation grows cotton for its own consumption.* Industry and commercial enterprise are extending themselves in every part. Nearly all the merchants in the Nation are native Cherokees. Agricultural pursuits, the most solid foundation of our national prosperity, engage the chief attention of the people.[13]

A census taken that year, and quoted by David in his dissertation, showed substantial growth in population, which had reached a low point toward the end of the last century. The count in 1825 showed 15,060 Cherokees living in the Eastern Nation—which included 1,277 slaves along with 147 white men and 73 white women who had married native Cherokees.

"Schools are increasing every year," Brown wrote; "learning is encouraged and rewarded. The young class acquire the English, and those of mature age the Cherokee system of learning." With some pride he noted that, with the Nation in a sound financial condition, a National Academy and library would shortly be established and a printing press was under consideration.[14]

In the fervor and eloquence of David's eulogy one could hear the echo of Chamberlin's exclamation, "Lo, what hath God wrought!"

The Ridge had been to Baltimore. On his frequent missions to Washington City—the most recent, to pay his respects to the defeated presidential candidate, Andrew Jackson—he often traveled by riverboat from Augusta to Savannah and thence by steamer to the Maryland port, which was now America's third-largest city. It was more crowded, busier than the capital, and its streets were unforgettably illuminated by gaslights suspended overhead.

When the autumn Councils were in session, New Town also was an animated, crowded city, with delegates and visitors from all parts of the Nation. The Ridge had once remarked with pride that "it is just like Baltimore." But he knew that when the Council adjourned the place would be a ghost town. For the buildings were not of tidy brick, but simply makeshift and impermanent affairs. The streets were no more than bridle paths worn smooth by horses' hooves; the lights at night were flaming pine cones that would disappear when the people who carried them disappeared. As a capital it was not the enduring monument that Cherokee progress called for.

He brooded over this as the October Council convened in 1825. Impending matters were first disposed of. Conscious of the United States' effective use of bribery in securing land cessions from neighboring tribes, it was resolved that: "The Principal Chiefs of the Nation shall in no wise hold any treaties or dispose of public property in any manner without the express authority of the Legislative Council in session." This restatement of the law passed in 1820 was given ominous weight by the affair of William McIntosh, the Creek chief who had tried to bribe John Ross and had just been assassinated by his own people for having ceded Creek lands without tribal sanction.

It was also decreed at this Council that "all gold, silver, lead, copper or brass mines, which may be found within the limits of the Cherokee Nation, shall be the public property of the Cherokee Nation," to be worked when and as the chiefs saw fit, with one quarter of the profits going to whoever discovered the mine. The presence of valuable minerals in the mountains, and the suspected existence of a vein of gold ore slanting southwest from North Carolina, had never greatly concerned the Nation. There was too much richness in the fertile fields and pastures to look elsewhere for support.

Finally, to The Ridge's gratification, it was resolved to build a permanent capital on a level tract of land near New Town at the junction of the Coosawattee and Oostanaula rivers in the geographical center of the Nation. It would be christened New Echota in fond tribute to the ancient Cherokee capital of Chota on the Little Tennessee. A two-acre city square and a main street sixty feet in width would sprout a grid of lesser streets for homes and businesses.

A hundred town lots of an acre each would be sold at auction and the proceeds would go toward the founding of the National Academy and the raising of a Council House, a Supreme Court building, and a printing press—the last a project which The Ridge had been suggesting for some months. In their anxiety to see quick, tangible results in the form of government quarters, the lofty conception of a National Academy was subtly pushed aside.

The press was the thing that gave wings to imagination. It was a project regarding which the Cherokees had no experience and little knowledge. But it must be kept in Cherokee hands and not farmed out to white promoters. With this in mind, it was resolved that $1,500 of that year's annuity would go toward the purchase of the press and type, presumably from Philadelphia or Boston, and that the rest should be raised by solicitation from friendly patrons in the North. Elias Boudinot was elected to tour the more promising cities, to gain sympathy and money for the project.

Elias would shortly be going North, in any event, to marry Harriet Gold, who was still enduring the ostracism of her family and friends in Cornwall. Boudinot started in Charleston, where he practiced his appeal for funds and polished and improved upon it before reaching Philadelphia. In the City of

Brotherly Love on May 26 he stood at the pulpit of the First Presbyterian Church in a ministerial frock coat, chaste broadcloth shirt, and silk cravat, looking, except for his bronze complexion, like a white American but speaking with the musical fervor of the Indian.

He told of the extraordinary advance of his people from the nomadic hunting life to that of peaceful trade and agriculture. He cited the rise of education and religion in the Nation, the improvement in morals, manners, local and central government. They were an "industrious and intelligent people" seeking "an equal standing with other nations of the earth."

Like David Brown, he drew on the 1825 census figures for a statistical profile of the Nation. "At this time," he noted, "there are 22,000 cattle; 7,600 horses; 46,000 swine; 2,500 sheep; 762 looms; 2,488 spinning wheels; 172 waggons; 2,943 ploughs; 10 sawmills; 31 grist-mills; 62 blacksmith shops; 8 cotton machines; 18 schools; 18 ferries, and a number of public roads. In one district there were, last winter, upwards of 1,000 volumes of good books; and 11 different periodical papers both religious and political were taken and read."[15]

And now came the moment to climax those achievements, for one of their number had given them an alphabet and a written language with which to further their education and establish better communication among themselves and with their valued neighbors in the United States. They would have a press with type cast in both English and Cherokee, for the printing of material of interest to the Nation and of interest to the world. If the kind people of the audience would bless their efforts with financial contributions . . .

Before ending his northern tour in Salem and Boston, after marrying Harriet Gold in Cornwall, Elias had collected $600 in donations. For the times it was a substantial amount and with additional funds from the annuity there would be enough to start negotiating for the purchase of a press. And Boudinot's industry had marked him as a worthy spokesman for the press, possibly as editor of a projected weekly journal. He could not, however, carry such a burden by himself. . . .

6
Rise of the *Phoenix*

THEY HAD traveled light, in heart and personal effects, as lovers should. Yet it had been an exhausting journey all the way from Boston, Massachusetts. More than seven weeks on the road—fifty days to be exact—driving their horse and four-wheel carriage over turnpikes, carriage paths, and rickety bridges in every kind of weather. So that it was not until late October 1825 that Samuel Austin Worcester and his bride arrived at Brainerd. Most of their few possessions, a feather bed, some linen blankets, Worcester's books and medical supplies, would arrive by steamer later.

At least Brainerd itself, in physical appearance, was a comforting and reassuring sight, and the surrounding country suggested the rolling hills of western Massachusetts. The well-kept quadrangle with its church and mission buildings nesting at the edges was not unlike a New England village common. To a young couple with youth and vigor and faith, this was a green felt-covered springboard to a wonderful new life of service.

Worcester, now twenty-seven, tall and wiry, with almost seraphic features beneath a tumble of dark wavy hair, had not been chosen haphazardly for this assignment. His life till now had been fortuitously tailored to it. He had been born in Peacham, Vermont, preceded by seven generations of preachers of the gospel. His father had been a printer before entering the ministry, and young Sam had learned to set type for his father's press, as well as cut wood, pitch hay, and tend to the livestock on his father's farm. As a boy he had studied at the Peacham Academy under Jeremiah Evarts, and later walked seventy-one miles to attend the college at Burlington, where his uncle Samuel Austin was the president.

From Burlington he was drawn to the Andover Theological Seminary, where he studied Latin, Greek, and Hebrew—to become an expert in linguistics. With this background and training it was only a short step to the Market

Street rooms of the Board of Foreign Missions, where he waited for an assignment to some foreign field—Polynesia, he supposed, or India. When Jeremiah
Evarts recommended he be sent to the Cherokee Nation, because of his knowledge of linguistics, Worcester felt he needed an assistant and he married her,
Ann Orr of Bedford, Massachusetts.

Ann was said to be "a woman of common sense, vivacity, and wit," not in-
considerable assets for the couple's chosen occupation. If Sam referred to her as
"an indefinite article and a disjunctive conjunction" he did so with semantic
affection. Theirs was a love that needed no restatement. For the life ahead, it
had to be that way.

Worcester's first goal at Brainerd was to master the Cherokee language, an
aim that had the approval of the Boston Board. His volunteer tutor was the
Cherokee half-breed Charles Reese, a member of the General Council and one
of the earlier converts of the mission. "I have been attending to Guyst's [sic] alphabet, with an hour's assistance from Mr. Reese," he wrote to Boston after
only two days in the Nation. "It seems to be the united opinion of all who have
formed an opinion, that his mode of writing the language must prevail, though
alterations may be made. The number of natives who have already learned it is
very great."[1]

It was Charles Reese who, after several weeks of observing his pupil's progress and devotion to his calling, gave him the Indian name of Atsenusti, or "the
Messenger." Said Reese of the blue-eyed dark-haired missionary with the face
of Galahad, "He is wise; he has something to say."[2]

Though Worcester learned to read and write the language fluently, he never
felt sure enough to speak it from the pulpit, a handicap he shared with almost
every other missionary. More and more he began to think of the projected press
and its obvious advantages. It would make possible the printing and dissemination of the Bible, the publication of textbooks, hymnals, and religious tracts.
With this in mind he journeyed to Hightower to visit Elias Boudinot, with
whose reputation (including his fondness for ball-play) he was well acquainted.

There seemed to be an instant rapport between the two. Both were about the
same age, zealous, intelligent, not too concerned with orthodoxy; and in Harriet's well-run ménage Worcester felt as much at home as in New England. "I
have more confidence in Boudinot as a translator than in any other," Worcester
wrote to Jeremiah Evarts, "and . . . my spending near a fortnight in his family
has given me quite a respect for his character."[3]

They operated well as a team together—first, working to systematize the
Cherokee language and master the parsing of the herculean verbs, which
Boudinot considered the most difficult in the world; then, planning for the
purchase and the operation of the press. Overnight Worcester became the
prime motivating force behind the project. In time he would be accused of taking it out of Cherokee hands, a charge that was far from true. As a printer in
his youth, he was on familiar grounds; with his Boston connections he was capable of taking over the commercial details. The press itself, however, would
remain a Cherokee institution, owned and operated by the Nation.

That autumn, 1826, things began to take shape. A press was ordered from the printing equipment firm of Baker & Greene in Boston, David Greene himself being a member of the American Board of Foreign Missions and giving them a favorable price. Two sets of type were ordered, to be cast in Cherokee and English characters, and Worcester sent a chart of Sequoyah's alphabet as guide. The press would be located at New Echota, in a building yet to be constructed, and Worcester and Ann would move to the Cherokee capital from Brainerd.

The pair turned their attention next to the matter of a weekly journal, to be printed partly in Cherokee, partly in English, as authorized by the General Council. What to call it? In his fund-raising tour Boudinot had told his audiences that the Cherokees, after centuries of barbarism, "must rise like the Phoenix" from the ashes of the past. Perhaps that reference cued the name for the projected paper, the *Cherokee Phoenix*.

The Indian title which would also grace the masthead, impossible to present in English characters, was perhaps more meaningful. In translation it trumpeted the promise: "I will arise."

By the spring of 1827 New Echota was taking on the appearance of a tidy little capital, though still a long way from The Ridge's memories of Baltimore. In point of fact, it would remain, except when the Council convened, little more than a crossroads Indian village with a few public buildings built of logs and shingle roofing, several stores, and half a dozen log or clapboard homes. But when the Council was in session, when tents sprang up around the village like a colony of moths and, in addition to the myriad campfires, people wandered to and fro with torches made of flaming candlewood—ah, there was a sight! The whole sky of northern Georgia seemed illuminated by the glow.

A New England visitor to New Echota found the Cherokee capital "truly an interesting and pleasant place," writing:

. . . the ground is as level and smooth as a house floor; the center of the Nation—a new place, laid out in city form—a spring called the public spring, about twice as large as our sawmill brook, near the center . . . Six new frame houses in sight besides the Council House, Court House, printing office, and four stores, all in sight . . . The stores in the Nation are as large as the best in our town in Litchfield County; their large wagons of six horses go to Augusta and bring a great load, and you will see a number of them together. There is much travel through this place. I have seen eleven of these large wagons pass by Mr. Boudinot's house in company.[4]

There was considerable bustle in the capital the last week of July, for tragedy had struck the Nation earlier in 1827. In January, the venerable Chief Pathkiller died, and within two weeks his Assistant Chief, Charles Hicks, succumbed from exposure to the winter's chill. The double deaths left the Nation sorrowful and rudderless. For the time being, the government devolved upon John Ross as President of the National Committee and The Ridge as Speaker of the Council. One of the reasons for this July assembly was to arrange for elections to fill the sudden vacancies.

But while the Nation mourned, Georgia saw reason for encouragement in the deaths of the Cherokee leaders. These two chiefs, the *Georgia Journal* noted, had been principal pillars of Cherokee resistance to removal. "Those who occupy their places are understood to be men of different disposition and character. An intelligent Cherokee is said to have made the remark, when he heard of the death of Charles Hicks, that the Cherokees will sell their land now; those who are left have their price. Now, therefore, is a most suitable moment to urge the claims of Georgia in that quarter. And we believe our Chief Magistrate will not let it pass unimproved."[5]

The *Georgia Journal* was wrong on two counts. Ross and The Ridge, and whoever succeeded them as permanent chiefs, were no less adamant against removal than their predecessors. And the Chief Magistrate, John Quincy Adams, was not overeager to press Georgia's claims against the Cherokees. The President did appoint three commissioners, all generals of the Army, to sound out the Indians on the subject—probably more to appease the Georgians than anything else. When the commissioners arrived at New Echota in July, the Council gently brushed them off. There was more important business to attend to.

Since the October Council of the year before—since as early as 1820, for that matter—the idea of a written constitution had been brewing. It hardly seemed essential from a practical point of view. The Nation had its written laws, gathering in number since 1819; it had reorganized its government along bicameral lines; it had established the machinery for free elections. But somehow the very idea of a written constitution seemed important at this stage. It would climax all the progress they had made in government. It would fit the pattern of democracy in other countries. But most of all, perhaps, it would be something they could hold up to the world—a shield, a battle standard, a declaration to Georgia, among others, of the permanence of their establishment.

And so this special constitutional convention had been called, with John Ross elected president of the assembly. It was Ross, in fact, who was credited with drafting the new constitution; and Ross who presented it to the assembled chiefs and delegates. Basically it did little more than collate the existing laws, reaffirm some, amplify others, and put them all in proper sequence. But the preamble alone suggested the loftier purpose of placing this constitution on a par with that of the United States:

We, the Representatives of the people of the Cherokee Nation, in Convention assembled, in order to establish justice, ensure tranquillity, promote our common welfare, and secure to ourselves and our posterity the blessings of liberty: acknowledging with humility and gratitude the goodness of the sovereign Ruler of the Universe, in offering us an opportunity so favorable to the design, and imploring His aid and direction in its accomplishment, do ordain and establish this Constitution for the Government of the Cherokee Nation.[6]

There was a significant addition to the sentiments expressed by Gouverneur Morris in the United States' preamble. The Cherokees committed themselves to a government under God; they declared themselves a Christian Nation. Not till America faced a time of crisis did the Union, in 1861, adopt the motto "In God We Trust," and not till a century later did Congress officially recognize the slogan—and then only as adding divine authority to coins and paper currency.

The first of the six articles of the constitution redefined the boundaries of the Nation and affirmed the Cherokee government's "Sovereignty and Jurisdiction" over this territory. Predictably, Georgia would take notice of this clause and regard it as one more infringement of its rights. Though Georgia's new governor, Virginia-born John Forsyth, was a son-in-law of the late Jonathan Meigs, his vision so far as the Cherokees were concerned was myopic. The very act of adopting a constitution meant that it was time for the Indians to go—since the President would expel them anyway as soon as Forsyth asked him to.

President Adams, however, generally approved the Cherokees' adoption of a constitution, though he sent Colonel Hugh Montgomery of the new Bureau of Indian Affairs to point out certain equivocal, if not objectionable, wordings. Adams took exception to the phrase "Sovereign and Independent," noting that this was of limited application. Cherokee sovereignty existed only within their boundaries; in relation to the United States their government was of a "purely municipal character." If the Cherokees winced slightly at the word "municipal" they let it pass; and let "Sovereign and Independent" stand.

Though the Cherokees were proud of their new constitution, ratification did not take place immediately nor was it achieved without at least some token opposition. In what was known as "White Path's Rebellion," a tradition-bound, full-blood chief of that name tried to organize a hard core of resistance in his native Turniptown. It was time, said White Path, to move in precisely the opposite direction: away from the white man's style of government and back to the ancient tribal ways.

The main body of Cherokees smiled tolerantly at the chief's views. "A noise which will end in noise only," declared Acting Chief Ross—which was how it ended. In time, after a brief suspension from the General Council, White Path returned to his seat in humble acceptance of the constitution.

Elections under the new regime would not be held till the following spring. Meanwhile John Ross carried on as Acting Chief, with William Hicks, son of the late Charles Hicks, serving as interim Assistant Chief. But the balance of 1827 was not without excitement and significant developments. For, pushing upriver from Savannah, strapped in the hold of a paddle-wheel steamer, was an article of greater import even than the constitution. The printing press was on its way.

While he was still at Brainerd, Samuel Worcester worked to make the visionary *Phoenix* a reality. At New Echota a building for the press was rising, a modest rectangular affair of logs with shingled roof, and doors at both ends. At the Boston end of the axis, Board Secretary Jeremiah Evarts worked with David Greene to find a suitable press and see to the casting of two sets of type, in Cherokee and English. To the workmen at the foundry Sequoyah's characters were like a Chinese puzzle; it would be a miracle if they got the faces right.

The General Council agreed to pay Boudinot a yearly salary of $300 as editor of the paper. A Tennessee printer named John Wheeler, mild-mannered and properly devout, was engaged for $400 a year—an inequality which gnawed at Boudinot's pride. Through Wheeler a second printer, named Isaac Harris, was contracted for, and it was his name that eventually graced the masthead.

Advance subscriptions were obtained—one from as far away as Germany—through a prospectus printed in Tennessee and mailed throughout the fall of 1827. Composed by Worcester, it defined the scope and purpose of the weekly journal. The *Phoenix* would present, wrote Worcester:

1. The laws and public documents of the Nation.
2. Account of the manners and customs of the Cherokees, and their progress in Education, Religion and the arts of civilized life; with such notice of other Indian tribes as our limited means of information will allow.
3. The principal interesting news of the day.
4. Interesting articles, calculated to promote Literature, Civilization and Religion among the Cherokees.[7]

Different subscription rates were quoted, to encourage prompt payment and to favor the Cherokee-speaking population. The prospectus noted that "To subscribers who can read English, the price of the paper is $2.50 annually, if paid in advance; $3, if payment is delayed six months; and $3.50, if not paid till the end of the year. To subscribers who can read only the Cherokee language, the price will be $2.00 in advance, or $2.50 to be paid within the year."

Newspapers and journals outside the Nation were invited to exchange their publications for copies of the forthcoming *Phoenix,* and long before the latter's appearance a table in the corner of the print shop was stacked with copies of the Boston *Statesman,* the Washington *National Intelligencer,* the New York *Mirror,* the New Hampshire *Patent & State Gazette, Niles' Weekly,* and even the Milledgeville *Journal* of Georgia. On these publications editor Boudinot would rely for national and international news and commentary.

In late November, as Sam and Ann Worcester were packing to move from Brainerd to New Echota, a letter arrived from Jeremiah Evarts saying in part:

The types & press, & furniture for the office are to be ready for shipping by the close of this week. The types & furniture have been ready for several weeks; but we have delayed purchasing a press, because we supposed the printer who would be employed, would wish to have some voice respecting the kind. We have this morning engaged one called the "union press"—it is an iron press; but seems simple in its structure—easily set up—& not likely to get out of repair.

Drawings of the press, with directions for putting it up and working it, will be forwarded to you. It weighs about lbs. 1000, the types & furniture—say—1200. All will be well packed & sent as soon as possible, to Augusta.[8]

The shipment, Evarts noted, would be sent to the care of John Ross and it would be up to Ross to get it from Augusta to New Echota. The matter of

Boudinot's dual role of editor and missionary evidently put the Board in something of a quandary. "I hope the council have made some provision for the support & employment of Mr. Boudinot," Evarts wrote, clearing the Board of this responsibility—fair enough, since the *Phoenix* was basically a Cherokee enterprise. As to Boudinot's connection with the Brainerd mission family, Evarts left the matter open, subject to future decision. Apparently Boudinot's fondness for ball-play was still a nettle in the missionary field.

At New Echota, befitting their image as partners, Worcester and Boudinot built almost identical houses close to one another on the central common: each two stories high, whitewashed and trimmed with gray, with double balconies, clapboard walls, and shingled roofs. For Harriet Boudinot and Ann Orr Worcester, both New England born of similar backgrounds, this proximity was heaven-sent. They could offer one another moral courage and companionship in the unpredictable and sometimes frightening future. Together, with feminine ingenuity, they fashioned of these twin plots in Georgia a little corner of New England.

Two days before Christmas, John Foster Wheeler arrived on the scene with Isaac Harris, a journeyman printer of unstable habits and embarrassing profanity. A young Cherokee half-breed named John Candy was taken on as an apprentice to the staff. With nothing to do until the press arrived, Wheeler and Harris attempted to learn the Cherokee alphabet and found it, according to Wheeler, "more incomprehensible than Greek. For myself, I could not distinguish a single word in the talk of the Indians with each other, for it seemed to be a continuance of sound."

Harris, for his part, dismissed the alphabet with a few well-chosen oaths. He would leave it up to Wheeler to set by hand the Cherokee columns in the paper. At which point it dawned on all concerned that, while type and press were on the way, they had made no provision for paper on which to print the journal. Harris hitched up a horse and started down the Federal Road to look for a paper supply in Tennessee. On his way he passed an itinerant peddler, touring the Nation with a large supply of spectacles. Their missions seemed happily coordinated; by the time Harris came back with the paper two weeks later, hundreds of Cherokees appeared in public wearing wire-rimmed glasses, like a flock of owls awaiting the rising of the *Phoenix*.

Down in Georgia a jaunty bit of doggerel was gaining popularity, put to an improvised tune by amateur troubadours:

> All I ask in this creation
> Is a pretty little wife and a big plantation
> Way up yonder in the Cherokee Nation.

Franklin Garrett, historian of the Atlanta yet to come, recorded an escapist version:

> I'm goin' for to leave my poor relation
> And get me a home in the Cherokee Nation.[9]

Either rendition reflected the restless itch of Georgians to get possession of those rich lands north of the Chattahoochee that had been promised to them for a quarter of a century. And none more anxious than Governor Forsyth, eager to accomplish what his predecessors had so notably failed to bring about: the removal of the Cherokees. On December 26, 1827, the Georgia legislature, under Forsyth's direction, passed the first state measure directly challenging the Cherokees' survival. It was the opening salvo of a siege that would continue for a decade and with ever-mounting fury.

In essence the act declared that all lands of the Cherokee Nation within the limits of the state of Georgia would hereafter fall under Georgia's laws so far as criminal jurisdiction went. It was presented and defended as an essential measure to protect the lives of Georgia citizens living on Cherokee territory. But the legislature left no doubt of its intentions. This was just a preliminary step.

The same legislature, that December, passed a revealing resolution: "That the policy which has been pursued by the United States toward the Cherokee Indians has not been in good faith toward Georgia . . . That all the lands, appropriated and unappropriated, which lie within the conventional limits of Georgia belong to her absolutely; that the title is in her; that the Indians are tenants at her will . . . and that Georgia has the right to extend her authority and her laws over the whole territory and to coerce obedience to them from all descriptions of people, be they white, red, or black, who may reside within her limits."[10]

Governor Troup, Forsyth's predecessor up to the previous November, had successfully secured the removal of the last of the Creeks from Georgia in defiance of President Adams' opposition. It was a hard act to follow, but Forsyth could not let himself be upstaged by the Cherokees. The legislature's resolution was a warning, but a barbed one. While it declared only the *right* of Georgia to extend its laws over the Indian territory, it left no doubt about the state's intentions. The federal government had better remove the Cherokees itself before the state took drastic action.

The resolution closed with a soft but deadly warning; Georgia would not use force to get her way *unless compelled to do so.*

The chiefs could not ignore Georgia's resolution or underestimate its implications. But nobody panicked in the Nation. Life went on much as before. The Georgia measure was too preposterous to be a serious threat. The President and the War Department would never tolerate its execution. But wiser heads—Ross and Hicks, John and Major Ridge—knew they had reached a point of crisis in the Nation's history. Would they be strong enough to weather it? God knows, they had taken every step possible to gain the strength.

Helen Hunt Jackson, author of *Ramona*, eloquently summarized this turn in Georgia-Cherokee relations:

What had so changed the attitude of Georgia to the Indians within her borders? Simply the fact that the Indians, finding themselves hemmed in on all sides by fast thickening, white settlements, had taken a firm stand that they would give up no more land. So long as they would cede and cede, and grant and grant tract after tract, and had millions of acres still left to cede and grant, the selfishness of white men took no alarm; but once consolidated into an empire, with fixed and inalienable boundaries, powerful, recognized, and determined, the Cherokee Nation would be a thorn in the flesh to her white neighbors. The doom of the Cherokees was sealed when they declared, once and for all, officially as a nation, that they would not sell another foot of land . . .[11]

Thursday, February 1, 1828, was a red-letter day for the Nation. Hauled by wagon from Augusta after a ten-week voyage from Boston, the press and type arrived at New Echota. With them came David Greene in person, to see that all was properly installed.

There was no fireplace in the twenty-by-thirty-foot print shop. With doors at either end and windows at the sides, there would have been no room for one. But the five men of the staff, Worcester, Boudinot, Wheeler, Harris, and Candy, along with David Greene, became at once too actively engaged to be aware of any chill.

There were endless details and adjustments to attend to. Wheeler and Harris, while waiting for the equipment, had built standard-size cases for the type, designed to fit beneath the windows. The 86-character Cherokee alphabet, however, demanded more space than anticipated and the cases had to be rebuilt. (The type "took over 100 boxes for figures, points, etc., to each case," Wheeler wrote.) Once rebuilt, the frames were found to be too high for the windows, and the windows in turn had to be removed from their sashes and raised by more than a foot.

For Greene there was no problem setting up the press, apart from its extraordinary weight. Its construction was simple. A cast-iron base held a tray for the hand-set type, over which a single sheet of paper would be laid. Just above the tray a horizontal metal plate hung from the end of a grooved shaft passing through a spiral-threaded cylinder. An immense protruding handle, swung full around, turned the shaft, lowered the plate, and pressed the paper evenly against the type. Only a single impression could be made at once; and in the case of the four-page *Phoenix,* only one page would be printed at a time.

The press was a monstrous thing, tyrannical and powerful, occupying almost a quarter of their limited space. But to Elias Boudinot, editor, it was a thing of glory. The voice of the Cherokees slept in its iron grasp, soon to ring out across the Nation. To Samuel Worcester the *Phoenix* was only one facet of the press which would also print copies of the Bible, hymnals, textbooks, and religious tracts. But to Elias it meant the *Phoenix* and the *Phoenix* only. It was his personal weapon with which to fight for Cherokee survival; and the recent act of the Georgia legislature gave him much to write about. He began to compose his initial editorial, dipping his quill pen in venom.

The third week of February was an almost sleepless period of pressure. Precisely how long it took to set the type by hand, in separate columns of Cherokee and English, is not recorded. Nor how long it took to print 500 copies of the *Phoenix*. The operation called for certain improvisations. With no inking rollers available, they were obliged to use balls of cotton wrapped in deerskin with which to spread the ink across the type.

It must have been a moment of extreme suspense when Wheeler or Harris gave the lever a full turn to make the first impression of the *Cherokee Phoenix*, Page One, Volume I, Number 1. The result, however, "was a very foul proof," according to Wheeler, "and a fatiguing job to correct it, as I did not know or understand a word of the language." But it got corrected; and with the date of Wednesday, February 21, 1828, printed beneath its double name in Cherokee and English, the *Cherokee Phoenix* took flight.

It circulated judiciously throughout the Nation, sometimes only a single copy to a village but read in turn by almost the entire populace, newly fitted out with pince-nez spectacles. It was read in the mission rooms in Boston and in homes on Beacon Hill; in staid New England villages and raucous frontier towns in Tennessee; by congressmen in Washington and (with consuming wrath) by Georgia senators in Milledgeville.

Eventually the *Phoenix* reached Sequoyah in the Western territory, who for the first time saw his syllabic characters in spiny print, precise as arrowheads. And in Zurich, Switzerland, the Baron de Campagne opened his copy with special satisfaction. His financial contributions to that strange and distant race of people in America had, he felt sure, helped to get the *Phoenix* started.

In 1828 reading and writing in the United States was given a lift with the publication of Noah Webster's pioneer two-volume *American Dictionary of the English Language*. But to the Cherokees both East and West the first issue of the *Phoenix* was of infinitely weightier significance. It was more important, even, than the transcription of their laws, their constitution, their multiple memorials to Congress, and Worcester's projected publication of the Bible. For it was all these things in one.

It contained its own lexicon of the native language, with Worcester's dissertation on Sequoyah's alphabet which made possible a form of writing "vastly more perfect than the English language . . . and I earnestly hope that the result of its application will be such as to be the just occasion of many thanksgivings to God." It began the printing for the first time of the Cherokee constitution drafted the year before, along with the collected laws of the Nation—all of which had not, till now, found general circulation. It presented the Lord's Prayer in both Cherokee and English. Language, government, religion—three subjects of vital concern to the Nation.

Nor did it ignore the present political situation of the Cherokees. Taking notice of Georgia's threat to extend its laws over Cherokee territory, Elias Boudinot's first editorial declared: "We will not intermeddle with the policies of our neighbours," and though concerned primarily with the interests of the Cherokees, "we will not return railing for railing, but consult mildness, for we

have been taught to believe that 'a soft answer turneth away wrath, but grievous words stir up anger.'"

Editor Boudinot closed his editorial with a placating paragraph:

We would now commit our feeble efforts to the good will and indulgence of the
public, praying that God will attend them with his blessings, and hoping for that
happy period, when all the Indian tribes of America shall arise, Phoenix like from
their ashes, and when the terms, "Indian depredations," "war whoop," "scalping
knife" and the like, shall become obsolete and for ever be "buried under deep
ground."[12]

The missionaries at Brainerd and other posts around the Nation had been
instructed by the American Board not to become involved in politics. At this
point, there was no pressure on them to become involved. But Elias Boudinot,
though officially a member of the Brainerd family, could not be bound by these
restrictions. The more he thought about Georgia's threat to extend its criminal
laws over the Nation, the angrier he became. Forgetting his vow not to "intermeddle with the policies of our neighbours," he delivered a head-on attack
against Georgia's manifesto of the previous year—writing in the *Phoenix* for
March 6, 1828:

What a pernicious effect must such a document as the report of the joint committee in the legislature of Georgia have on the interests and improvement of the Indians? Who will expect from the Cherokees a rapid progress in education, religion,
agriculture, and the various arts of civilized life when resolutions are passed in a
civilized and Christian legislature (whose daily sessions, we are told, commence
with a prayer to Almighty God) to wrest their country from them, and strange to
tell, with the point of the bayonet, if nothing else will do? Is it in the nature of
things, that the Cherokees will build good and comfortable houses and make them
great farms, when they know not but their possessions will fall into the hands of
strangers & invaders? How is it possible that they will establish for themselves good
laws, when an attempt is made to crush their first feeble effort toward it?[13]

In a way, a woman's way, Harriet was as troubled as her husband about the
situation and the life that they had undertaken. She shared her husband's anxiety over the future, especially as concerned herself and Elias. But she never regretted the decision made in Cornwall. "These months were trying ones to me,"
she wrote, "yet I number among them some of the happiest hours of my life—
when a consciousness of doing right was my only consolation . . . The place of
my birth is dear to me but I love this people and with them I wish to live and
die."

Her love, however, was sometimes sorely tried by the exigencies of tribal life.
She was not Boudinot's wife only. By Cherokee custom she had married the
whole family. She was sister in more than name to Elias' brothers and sisters,
aunt to innumerable russet-skinned children; their parents and grandparents
were hers as well. She was sometimes expected to cook and keep house for as

many as twenty or thirty of her kinfolk at a time—for such was the privilege of a sister, aunt, and daughter.

She thought often, with empty longing, of the comforting quiet of the Litchfield Hills. "I would like to visit you," she wrote to her family, "but it is not likely we shall in several years if ever." Did they speak kindly of her, she asked, in Cornwall? Or did the town still nurse its feeling of resentment and hostility toward her?[14]

Sophia Sawyer was also in an emotional turmoil. She had been removed from Brainerd. No one told her precisely why; but her unorthodox behavior, and habit of saying what she thought, might have been among the causes. And her methods of teaching—popular with the Cherokees but not with her fellow missionaries. Anxious to have her pupils reading English, she had given them, not the Bible or verses from the hymns, but copies of the *Youth's Companion*.

So, "for her own good," they sent her down to Elizur Butler's newly opened mission school at Haweiss, southwest of New Echota. "I have been cast down, but not destroyed by removal from this station," she wrote to Jeremiah Evarts. Her great regret was the strong attachments she had formed among the children. "Leaving them is to die a little." And it broke her heart when they, on hearing of her departure, asked, "Don't you love us any more?" Yes, she loved them; she would have to find others at Haweiss to give her limitless affection to.

Haweiss was not far distant from New Echota, and on an early visit to that town Sophia renewed her friendship with Elias Boudinot. If she had shared the missionaries' doubt about Elias' future (he would never live down that ballplay), she found him now "diffusing happiness all around . . . a light to his people," and destined to be "a star in his kingdom of glory." At New Echota she stayed with Ann and Samuel Worcester—surprisingly, since Worcester had been one of her well-meaning critics in the Brainerd days. That she was entertained with warmth and understanding seems evident in her words to Evarts: "I feel like one shipwrecked & thrown on a peaceful shore by the boisterous waves."[15]

Worcester himself was up to his neck, with Boudinot, in shaping the early issues of the *Phoenix*. Physically the *Phoenix* stacked up well against the newspapers of New York and Philadelphia, New England and the South. Its four large-size pages contained five columns of type in an approximate ratio of three columns in English to two in Cherokee. The allocation was not disproportionate. Since each of Sequoyah's characters stood for a whole syllable, it required less space to express a thought in Cherokee than in English.

National news was of necessity obtained from the journals received in exchange, which shortly numbered more than a hundred. And from these, too, editor Boudinot culled most of the miscellaneous material "of general interest" which the prospectus promised to its readers. The articles ranged far afield, covering the Excavations of Pompeii, the Beneficial Effects of Laughter, Sunset in the Alps, the Probable Collision of the Earth and a Comet.

There were few advertisements; and none whatever for the patent-medicine nostrums that abounded in journals outside the Nation. But the personal welfare of its readers was considered in such articles as "Recipes for Insuring Health," "Tight Lacing and Thin Clothing," "Female Delicacy," and "The Evils of Alcohol."

Contributions from readers, especially in the form of letters, were encouraged; and, with the Nation agog over its new ability to write, the little print shop was deluged with mail. While United States postal service had existed in the territory since 1819, with offices at Rossville and Spring Place, the demands of the press required the opening of another office at New Echota. Samuel Worcester was appointed, by the federal government, postmaster of the station.

Worcester was working on his translation of St. Matthew, writing weekly articles for the *Phoenix*, corresponding regularly with the Boston Board of Foreign Missions to keep them posted on missionary work in progress. Though he chafed against this added burden of struggling with the mail, the appointment would be his brief salvation in the years ahead. For the Cherokees, at this peak moment of achievement, were standing on the brink of peril. And Worcester himself was closer to that brink than he imagined.

7

David and Goliath

BLESSED ARE the meek: for they shall inherit the earth. Blessed are they which hunger and thirst after righteousness: for they shall be filled. Blessed are the merciful . . . the pure in heart . . . the peacemakers . . .

They were noble words, said the venerable Chief Yonaguska, hearing the gospel read to him by Daniel Butrick from Worcester's translation of St. Matthew. The chief, however, appeared to have some reservations.

"It seems to be a good book," Yonaguska remarked thoughtfully, "but it is strange that the white people are not better, after having had it so long."[1]

It was as far as the Cherokees would go in condemning those who persecuted them, for John Ross was teaching them forbearance. The whites of Georgia who wanted them removed simply did not understand the situation, did not realize how far the Cherokees had gone in building a stable, law-abiding nation. They would either come to their senses, or the President in Washington would remind them of their obligations under previous, inviolable treaties.

Even the militant Elias Boudinot, though not denying that a certain animosity existed between the Cherokees and Georgia, urged the readers of the *Phoenix* to be moderate in attitude toward their southern neighbors. There were many Georgians, he wrote, "who are real friends to the Indians; many whose friendship we greatly prize." He quoted a correspondent who had expressed, in a letter to the paper, the hope that religious tolerance would take the place of racial prejudice, to the end that "all commotions and angry feelings shall be buried in oblivion, and all become the family of God . . ."[2]

Governor Forsyth, however, harbored no such charitable thoughts. When the *Phoenix* reached his desk in the capitol building in Milledgeville, he read for the first time the Cherokees' new constitution and considered it "presumptuous." First the missionary schools spreading education in the Nation. Then a written language of their own, with their own recorded laws. Then a supreme court, with their own judicial system. Then a constitution. Then a national newspaper . . .

Things had been allowed to go too far. The Cherokees were getting too big for their breeches. He rolled up his copy of the *Phoenix* containing sections of the constitution and mailed it to John Quincy Adams. What did the President propose to do about this arrogant creation of "an independent government within the limits of the state?"

Left to himself, Adams would have chosen to do nothing. He shunted the problem off on his cabinet, who transferred it to the Congress. Congress had already appropriated $50,000 for effecting, or at least promoting, the removal of the Cherokees from Georgia, and now the War Department sent Colonel Hugh Montgomery to investigate the situation and report back on his findings. Before Montgomery even got under way, Forsyth warned him by letter that "the Cherokees in Georgia will be inevitably subjected to the State laws if the compact made in 1802 is not speedily executed by the U. States."[3]

Montgomery toured the Nation with an open mind. As Indian Agent for many years there was not much new for him to learn. He was authorized to offer, by way of innocent bribery, rifles and blankets and transportation costs to any families wishing to enroll for emigration. He found no takers. Voluntary removal, he reported, was "a lost issue. Removal, if accomplished at all, must be accomplished by coercion"—not something Montgomery was willing to advise.

This was an election year in both the United States and the Cherokee Nation—for the latter, the first elections to be held under the new constitution. It was a test of the working of democracy among the Cherokees, and The Ridge exhorted the people to choose wisely and choose well. He himself would have qualified as a candidate for Principal Chief, but it was time, he believed, for younger men to take the reins. He cited the $50,000 congressional appropriation to force a land cession upon the Nation, and the need for staunch leaders to resist it.

"Let us hold fast to the country which we yet retain," he exhorted. "Let us direct our efforts to agriculture, and to the increase of wealth, and to the promotion of knowledge."[4]

Politicking as practiced in the United States was unfamiliar to the Nation. Yet the people responded with vigor to the electioneering campaigns, most of them conducted in low key. Boudinot opened the columns of the *Phoenix* to prospective candidates for office (though reserving the right to withhold communications he considered inflammatory or divisive), and one who signed himself Utaletah invoked his followers to handle with care the "privilege" of free elections:

The welfare of our country should be the order of the day with all who have the interest of their native land at heart. Our Nation, as a political body, has reached an important crisis, and bids fair for rapid progress in the path of civilization, the arts and the sciences . . . that is gradually gaining an ascendancy amongst us equalled by no other Indian Tribe . . . It is but just to ourselves and to our country, to endeavor to maintain the eminence we have attained to. . . .

The Committee should be composed of men of education, and good knowledge in the affairs of our Nation; while the Council should be composed of full blooded Cherokees, known for love of their country, the land of their forefathers, and also celebrated for their good natural sense, justice and firmness.[5]

Elections were held in the several districts toward the end of the summer, in anticipation of the autumn Council. As an unnecessary precaution some of the missionaries, including Isaac Proctor, were asked to supervise the procedure when the votes were taken in the local Council Houses. They were pleasantly surprised at the good order that prevailed. "There was nothing of that intrigue and unfairness which is to be seen at elections in some of the civilized states," recorded Proctor.

Since the deaths early in 1827 of Chiefs Pathkiller and Charles Hicks, John Ross and William Hicks had served as interim Chief and Assistant Chief respectively. While Ross's reputation for integrity remained high, William Hicks was rumored to be secretly preaching removal and was accused of having discussed the matter with Hugh Montgomery. That rumor ended his political career; and at the October Council, John Ross was overhwelmingly elected to retain the office of Principal Chief, while Ross's kinsman George Lowrey replaced the disgruntled Hicks as Assistant Chief. The Ridge was raised from Speaker of the Council to the newly created post of Adviser to the Chief.

Going Snake replaced The Ridge as Speaker of the Council, and John Ridge, after an unpleasant interval, replaced half-breed Alexander McCoy as Clerk of the Council. Like William Hicks, McCoy was suspect. It was learned he had consulted United States agents as to what he might get for his property if he agreed to enroll for emigration to the West. On learning of this, the Council requested his resignation.

John Martin, a judge of the Supreme Court, was elected Treasurer of the Nation, an amorphous post that seemed to exist in name alone. For there was no real treasury as such. Even at this advanced stage of development the Nation did not issue its own currency but relied on that of neighboring states. Its principal income of $7,500, from annuities from the United States, was paid directly to John Ross, and went out as fast as it came in. The October Council alone cost more than $5,000, most of it going for the salaries and expenses of delegates and for the mountains of provisions—beef, venison, pheasant—spread out by hired chefs on sheltered tables of the Council grounds.

Treasurer Martin accordingly found little to keep him busy in New Echota and stayed much of the time at home. Had he thought it his duty to be present in the capital, he would hardly have found a proper place to sit. This situation caused one worried citizen, signing himself "A Cherokee," to complain to the *Phoenix:* "A seat of government without a treasury is like a coat without a pocket." He urged the Council to clothe its "naked metropolis."[6]

If the plaint was lighthearted, the flaw was very real. The lack of a national treasury and of an independent fiscal policy was too obvious a weakness for the Cherokees' enemies to overlook—for long.

As the government otherwise reached maturity, confirmed by the 1828 free elections, the little capital of New Echota also reached completion. Besides the print shop there was a building for the Supreme Court with a judge's bench and jury box and pinewood seats for the public, and a Council House that departed from the ancient conical architecture. It was described as "a spacious rectangular log building of two stories, with brick chimneys and fireplaces, glass windows, sawed plank floors, and a stairway that led to upper conference chambers."

Missing was any sign of a National Academy with its library and musuem which had been the glowing core of the original imaginative dream. The press and the *Phoenix* had seemed to divert attention from that goal, which now would never be realized. Citizens of New Orleans, hearing of the project, had raised funds for two world globes to be donated to the academy and/or museum, which David Brown brought back from the Crescent City. They gathered dust in David's home, which, in the light of unforeseen events, was anything but a safe repository.

Commercial ventures, however, found a foothold in the little capital, with four stores (only two of which were open the year round); and adjoining the two-acre green were a number of substantial residences to give the town a settled look. The homes of Elijah Hicks and Alexander McCoy, which had been there before the town was started, still remained, and the clapboard, balconied houses built for Elias Boudinot and Samuel Worcester were landmarks in the community. They would have looked appropriate in Harriet Gold Boudinot's Connecticut or Ann Orr Worcester's Massachusetts.

John Ross had long since moved from Ross's Landing to be closer to the capital. He had built a comfortable home a mile from The Ridge's at the junction of the Etowah and Coosa rivers—captioning his letters "Head of Coosa"—planted orchards and flowering magnolias, and decorated the sloping lawns with strutting peacocks. No one ridiculed this show of affluence and elegance. He was the Principal Chief; his image was the image of the Nation.

Two hundred miles up the Federal Road, at the Hermitage in Nashville, another newly chosen head of state received the news of his election. Andrew Jackson had won 56 per cent of the popular vote for President and 178 electoral votes against 83 for the incumbent Adams. That evening his wife Rachel complained of feeling faint; two days later she was dead, shrouding in grief and bitterness Old Hickory's final victory. Only weeks earlier the Indian youth Lincoyer, whom the general had adopted during the Creek campaign, had succumbed to tuberculosis. Death seemed anxious to accompany Jackson to the White House.

There was no question where Jackson stood on Indian removal. The Battle of Horseshoe Bend had long since been eclipsed by the Battle of New Orleans, and the general's viewpoint had shifted from that of leader of the humble to commander of the great. Though the Jacksonian Age would label him "Man of the People," he was his own man and he walked alone. Those who blocked his forward thrust were destined to be hurled aside. And the Indians, he was convinced, stood squarely in the path of progress.

As to where the Indians stood on Andrew Jackson, Chief Junaluska probably expressed it best. "If I had known that Jackson was going to drive us from our homes," said Junaluska, "I would have killed him that day at the Horseshoe."[7]

One who stood squarely in Jackson's path—awaiting their head-on confrontation with no thought of budging—was John Ross. The five-foot five-inch Ross, so recently chosen Principal Chief of his Nation, might look physically puny compared with his adversary in the White House, over six feet tall. But in the inevitable battle that was brewing between David and Goliath, the Cherokees' faith in Ross would never waver. "They look upon him as some sort of god," protested future governor George Rockingham Gilmer. Gilmer was right, even with reference to the white man's God. One Cherokee told William Chamberlin that he would believe in the Gospels only if John Ross endorsed them.

Jackson's election gave vicious impulse to the drive for Indian removal. On December 20, 1828, Governor Forsyth signed a bill declaring that as of June 1, 1830, all Cherokee territory in the state would be subject to the laws of Georgia and would, in fact, be partitioned among adjacent Georgian counties. Cherokee sovereignty was wiped out in a single sentence: "All laws, usages, and customs made, established, and in force in the said territory, are hereby declared null and void."[8]

The act came as no surprise. Georgia's intentions had been signaled by the similarly worded resolution passed the year before. And once again the state, by postponing the effective date to June 1830, was giving the federal government time to avoid a divisive confrontation—time, as Forsyth put it, to "enable the President to execute the Compact of 1802." As if Jackson would consider any treaty, any compact, binding!

This time the Cherokees were more alarmed. The earlier resolution had been regarded as simply a statement of Georgia's discontent. This measure, if implemented, could destroy the Nation. That unthinkable catastrophe became a possibility with Andrew Jackson in the White House. Concerning the Cherokees the President-elect had remarked to Georgia congressmen, which now included Georgia's Wilson Lumpkin: "Build a fire under them. When it gets hot enough, they'll move."[9]

Georgia was building a fire under them.

A memorial of protest was drafted by the Council, in which it was stressed that the Cherokees had never been a party of the Compact of 1802 and would never surrender their rights. It bore the signatures of 3,095 Cherokee citizens and officials, and shortly after the first of the year John Ross was authorized to carry it to Washington.

The timing was bad. It marked the raucous birth of a new federal administration, the administration of the common man, the Tennessee backwoodsman, the Irish immigrant, the land-hungry pioneer. The capital was jammed as never before with favor-seeking opportunists. Jackson was holed up at Gadsby's Hotel, labeled "the Wigwam" in his honor, and absorbed with the forming of a cabinet. He had no time for his former adjutant, now Principal Chief of the Cherokees.

His already chosen Secretary of War, John Henry Eaton, was romantically and hopelessly involved with the American Pompadour, Peggy O'Neill, a tavern keeper's daughter who was whipping up a social hurricane in Washington. Though Indian affairs were still the province of the War Department, Eaton's knowledge of the problem was abysmal. He favored removal simply because "there is more game to be had in the West"—believing the Cherokees still relied on hunting and fishing for survival.[10]

Thus the Cherokee memorial suffered the fate of many more to come. It simply lay there until pigeonholed. The era of the common man did not include the Indian. Least of all an educated and uncommon Indian.

Ross returned to Head of Coosa without waiting for the President's inauguration. But on March 4, 1829, a curious situation existed on the continent. Two nations, one within the other, both claiming sovereign independence, both headed by exceptionally strong and resolute executives. True, there were tremendous differences in the size of the nations. The Cherokee Nation numbered between sixteen and eighteen thousand people; the United States was approaching the twelve-million mark. But the weight of justice could, if properly applied, even up such inequalities.

Crowding the Cherokee Nation on the south was the sovereign state of Georgia. It was geographically the largest in the Union, its half-million population ranking tenth among the twenty-seven states. But it was a land-hungry population nonetheless; and Georgia too was a gateway on the route to the expanding West. Moreover, the northern states were outstripping the South in population and prosperity; the Cherokees were a handicap to Georgia's Manifest Destiny.

It was not yet a war. But with Jackson's election, the battle lines were drawn. The Cherokee Nation was caught in a pincer movement, facing potential enemies on two fronts: to the north the United States, preparing to evict them; on the south, Georgia preparing to invade them. Nonbelligerent resistance was Ross's open policy; "Remain united," was his battle cry. But had the Cherokees sufficient weapons for a two-front war?

The Nation would need allies. And it had them.

The missionaries, as noted, had been cautioned not to engage in political controversies. But it was hard for an idealist like Samuel Worcester to stand aloof from what so vitally concerned his people—his adopted people. Especially when teamed so closely with Elias Boudinot, who was outspoken against the United States and Georgia on the question of removal.

In the first issue of the *Phoenix* the editor had written: "We will invariably state the will of the majority of our people on the subject of the present controversy with Georgia, and the present removal policy of the United States." Fair warning. Boudinot did not need to manufacture words himself. With Jackson in the White House and with Georgia's policy made plain, readers by the dozen sent their protests to the *Phoenix*.

"The lands we possess are the gift of our Creator," wrote a group of citizens from the deep-mountain Valley Town district. "They are moreover recognized by the United States, and *guaranteed to us forever* . . . Within these limits we consider ourselves at home, and have no doubt to the goodness of our title . . .

"Our Creator has not given us the land beyond the Mississippi, but has given it to other people; and why should we wish to enter upon their possessions?"[11]

Such reasoning, however naïve, appealed to the missionaries, who were definitely on the side of the Creator. They were not of one mind on every issue. For some time the Brainerd-oriented group continued to look askance at the overactive Methodists; they seemed to put too much joy into religion; and Elias Boudinot uncharitably published an editorial criticizing their methods of evangelism. At first, the Methodist missionary N. D. Scales sent to the *Phoenix* a well-reasoned rebuttal, which Elias refused to print. It had come with postage due. Boudinot's curt editorial reply: "According to the terms of our paper, we expect all communications to be post paid."

This was the smallest of tempests in a teapot, and Boudinot apologized to the Reverend Scales. Thereafter the missionaries worked together in extraordinary harmony. Sectarian lines, if drawn at all, were hypothetical. Congregationalists from Brainerd preached at Methodist gatherings; Moravians spoke to Evan Jones's Baptist congregations; the irrepressible Daniel Butrick preached to anybody who would listen. In short, the missionaries formed one influential body, walking a thin line between preaching the gospel and defending the rights of their disciples.

Too thin a line, thought Governor Forsyth, who complained to Colonel Thomas McKenney, head of the Bureau of Indian Affairs in Washington, that the missionaries were exhorting the Cherokees to defy the laws of Georgia, and forming a hard core of resistance to removal. McKenney passed the complaint on to the Board of Foreign Missions, as Jeremiah Evarts reported to Sam Worcester. "The charge," wrote Evarts, "was interfering with the press, & writing scurrilous articles respecting officers of government & other public men."[12]

Worcester had written no scurrilous articles, though some of Boudinot's editorials could be interpreted as such. And while Worcester wrote a disclaimer for publication in the *Phoenix,* stating that the editor's views were his and his alone, the opinion still prevailed in Georgia that Worcester was the man behind the pen.

It was safe to say that Evarts represented Boston's attitude in the affair. They would stand behind the missionaries, come what may.

"Do what is right," the secretary wrote to Worcester, "& you need not fear."[13]

Boudinot was temporarily restrained from further inflammatory editorials by discord at the press. Isaac Harris had not worked out as printer. He was quarrelsome, independent, and profane. From the start, he and Boudinot had been at swords' points. Elias threatened to resign unless the printer was replaced by "a man whose influence shall be in favor of good things." The Council sided with Boudinot and fired Harris. When the latter refused to leave the print shop, Assistant Chief George Lowrey stormed into the building and physically threw him out.

John Wheeler, stable and faithful, took Harris's place; and on its first anniversary in February 1829, the name of the *Phoenix* was expanded to become the *Cherokee Phoenix and Indians' Advocate*. The new name suggested a new spirit of crusade. As the paper began its second year of publication Boudinot reminded his readers that the *Phoenix* was "sacred to the cause of Indians," and vowed to pay particular attention to the government's policy of Indian removal "and objections thereto."

He added a plaintive note applicable to fledgling journals everywhere: "Thus far the *Phoenix* has been a dead expense to the proprietors."[14]

Both Boudinot and Worcester were having company that year. Visiting the Boudinots were Harriet's parents, Benjamin and Eleanor Gold, who had journeyed from Cornwall by horse and buggy, relieving the tedium "by song & a pinch of snuff as we passed along the country." Their first stop in Indian territory was at the home of Lewis Ross, John's brother, which reassured them as to the nature of Harriet's adopted land.

"Mr. Ross's house," wrote Gold to his cousin Hezekiah Gold in Cornwall, "is a large & elegant white House as handsomely furnished & handsomely situated as almost any house in Litchfield County—he appears to be rich & no doubt is so. He has around his House about 20 Negro slaves who paid good attention to us two nights—& when we offered to pay a bill they told us that Mr. Ross would not take anything for entertainment of any people who had connection with the Nation."[15]

They had feared that Harriet's marriage might have turned out as badly as predicted in New England, and were again reassured on their arrival at New Echota. The Boudinot house, reported Gold, was "well done off and well furnished with the comforts of life. They get their supplies of clothes and groceries—they have their year's store of teas, clothes, paper, ink, etc. from Boston, and their sugar, molasses, etc., from Augusta. They have two or three barrels of flour on hand at once."

Elias himself, though still smarting from his treatment by the citizens of Cornwall, was granted a measure of approval. The Golds found that "Mr. Boudinot has much good company and is respected all over the United States . . . Harriet says she envies the situation of no one in Connecticut." The Golds were also delighted with their three bright, "Yankee-looking" grandchildren—Mary, William, and Eleanor—the last attending Miss Sophia's school "kept in the Court House about 30 yards from her Father's House."

Miss Sophia, it seemed, had found her niche in Cherokee missionary life. She was now staying at the Worcesters' house in New Echota, despite the fact that three years earlier Sam Worcester had considered her a nearly hopeless case, too "fiery," too "intractable." It was partly on Worcester's recommendation that she had been sent from Brainerd to the mission school at Haweiss. That had not worked out any better, and David Greene had written from Boston suggesting that the Worcesters take her in at New Echota.

"I do not know how far she may be permanently useful in your family,"

Greene wrote, "yet I do not think of any place where she can probably be more contented & turn her labors to better account. Perhaps she may do something at teaching a few scholars in the place." In any event, the Worcesters' stable and devout ménage should straighten her out if anything could.[16]

It did more than that. At New Echota, Miss Sophia's soul took flight. "Let this be a new era in my life," she wrote to David Greene, "when angels will love me . . ." Formerly, at Brainerd, "my feelings blinded me . . . I had no faith." But now: "Within a few more revolutions of the planet, I shall walk the streets of the new Jerusalem, & associate with glorified spirits—shall understand the mysteries—my soul will be expanded."[17]

Samuel Worcester could not have failed to respond to Miss Sophia's transports. She lived on emotional peaks, and it was such a far drop to the valleys. He felt protective, and he and Ann treated her, as Sophia wrote, with "utmost kindness." As to her feelings for Worcester—though she had once thought him the root of all her difficulties, he having been critical of her in the past—she now was filled with only "delicacy and tenderness" toward him. "Should I not have his affections, it would be insupportable." Ah, Sophia, Sophia! If only the world were more responsive to the heart . . .

David Greene had suggested she might do a little teaching. Worcester arranged to have the courthouse during the long periods when it was not in use, and here Sophia eagerly set up school. As teacher and principal in one, free of restraint, her fiery energy found a fruitful outlet. Her girls were the children of neighborhood families: the daughters of Vanns, Martins, Fields, Hickses, and McCoys, besides young Eleanor Boudinot and little Ann Eliza Worcester.

Her curriculum explored such intriguing avenues as celestial phenomena, the stories in the *Youth's Companion,* world-affairs articles in *Parley's Magazine,* and the study of geography with special emphasis on animals and the sad plight of the Greeks. The latter prompted her students to donate thirty cents each, or $3.60, to a fund for the relief of Greek children. Perhaps they saw in the struggles of that alien people something akin to what they were facing in America.

As of the moment, what they were facing seemed far from hopeless. Georgia's law annexing the Nation would not be in effect for another year, and anything could happen in a year. While impatient Georgians were already trespassing upon their territory, staking out premature claims on Cherokee land, Hugh Montgomery, United States Indian Agent, was counted on to prevent undue abuses. The Cherokees had patience; sentiment in their favor was mounting in the North; and time was on their side.

They could not have foreseen the mortal blow that fell upon them next. Gold was discovered in the Georgia mountains in July 1829.

The presence of precious metals in the region had been known for years if not for centuries. De Soto had apparently discovered gold in the southern Alleghenies, and the Spaniards had left traces of their mines. Since the turn of the century, 1804 to be exact, virtually all the gold mined in the United States came from North Carolina, more than $20,000,000 of it, but the Cherokees had long since lost their portion of the gold-producing country. And their same indifference to the fiscal side of government applied to their regard for mineral wealth. They did not covet its possession or regret its lack.

When, however, gold was discovered in Burke County in 1828, the obvious path of the vein led like a poisoned arrow into northern Georgia, piercing the heart of the Cherokee Nation.

Those who discover gold are not eager to release the facts. There were many versions. A young slave found a nugget just thirty miles east of New Echota and in ignorance displayed it to his master; an Indian youth living on Ward Creek sold a gold "pebble" to a Yankee trader. Most probably the news leaked out, part rumor, part distorted fact, over a period of some months.

But by mid-July the rush was on. It became a stampede, impossible to check. Seemingly overnight four thousand gold-seekers, mostly from Georgia and mostly white, poured into the region to dig and pan for gold at the site that was later named Dahlonega, meaning "yellow metal." In subsequent months their numbers would swell to ten thousand or more, and the gold extracted would amount in value to more than $16,500,000, second-largest strike in the history of the continent up to then.

An unidentified prospector remembered: "Within a few days it seemed as if the world must have heard of it, for men came from every state . . . They came afoot, on horseback, and in wagons, acting more like crazy men than anything else." Raucous tent and shack communities sprang up at Dahlonega and nearby Auraria in a pattern followed twenty years later at the Comstock Lode.

"The dust became a medium of circulation," wrote one observer, "and miners were accustomed to carry about with them quills filled with gold, and a pair of small hand scales, on which they weighed out gold at regular rates; for instance, 3½ grains of gold was the customary equivalent of a pint of whisky."[18]

Worcester and the missionaries deplored this overwhelming flood of greed and lust. But not on moral grounds alone. They saw the discovery of gold as spelling doom for the Indian Nation. While a few prominent citizens such as Elijah Hicks and Ross's nephew William S. Coodey joined the impetuous miners in panning for the precious metal, others like John Huss and Archibald Downing, mission converts, along with several members of Dr. Butler's congregation at the Haweiss Mission, visited the gold fields to conduct religious services. So perhaps the good and evil balanced out.

As a body politic the Nation took no official interest in the gold fields; perhaps a pity, in that they could have used the profits to finance the *Phoenix,* the maintenance of public works and buildings, and the strengthening of their almost nonexistent treasury.

Not that the event was underestimated. The gold strike was a matter of concern to both the Cherokee General Council and the Georgia legislature. For the latter it represented another telling reason why the Cherokees should be expelled, and quickly, before they exploited the mineral wealth which would soon come under Georgia's jurisdiction. For the Cherokees it was one more reason to strengthen their defenses against the inevitable added pressure for removal.

There were weak points in those defenses. Individuals like Alexander McCoy and William Hicks, embittered at being removed from office, might well be susceptible to bribes from United States or Georgia agents, and induced to sell their extensive acreage. Enough of such private deals would erode the territory bite by bite and achieve the goal of general cession.

The October Council focused on this problem. A bill was passed strengthening the previous law that decreed death for any Cherokee who sold or ceded his land without the sanction of the Nation. The new measure specified:

Be it further resolved, that any person or persons, who shall violate the provisions of this act, and shall refuse, by resistance, to appear at the place designated for trial, or abscond, are hereby declared to be outlaws; and any person or persons, citizens of this Nation, may kill him or them so offending, in any manner most convenient, within the limits of this Nation, and shall not be held accountable for same.[19]

There were no dissenting voices in the passing of this act. The Ridge and The Ridge's son John, the latter now Council Clerk, and all of the eight district chiefs subscribed to it. The aging Chief Womankiller of the Hickory Log district made an eloquent appeal in behalf of those ancient Cherokees "who now sleep in the dust." He knew how they might feel because he now stood on the edge of the grave himself, and he said:

My sun of existence is now fast approaching to its sitting, and my aged bones will soon be laid underground, and I wish them laid in the bosom of this earth we have received from our fathers who had it from the Great Being above. When I shall sleep in forgetfulness, I hope my bones will not be deserted by you. I do not speak this in fear of any of you, as the evidence of your attachment of the country is proved in the bill now before your consideration.

I am told that the Government of the United States will spoil their treaties with us and sink our National Council under their feet. It may be so, but it shall not be with our consent, or by the misconduct of our people. We hold them by the golden chain of friendship, made when our friendship was worth the price, and if they act the tyrant and kill us for our lands, we shall, in a state of unoffending innocence, sleep with thousands of our departed people. My feeble limbs will not allow me to stand longer. I can say no more . . .[20]

Meeting two months later, in mid-December 1829, the Georgia legislature took account of what they regarded as a new note of defiance in the Nation. The Cherokees were gaining support for their position in the northern states and cities. True, there were many in Georgia sympathetic to their plight, and not a few who questioned Georgia's right to interfere or impose its authority on the Nation. But now there was gold, and gold had a perverse effect upon man's reason.

Furthermore, President Jackson in his first address to Congress on December 8 had come out in favor of Indian removal. The message had not been harsh or hostile. The Indian emigration should be "voluntary, for it would be cruel and unjust to compel them to abandon the graves of their fathers and seek a home in a distant land." But for their own good, they should go, nonetheless; or else Georgia's claims of jurisdiction would be upheld by the United States and the Cherokees would have to accept absorption by the state.[21]

While Georgia's authority would not be imposed upon the Nation until the following June of 1830, there were steps to be taken meanwhile that might nudge the Indians toward compliance. To measures already passed Georgia appended some new restrictive acts. One virtually stripped the Indians of any right in a court of justice. No Indian would be allowed to testify at a trial involving white men; no Indian contract or testimony was valid without two white witnesses.

Taking cognizance of the discovery of gold in Cherokee territory, the legislature further enacted that no Indian could engage "in digging for gold in said land, and taking therefrom great amounts of value, thereby appropriating riches to themselves which of right equally belong to every other citizen of the state . . ." No provision was made for interloping Georgians digging Cherokee gold from Cherokee mines.[22]

Taking note further of the Cherokee law decreeing death for all who sold or ceded Cherokee lands, and the shackles that that measure put upon removal, the Georgia legislature tacked on an act to negate the Cherokee decree, declaring that "it shall not be lawful for any person or body of persons . . . to prevent, or deter any Indian, head man, chief, or warrior of said Nation . . . from selling or ceding to the United States, for the use of Georgia, the whole or any part of said territory . . ."

The penalty for violators was "confinement at hard labor in the penitentiary for a term not exceeding four years at the discretion of the court." The same penalty was applied to any persons or body of persons preventing, by force or threat, individual Cherokees from enrolling for emigration or from actually moving to the West. The new bill also banned all further meetings of the Cherokee Council and all political assemblies on Georgia soil, except for the purpose of negotiating land cessions.

Again, the new measures would take effect on the date established for previous enactments, on June 1830, now only six months off.

The hammer blows were falling fast as the Cherokees faced the greatest crisis in their history. But they did not go uncountered. In Massachusetts, Jeremiah Evarts, secretary of the American Board, began releasing to the press a series of letters over the pseudonym William Penn, which appeared, among other places, in the Washington *National Intelligencer* and were reprinted in the *Phoenix*. One of the first of these, published in the autumn of 1829, seemed little less than a call to war.[23]

The writer suggested that "the Indians had better stand to their arms" rather than be forced to emigrate or "be trampled as the serfs of Georgia . . . We would rather have a civil war, were there no alternative . . . We would take up arms for the Indians, in such a war, with as much confidence of our duty as we would stand with our bayonets on the shores of the Atlantic, to repel the assaults of the most barbarous invader."

With South Carolina already taking a belligerent stand against the protective "Tariff of Abominations"—a stand that well might lead to civil war—these were inflammatory words. But there was more to come, directed at the "perfidy" of Georgia's contemplated moves against the Cherokees:

Let the vials of God's wrath be poured out in plague, and storm, and desolation; let our navies be scattered to the four winds of Heaven; let our corn be blasted in the fields; let our first born be consumed with the stroke of the pestilence; let us be visited with earthquakes, and given as a prey to the devouring fire; but let us not be left to commit so great an outrage on the laws of nations and of God; let us not be abandoned to the degradation of national perjury, and, as its certain consequence, to some signal addition of national woe.[24]

To Georgia's Senator Wilson Lumpkin, coming in from the wings to center stage in the Georgia-Cherokee dispute, these were the wild words of a maniac. The Virginia-born Lumpkin, now thirty-seven, had by his own admission been long concerned with the fate of the Cherokees, "that unfortunate race," and had early maintained that their hope of prosperity lay only in the West, where they would be free of pressure from Georgians like himself. When he spoke of thinking of the Cherokees' own good, there is reason to believe he meant it.

He had been active in the early planning of the railroads that would someday make Atlanta a crossroads of America (in fact, that city was first named Marthasville for Lumpkin's daughter), and had surveyed the route of the Western & Atlantic, which General Sherman would use as his lifeline in besieging the Gate City. As a surveyor, Lumpkin traveled often through the Cherokee Nation, where he became acquainted with the leading chiefs and families, the Ridges, Rosses, Vanns, Fields, Hickses. As a congressman, he had served on several committees concerned with Indian problems, and considered himself an informed, broad-minded authority on Indian affairs.

But tolerance exploded on reading the material of "William Penn," whom he readily identified as the Boston secretary of a "new sect" and whose writing he found infused with a "savage, superstitious, and diabolical spirit." There had been many verbal attacks upon the missionaries for encouraging the Indians, obliquely if not directly, to hold fast to their lands. But in reprinting in the *Phoenix* Lumpkin's reply to William Penn, Worcester and Boudinot must have realized that the missionaries were in trouble.

This "Christian party in politics," Lumpkin told the U. S. Senate, had become the first "concerted and united opposition" to the government's plans for Indian emigration. Not strictly true, since the whole Cherokee Nation was concerted and united in its opposition to removal. But Lumpkin had found a vulnerable target. He would leave the rest to Gilmer and the Georgia legislature. If he expected them soon to take action, he would not be disappointed.

The Nation was under attack at home as well, as white prospectors in increasing numbers poured into the gold fields. Clashes between the Cherokee miners and the whites from Tennessee, Georgia, Alabama, and North Carolina became frequent. In these brawls the Cherokees were hopelessly outnumbered. The General Council called on the Indian Agent, Hugh Montgomery, to remove trespassers as violators of the Federal Intercourse Act, and Montgomery in turn called on the federal government for troops. A battalion of blue-coated regulars arrived at Dahlonega, but found it impossible to maintain order. They tended to side with the Indians as rightful owners of the land and mines, but as fast as one dispute was settled, another broke out elsewhere.

"I fear the gold mines will prove a greater disadvantage to the Cherokees than the laws of Georgia," Worcester wrote to the Board in Boston. "Many have preferred digging gold the past season to raising corn; and will probably suffer for it during the winter . . . The iniquity practiced at the mines cannot be described. Hardly any sin can be mentioned but what is practiced."[25]

Not all the miners struck it rich, by any means. But many white prospectors looked around them and began to covet what they saw: rich pasture lands sustaining herds of sheep and cattle, fields of corn and cotton and potatoes, fruit-bearing orchards, comfortable farms. There was another sort of fortune in this bountiful land and they began to stake their claims.

Homes that had been abandoned in 1818, and earlier, by Cherokees emigrating to the West were summarily appropriated by the white invaders. Farms were "purchased" with spurious deeds of sale which, once Georgia took over the territory in the spring, would be incontestable in a court of law. It was open season for pillaging and theft. Bands of armed marauders from what was known as the Pony Club made surreptitious raids on Cherokee plantations, making off with horses, livestock, any property that they could swiftly lay their hands on.

Particularly victimized were those Cherokees living along the old Cherokee-Creek border in the southwestern section of the Nation, where Georgia squatters moved in by the score, bringing their families, their wagonloads of household furniture, their rifles and farming implements. As Indian Agent, it was Hugh Montgomery's job to oust them, under the congressional act that forbade whites from intruding in the territory. But Montgomery left it up to Jackson, and the President called on the dependable John Coffee, living now in Alabama, to investigate.

Coffee met with the Ridges and twenty of the leading chiefs at John Ross's house at Head of Coosa. Here The Ridge told him, according to Coffee, "of many depredations committed in his Nation by intruders and the frontier inhabitants of Georgia, and he requested me to represent them to our Govt. inasmuch as the agent . . . neglected to do his duty in that respect."

Coffee informed the group that the government could do little for them. It was purely a local or domestic problem, and as such it was up to the Cherokees themselves to oust the intruders. More specifically, up to John Ross as the Nation's Principal Chief.

Ross took the matter under advisement—any action would have to have the approval of the General Council. Assistant Chief George Lowrey proclaimed January 1, 1830, a day of fasting and prayer "for all Christian Cherokees," which Elias Boudinot in the *Phoenix* declared highly appropriate to "the peculiar situation of the Nation."

The situation was more than peculiar. The new year that was hanging over them was fraught with peril. The warning had been spelled out for them by Andrew Jackson in the White House, by Wilson Lumpkin in the Congress, and by Governor George Rockingham Gilmer taking over for Forsyth in the Georgia capital. It had reverberated in the West, where three thousand Cherokees under Oolooteka, or Chief John Jolly, felt that their own destiny was linked with that of their brothers in the East. Injustice recognized no geographical boundaries.

In the West one adopted Cherokee had been fighting a battle of his own—and losing. As "the Raven"—Sam Houston—had predicted at the Battle of Horseshoe Bend, the world had heard much of the young man. From successful Nashville lawyer he had gone on to Congress; then, as Andrew Jackson's candidate, been elected governor of Tennessee. At this high point in his career, he married Eliza Allen of a distinguished Nashville family. Then catastrophe.

Within two weeks he threw over the governorship, left Eliza, and sought oblivion in alcohol, giving no explanation for this unpredictable conduct beyond the written statement that he was "overwhelmed by sudden calamities, *which from their nature preclude all investigation.*" Hitting bottom, he did one predictable thing. He sought refuge, as he had in his youth, among the Cherokees. Making his way to the Arkansas, he rejoined his foster father Chief John Jolly, donned Indian dress again, and made his home with Jolly's family.

The Cherokees welcomed the Raven back with open arms. He was a dissipated wreck, still addicted to the bottle, but they forgave him his delinquencies. "My son the Raven has walked straight," insisted Chief Jolly. "His path is not crooked. . . . He is beloved by all my people"—while Houston himself "felt like a weary wanderer returned at last to his father's house."[26]

The Raven, the Cherokees felt, could do much for his adopted people. He became so popular and active among them that it was not inconceivable that he might become Principal Chief of the Cherokees in the West, succeeding Jolly. Meanwhile they sent him as their ambassador to Washington. He was a friend of the President—for which they forgave him, knowing that with that connection he could better serve their interests and the interests of their troubled brothers in the East.

Houston started for the capital in the winter of 1829–30, still wearing Indian buckskin, purple robe, and moccasins. On the way, fancying himself a poet, he composed a tribute in verse to the noble Cherokees which began with the lines:

> There is a proud undying thought in man,
> That bids his soul still upward look,
> To fame's proud cliff![27]

It might seem unclear whether he was writing of the Cherokees or of himself. Time would clarify that point.

8

Circumstances
Long Dreaded

THE RIDGE had not donned battle dress since the Creek War and his campaign days with General Jackson. Then he had been in his early forties. Now, in 1830, he was sixty; but still sturdy, muscular, and vigorous. His iron-gray hair reflected an iron constitution. Though he held no official position in the Nation, having deferred to the younger chiefs whose education he had helped promote, he was still a figure to be reckoned with. Youth held the key to the future; he was custodian of the past.

He was not about to wear the major's uniform which Jackson had presented to him. Stripped to the waist, in buckskin trousers and moccasins, his massive torso was gaudily stained with the red war paint derived from hematite; over his dense curled hair he fitted a buffalo head with horns, a theatrical prop no doubt from the tribal artifacts which Boudinot had formerly collected for the now defunct Academy Museum.

With him on that early January morning at the Ridge plantation on the Oostanaula were some sixty Cherokee braves similarly streaked with crimson paint, some with head feathers, some with stained buffalo robes around their shoulders, all with rifles, knives, and tomahawks. Their faces were so hideously camouflaged with black and crimson ocher that only nine were later recognized —which was their purpose. They were a murderous-looking crew, and that too was intentional.

For Ross had readily gained the Council's approval for expelling white trespassers from the Nation, by whatever means were needed. He had called on The Ridge to recruit the necessary volunteers. The Ridge "had a bunch of drunken Indians drilling for a week," Governor Gilmer later complained to Jackson, adding that General Coffee had reviewed, and presumably approved, this little army. But Gilmer's report seems hardly likely. Coffee was not involved. The Indians were not drunk. They did no drilling. They were doing what came spontaneously to a proud and injured people.

Whooping and firing their guns in warning, they galloped southward through Vann's Valley and down along the Georgia-Alabama border, taking possession of each farm or plantation which the Georgia interlopers occupied. Surrounding each house, they gave the occupants time to evacuate the premises and load their personal possessions onto wagons (only once did they meet resistance which forced them to hack down the door). Then they burned the building to the ground. The destruction, they felt, was justified. It was Cherokee property they were burning. If they left it intact the intruders would return.

Word of the Viking-like foray reached the sheriff at Carrollton, who organized a counter-thrust by some two dozen armed and mounted deputies. They sought to intercept The Ridge's force at Cedartown but found on arrival that the bulk of the Indian band had come and gone, leaving the countryside scarred by smoldering ruins. In one of those ruins, however, surrounding a broached keg of whiskey, were five braves who had slipped from The Ridge's command and returned to celebrate.

Ross had given strict orders, seconded by The Ridge, that no spirits were to be consumed by any of the force. But the discovery of the keg had been too much for the delinquent five. They were roaring drunk by the time the sheriff's deputies arrived. One escaped; the other four were taken into custody and escorted to Carrollton. A Cherokee named Chewoyee, who was too drunk to stay in the saddle, was brutally beaten and left dying on the trail. Two of the others escaped as the group neared Carrollton, leaving only a single prisoner to occupy the county jail.

WAR IN GEORGIA screamed the newspaper headlines as reports of the escapade reached eastern cities. And briefly it looked like all-out war as bands of whites organized for swift retaliation. "Such has been the excitement produced by the outrage," Governor Gilmer observed, "that it has been with the utmost difficulty that the people have been restrained from taking ample vengeance on the perpetrators." Threats on the life and property of John Ross and The Ridge caused cordons of Indians to stand guard around their premises. On both sides, hunt-and-destroy missions roamed the southern portions of the Nation; and while there were frequent rifle skirmishes, no major battle occurred.

It had been an unfortunate incident, however much provoked, as Elias Boudinot discerned in his *Phoenix* editorial on the event:

This is a circumstance which we have for a long time dreaded, and which has been brought about by the neglect of the executive to remove the great nuisance to the Cherokees . . . It has been the desire of our enemies that the Cherokees may be urged to some desperate act—thus far this desire has never been realized . . . If our words will have any weight with our countrymen in this very trying time, we would say, *forbear, forbear*—revenge not, but leave vengeance "to whom vengeance belongest."[1]

Ross concurred, to the extent of declaring that from now on the Nation would take its troubles to the courts. But those who liked to make the most of "Indian depredations"—a favorite synonym for any act surpassing passive obeisance—played up this "barbarous and savage" onslaught. Citizens, it was said, had been driven from their houses to die in the snow; little children had been cruelly treated; the homes that had been burned belonged lawfully to whites—at least, they would when Georgia's new law became effective.

In Congress, Wilson Lumpkin, among others, saw an opportune time to present the first Indian Removal Bill. It was essentially an implementation of Jackson's message of December 8. The measure provided for ample territory west of the Mississippi to be guaranteed to the five Southeastern tribes, "as long as they shall occupy it," in exchange for their respective territories in the East. The bill also provided for a fund of $500,000 to pay the cost of transportation, reimburse the Indians for their abandoned properties, and provide subsistence during their first year in the West.[2]

Up to now, few bills had ever been so hotly debated in Congress, and most of the speeches, pro and con, Boudinot reprinted in the *Phoenix*. While the measure applied to all Five Civilized Tribes, the Cherokee-Georgia controversy centered the issue on the Cherokees, and much of the inflammatory wrangling in Congress focused on this controversy. The Seminoles, the Choctaws, the Chickasaws, and the remaining Creeks were all encompassed in the removal proposal, but the rapid rise of the Cherokees to the status of a civilized society drew special attention to their case.

The most eloquent nonstop defense of the Indians was delivered in April by New Jersey Senator Theodore Frelinghuysen, who spoke for six hours over a period of three days. As an example of the reason, clarity, and moderation so rare in political oratory, no quoted extract could do it justice. Comparing the proposal with the tragic partition of Poland, still vivid in world memory, Frelinghuysen reviewed United States policy toward the Indians from American Independence to the current year—the long record of broken treaties with a people whose rightful possession of their lands predated by centuries the coming of the white man—and left it up to the conscience of America to protect "our public honor."[3]

The conscience of America was, however, colored by geography and social climate. The conscience of Puritan New England, where William Lloyd Garrison gave Frelinghuysen the lifelong title of "Christian Statesman," was not the same as that of the southern border states, where Garrison, in turn, would become despised for his Abolitionist pronouncements. Senator Edward Everett of Vermont also appealed to America's elusive conscience, but spoke with less restraint and better aim.

Declaring, "It is all unmingled, unmitigated evil," Everett castigated the drive to remove the Cherokees as one that "cannot come to good. It cannot, as it professes, elevate the Indians. It must and will depress, dishearten, and crush them."

"Sir," Everett told the Speaker of the House on May 19, "if Georgia will recede [yield], she will do more for the Union, and more for herself, than if she would add to her domain the lands of all the Indians, though they were paved with gold.

"The evil, Sir, is enormous; the inevitable suffering incalculable. Do not stain the fair name of the country . . ."

The world was listening, Everett told the Senate; the world would long remember. No political word play could justify such heinous injustice, or "satisfy the severe judgment of enlightened Europe. Our friends will view this measure with sorrow, and our enemies alone with joy.

"And we ourselves, Sir, when the interests and passions of the day are past, shall look back upon it, I fear, with self-reproach, and a regret as bitter as unavailing."[4]

The reference to foreign opinion was pertinent. In Europe the fate of the Cherokees was getting wide publicity. British author Frances Milton Trollope, in Washington that year, noted in her famous *Domestic Manners of the Americans* that the oppression of the Cherokees stood for all that was deplorable in the United States. "If the American character may be judged by their conduct in this matter," Mrs. Trollope wrote, "they are most lamentably deficient in every feeling of honor and integrity, treacherous and false almost beyond belief in their intercourse with the unhappy Indians."

From Senator Peleg Sprague of Maine, from homespun Davy Crockett of Jackson's Tennessee, came moving appeals in the Cherokees' behalf. Sprague compared Georgia's position with that of Shylock demanding his last pound of flesh. "Who can look an Indian in the face and say to him, 'We and our fathers for more than forty years have made to you the most solemn promises; we now violate and trample on them all, but offer you in their stead another guarantee.' "[5]

As the bill approached a Senate vote Wilson Lumpkin rose predictably in its defense. He reminded the assembly that he himself, in his youth, had lived in the frontier shadow of the tomahawk and scalping knife, and knew whereof he spoke. He did not blame the Indians for this unhappy situation; he blamed the United States government for not sooner removing them to a land more suited to their purpose. And he blamed particularly "the wicked influence of designing men, veiled in the garb of philanthropy and Christian benevolence" who "excited the Cherokee to a course that will end in their speedy destruction . . ."[6]

Lumpkin lashed back at the arguments of Jeremiah Evarts in the William Penn letters appearing in eastern periodicals. He attacked the Principal Chiefs of the Cherokees, the men obsessed with privilege and power, who had betrayed "the poor degraded Indians." Granted a new life in the benevolent West —free of the missionaries, the "absolute rulers" among their chiefs, the misguided philanthropists who wished to perpetuate their misery—they could share with Western Cherokees "the prospect of comfort and future blessings."

While this debate held the center of the stage in Washington, a curious little drama was enacted in the wings. Sam Houston, the Raven, had arrived from Arkansas. Still in Indian raiment with silver ornaments that jangled as he walked, he caused a sensation among the dark-suited congressmen in claw-hammer coats. He was here, it turned out, not to plead for justice for the Indians. There was something more at stake: the matter of furnishing rations to the 80,000 Indians destined for removal to the West. Thomas McKenney of the Bureau of Indian Affairs had estimated the cost at $4,400,000 and was soliciting bids from likely contractors. Houston wanted a piece of the action.

The Raven approached McKenney and offered to supply the Indians during their journey at a cost of 18 cents a head per day. McKenney considered the bid extortionary, and was backed up by the Washington *Telegraph,* which revealed that other bids had been as low as 6 cents. Houston shaved his price to 13 cents, and when this too was rejected he took the matter up with President Jackson and Secretary Eaton.

In blatant chicanery these two contrived to give the bid to their old friend Houston, going over McKenney's head. McKenney threatened to expose the scandal, blocked the deal, and as a consequence was fired from his job. Jackson and Eaton wriggled out of the scandal by announcing that, since the Indians were not immediately emigrating anyway, all bids were temporarily suspended.

All things considered, it was a minor bit of tawdriness, hardly deserving a footnote in history. Its significance lay in the fact that—long before the Indians were scheduled to emigrate, even before the Removal Bill was voted on—men in high office were conspiring to see that chosen individuals made a profit from the Indians' expulsion. And it is sad that Sam Houston should have been among them. He returned to the West, not entirely discredited, but once again a somewhat lonely, broken man.

McKenney should have emerged as something of a hero from this incident. But he wrote his own sorry footnote to the year's developments. Convinced that his job was in jeopardy for his failure to see eye to eye with the President on Indian removal, he switched sides at the last moment to try to retain his position. Or perhaps, to give him the benefit of the doubt, he genuinely came to believe that the Cherokees might be better off beyond the Mississippi.

Since a big stumbling block to removal was the stand of men like Samuel Worcester, Elias Boudinot and his *Phoenix,* Jeremiah Evarts and the Boston Board of Foreign Missions, McKenney formed a counter-group called the Indian Board for the Emigration, Preservation, and Improvement of the Aboriginals of America. To this impressive name he attached a small band of clergymen and laymen from the Dutch Reformed Church of New York, and exhorted them to speak out in favor of Indian removal—at the same time calling the President's and Secretary Eaton's attention to this effort. "I have never had such hopes for the Indians before," he wrote to Eaton. "I shall be surprised if this group does not carry all before it."[7]

The effort fizzled—"struck by paralysis," McKenney confessed. It did not save his job with the Indian Bureau, but it lost him his sixteen-year-long friendship with the Cherokees. "His cynical use of the native clergymen and the Indians was unworthy of him," noted his biographer. McKenney devoted the rest of his life to his justifiably famous gallery of Indian portraits—including paintings of John and Major Ridge, Sequoyah, David Vann, and John Ross—done at times when he played host to these visiting Cherokees in Washington.

As the day approached when Georgia laws and Georgia's authority would be extended to the Nation, Elias Boudinot was a man in torment.

What would happen to the *Phoenix?*

Would the Cherokees lose their free voice and their only source of information?

Should he tread softly to avoid provoking confiscation by the state?

Or should he, as editor, maintain a militant stance in defense of Cherokee independence and in defiance of Georgia's claims and Jackson's Indian Removal Bill?

He chose the latter course—for now. In this he had the unqualified support not only of Ross, George Lowrey, John and Major Ridge, and other principal leaders of the Nation, but Samuel Worcester and the missionary colony as well. For the missionaries had all but abandoned their position of neutrality. Daniel Butrick, still tormented by self-doubt, thought the Cherokees should be "strengthened in this particular crisis," but for now would leave it up to God. Elizur Butler took it up with Jeremiah Evarts, writing in September 1830:

When I consider what God has done for this people; their improvements the last ten years; the justice of their cause; the injust ground their enemies stand on . . . I cannot but think favourably of the issue of their contest with Georgia.

I have never seen the Cherokees more united than they now are. It is not known that anyone now thinks of emigrating . . . They feel that their cause is the cause of justice, and that their rights will be maintained in the Federal Court . . .

Mr. Ross told me a few days since his hopes of success over Geo. were never greater. The uncommon union of the Cherokees was a great encouragement.[8]

Butler would all too soon realize how deeply his own fate was linked with the dispute.

In the columns of the *Phoenix,* Elias Boudinot hammered at Georgia's imposition of its laws upon the Nation. He reprinted Edward Everett's speech before the House in which Everett pointed out the discriminatory nature of those laws:

Unprincipled white men have but to cross the Cherokee line; they have but to choose the time and the place, where the eye of no white man can rest upon them, and they may burn the dwelling, waste the farm, plunder the property, assault the person, murder the children of the Cherokee subjects of Georgia, and, though hundreds of the tribe may be looking on, there is not one of them that can be permitted to bear witness against the spoiler.

When I am asked, then, what the Cherokee has to fear from the law of Georgia, I answer that, by that law, he is left at the mercy of the firebrand and the dagger of every unprincipled wretch in the community.[9]

There was no lack of proof for Everett's charge. Already examples were piling up of assaults upon innocent Cherokees. In the *Phoenix* for May 29, 1830, Boudinot reported the case of a farmer who was approached by a band of white men offering to buy his horses. When he refused to sell, they turned the animals loose from the corral. As the farmer ran to recover the horses, leaving his home unattended, the marauders entered the house and beat his wife into insensibility.

Yet the injured man and his wife had no avenue of recourse. For, noted Boudinot, "we cannot be a party or a witness in any of the courts where a white man is a party. Here is the secret. *Full license to our oppressors, and every avenue of justice closed against us.* Yes, this is the bitter cup prepared for us by a *republican* and religious government—we shall drink it to the very dregs."[10]

In other instances cattle were stolen, homes plundered, and women violated while the owners were absent. In the gold fields federal troops were helpless against chaotic clashes between Cherokees and whites from Tennessee and Georgia. The number of false claims brought against the Indians, which led to their arrest and appearance before Judge Augustin Clayton of the superior court in Lawrenceville, taxed that magistrate's patience.

Matters came to a head when three prominent Cherokees, Elijah Hicks, Fred Thompson, and John Rogers (the last from a family that would one day produce the philosopher-humorist Will Rogers), were brought before the judge for defying Georgia's law and extracting gold from the Dahlonega mines. Clayton was a loyal Georgian and a strong states' righter. He was also a fair and reasonable man. Aware that some two thousand whites were also unlawfully panning for gold forbidden to the Cherokees, he released the three culprits—who were forced only to pay a fine amounting to the per diem salary of the county sheriff. Clayton then wrote to Governor Gilmer suggesting he ask the President to recall the federal troops; they were just cluttering up the courts with time-consuming cases.

Gilmer followed the judge's advice. He wrote to Jackson that the presence of United States soldiers was an affront to Georgia; the state could handle the situation at the mines. Jackson was more than happy to recall the troops. To replace them, Gilmer appointed a sixty-man guard to keep order at Dahlonega—a force which was later expanded to enforce the law in the Nation as a whole.

The Georgia Guard! It was a name to strike terror in the hearts of isolated Cherokee farmers, wealthy planters, even the missionaries, whose homes were subject to invasion. Most of the Guard were untrained, poorly disciplined, and ill equipped. The state armory supplied their rifles; they wore whatever makeshift uniforms appealed to them. Yet for all their callousness and seeming lack of sensitivity, they were not much different from the common state militias of the time—essentially vigilantes, with the vigilante's self-importance and disdain for civil rights.

And for the record, in fairness to Georgia, let it be noted that these were of the same stock that, in the later Civil War, marched out in pitifully small numbers to check General Sherman's armies at the gates of Atlanta. They fought magnificently and, if they had to, died magnificently. Perhaps it is crisis and adversity, such as the Cherokees were facing, that bring out the best in human character.

May 28, 1830—a day that intended to lower the curtain forever on the sovereign Cherokee Nation in the East. Having passed the House, the Indian Removal Bill was ratified in the Senate by a margin of eight votes.

Having lived under the threat of enforced removal for a quarter of a century, the act brought neither shock nor surrender to the Nation. Though those who had fought for Andrew Jackson and for Georgia in the Creek War had now been rewarded with base ingratitude, "they are not yet vanquished," as an anonymous correspondent told the readers of the *Phoenix*. And John Ross reminded his people of a significant clause in the Removal Bill which provided that "nothing in this act shall be considered as authorizing the violation of any existing treaty between the United States and any of the existing tribes."

Surely, any attempt to remove the Cherokees by force, or any violation of their territory, would be contrary to the treaties of Hopewell and Holston, which had guaranteed forever their territorial integrity and independence. Regardless of the Removal Bill, regardless of Georgia's threatened annexation of the Nation, the Cherokees had only to stand fast and let justice take its course.

. . . such stuff as dreams are made on!

Jackson, too, was aware that the bill could be legally implemented only by separate treaties with the different tribes. To this end he invited representatives of the Creeks, the Choctaws, the Chickasaws, and the Cherokees to meet with him in August, at the Hermitage in Nashville, to discuss terms.

In case the Cherokees balked at doing so, he had a persuasive weapon in their weak financial position. Government annuities, due them for previous land sales to the United States, had till now been paid directly to John Ross for deposit in the National Treasury. This gave Ross exceptional powers, and he and his fellow chiefs were, in government eyes, the core of opposition to removal. One way to tie their hands was to keep this money out of their reach.

Jackson advised, and Eaton announced, a new policy for the payment of annuities. Henceforth the money would not go to Ross in a lump sum. It would be distributed to individual Cherokees on their personal application at the Indian Agency in Tellico. Some Indians would have to travel a hundred miles or more to collect their share, which could amount to as little as forty-two cents. But at least the payments would be kept from Ross's hands, and the government could not be accused of reneging on money that was due.

Regarding Jackson's proposal to meet the Indians in Nashville, Jeremiah Evarts wrote to Ross from Boston, recommending that he do so and take with him Elijah Hicks, George Lowrey, and the Ridges. To strengthen Ross's hand, Evarts sent him a digest of legal opinions on the issue—his own and those of Daniel Webster and former Attorney General William Wirt. In the light of these, he recommended:

1. Tell him—Jackson—frankly that you think the U.S. is bound to protect the Cherokees against the laws of Georgia; and that you wish to have the matter decided by the Supreme Court.

2. Tell him that you cannot think of making a treaty until you get a decision on the question.[11]

Evarts also advised Ross and his delegation, if they went to Nashville, to insist that any treaty made with the President should be subject to the full approval of the General Council and the national majority; that such a treaty "will be made by you *as a nation;* that it will be ratified by the Senate, and that your national character will thereafter be respected"; and, further, that the delegates expected the President to protect the Cherokee Nation against intruders and unjust claims prior to their voluntary emigration.

Get everything down in writing, Evarts urged, aware of the impermanence of presidential promises. That being accomplished, "you may be assured that if you get your case fairly before the Supreme Court your rights will be defended. It is so clear a case that the court cannot mistake it. All the great lawyers in the country are on your side."

Regardless of what immediate use Ross made of this advice, it charted a clear-cut course to follow. His mind was made up. There was nothing to be gained by further talks with Andrew Jackson. "I knew that the perpetrator of a wrong never forgives his victim," he later wrote. Nevertheless, he called for a special Council to assemble in July, to discuss the wisdom of further negotiations with the President and more particularly to consider Evarts' suggestion of taking their case to the United States Supreme Court.

Theoretically the Cherokee Nation, as an independent and sovereign republic, had ceased to exist as of June 1, 1830—the date when Georgia's confiscatory laws supposedly became effective. Governor Gilmer, however, was reluctant to move too fast toward this extremity. There was too much resentment, even in his own state, against undue oppression of the Cherokees. He settled, for now, for installing units of the Georgia Guard at key points throughout the Nation, notably the gold fields, more as a show of authority than for outright law enforcement.

The Guard had substantial nuisance value. They made summary arrests for imagined insults to their dignity. Indians were humiliated in the courts, dragged before jaundiced judges on fraudulent complaints; kicked, beaten, prodded, and reviled when they failed to jump to orders. Cherokees normally sober were plied with liquor, then thrown into the local jail for being drunk. Others were charged with disturbing the peace when resisting unwarranted arrest.

Yet the Cherokee Nation remained alive and sound long past the June 1 date for its extinction. Each new humiliation, each new prod from Georgia, strengthened its resolve.

In defiance of the edict that forbade political assemblies on Georgia soil, the General Council met as customary at New Echota in mid-July. Though the

Georgia Guard stood by at a respectful distance, assigned to watch for signs of insurrection in the Nation, they did not interfere. The Council quickly dispensed with Jackson's invitation to the Hermitage. They would send no delegates to the meeting. In a formal resolution it was stated:

We have no desire to see the President on the business of entering into a treaty for exchange of lands . . . Inclination to remove from this land has no abiding place in our hearts, and when we move we shall move by the course of nature to sleep under the ground which the Great Spirit gave to our ancestors and which now covers them in their undisturbed repose.[12]

This settled, the Council spent the next two days considering Evarts' suggestion that they take their case to the United States Supreme Court. John Ross was authorized to hire such attorneys as might be needed to instigate this action, though with Jackson's tactic of diverting annuity payments from the Nation's Treasury there was not enough money to cover legal fees. They would have to cross that bridge, by some means, when they came to it.

Before dispersing, the General Council drafted another memorial of protest, this one addressed to the American people as a whole. A democracy, it seems, requires endless paper work, much of it repetitious, but all somehow essential to the process. The number of memorials written and submitted by the Cherokees to various agencies and groups is hard to present in chronological order. They would make a large-size, cumbersome volume in themselves. But all were pertinent; all were eloquently written.

Stating simply, "We wish to remain in the land of our fathers," the memorial added that "if compelled to leave our country, we see nothing but ruin before us." Actually, throughout that year, small bands of discontents—the dropouts of Cherokee society—had voluntarily gone West in pursuit of rainbows, settling in the Arkansas. George Vashon, the Indian Agent in that territory, had written to Thomas McKenney that "the five hundred Cherokees who reached here this year have been forced to sell their claims on the government for provisions to relieve their suffering.

"It is greatly to be regretted that the long continued delay of payment has operated to place these unfortunate people so much in the pitiless power of speculators."[13]

If the Eastern Cherokees knew of this breakdown in promised payments to the emigrating Indians, they had also their own reports on conditions in the West. It was territory unfamiliar to them, occupied by hostile tribes such as the Osages who would look upon them as intruders. It was not suitable to agriculture, "badly supplied with wood and water." Above all, "it is not the land of our birth, nor of our affections."

In the light, or shadow, of these disadvantages, "Shall we be compelled by a civilized and Christian people, with whom we have lived in perfect peace for the last forty years, and for whom we have willingly bled in war, to bid a final adieu to our homes, our farms, our streams and our beautiful forests?"

The memorial closed with an appeal to all Americans "to remember the great law of love. 'Do to others as you would that others should do to you.' Let them remember that of all the nations on the earth, they are under the greatest obligation to obey this law."[14]

The document was signed by Ross's brother Lewis as President of the Committee, Going Snake as Speaker of the Council, and John Ridge as Council Clerk, as well as by all members of the National Committee and the legislative branch. A deputation composed of Richard Taylor, John Ridge, and Ross's nephew William S. Coodey was authorized to carry the document to Washington, present it to the Congress, and further present their case to the President and War Secretary Eaton.

Meanwhile John Ross remained in the Nation to find lawyers who might take their case to the Supreme Court. Cued by Evarts' query, "Have you a good safe lawyer in Georgia, whom you can trust?" he engaged the firm of Judge William Underwood and Thomas Harris to represent the Nation, relying on affluent Cherokees like himself to contribute to the legal fees.

But Underwood and Harris were a Georgia firm, with license to practice only in the state courts. The Cherokees needed national representation if they were to carry their case to the United States Supreme Court. And in this they had a stroke of luck.

At age fifty-eight William Wirt of Baltimore had reached his modest peak of fame as a constitutional attorney. He had gained distinction as one of the lawyers prosecuting Aaron Burr (whom Andrew Jackson, at the time, had openly defended). Partially for this service President Monroe had named him United States Attorney General. John Quincy Adams had kept Wirt in office, to give him more than twelve years' service at the post; but Jackson, having little use for a strict constitutionalist, dismissed him.

Wirt was at his best espousing causes that gave full scope to his powers of oratory. The more emotional an issue, the better he could handle it and the more it appealed to his crusading spirit. Even before Jeremiah Evarts mentioned his name to Ross as a likely attorney for the Cherokees, Wirt had taken up the cudgel for the Indians. He had criticized Jackson's Removal Bill; had conferred with Evarts on the strategy for Cherokee resistance; had astounded Governor Gilmer by gratuitously advising him of the weakness of Georgia's case against the Cherokees.

When John Ross approached him, Wirt readily agreed to carry the Cherokees-versus-Georgia issue to the Supreme Court bench. Jeremiah Evarts, whom Wirt put on a par with Thomas Jefferson and Patrick Henry, had written to Ross: "Again I see that Georgia is arresting Cherokee gold-diggers. Let one of them go to jail, and then bring an action for false imprisonment before a Georgia court, expecting the court to decide against him, and then carry it by writ of error to the Supreme Court of the U.S."[15]

In other words, find a test case which epitomized the conflict, and one in which there was more than an even chance of winning.

Wirt fortuitously found precisely such a case. A Cherokee named Corn Tassel had been convicted of murder and sentenced to hang by the Hall County

Superior Court in Gainesville, Georgia. Since the Cherokees still considered Hall County within the Nation, the Indians should have jurisdiction of the case. Wirt jumped at the opportunity and drafted an appeal. For the first time in New World history American Indians would take their plea for justice to the United States Supreme Court.

While waiting for the Court's decision the General Council met again at New Echota in defiance of Georgia law. Possibly with the feeling that this might be the last assembly in their capital, Cherokees from every corner of the Nation gravitated to the Council grounds, by foot, on horse, or in carriages, bringing their families and provisions, making New Echota a fire-lit glowing Camelot above the Georgia plains.

Standing in the background in the Council House was a detached sphinx-like observer, a vaguely familiar figure from the past. John Lowrey, almost twenty years before, had fought with the Cherokee six hundred in the Creek campaign. A few like The Ridge and Ross remembered the former colonel, but were forced to ask him for his credentials.

Lowrey, it appeared, was now a United States agent assigned by John Eaton to infiltrate the meeting and somehow persuade the Cherokees to accept a treaty for removal. His switch from loyal Cherokee to government accomplice may have been sincere; at least the reasons he advanced, though heard before, were sound. Guaranteed territory in the West; funds for transportation, for subsistence in their new homes, for schools and teachers. There was something to be said for these provisos.

Out of respect for old-time association the Council heard him out. Then John Ross replied in words that hardly needed repetition. "The Cherokees have long since come to the conclusion never again to cede *another foot* of land . . . they now only ask from the Federal Government the protection of those rights which have been solemnly guaranteed to them under former treaties. The offer of new guarantees can be no inducement to treat."[16]

This business settled, elections were held for new officers designed to strengthen the Council and the cause of unity. John Ridge was chosen President of the National Committee, a post that put him second in authority to Ross, who remained in office as Principal Chief. In Cherokee eyes the years were making something of a monument of Ross. They crowded around his horse whenever he entered a village; jostled each other to shake him by the hand; listened with rapt attention to his every word. It was only those like Wilson Lumpkin who could dare deny his influence. Wrote Senator Lumpkin, in words forecasting future strategy: "John Ross, when compared with such men as John Ridge and Elias Boudinot, is a mere *pigmy.*"

Two months after the Council adjourned President Jackson delivered his second message to the Congress. Miffed at being slighted by the Cherokees that summer when he invited the Indians to Nashville, no doubt equally miffed by the current appeal to the Supreme Court, he sounded less conciliatory than in his initial message of a year before. He announced that two important tribes, the Choctaws and the Chickasaws, had made treaties for removal to the West, and expressed the belief that "their example will induce the remaining tribes also to seek the same advantages."

But to those still holding out, the President's warning was explicit. The United States government would not intervene with Georgia's right, or any state's right, to expel the Indians within its boundaries. There was no alternative to emigration other than annihilation "as one by one many powerful tribes have vanished from the earth."[17]

The Cherokees had little time to worry over threats. A week later, on December 12, 1830, the Supreme Court cited the state of Georgia to appear before the bench and show cause why a writ of error should not be issued in the Corn Tassel murder case. If not yet a total victory, it plainly forecast a victory of sorts. The Cherokee right of appeal had been established; the Indians had a voice before the bar.

Georgia not only ignored the citation and failed to appear in court, but took the one step calculated to evince contempt for the decision. It hanged Corn Tassel without delay. Still smarting at the Indians' move to block the sentence, Senator Lumpkin wrote to the President:

It appears to me that the rulers of the Cherokees have sufficient intelligence to see the utter imbecility of placing any further reliance upon the Supreme Court to sustain their pretensions . . . Georgia is not accountable to the Supreme Court or any other tribunal on earth . . .[18]

South Carolina was having similar thoughts, concerning the protective tariff which northern legislatures were imposing on the country. It was even rumored that the state might withdraw from the Union if the "Tariff of Abominations" was not revoked. If Georgia and South Carolina should together defy the federal government, what other states might follow, with the possibility of civil war? For now, it was just a threat, but a threat which strengthened Georgia's hand on the question of Indian removal.

Lest anyone question Georgia's sincerity or intentions, the state legislature took further steps to consolidate their dominance of the Cherokee Nation. A bill was passed which ordered that the territory be surveyed and subdivided into land lots of 160 acres and "gold lots" of 40 acres each—these to be later distributed by lottery to native Georgians. The legislators also reiterated and strengthened the ban on any future meetings of the Cherokee Council, *except for purposes of treating for removal.*

Georgia, it was argued, had been as tolerant and forbearing as the Cherokees had been impudent and obstinate. Senator Lumpkin believed that one reason for their obstinacy was the "religious fanaticism" instilled in them by the missionaries. Governor Gilmer held the same belief, and took steps in December 1830 to emasculate the group. Few of them were Georgians anyway. They were outsiders, most of them Northerners, and probably Abolitionists to boot.

There was a way to spike their guns, however. Gilmer persuaded the state legislature to enact a law requiring all white persons living in the territory to obtain a license from the governor or one of his surrogates, said license to be had only upon taking an oath of allegiance to the state of Georgia. Once they had paid this obeisance to the state's authority, the missionaries would be under Gilmer's thumb.

The Cherokee deputation headed by Ridge, Coodey, and Taylor arrived at Washington City in mid-November and checked in at the Indian Queen Hotel, to be welcomed once again by host Jesse Brown, who had come to look upon these Indians as discriminating patrons. The Ridge had long since set a standard of decorum to be followed by Cherokee emissaries in the capital, and son John and his associates observed the pattern. A newspaper correspondent who kept track of their visit found them "well-dressed gentlemen of good manners—themselves good society for any sensible man—sitting at the publick tables throughout the City—undistinguished from the common mass except it be in superior delicacy of feeling."[19]

Perhaps because of his advanced age Richard Taylor stood out least among the group. He was self-effacing, dour, and silent, paying attention only to the long-stemmed silver pipe which General Washington had presented to his fore-bears many years before. Ridge and Coodey, however, impressed the reporter as "men of liberal education, polished in their manners, and worthy of our society. The propriety and dignity of their demeanor are not simply exceptionable, but commanding, prepossessing, and attractive."

Despite their youth, the writer found the two younger men well informed and knowledgeable. "They enforce respect and esteem. They actually know more of the institutions, laws, and government of the United States than a large fraction of those who occupy seats in the House of Representatives; and this may be said without dishonouring that body."

The delegates had come to see the President and Secretary Eaton and obtain their views, as well as express their own views, on Georgia's step-by-step destruction of their Nation. There was no misreading Georgia's move to survey the territory, chop it up into lots, and distribute the whole by lottery. It would end their national existence, and they sought a "direct and frank" assurance of United States' protection.

Eaton, whose ignorance of the situation was colossal, gave them only evasive answers. When they pressed him on other scores, such as the diversion of annuity payments from the Cherokee Treasury and the "oppression our citizens have endured from the Georgians," Eaton dismissed them as having no authority to present such matters to the government. The only Cherokee delegation that would be recognized by his department, or by the President, was one which came "with written authority to discuss a removal treaty."

But if the delegates had no footing in government circles, they found plenty of support and sympathy outside those circles. "The kind condolence of acquaintances and friends of Indians throughout the U.S.," John Ridge wrote to his father-in-law in Cornwall, "comes upon the ear like soft music of other days." And he believed the Cherokees had a good friend in Henry Clay, who might replace Jackson in the 1832 elections. "It is to a change of this administration that we must now wait for relief."[20]

To Elias Boudinot he sent similar assurance, writing for publication in the *Phoenix:* "From private and public sources, we are induced to believe that Henry Clay is our friend, and will enforce the treaties. Bear up my friends for two years longer, and we are victorious—let the people understand that."

William Wirt meanwhile, undeterred by defeat in Corn Tassel's case, was preparing his next appeal to the Supreme Court. He demanded an injunction to stop Georgia from extending her laws over the Cherokee Nation, from intruding on Cherokee territory, and from violating in any other way the sovereignty and independence of the Nation. It was a bold move, putting the whole affair in Marshall's lap.

"What the fate of the motion will be," Wirt wrote to Ross, "it is impossible for any lawyer to predict with certainty; for the case is perfectly new, there being no precedent to guide us . . . Your counsel will support it with all the zeal and ability that Heaven has given them and the issue will be with Providence."[21]

The Cherokees had more than a passing acquaintance with Providence. They had learned to put more faith in its wardenry than in the government of the United States. And that winter in Washington the natives witnessed a strange event. Scores of red Indians, in harmony and sympathy with one another, united to observe a day of prayer and fasting. Jesse Brown, manager of the Indian Queen Hotel, had never known a time when the platters of sliced beef and crystal decanters of whiskey went untouched, and the gracious high-ceilinged chambers resounded to hymns and prayers instead of Saturnalia.

Puzzling people, these Cherokees.

9

A New Species
of Courage

"Do what is right, and you need not fear."

So Jeremiah Evarts had written to Samuel Worcester, following charges made against the latter for his "scurrilous articles" in the *Phoenix*. Evarts' advice was directed at the missionaries as a whole. None had written scurrilous articles (Elias Boudinot, though a convert, was in a category by himself), but all had taken a stand sympathetic to the Indians' position.

The ever-outgoing Methodists were more than merely sympathetic. Late in September 1830 they had met at Chatooga to draft a strongly worded resolution defending the right of the Cherokees to remain where they were and condemning federal and state attempts to move them. The resolution was signed by such Methodist stalwarts as Nicholas Scales, James J. Trott, and Dickson McCleod, who would be more involved in the Cherokees' future than they realized.

Elias Boudinot seized on this gesture as a means of prodding the rest of the missionary colony to take a more aggressive stance. He reprinted the Methodist resolution in the *Phoenix* for October 1, 1830, and appended his own editorial comment:

The time has come when it is the duty of every friend of justice and humanity to speak out and express his opinion, and raise his voice in favor of oppressed innocence. Why should not missionaries, the true friends of the Indians, who toil day and night for their spiritual good, be permitted to exercise the sacred right of freemen, *liberty of speech* and *freedom of opinion?*

An act passed by the Georgia legislature on the previous December 22, which required all white residents living in Cherokee territory to obtain a license from the state, added muscle to Boudinot's suggestion. It appeared directed especially at the missionaries, cornering them in a dilemma. To take the required oath of allegiance to Georgia would cancel their citizenship in their native states. More important, it would cancel much of their influence with the Cherokees. They would be surrendering to Georgia at the same time that they posed as spiritual champions of the Cherokees. They had worked to make the Nation strong and civilized. Could they desert it on the threshold of that goal?

There was a delicate moral balance here, and men like Samuel Worcester felt it keenly. There were rational reasons for advocating emigration to the West. When Worcester saw the Cherokees humiliated and degraded by the Georgia Guard, encouraged to drink to excess by the now unregulated sale of whiskey, bewildered by oppression, apprehensive of the future, sinking daily into inescapable despair, was it not in their interest to advise them to remove from all of this?

Yet to do so, what was the moral issue there? Was it not saying to the Cherokees: Life has become too difficult for you in this environment. Abandon your goals and your achievements, leave your ancestral homes, seek a land of milk and honey somewhere else. Fight the good fight no longer; your enemies are too much for you.

Would that be keeping the faith? The kind of faith they sought to teach? Worcester thought not; the Cherokees should stay and fight.

Believing the time had come to stand up and be counted, the missionaries of the American Board, along with representatives of the Moravians and Baptists, met at New Echota on December 29, 1830, to formulate a policy. Daniel Butrick was elected chairman of the meeting and Samuel Worcester secretary. What came out of the convocation was not only a statement of the missionaries' views, but a significant summary of the Nation's progress at this summit in its history.[1]

Their manifesto was prefaced by resolutions disavowing any political interest in the Indian dispute, or any intended interference in the matter. Their interest was on moral grounds; and on moral grounds the removal of the Indians, or the subjection of the Nation to its neighbor states, could bring only disaster to the Cherokees, "arresting their progress in religion, civilization, learning, and the useful arts."

That progress alone was sufficient argument for their remaining on the land which they had tended, cultivated, and improved; on which they had built their homes, and schools, and churches; maintained roads, and mills, and trading posts, and ferries. The memorandum cited the advancements made in housing, agriculture, spinning and weaving, and the manufacture of clothing which compared in style and quality with that of white society.

Progress in education had been rapid, but admittedly there was room for much improvement. Not many Cherokees could read and write English, though in Sequoyah's language literacy was high. Polygamy had been all but eliminated; superstition was rapidly dying out; and intemperance, that *bête noire* of the Indian race, had been greatly reduced by the Nation's "wholesome laws." When it came to religious statistics, the American Board may have been embarrassed; the Methodists had more church members than all the other denominations combined.

In gentle language the manifesto dispelled the myths that the Cherokees' enemies used against them:

1. That the Cherokees were under the collective thumb of their half-breed, aristocratic, wealthy chiefs, and that under that circumstance free speech was denied to them;

2. That living in the East adjacent to more populous and influential white communities exposed them to practices and vices that they could not handle;

3. That the missionaries were playing devil's advocates, opposing states' rights and Indian removal in the guise of evangelism.

All three of these charges they refuted. "That the Indians of mixed blood possess, in a considerable degree, that superior influence which naturally attends superior knowledge, cannot be doubted." Nevertheless, "freedom of speech exists nowhere more unrestrained than here." If a few individual Cherokees were reluctant to court unpopularity by speaking out in favor of removal, that was only natural in a community where "there exists an overwhelming torrent in opposition to removal."

Living in the East and rubbing shoulders with white neighbors was, all things considered, an advantage, despite the evils of drink and other vices which the white man introduced. The exposure to a more advanced, and possibly more civilized, society had improved the life style, manners, and possessions of the Indians. "To deprive them of these advantages, while in their present state, would be an incalculable evil."

Finally, the missionaries no more strove to influence the Indians politically than they sought credit for the great and rapid progress of the Nation.

But. Those who worked for the salvation of the Indians could not help having their own opinions on the crisis which now faced the Cherokees, and "it is impossible that our views should be unknown to them." These views were the same as those shared by the Cherokees: that removal by the federal government, or extension of state laws over the Nation, were flagrant violations of their rights as guaranteed them by repeated treaties.

The Cherokees were nearly at the crest of their long climb toward the uppermost rung of civilization. Soon, very soon, they would be on a level with the whites. The missionaries were opposed to any measure destined to arrest that progress:

If the free expression of such an opinion be a crime, to the charge of that crime we plead guilty. If we withheld our opinion when called for, we could not hold up our heads as preachers of righteousness among a people who would universally regard us as abettors of iniquity.

The Prudential Committee of the Board of Foreign Missions, headed by Jeremiah Evarts and concerned with matters of Board policy, endorsed the missionaries' stand. Appealing to the religious conscience of America, the members drafted another memorial, more theological in tone, to be sent to the Congress when it next convened. It sought to arouse compassion as a prerequisite of justice. Of the Cherokees it was asserted:

They have no expectancy from earth. Their hearts are sickened by disappointment. They are gathering up their wasted and lost affections—arming their wounded spirits with a new species of courage—and beginning to lift their eyes up where Jehovah dwells. We (Christians once) have taken their lands, and they have taken our religion.[2]

There was a note of warning in the phrase "a new species of courage." The Board no doubt referred to courage gained through prayer, and the Cherokees had learned to pray. And in its conclusion the memorial posed a question: would not the God of Wrath hear those prayers and bring destruction to the Cherokees' oppressors?

The publication of the missionaries' manifesto gained the admiration of most Northerners, the gratitude of the Cherokees, and the animosity of Georgia's leaders. The men of God were still a bunch of radical fanatics in the eyes of Governor Gilmer and Senator Wilson Lumpkin. Making their views known solved no problems for the missionaries. But for some of them it compounded the existing problems.

Daniel Butrick, who had chaired the convention at New Echota, was among those deeply troubled. If he should render unto Caesar that which was Caesar's, then he should go along with Georgia, take the oath, get a license, and stay put. Otherwise he should leave the territory altogether, and avoid any confrontation with the state officials. He wrote to the Board in Boston for advice. The advice was unequivocal: Stay where you are. Mark time. See what develops.

The whole Nation seemed at an ill-marked crossroads. On March 1 the new laws would take effect. Already surveyors were moving through the Nation with their "white man's cheaters," compasses and plumb lines, marking out plots for distribution by state lottery. All whites in the territory failing to obtain a license would be subject to four years in the Georgia penitentiary. And any minute now the Supreme Court should be rendering a verdict on Wirt's second bill of injunction against the state of Georgia.

John Marshall of Virginia, a septuagenarian who had practiced law for half a century and been Supreme Court Justice for thirty years, was a man of giant decisions. Tall, patriarchal, and given to wearing dusty "antique" clothes, he was unvarnished in appearance. But the force of his personality gave the Court a weight and dignity it had never had before and would never altogether lose. To him the Constitution was no abstraction. It was solid as a rock: an institution, he maintained, "intended to endure for ages to come, and consequently, to be adapted to the various *crises* of human affairs."

Personally Marshall had no use for Andrew Jackson, having campaigned against the President's election. He had no partiality for William Wirt either, though he, Marshall, had presided over the prosecution of Aaron Burr and been hanged in effigy for his decision. He was his own man and the Constitution's man. And in the current crisis in American-Indian history, whatever his sympathies, Marshall stuck to the words and spirit of the Constitution.

Basically, his was the ruling handed down by the Supreme Court on March 5, 1831. He recognized Georgia's threat "to annihilate the Cherokees as a political society," and added: "If courts were permitted to indulge their sympathies, a case better calculated to excite them can scarcely be imagined." His written decision took a humanitarian view of the Cherokees' plight:

A people once numerous, powerful, and truly independent, found by our ancestors in the quiet and uncontrolled possession of an ample domain, gradually sinking beneath our superior policy, our arts and our arms, have yielded their lands by successive treaties, each of which contains a solemn guarantee of the residue, until they retain no more of their formerly extensive territory than is deemed necessary for their comfortable subsistence.[3]

But the question was one of jurisdiction. It came down to a matter of words, and the words of the Constitution were like the bricks of a building's foundation, immovable and irreplaceable. The Constitution gave the courts power to arbitrate disputes "between a state or the citizens thereof, and foreign states, citizens, or subjects." The Cherokees were not a state, and could not be considered a foreign nation because as a nation "it is not foreign to the United States." Consequently:

If it be true that the Cherokee nation have rights, this is not the tribunal in which those rights are to be asserted. If it be true that wrongs have been inflicted, and that still greater are to be apprehended, this is not the tribunal which can redress the past or prevent the future.

The motion for an injunction is denied.[4]

The Cherokees had expected a ruling in their favor, though Wirt had cautioned against undue optimism. Now their mountain walls seemed shaken. John Ross toured the Nation, putting the best light possible on the verdict. It was not a fatal blow, he told his people. There was much that was favorable in the Court's decision. Marshall had adhered to a strict interpretation of the Constitution, at the same time stating that "the Indians are acknowledged to have an unquestionable right to the lands they occupy, until that right shall be extinguished by a voluntary cession to our government . . ."[5]

Georgians rejoiced at the Supreme Court verdict. They had been given a green light; they were ready to take over. The *Phoenix* in March and April reported sundry incursions from the south. A group of ten armed men severely beat a Cherokee husband and wife, "causing a flow of blood because they quietly did not suffer themselves to be robbed of their property."

At the gold fields mounted guardsmen sought to intimidate the miners by charging at innocent groups and forcing them to scatter to avoid the horses' hooves. One aged Cherokee was severely wounded for ignoring an order to open a gate for the intrepid cavalry. Another aging Indian, despondent at what he saw occurring, hanged himself from a tree outside his home. The occupying troops finally sought to settle things by burning down the miners' shacks, destroying their picks and shovels and tools of trade, and generally rendering Dahlonega and Auraria enemy-infested ghost towns.

The Pony Club had a field day. Colonel Jacob R. Brooks of the Georgia Guard, whose duty it was to check their operations, looked the other way. After all, it was only innocent sport akin to squirrel shooting. The night riders had their own merry ballad with which to serenade their victims. Sung to an improvised tune with the lilt of Robert Burns, a few lines went:

> Go, nature's child.
> Your home's the wild;
> Our venom cannot gripe ye
> If once you'll roam,
> And make your home
> Beyond the Mississippi.[6]

Thievery was not the sole goal of these pranksters. As their ballad suggested, they would direct their venom at making life intolerable for Indians on this side of the Mississippi. A Cherokee farmer's wife, approached by two white men demanding corn, was unable to oblige them. The corn had not yet ripened in the field. The strangers went to verify this fact and soon the field was set ablaze. As the housewife attempted to put out the fire, the two whites perched on a fence and applauded her efforts with whoops and laughter.

Southern gallantry appeared to have taken a turn for the worse. Elias Boudinot was prompted to print a notice in the *Phoenix*.

CHEROKEE WOMEN, BEWARE

It is said that the Georgia Guard have received orders, from the Governor we suppose, to inflict corporeal punishment on such females as shall hereafter be guilty of insulting them . . . According to our understanding of insult, we think, first, it is very undignified for a female to exercise it under any circumstances; and second, it is equally undignified for any gentleman to inflict a corporeal punishment on a female who may be guilty of such a crime.[7]

Complaints to Governor Gilmer of the Georgia Guard's brutality brought little response. Gilmer passed the charges on to Colonel J. W. A. Sanford, who denied the "foul aspersions cast upon the Guard & upon those conducting its operations. Emanating as they do from that most polluted of all receptacles, the *Cherokee Phoenix,* they would have passed me as does the idle wind but for their dissemination abroad. They are false, Sir, as false as the canting and hypocritical fanatic who indites them."

Boudinot himself came in for attack from Colonel Charles H. Nelson, martinet officer of the Guard. Among other offenses Elias had referred to Andrew Jackson in an editorial as "our false and faithless father." Boudinot escaped serious chastisement through Nelson's belief that the editor was "not possessed of sufficient talent to write." The offensive article must have been composed by someone else. Boudinot was threatened with a whipping, lectured instead by Colonel Nelson, and given what amounted to a stay of execution.

But Nelson and the Georgia Guard would not go lightly with the missionaries. In fact, baiting these men of God was part of their new recreation. Sam Worcester received a letter, which he handed to Boudinot for publication in the *Phoenix* of April 30, 1831. The writer told of witnessing, near the Cherokee town of Tensewaytee, a baptismal ceremony which involved submersion in the river:

After the solemnity of baptism was performed . . . but before the congregation had retired from the water the following . . . scene took place among the Geo. Guard. Three of their number pretended that they were so powerfully moved by the Spirit, that they mounted their fine horses, returned to the place of baptism, telling the people to get out of their way or else they would ride over them, for they were determined to baptize their horses in the same place. They rode into the water mocking religion and repeating the blessed words of our sacred Saviour.[8]

Plainly it was the missionaries who were now a major target. All who failed to obtain a license by taking the oath of allegiance were hereafter subject to four years in the penitentiary. No time was wasted after the March deadline to enforce the law. On March 12 Colonel Nelson led a mounted company on the first official roundup. Their orders were to arrest among others John Thompson at Hightower, Samuel Worcester at New Echota, Isaac Proctor at Carmel, and Elizur Butler at Haweiss. Butler happened to be in North Carolina at the time and so escaped the net.[9]

The Guard carried no warrants. The official charge against their captives was failure to take the oath of allegiance and obtain a license. But Governor Gilmer had a deeper grievance, expressed in a letter to Samuel Worcester in which he accused the missionaries of "opposing the humane policy of the general government" and "exciting the Indians to oppose the jurisdiction of the state."

Those who were arrested—Worcester, Thompson, and Proctor—offered no resistance. It would have been of little use. The Supreme Court ruling was, for now, against them; and the colonel told his captives that even had the Court ruled in their favor, Georgia would not have recognized the verdict and would have sent 10,000 troops into the Nation to enforce its laws.

Daniel Butrick, ever in a tizzy, saw the writing on the wall. Any minute the Georgia Guard might haul him off to jail, "where my usefulness would be ended." He escaped the initial roundup by being away from home at the time of Isaac Proctor's arrest. Now he decided to stay out of Georgia's reach, at Brainerd, and leave his wife Elizabeth to handle the mission at Carmel. Georgia's law regarding white residents did not apply to women.

The stranded Elizabeth was made of sterner stuff. She did not blame her husband for seeking refuge in Tennessee; she resented the circumstances which had forced him out of Georgia. Spunkily she wrote to Colonel J. W. A. Sanford of the Georgia Guard: "We wish to be considered as Cherokees, continue here as long as they do, have their people as our people, our God their God." And she promised the colonel that she herself would continue to exercise "the privilege of laboring here at this place for the good of this people."

There was more comic-opera travesty than violence in the roundup operation. As John Ridge observed with some amusement, the separate units of the Georgia Guard were preceded by a wagon bearing an outsized drum which was whacked by a young recruit. Following the drum a fifer tootled a martial air. Muskets at the ready, the mounted troops approached each mission in ranked array like medieval troops about to storm a castle.

The seizures were made with ritualistic courtesy, the prisoners being given time to take leave of their families and gather up their personal belongings. Then, to the sound of drum and fife, they were marched off, sixty miles or so to the southeast, to be delivered to the civil authorities in Lawrenceville.

While awaiting trial the missionaries were treated with consideration and considerable public sympathy. Prominent Georgia citizens, among them General Edward Harden, interceded in their behalf. While Georgia sentiment favored removal of the Indians, it did not, outside the legislature, favor the use of force. "Jurisdiction, but not oppression, seems to be the prevailing cry," noted Worcester.

The Georgia law firm of Underwood and Harris, hired earlier by Ross to handle Cherokee affairs, appeared with the prisoners before Judge Augustin Clayton at the Gwinnett County Superior Court on March 15. The attorneys applied for a writ of habeas corpus on the grounds of unconstitutional arrest. Judge Clayton put his own interpretation on the case. Worcester, Thompson, and Butler being in charge of government funds for the benefit of the Indians, and also being United States postmasters at their separate stations, were federal employees and not subject to state law. He dismissed all three of them.

Worcester returned to New Echota and to his wife Ann, who had just been delivered of a third daughter, Jerusha, and was making a slow recovery from labor. His retracted arrest had, he felt, been a victory for the missionaries and the Cherokees. The release of the prisoners was a vindication of both their work among the Indians and their right to continue in that work. There was nothing more to fear.

Governor Gilmer had an opposite reaction. Indignantly he wrote to Eaton demanding to know if the Secretary considered the missionaries agents of the government simply because they handled federal funds. Eaton replied that he did not. Still, they *were* employees of the U. S. Postal Service. How was that problem to be solved?

Easy. Gilmer would ask the President to fire them.

In Washington the Cherokee delegation of Ridge, Coodey, and Taylor called on the President to discuss the Supreme Court verdict. They were not, as John Ridge wrote to Boudinot, seeking any favors or special dispensations. Rather, they took the attitude that the Supreme Court's decision was generally favorable to their position. The Court had simply waived the right of jurisdiction, while noting the justice of their case.

But the conversation on March 6, as Ridge reported, took a different turn.

"I am glad to see you," said the President, "particularly at this time. I knew or thought I knew, that your claims before the Supreme Court could not be supported. The Court has sustained my views with regard to your Nation."

That was far from the opinion of the Cherokees. But the talk was friendly and the delegates did not interrupt.

"What I blame you for," said Jackson, "is letting the lawyers falsely take your money, with promises—promises they may yet make, even after this—that they can make you safe."

"But," said Ridge, "you cannot blame the Cherokees for attempting to uphold their rights before the proper tribunals."

"Oh, no," said Jackson, "don't misunderstand me. I only blame you for suffering the lawyers to fleece you." Then, with an apologetic cough: "I have been a lawyer myself long enough to know how lawyers will talk to obtain their client's money.

"I am the friend of the Cherokees," the President went on. "They fought with me in the war and freely shed their blood with the blood of my soldiers in defending the United States and how could I be otherwise than their friend?"[10]

Had Ridge been tempted to suggest that Jackson show his friendship in a manner quite the opposite of driving them from their homes, there was no chance to express himself. The interview was interrupted by the arrival of a Georgia delegation—no doubt seeking the President's congratulations for their victory in court. As the President said farewell to his Cherokee guests, warmly shaking each one's hand, his final message held a somber warning:

"You can live on your lands in Georgia if you choose, but I cannot interfere with the laws of that state to protect you."[11]

How long after that the President gave the order to discharge the missionaries from their postal jobs is hard to say. But under the date of May 16 Samuel Worcester received a letter from the governor, very formal, very firm. It noted that Worcester had remained in the territory without a license, claiming exemption from the law by virtue of holding the office of postmaster at New Echota.

"You have, no doubt, been informed of your dismissal from that office," Gilmer wrote. "That you may be under no mistake as to this matter, you are also informed that the United States Government does not recognize, as its agents, the missionaries acting under the direction of the American Board of Foreign Missions." The letter continued:

I am still desirous of giving you, and all others similarly situated, an opportunity of avoiding the punishment which will certainly follow your further residence within the State contrary to its laws . . . Col. Sanford, the commander of the guard, will . . . delay your arrest until you shall have an opportunity of leaving the State.[12]

A similar notice went to Butler and Thompson, whom Clayton had released from their earlier detainment, and to other leading missionaries. The Moravians prudently left their missions in the hands of women teachers while the men sought sanctuary in North Carolina, where the Baptists were already safe. Many American Board workers also left the state, most of them repairing to Brainerd, now partially recovered from its fire of the year before.

Worcester, however, held his ground. Both Ann and the baby were sick; he would not leave them. Nor did he intend to submit to Gilmer's threats. He thought that matter over for four weeks—during which Colonel Sanford left him alone—and finally replied on June 10 to Gilmer's ultimatum. He denied the governor's charges that he and other missionaries had incited the Indians to resist the laws of Georgia or the policies of the United States. But he did not deny believing that the Cherokee position was the right one; that Georgia had no claim upon the territory of the Nation.

That being the case, he would remain at his post in New Echota; "and if I suffer in consequence of continuing to preach the gospel and diffuse the written word of God among this people, I trust that I shall be sustained by a conscience void of offence, and by the anticipation of a righteous decision at that tribunal from which there is no appeal."[13]

John Ross stood solidly behind the missionaries, pronouncing Georgia's law "ridiculously absurd" and writing to Elias Boudinot that "I do hope our white citizens will not be so ignorant of their own rights as to be frightened out of their true interest and expatriate themselves by licking the usurper's hand." Worcester received more meaningful support from his early idol of boyhood days in Vermont—Jeremiah Evarts.

Though failing in health, Evarts continued to fight the missionaries' battle from the Mission Rooms in Boston, writing to Worcester: "By standing firm in this case, & being willing to suffer for righteousness' sake, you will do much to encourage the Cherokees . . . it is the very point, in my judgment, where they will lose their country, & their earthly all, if Georgia shall finally prevail against them."[14]

Men like Worcester, "men of a select character," wrote Evarts, might well be called upon by God to sacrifice their lives, if need be, for the Cherokees. With prophetic insight he made clear what he was thinking of:

If Georgia should carry some of you to prison, the fact would rouse this whole country, in a manner unlike anything which has yet been experienced . . . I think I never knew, or read of, a case in which so much good would be done, by submitting (only a few persons) to a groundless & most odious persecution. You would not only benefit the Cherokees, but your case would be known through the civilized world. You would do good to the poor and oppressed everywhere.[15]

Sam Worcester would cherish those lines for the balance of his life. For they were among the last words Evarts ever wrote. Returning home that spring from Cuba, which he had visited briefly for his health, Evarts was put ashore at Charleston, South Carolina, where he died on May 11, 1831.

Sophia Sawyer, who grasped at stars and rainbows and all things unattainable, had found a hero. Samuel Worcester, she knew, had been skeptical of her abilities and thought her giddy (though he never used that word). Yet he had treated her with avuncular consideration at New Echota. Her devotion, ever seeking a target, responded to his kindness. He whom she had regarded as an enemy was now a friend. Her adoration soared when, on July 7, a detachment of the Georgia Guard under Sergeant Jacob Brooks stopped at the Worcester house to arrest her patron for the second time. He was about to become a martyr, and martyrdom meant instant sainthood in her eyes.

Worcester protested to Brooks that his wife was sick; he could not leave her. But Brooks was under orders, and the following morning the missionary fell in line behind the baggage wagon and the small detachment started on its circuitous march to Camp Gilmer outside Lawrenceville in Georgia. A new wave of arrests was under way.

The company snowballed in numbers as it proceeded, picking up other guards and prisoners along the way. On meeting with Colonel Nelson's detachment, the Methodist minister James J. Trott was added to the cavalcade, along with a Cherokee miner arrested at the gold fields and chained to the wagon for security. Chance added another prisoner to the column when they encountered the Methodist preacher Dickson McCleod riding in the opposite direction. Surprised to see his fellow worker Trott in custody, McCleod asked the reason for his arrest. He was told that this was the Georgia Guard; they did not need a reason.

"It seems they proceed more by orders than by law," said the unwary Methodist.[16]

Though McCleod was a resident of Tennessee, the remark was made in territory that allegedly belonged to Georgia. He was promptly arrested, ordered to fall in with the other prisoners, and forced to keep to the center of the road, where the mud and water were most malefic.

They stopped for the night at the house of a man named Dawson, where Trott, McCleod, and Worcester were shackled by the ankles, and the Cherokee chained by the neck to the wall. The next morning Elizur Butler was added to the group of prisoners, having been picked up two days earlier at Haweiss Mission. He had fared the worst of any of them, having been forced to make the early stages of the journey chained to the neck of a guardsman's horse.

During the march, as Worcester later wrote to Boudinot, the missionaries suffered most from "the profaneness and obscenity of [Sergeant Jacob] Brooks' language that could not be exceeded by any thing which the most depraved and polluted imagination could conceive. Not only the person who had given the offence, nor only the prisoners, but all missionaries, all ministers of the Gospel, and religion itself, were the subject of his railing."

Divorcing the speaker from the words themselves, Worcester found consolation in a phrase that Brooks repeated as a taunt: "Fear not, little flock, for it is your Father's good pleasure to give you the kingdom."

The abused and failing Dr. Butler, chained by the neck to the escorting horse, likewise had reason to find consolation in a strange event. When night came, he pointed out to his mounted guard that should he stumble in the dark he would be garroted by the chain around his neck. The guard begrudgingly permitted him to mount the horse and ride behind the saddle. The extra load or the darkened trail was too much for the animal. It stumbled and fell on both the riders, hurting Butler scarcely at all but seriously injuring the guard.

They approached Camp Gilmer on Sunday, July 10, to be told by Brooks: "There is where all the enemies of the state of Georgia will have to land; there and in hell." Their actual cell, though devoid of comfort, was no worse than the average jail; they had enough blankets, food, and water, and were permitted to widen the slits between the planking for extra ventilation. During the following week, more captives arrived to swell the prison population to eleven —all white and most of them missionaries, save the single Cherokee.

The following Sunday, Trott and Worcester requested permission to hold religious services in the jail, for the prisoners and as many of the Georgia Guard and local residents who cared to come. Colonel Nelson replied that he considered the request "an impertinent one." Their arrest had been for the purpose of restraining their activities, not promoting them. "If your object be true piety you can enjoy it where you are."

On July 23 the case of the controversial eleven was heard before the Gwinnett County Superior Court, with the accused represented by Underwood and Harris. Samuel Worcester was additionally defended by the Vermont-born lawyer Elisha W. Chester. All were indicted by Judge Clayton and released on bond, pending trial in the state supreme court in September.

Worcester returned home to Ann, who needed him more than ever now. She still ran a fever, and little Jerusha had never been well. Though he was out on bail, Worcester's freedom was insecure. He had been told of a letter from Gilmer to Colonel Sanford in which the governor said of the prisoners, "If they are released by the courts, or give bail and return [to their homes], arrest them again." Worcester would be no use to Ann or the children in jail. Reluctantly, he left his family and crossed the border into Tennessee, to await at Brainerd his September trial.

Even this respite was short-lived. On August 14 his daughter Jerusha died. Worcester hurried home on hearing the news. He was too late for the funeral, which was conducted in his absence by Elias Boudinot. He was not too late, however, for the Georgia Guard, which arrived almost simultaneously, and arrested him for trespassing on Georgia soil. Back he went to the Lawrenceville jail, to be joined before too long by the rest of his co-defenders.

The trial which was held on September 15 was something of a travesty; it was a court of conviction not of justice. "The address of the judge on pronouncing the sentence of the court will doubtless be given to the public," Worcester wrote to Boudinot, "and of its character the public must judge."[17]

Aware of the ground swell of public opinion, Clayton did not castigate or denigrate the prisoners. They might be worthy men and Christians, but it "was the duty of every Christian to submit to civil authority" and on that point they were guilty. He sentenced all eleven to four years' hard labor in the penitentiary.

Governor Gilmer, serving his last months in office, was also aware of public sympathy for the missionaries. He did not want them elevated to the role of martyrs. By the time they reached the Milledgeville Penitentiary he sent word that all would be pardoned who either took the oath of allegiance to the state or withdrew beyond its boundaries. Nine of the eleven took advantage of the offer and were freed. Only two, Samuel Worcester and Elizur Butler, refused.

Prison officials argued for hours with the intransigent couple. For theatrical effect, the prison gate was opened and shut throughout the interview, its rusty hinges grating ominously on the ear, to remind them of the grim alternative to freedom. The metallic clanking had the opposite effect. Worcester and Butler remained firm and, posthumously, Jeremiah Evarts had his martyrs. That night the couple were taken to their detention quarters in the penitentiary, dressed in prison garb, and introduced to their unsavory cellmates.

In thirty years to come the Milledgeville Penitentiary would gain a reputation not unlike that of Andersonville, the infamous Civil War stockade. It harbored no such horrors now. Destroyed by fire earlier in the year, it had been hastily rebuilt into four large chambers, adequately light and airy. Their fellow prisoners were ordinary thieves and cutthroats, but they treated the two missionaries with reserved respect.

"God, in his great kindness, has given [me] a cheerful heart," wrote Worcester to the Board in Boston, adding of himself and Butler, "we get along with a good deal of comfort."[18]

The "hard labour" to which they had been sentenced was anything but arduous. Elizur Butler was given a cobbler's bench and applied himself to learning the shoemaker's art; life in the mission had taught him that practical skills were never wasted. Samuel Worcester, less dexterous than his companion, took up carpentry, making small cabinets and boxes, some of which he sent as gifts to the Mission Rooms in Boston. The Board members smiled tolerantly at these efforts; none of the cabinets seemed aligned, none of the lids would fit the boxes.

Besides relative physical comfort in the jail there was spiritual comfort also, "the consolation of believing that we enjoy the sympathy of Christians extensively," as Worcester wrote to Elias Boudinot. The two men were allowed to preach on Sundays to the other inmates and to such of the Georgia citizens as cared to come. Of these latter, Worcester noted, "while they do not approve of the course we have taken, nevertheless [they] give us credit for the uprightness of our motives."[19]

While Ann Worcester and Lucy Butler were stranded at New Echota and Haweiss, running the missions in the absence of their husbands, they were not without loyal friends among the Cherokees. A collection was taken for money with which to visit their husbands and take blankets to the prisoners. In November, Ann and Lucy started for Milledgeville with the Chamberlins. On their way, the party was overtaken by a group of hard-riding Cherokees who had just collected $2.12 to add to the fund. "This is very little to do for those who are suffering for us," their spokesman said, "but we will try to get more."[20]

Of great consolation to the prisoners were the touching letters from the Indians, which came from every corner of the Nation. In pairs and caucuses the Cherokees assembled to compose their messages of gratitude and tribute, expressed laboriously in Sequoyah's calisthenic characters. "Because of your courage," wrote Little Turtle, speaking also for his comrades, "I am not afraid of what the Georgians are doing. I do not feel sorry that you are willing to go to prison, for you have done no wrong, and I do not think you will be unhappy."[21]

Worcester must have thought of Jeremiah Evarts' words, "Courage is the thing they want—long continued courage." A hundred years later Marion Starkey, chronicler of Cherokee civilization, said of Worcester's intransigence, "One act of courage makes the whole world braver." True indeed. It was a priceless ingredient that Worcester was giving to the Cherokees. It would serve them well.

There was another, more practical aspect of the case. Though he would never know it, Evarts had found his cause célèbre in the martyrdom of Worcester. Attorney William Wirt wasted no time in preparing yet another case for the Supreme Court. This one was different. The rights of the Indians were not involved, those rights apparently too nebulous or nonexistent to carry weight in court. This case concerned the rights of a white man as protected by the Constitution. Samuel Worcester vs. the State of Georgia.

Samuel Worcester in this context was not a man alone. For this brief moment in Indian history he was the Cherokee Nation. In him rested a last hope of the red man everywhere. When the court convened in January 1832, it would face one of the gravest decisions in the conscience of America.

10

"We Are Distressed . . . Distressed!"

AGAIN IT was autumn. The air was heavy with wood smoke as the Indians burned the underbrush beneath their chestnut groves. Forest leaves whipped up a storm of gold and scarlet. New Echota drowsed in the October sunshine, bare of the crowds that normally, this time of year, trampled flat the grassy meadow that surrounded the town hall, the Council House, and the print shop of the *Phoenix*.

Elias Boudinot, in the absence of his partner Worcester, was having his troubles with the *Phoenix*—and the mails. The new postmaster, William J. Tarvin, who replaced the imprisoned missionary, was principally concerned with selling liquor to the Indians, having been a licensed trader prior to his appointment. When Boudinot protested editorially against this violation of the law, Tarvin retaliated by withholding letters and packages destined for the *Phoenix*, thus delaying not only supplies but newspapers normally received in exchange, on which Boudinot relied for much of his material.

This "New Era," Boudinot wrote in the *Phoenix* for July 11, 1831, "has not only wrested from us our rights and privileges as a people, but it has closed the channel through which we could formerly obtain our news. By this means the resources of the *Phoenix* are cut off. We must now depend, if we continue our labors, upon our patrons at home and abroad." On this, the close of the third year of publication, 1831, the editor was not only short of outside news; the restrictive acts of Georgia had rendered the *Phoenix* short of funds.

The newspaper's columns did not, however, lack for copy. Letters poured in on the Cherokee-Georgia controversy, many escaping Tarvin's censorship (or perhaps the abusive ones were deliberately allowed to pass). Boudinot himself had written no inflammatory articles condemning Worcester's arrest; he let the facts speak for themselves; but he did vent his spleen on the oppressions of the Georgia Guard and the depredations of the Pony Club. And the targets of his attack struck back.

One Georgia citizen who signed himself Ralph Scruggs, addressing the editor as a "d——d little frog eater," charged that "the treatment you and your countrymen are receiving is in payment of your d——d rascally treatment you have treated the whitemen when you had the power to do so . . . you d——d mountain ranger and wolf eater."[1]

Another correspondent sent in a drawing of an Indian hanging by the neck, with such superimposed captions as "Hang the Traitor," "Cut his Throat," and "Shoot him." Boudinot made an engraving of the illustration and presented it on a front page of the *Phoenix*.[2]

In more direct fashion Colonel Nelson of the Georgia Guard stomped into the *Phoenix* office to reprimand the editor, sharply accusing him of publishing "libelous articles" against the state of Georgia and the Guard. As Boudinot reported to his readers:

He [Nelson] also observed that as they could not prosecute for libel, the only way we could be punished would be . . . to tie us to a tree and give us a sound whipping . . .

We are not aware of having slandered Georgia or the Guard, and if we have, we think it a very poor way indeed to convince the world of it by flagellating us . . . Truth *has* been our object and truth *shall* be our object.[3]

Boudinot's writings were so literate that Nelson concluded that no full-blood Indian could have been the author of them. He regarded the editor as an "ignorant sort of man . . . not possessing sufficient talents to write the editorials in the *Phoenix*." Plainly these had been composed by Samuel Worcester, who, like missionaries generally, was conspiring to incite the Indians against the state authorities.

Others expressed the same belief, to the point that Worcester, before his incarceration, had submitted a written denial to the paper. He was a strong supporter of the *Phoenix,* but was not its editor and had never written anything for its columns "except now and then a notice . . ." Few Georgians, and surely not Nelson, credited the disclaimer. Boudinot remained free, but the *Phoenix* was on parole.

Daniel Butrick was among the soldiers of retreat at Brainerd. His wife Elizabeth was running the Haweiss Mission in his absence. He himself had been branded a traitor by William Chamberlin for having left his post while men like Samuel Worcester chose imprisonment over surrender. More to his mortification, the American Board of Foreign Missions had apparently decided to ignore him. "Though I have written again and again," he complained in January 1832, "stating my reasons for dissenting from the opinion of Mr. Worcester, yet month after month passes & I cannot obtain a word in reply."

That he was toubled in conscience seems apparent from his journal, in which he secretly vented his anger and frustration. His admiration for the Cherokees had not diminished; he believed in their cause; he reviled their persecutors. But at this point he could only take his fury out in words. Under the caption "A good word for Indians," dated January 11, he let himself go:

American citizens are so much worse than the Indians that the latter cannot live near them . . . without having their property torn from them, their minds corrupted, and their virgins debauched. Therefore they must leave and retire to the more virtuous and civilized inhabitants of the forest.

"And who will say that this is not correct reasoning?" Butrick asked his diary. "Facts sufficiently establish this point."

While the white man can go and come without fear of robbery, oppression, and murder, the poor Indian must watch night and day to preserve one little pony to plough his field, or one poor cow to nourish his family, or one creature of any kind to furnish his meat. Or, if riding alone, he is in constant danger of having his horse torn from him by the hands of ruffians. If seeking the fruit of his own soil, he is in danger of being seized, dragged to prison, and most infamous punishments.

"And what can he do?" Butrick asked himself rhetorically. "He cannot live with such wretches. He must go to the western wilderness & associate with more virtuous company." Having satisfied his conscience on these points, Butrick spread his rage around the globe:

Let all the nations of the world know this. Let France and England know it. Let Spain know that the bloody hands of her Cortes and Pizarro are white when compared with those of American citizens . . . Let Italy know it. Let the Pope be told . . . Let Africa hear it. O let the lions of the torrid zone know that the poor Indians would gladly receive asylum with them, if so they might escape the mammoth jaws of United States citizens.[4]

It was as good a summary of the situation as one could offer, and no doubt Butrick felt better having written it. Though a fugitive, it was reasonably safe for him to make sneak trips into Georgia on occasions. He would have liked to visit Lucy Butler, Elizur's wife, at Haweiss, but the last time he had done so he had felt so guilty and so uncomfortable that he decided to forgo further exposure to her accusing eyes.

For her part, Lucy was having trouble keeping the school going without her husband. Delight Sargent had come down from Brainerd to help out, but for three months only. Lucy had thought of closing down at the end of the year, but, as she wrote to David Greene, "I hardly know what answer to give the Cherokees, when they inquire what time they must return their children to school." Not able to find an answer, Lucy kept on with her teaching.

So it was with the other white women in the Nation who had cast their lot with the Cherokees, and had lost their husbands as a consequence. They could find no answers—so they stayed where they were, alone, and kept on working.

Sophia Sawyer, for example. She remained at New Echota, helping Ann Worcester with the children and teaching at the courthouse. She was especially proud of two black pupils in her class, sons of slaves from neighboring plantations. Being a woman and thus immune from the licensing law, Sophia herself had nothing to fear from the Georgia Guard. But the blacks were something else again, a weak point in her armor.

The Guard called at the school one day in January, waited politely until class let out, and then confronted Miss Sophia. Did she not know, the corporal asked, that it was against the laws of Georgia to teach "Nigras"?

Yes, said Sophia, but thankfully this was not Georgia; this was the Cherokee Nation, which was far too civilized to make such laws.

"No, ma'am," said the corporal stubbornly. "This here's Georgia."

Miss Sophia held her ground. "That is for the Supreme Court to decide," she said.[5]

Sophia, her associates knew, could be difficult at times. She was difficult now. Only over her dead body would the soldiers enter her school again and now, she told them, they had better go before she lost her temper. With surprising docility, like others confronted by Sophia's wrath, the Guard withdrew. But their purpose had been accomplished. The two black children, intimidated by the very presence of the soldiers, failed thereafter to show up for school.

Under pressure from Georgia, Andrew Jackson made a gesture toward fulfilling his pledge to remove the Indians. In the fall of 1831 he appointed one of his cronies, former congressman Benjamin F. Currey, to the office of Superintendent of Indian Removal. War Secretary Lewis Cass, succeeding John Eaton, laid down the rules for Currey's procedure. Each family willing to accept the government's terms for emigration would receive "a good rifle, a blanket, and kettle, and pound of tobacco." Payments would be made for the "improvements" they abandoned; their livestock would be purchased; and their transportation West would be provided for them.

"Let them know," wrote Cass to Currey, "that the President feels for their situation, that he has satisfied himself that they had better remove and soon, and that where we wish them to go, they will find a mild climate, a fertile Country, and the means of preserving their institutions, without the interference of the white people. And let them Know, that we leave the choice to them, trusting that the Great Spirit, who made the white man and the red, will open their eyes to see the path they ought to travel."[6]

Few eyes were opened to that path. In succeeding months Currey and his assistants, one of them Major W. M. Davis on assignment from the Army, worked hard to enroll a sufficient party for removal to the West. They labored against forbidding odds. The Superintendent attributed the resistance to the fact that the Cherokees had been intimidated by their chiefs, threatened with whipping if they acquiesced. More truthfully Currey confessed that he and his agents, many of whom were Georgians, were regarded by the Indians as "enemies"—and "the natives would not listen to a word they said."

In December enrollment increased as some Cherokees sought escape from the hardships of winter. Currey estimated that he would have a thousand prospective emigrants by spring. He ordered from the government a fleet of sixteen flatboats to start them on their journey. By March, however, there were only 180 Cherokees quartered in huts on the banks of the Hiwassee River, waiting to embark. The Superintendent delayed their start till the number rose to 380 persons, almost a third of whom were black.

Most of the emigrants were ne'er-do-wells and drifters, seeking a handout in the West. They were expendable; their departure only strengthened the homogeneous will of those remaining. In fact, never had the Cherokees been more united. Never had the constricting forces of adversity compressed them into such a firm amalgam, hard as armor plate. This became apparent as the time for the October Council neared.

Most members of the General Council were inclined to meet at New Echota, in defiance of Georgia's law forbidding such assembly. John Ross invited the leaders to his home at Head of Coosa to debate the matter. The Ridge was firm; a Nation should not desert its capital in the face of a besieging enemy. But his son John teamed with Elias Boudinot in urging that the Council gather elsewhere. At New Echota the meeting might be interrupted by the Georgia Guard; the members would be threatened with arrest; if arrested there was certain to be trouble. Ross agreed, and it was resolved that "the seat of government should be removed beyond the limits of Georgia." As a consequence, though the Georgia Guard raided New Echota on the date of the expected Council, they found the Indian capital a deserted city.

The new site selected for the Council was Chatooga, just across the Alabama border. A campground for district and religious meetings, it provided tables and benches, a platform for the speakers, and branches supported on forked sticks as shelters from the weather. But Chatooga was a considerable distance from the center of the Nation, a journey of a hundred miles or more for many of the chiefs. Nor could it compare with the comforts of the Council House at New Echota, of which the members were so proud. But to meet at all was a moral victory for which discomfort was small price to pay.

Ross addressed the assembly on the state of the Nation, extolling the virtues and rewards of unity. He noted that few had succumbed to Benjamin Currey's wiles; Washington should get the message; the Cherokees were of one mind on removal. Reviewing the progress the Nation had made despite all obstacles, he asserted that because of this progress the day was not far distant when "an incorporation into the great family of the American Republic" would be the happy lot of every Cherokee.

For Ross was pursuing yet another dream. To solve all its problems, the Cherokee Nation would become a state, and would take its sovereign place within the framework of the Union. Georgia would no longer be an enemy, but a neighbor. So with Tennessee and Alabama and North Carolina. All would be equal—the white, the red, the black—in this southeastern utopia. All they had to do to qualify as a new star in the spangled banner was to demonstrate their civic and moral responsibility, their dedication to American principles of government and education, their devotion to the Christian faith.

. . . *such stuff as dreams are made on.*

The Council also considered more immediate and practical programs. In what had become an annual pattern another delegation would be sent to Washington to present the Cherokees' grievances to Cass and Jackson. Ross picked the three he thought were most invulnerable to government trickery and bribery: John Ridge, William Shorey Coodey, and John Martin (replacing Richard Taylor of the year before).

At the same time, heeding Elias Boudinot's plea that the *Phoenix* was badly in need of funds to continue the Nation's battle for survival, the editor was "authorized to take a journey through the U.S. to solicit donations in money from all individuals disposed to . . . aid the Cherokee Nation . . . in its present struggle with . . . all those who are exerting their influence to eject our people from their native land." Boudinot's brother, Stand Watie, would serve as editor of the *Phoenix* in his absence.

Ross had planned to ride part of the way north with the delegation. But the night before their departure, November 30, 1831, he was forced to change his mind. A lanky, rifle-toting stranger called at Head of Coosa, where Ross was chatting with his younger brother Andrew. The man explained that a highway robber had stolen his horse, and the thief was now trapped at the ferry landing hoping to escape across the river. Would the Ross brothers help him apprehend the culprit?

John and Andrew joined the stranger in his mission. The thief was indeed at the ferry, but only as a co-conspirator in a clumsy plot. For the stranger suddenly dropped behind his volunteer helpers, shouldered his rifle, and shouted:

"Ross! I've wanted to kill you for a long time, and I'll be damned if I don't do it now!"

John and Andrew spurred their horses to a gallop, veering right and left, before the assassin could get them in his sights. The murder attempt was later attributed to renegades in the Pony Club, without, perhaps, political significance. But the incident served notice that, as the Georgia-Cherokee dispute continued, violence would become an increasing factor in the conflict.[7]

In Washington the three-man delegation put up at the Indian Queen Hotel prepared to discuss their grievances with Secretary Cass. But some of the wind was taken from their sails with the discovery that there was another delegation in the capital, this one composed of Western Cherokees who were anxious to further the President's removal program. The selling of Cherokee lands in the East (which did not belong to the Westerners anyway) would bring people and money and land guarantees to the Cherokee towns beyond the Mississippi. And they subscribed to Chief John Jolly's thesis that if all the tribes united in the West they could build a wall against American encroachment from the East.

Perhaps Chief Jolly shared his adopted son's conviction that "the age of the

Indian in the East has passed." Sam Houston had reason to be bitter. He had returned from Washington in some disgrace, having failed to get the Indian rations contract. And he had fallen from grace in other ways as well. In the summer of 1830 the Raven had married (or "shared the blanket" with) Jolly's niece Talihina of the distinguished Rogers family, hoping for consolation in her arms.

But the old bane persisted. As he confessed, he "buried his sorrows in the flowing bowl," until the Indians changed his sobriquet from the Raven to Ootsetee Ardeetahskee, or "Big Drunk." Intoxicated one night, he assaulted his foster father and was knocked insensible by the chief's defenders, for which he was forced to apologize before the Council. Sam Houston had hit bottom. But he was still a Cherokee, he insisted; he would still be heard from.

In Washington, Jackson was naturally partial to the Western delegation, even though they were without authority to negotiate for their Eastern brothers. He received the Westerners and ignored John Ridge and his associates. This was disheartening enough; but inciting more bitterness was the fact that, on their way to Washington, the Western delegates had stopped off in Tennessee and recruited two discontented deputies from Cherokee Nation East, specifically the remote Aquohee District: John Walker and James Starr.

Walker and Starr. Names that would go down in infamy. John Walker, Jr., was the malcontent son of Major Walker who had fought with the Cherokee forces at Horseshoe Bend. John had gained some influence and stature by marrying the niece of the former Indian Agent Jonathan Meigs. What prompted him to turn against the majority of his compatriots is a mystery. James Starr appears to have been no more than a fellow traveler, following the course of least resistance—an attitude that made both men useful tools for Andrew Jackson.

Though Ridge's delegates succeeded in placing their memorial into the hands of Cass, it got them nowhere. The Secretary told them in reply that the President was their friend. He was conscious of their difficulties. But "he is convinced there is no remedy but in a removal beyond the immediate contact of the white people. As to coercion none will be applied . . . You are free to remain with the privileges and disabilities of other citizens." However, "every dictate of prudence requires that you should abandon your residence, and establish yourselves in a country where abundance, peace and improvement are offered to you."

Then Cass, perhaps unconsciously, dropped a delayed-action time bomb:

I do not address you as I should the great body of your people. You are well educated and intelligent, able to appreciate the value of our institutions, and fitted to enjoy them. Not so with your countrymen generally. As therefore you must judge for them, I trust you will view their situation as it is, and inquire what is best for them.[8]

In other words, they represented a select group—capable of judging for the whole, wiser and more gifted than their fellows. To a man like John Ridge,

vain and confident, it was food for thought. Perhaps at this moment he began
to reconsider his position.

There was little more the delegates could do in Washington. Leaving Martin
and Coodey to handle whatever came up, Ridge decided to accompany
Boudinot on the latter's fund-raising tour. They went by stage to Philadelphia,
where Boudinot had lectured seven years before and where Ridge, as he informed John Ross, anticipated "a great & vigorous expression of indignation
from this city against the cruelties of Georgia, and the policy of the U.S. . . ."

The indignation surfaced quickly in the City of Brotherly Love. Newspaper
publisher Matthew Carey at a fund-raising dinner for the speakers toasted
"Confusion to the Councils of Georgia and the Administration in relation to
the Cherokees." Colonel Thomas McKenney, former Superintendent of Indian
Affairs, was staying in Philadelphia to see to the publication of his portfolio of
Indian portraits. He was quick to resume his battle with Andrew Jackson over
Cherokee removal, and offered, as Ridge informed Ross, "to publish in this city
short letters addressed to the President which shall strike him as the lightning
strikes the branchless pine."

Moving on to New York, the speakers made a similarly good impression.
Describing John Ridge, a reporter for the *Commercial Advertiser* wrote that he

is rather tall and slender in his person, erect, with a profusion of black hair, a shade
less swarthy, and with less prominence of cheekbones than our western Indians. His
voice is full and melodious, his elocution fluent, and without the least observable
tincture of foreign accent or Indian. Even his metaphors were rarely drawn from
the forest, and he held little or none of that vehement action that characterizes the
orators of uncivilized tribes.[9]

More to the point, the reporter noted that Ridge presented the Indian case,
"the simple story of their wrongs," with "unaffected and irresistible power . . .
His narrative of the brutalities of the Georgia Guard towards the Missionaries
. . . was sufficient to fire the blood and rouse the indignation of every American deserving the name of man." By the end of their New York appearance a
committee headed by Mayor Philip Hone collected $800 for Boudinot's *Phoenix*
and composed a memorial addressed to Congresss signed by six thousand citizens.

But it was in New England that the two crusaders enjoyed their heartiest
ovation. Perhaps they brought with them some of the glamour they had once
enjoyed as the "Young Men of Cornwall." And they had such distinguished
sponsors as John Pickering and Henry Ward and Lyman Beecher. "You gave
us good advice; we followed it; we were happy," Boudinot told an enthralled
New Haven gathering. Then his voice broke as he recounted all that the Cherokees had suffered at the hands of Georgia and a fickle Washington administration. For a moment he showed signs of a disturbing instability.

"What shall we do?" he asked his audience in distraction. "We are distressed
. . . distressed!"[10]

It was in Boston, at the close of their New England tour, that Ridge and Boudinot shared with their hosts at the Mission Rooms the news of a Cherokee triumph they had hardly dared to hope for. The case of *Worcester* vs. *Georgia* had been reviewed by the Supreme Court, and on March 3, 1832, Chief Justice Marshall rendered his decision.

In brief, the written opinion stated that the Georgia court which had sentenced Worcester had acted under "a law which is void, as being repugnant to the constitution, treaties, and laws of the United States." It ought, therefore, "to be reversed and annulled."

Elias Boudinot, so lately stricken with distress, wasted no time in writing to Stand Watie at New Echota, "It is a glorious news . . . a great triumph on the part of the Cherokees . . . The question is forever settled as to who is right and who is wrong . . ." The sedate and aging Reverend Lyman Beecher, who knew both Ridge and Boudinot from Cornwall days, happened to call at the Mission Rooms when the word arrived. As Boudinot wrote to Stand Watie,

I asked him whether he had heard the news from Washington. He said, "No, what is it?" I told him the Supreme C. had decided in favor of the missionaries. He jumped up, clapped his hands, took hold of my hand and said, "God be praised," and ran right out to tell his daughter and his family. These little incidents manifest the feeling, the intense feeling, on the question.[11]

Less emotional, more analytical than Boudinot, John Ridge received the Court's opinion with reserve and skepticism. He could not share his companion's conviction that the question was forever settled as to who was right and who was wrong. He himself, perhaps, was wavering at this point. In any event, blind optimism could be dangerous. In contrast to Boudinot's enthusiasm he sent to the stand-in editor of the *Phoenix* some words of caution.

Yes indeed, he told Stand Watie, the Supreme Court's verdict was a cause for satisfaction. But take care! It was a long step from decision to enforcement. "You . . . ought to advise our people that the contest is not over . . . the Chicken Snake General Jackson has time to crawl and hide in the luxuriant grass of his nefarious hypocrisy until his responsibility is fastened upon by an execution of the Supreme Court at their next session. Then we shall see how strong the links are to the chain that connects the states to the Federal Union."[12]

John had seen how the Western delegation had gained precedence in Washington. He had heard from the lips of Lewis Cass that the Secretary was prepared to recognize virtually any deputation ready to discuss removal terms. Specifically, this meant men like Starr and Walker, professing to hold authority and influence they did not, in fact, possess.

"In view of these facts," Ridge cautioned his cousin, "you should be on your guard . . . we shall live to tread on the necks of traitors."

How right he was! And, in many ways, how blind!

Predictably there was outrage in the state of Georgia, where Wilson Lumpkin was beginning his first term as governor. Even Lumpkin's political opponent, former Governor George M. Troup, agreed with his adversary that the Court's ruling was a flagrant violation of Georgia's rights; while Lumpkin himself vowed to meet the verdict with "determined resistance." Both were secure in the support of Andrew Jackson, who allegedly declared: "John Marshall has made his decision, now let him enforce it."[13]

Thus, at its moment of greatest triumph, dark clouds hung above the Nation. But none was visible to the great mass of the Cherokees, who read in the *Phoenix* of this new and happy turn in their affairs. Chief Ross had been right, as always, in declaring, "United we stand." They had stood united, and now it seemed that they would stand forever.

Throughout the Nation the Indians rejoiced as they had rarely had occasion to rejoice before. The mountain Cherokees strapped tortoise-shell rattlers to their ankles, donned feathered headdress, and danced the night away. At the ball-play grounds the betting was heavy and the contests wild and unrestrained. In villages and valleys there was feasting and revelry surpassing even the Green Corn Festivals. Some effervescent individuals tapped a whiskey keg and were eagerly arrested by the Georgia Guard, to be carted off to jail in a sublime euphoria.

While Benjamin Currey and his agents continued to canvass the territory for prospective emigrants, their efforts were blown to shreds by the Supreme Court ruling. Major Davis, who had not had time to know or understand the Cherokees, was bewildered by their lunatic festivity. He considered the celebrating Cherokees (as he wrote to his superiors in Washington) a "deluded people" who "believed in the reality of the Court's decision, and were rejoicing, yelling, and whooping in every direction."

"Indeed," Davis wrote to Secretary Cass, "such was their audacity that they sent private emissaries into our camp on the Hiwassee River, before the emigrants embarked for Arkansas, and persuaded them not to go; that if they would remain they would be protected; which produced some disaffection among them . . . Finally, the agitation and disorder among them increased to such a degree, that . . . we had to plant a strong chain of sentinels around their camp, composed of white men who had volunteered their services to protect the disaffected from making their escape."[14]

Despite his warning to Stand Watie that too much optimism might be dangerous, John Ridge confessed to his cousin, "Since the decision of the Supreme Court I have felt greatly revived—a new man—I feel independent . . . How much gratitude we owe to the good men Mr. Worcester and Dr. Butler."[15]

Every Cherokee in the Nation felt revived and newly free and filled with gratitude for the two who had suffered imprisonment to bring this happy circumstance about. But it was puzzling that the missionaries still remained in jail. This was no fault of their lawyers. Underwood and Elisha Chester moved in the Superior Court of Georgia that Marshall's mandate be acknowledged and the prisoners discharged. The court refused. On Judge Clayton's advice Chester wrote to Governor Lumpkin requesting the dismissal of the prisoners. Lumpkin's response was terse:

"You got around Clayton, but you shall not get around me."

So Worcester went on with his carpentry and cabinetmaking and Butler tapped away at his cobbler's bench. Both remained outwardly cheerful, continued to hold Sunday services, seemed not too concerned about the delay in their release. In prison they served as symbols of state oppression. By inference, this aroused sympathy for the Cherokees—which was largely their purpose in submitting to their jailers in the first place.

True, Governor Lumpkin had made it clear that they could gain their release at any time, by taking the oath or leaving the state. To do either, Worcester felt, would be to betray the Cherokees.

There were, however, troubling considerations. Well-meaning citizens, not all of them Georgians, wrote to question Worcester's stand. The missionaries had won their case; their cause was vindicated. Even though Georgia ignored the Supreme Court mandate, was there any real point in staying in jail? If Georgia continued to defy the ruling, were not the Cherokees doomed beyond all help?

Nullification, now a burning issue, was another troubling consideration. South Carolina seemed ready to go to war rather than accept the Tariff of Abominations. The rebellion of one state alone could probably be dealt with. But what if Georgia were to join her? As might happen if the federal government tried to enforce the Supreme Court mandate. Jeremiah Evarts had written, of Georgia's oppression of the Cherokees, "We would rather have a civil war, were there no alternative." Was Worcester ready to accept such grave responsibility?

He discussed the matter with Elisha Chester, who had been in touch with Andrew Jackson during the Supreme Court trial. Jackson was reportedly adamant in his opposition to South Carolina's mutinous stand. The state, the President said, was in all ways subject to federal law. How, then, could he support Georgia in her similar defiance of the government? An obvious answer was that Jackson had a double standard covering such embarrassments. But Chester did not say so.

In fact, though he listened attentively to Worcester's troubled questioning, Chester was strangely evasive.

He had reason to be.

As it turned out, April was the cruelest month. Dark rumors suddenly assailed the Nation, quieting the joyous celebrations that had heralded the March decision of the Court. The first jolt came from Congressman Daniel Newnan of Georgia, who wrote to the press, regarding John Ridge's commission in Washington, "The Cherokee Delegation have at last consented to recommend to their people to make a treaty with the government upon the general basis that they shall acquire a patent for lands over the Mississippi . . ."

Reprinted by Stand Watie in the *Phoenix,* the report brought shock and consternation to the Cherokees. Both Ridge and Coodey wrote letters of denial that were published in the Washington *National Intelligencer.* But the terrible doubt remained. What were the delegates up to in Washington? In the wake of victory were they selling out the Nation for some secret, personal considerations? Were Starr and Walker the traitors, or were Martin, Ridge, and Coodey?

Hard upon that came rumors that Samuel Worcester had given up the fight, and was seeking a pardon from the governor. Elisha Chester, it was said, had so reported to John Ross. The missionaries were planning to seek a pardon from the governor before testing their case again in the Supreme Court. That being so, justice from Georgia for the Cherokees was out of the question, since Jackson was openly siding with the state. As leader of the Nation, it was up to Ross to make the best deal possible for the Cherokees and settle for removal.

There had been other such rumors, one deriving from David Addison Reese of Georgia, a distant cousin of Elias Boudinot and professed friend of the Cherokees. Reese had heard from an "unimpeachable source" of Worcester's alleged defection. Though Ann Worcester stoutly defended her husband and denied the rumor, all but calling Reese a liar, John Ross when questioned seemed less positive and more bewildered. He didn't trust Reese. He couldn't make Chester out. He couldn't unravel the tangled threads of hearsay, innuendos, dubious reports.

A final blow to Cherokee confidence came when Ross proclaimed July 19 a day of prayer and fasting. It would be, the proclamation read, a "day of tribulation and sorrow, as the time appears to be fast hastening when the destiny of this people must be sealed. Whether it has been directed by the wonted depravity and wickedness of man, or by the unsearchable and mysterious will of an allwise Being, it equally becomes us, as a rational and Christian community, humbly to bow in humiliation . . ."[16]

What words were these to signal such a triumph as the Nation had experienced? What sort of crisis was the chief referring to? Why was this a time for "tribulation and sorrow," a time for heads bowed in humiliation?

While Elias Boudinot, in a *Phoenix* editorial, applauded the proclamation— "What could be more proper!"—he did so in disturbing words. "We have need to go to the Ruler of the universe," the editor wrote, "in this day of deep affliction. We have been too long trusting to an arm of flesh, which has proven to be but a broken reed."[17]

The Cherokees were puzzled. Which way the wind—was it fair or foul?

A pall of doubt hung over the Nation as the people looked around them and observed the signs. The missionaries were still in jail. Surveyors still roamed the land with ax and compass. Was it possible that the Supreme Court had no power, that its word would go unheeded? Surely not! If one could not have faith in the honor of the United States government and its institutions, one could not have faith in the Cherokee Nation's government and institutions which were modeled in their image.

Unthinkable! Or was it . . . ?

Had it only been possible to know the truth—that David Reese's story about Samuel Worcester had been pure fabrication, that Elisha Chester was, in essence, a double agent, having made a pact in Washington with Andrew Jackson to use his influence to persuade the Cherokees to come to terms. All this would come out in time—and only minor injury, not mortal harm, would result from their respective machinations.

But what would be revealed more slowly and would augur more disaster for the Nation was the sign of division developing within the ranks. The Cherokee story has been analyzed from one side or the other, pitting the heroes against the villains. But there were no heroes and no villains. There was not even a clear right or wrong. There was only the conflict that is part of every human conscience.

To go back a month or so, and pick up clues. When John Ridge and Boudinot returned to Washington from their New England speaking tour, they learned quickly of Jackson's attitude toward the Supreme Court decision. The President made no bones about it; he would not force Georgia to obey the mandate. Ridge went directly to the White House to confront the President. He wanted an explanation. What, he asked, could the Cherokees expect? Would the power of the United States support them against Georgia?

No, said the President frankly, it would not. He advised the young man to go home and tell his people that no hope remained; that their only salvation lay in accepting the government's terms and moving West. Presumably Ridge made no reply. Certainly there is no record among Jackson's papers that he verbally or otherwise accepted the decision.

Perhaps, however, John showed enough dismay to justify Jackson's writing some days later to his friend John Coffee, "I believe Ridge has expressed despair, and [has concluded] that it is better for them to treat and move." Perhaps, too, that letter was one source of the rumor of John's wavering position.[18]

Amos Kendall, a close political friend of Jackson's and a member of the "Kitchen Cabinet," was possibly present at the Ridge-Jackson meeting. In any event, his report of the interview suggests that this was the instant when Ridge shifted his position:

Ridge left the President with the melancholy feeling that he had the truth. From that moment he was convinced that the only alternative to save his people from moral and physical death was to make the best terms they could with the government, and remove out of the limits of the States.[19]

If Ridge changed his mind while still in Washington, it is probable that he brought John Martin and William Coodey over to his way of thinking. And it is probable, too, that when he returned to Running Waters in mid-May, he confessed this reversal of position to his father, Major Ridge. The Ridge might not have understood it; his life had been dedicated to the Cherokees' survival and their national integrity; it was he who assassinated Doublehead for betraying that integrity. And here was his own son John declaring for removal.

It must have been a bitter moment for The Ridge. But much as he had stood for the old ways and the old traditions, he had stood for education and leadership among the young. John had had that education; he had been trained for leadership; The Ridge himself had yielded much of his authority in the Council to his son. Whatever position John took he would take as well, and stand beside him.

For a man so old, who had traveled so far, it was total surrender, a final renunciation of the past. And for The Ridge there was not much remaining but the past. He was a gnarled oak in the forest, no longer able to bend with the wind; able only, if the storm blew wild enough, to fall. There was an unconfirmed rumor that he called at the Moravian Mission, telling Brother Clauder he wanted "to seek the good now"; he wanted, at long last, to become a Christian and to be baptized; there was not much time left.

Elias Boudinot, too, was going through a difficult conversion. In his absence the *Phoenix,* under Stand Watie's direction, had published the rumors of John Ridge's double-dealing in Washington and Worcester's surrender to the governor of Georgia. Watie saw these as a threat to national security, a call to arms. Let the people be forewarned, and strengthen their resistance.

Boudinot was not so sure. With the federal government and the state of Georgia both ignoring the Supreme Court ruling, was there any real hope left in the East? Perhaps it was time to reverse one's stand and consider the possible wisdom of removal.

To Ross and the Council majority, the course was clear; the Cherokees would hold firm to their eastern territories. To John Ridge and Boudinot, the West began to loom as an alternative; at least there were two sides to the question, and both should be considered. With these diverse but perhaps reconcilable attitudes, the General Council assembled at Red Clay, Tennessee, the last week of July.

Red Clay was aptly named. Adjoining a large spring with four effervescent satellites, the Council grounds rested on a shallow saucer of crimson earth baked brick-hard from the summer's heat. Except for a crude shed hastily constructed as a Council House there was no shelter beyond that afforded by the oaks and chestnuts and spindly cedars that seemed to have marched down from surrounding hills.

Three tasks awaited the grim-faced members who assembled there on July 23. One was to hear and appraise the report of their delegation back from Washington. Another was to consider the matter of national elections, which would normally be held that year but which had been proscribed by Georgia law. The third was to listen, at Jackson's request, to the government's latest terms for removal, which would be presented by his emissary. That emissary proved to be none other than Elisha Chester, who was appearing for the first time in his true light as an agent of the federal administration.

John Ross opened the sessions with an address to the Cherokee Nation as a whole in which he praised the "prudence, unanimity and firmness of the people in clinging to Our Common Cause." He saw no despair in what he called "the embarrassment of our present situation . . . if the people will but continue constant and be sensible and true to their own interest."

Ross was not the practiced orator that John Ridge had become. Nor could he match The Ridge in eloquence and powerful delivery. He was practical, didactic, unemotional. He spoke in a monotone. His metaphors lacked imagination. But he was believed—perhaps for just those reasons.

There was nothing unusual in his address, except perhaps an almost hidden reference: "A man who will forsake his country in time of adversity and will co-operate with those who oppress his own kindred is no more than a traitor and should be viewed and shunned as such."[20]

All eyes most likely turned to Starr and Walker, who were sitting in the audience, while Starr and Walker would have turned their eyes upon Elisha Chester, who had the unhappy task of reading Secretary Cass's letter to the Cherokees. It was a letter advocating their removal—the same old arguments, the same old terms, the same old promises, the same old guarantees. But one paragraph was startlingly new. The Council was surprised to learn from Cass that the President believed the Cherokees had had a change of heart on the subject of removal and were ready to talk terms!

Where did such an idea come from? Starr and Walker? Ridge's recent mission to the capital? Suspicion is a vicious and divisive cancer on the body politic. If Cass's message accomplished nothing else it helped to spread doubt and distrust among an already disillusioned people. The discussion became bitter, tempers frayed, as John Ridge and Boudinot spoke in favor of at least considering the new proposals—a suggestion that had all the impact of an earthquake.

In the end the Council curtly rejected Cass's proposition, and as much as told Chester he was not the man to present it anyway—a wolf in sheep's clothing, professing friendship for the missionaries and the Indians and taking pay and orders from the President. They would answer Cass personally and in full, and did, in a letter dated August 6 that was signed by the entire Council. Among the signatories were the names of John and Major Ridge (Boudinot was not a Council member). If they had made their minds up on the matter of removal, they would coast along for now with the majority.[21]

The first four sentences scotched the rumor that the Cherokees had changed their minds; they had not; they found the government's assumption and the arguments "objectionable." The rest of the letter presented Cherokee grievances against the state of Georgia, and the massive violation of their rights which the United States had promised to protect. How, now, could agents of the United States approach the Cherokees with further promises, more guarantees, another treaty to be signed—having ignored all existing guarantees and treaties up to now?

Last on the Council's agenda was the matter of national elections, an institution that the Cherokees regarded with the utmost pride. These had been forbidden by the same Georgia law that prohibited meetings of the General Council and denied the Cherokees control of their affairs. Some members urged that they hold elections anyway. But the consensus favored avoiding any further conflict with the state; they had enough trouble as it was. It was voted to suspend elections until further notice. Ross and Lowrey, whose terms would normally expire in October, would remain in office as Principal Chief and Assistant Chief, respectively, until elections, at some time in the future, were resumed.

The move did much to widen the growing hiatus between Ridge and Ross. Though Ross's following was great, and no doubt he would have been returned to office anyway, John Ridge had every reason to believe he had a chance in new elections. He was better educated, more articulate than Ross. His father's name was one that carried weight throughout the Nation. He had had experience by now in dealing with executives in Washington. He would bide his time, however, until the annual October Council three months hence.

The meeting ended in a climate of discord and acrimony. Before returning to Head of Coosa, Ross got hold of Boudinot. He cautioned the editor of the *Phoenix* not to publish any report of dissension in the Council. To do so would only encourage the enemy. The Nation must appear of one mind on the subject of removal. If Elias had any personal feelings on the matter, he must keep them to himself.

Summer was like a heady tonic to Sophia Sawyer. The chatter of streams, the scent of wild roses, the song of the thrasher, called her to the mountains. By August—when her pupils left school anyway, supposedly to help with the crops but more truthfully to attend the Green Corn Festival—the lure was irresistible. Besides, she was curious. She sensed the deep currents of trouble running through the Nation. She wanted to get out and talk and listen to the people.

Worcester was still in the penitentiary, but Ann had recovered fully and was able to handle the household by herself. So when the Reverend Evan Jones, Baptist preacher at Valley Town, invited Miss Sophia to accompany him on a circuit of northeastern villages and missions in the Smoky Mountain region, she donned Indian buckskin and riding boots and willingly followed him into the wilderness.

The trails were steep, the heights forbidding, and once her horse threatened to plunge her down a precipice. But Sophia stayed her fears by "realizing, if I ever did, that 'in God we live, move, and have our being.'" She found the scenery "magnificent" and only wished she had the powers to describe it. And her abiding faith in the male sex was strengthened as, at each perilous turn in the trail, "Mr. Jones, with truly Christian fortitude, moved calmly and quietly forward bidding me to follow."[22]

Whatever the day of the week, wherever they stopped in the Valley Town district, their coming occasioned meetings, rallies, even baptismal ceremonies. A bent and wizened Indian of over ninety years of age, recorded Miss Sophia, trudged twelve miles over the mountains to be baptized by the Reverend Jones. Local ministers sought the advice of the more experienced circuit preacher. People crowded around him to discuss the intricate difference between right and wrong. Uppermost in their minds were the rumors of imminent and forced removal to the West. Regarding the government officials proposing such a course, they asked:

"How can we trust them when they are breaking the most solemn treaties? Here are our homes, our firesides, our cultivated fields, our gardens of fruits."

They added to this list of treasured possessions the graves of their ancestors, saying:

"Let us die with them. If we leave this country, these hills and valleys and this mountain air, we shall sicken and die. And what would we get in exchange, in the West? Perhaps war on our arrival, or if we remain, a few years of peace while we cultivate the land, until the white man will trade our rights again. Where can we find rest or protection?"[23]

Miss Sophia did not have the answer, even as applying to herself. She returned to New Echota with a heavy heart, weeping without tears for her suffering people. Wherever they went, there would she go also. She knew that now. And she knew that the moment of decision was not far away.

11

A House Divided

AT HIS DESK in the print shop, with the lazy drone of bees outside the window and the heat like a blanket on the village, Elias Boudinot struggled to compose a letter. Ordinarily writing came easily to him; words tumbled out in a torrent of conviction. But this was different. This was a letter to John Ross. Dated August 1, 1832, it stated that Elias, after more than four years of service, was quitting as editor of the *Phoenix*.

With the chained emotions of the Indian, Elias kept his reasons simple. The $300 salary was inadequate for his needs. His health was suffering from the exacting indoor work. The financial problems which the *Phoenix* faced made it unlikely that the paper could continue. On top of this, he told his chief, the *Phoenix* had fulfilled its mission and "done all that it was supposed to do, in defending Cherokee rights, and in presenting Indian grievances to United States people."

Then, painfully, he came to the crux of the matter—his open-minded presentation of the pros and cons of Indian removal:

> I could not consent to be the conductor of the paper without having the privilege and the right of discussing those important matters—and from what I have seen and heard, were I to assume that privilege, my usefulness would be paralyzed, by being considered, as I unfortunately already have been, an enemy to the interest of my beloved country and people . . . I should think it my duty to tell them the whole truth; I cannot tell them that we will be reinstated in our rights when I have no such hope . . .[1]

As his protest suggested, Boudinot was not so much resigning as being forced from his position by John Ross's censorship. Earlier the chief had written to him regarding the editorial policy of the *Phoenix,* stating: "The toleration of diversified views in the columns of such a paper would not fail to create fermentation and confusion among our citizens, and in the end prove injurious to the welfare of the Nation. The love of our country demands unity of sentiment and action for the good of all."[2]

As to love of country there was little difference between Ross and Boudinot. ("I love my country and I love my people as my own heart bears me witness," Boudinot had written in his letter.) But to Elias "action for the good of all" meant something different from what it did to Ross. He was not siding with Georgia and the United States. Though the white man had given him an education, a wife, even an income through the missionaries, the white man's society and government had betrayed the Nation—tricked it with broken treaties, degraded it with humiliating laws, corrupted it with Anglo-Saxon vices.

Boudinot did not ratify those ugly truths. But he could not see his people crushed by the hopeless odds against them. They must remove beyond the reaches of destruction. He would not use his cherished *Phoenix* further to deceive them. He would rather see the paper die—perhaps to rise from its ashes at some other time and place.

"I have done what I could . . . I have served my country, I hope with fidelity," Boudinot added to the announcement of his resignation published in the *Phoenix*.

But Ross, while he accepted Boudinot's resignation, could not share the editor's opinion that the *Phoenix* could and should be discontinued. "I deem it to be essentially important that the paper should be kept up," he wrote to Boudinot. It had "been greatly instrumental in the diffusion of science and general knowledge among our citizens" and "the pecuniary embarrassments of the Nation by no means ought to influence you to discontinue the paper, if a suitable person can be found to conduct it."[3]

Ross had a suitable person in mind: his brother-in-law Elijah Hicks. The principal thing in Elijah's favor was his loyalty to Ross's views and his fanatic hatred of the Nation's enemies. As the son of Charles Renatus Hicks, former Principal Chief of the Nation, he was not without stature, not without intelligence and courage; but he wore those qualities as blinders. Under his direction the *Phoenix* would become more an instrument of propaganda than one of knowledge and enlightenment.

To give Hicks his due, he was taking the helm at an inauspicious time. The lottery wheels would soon start spinning down in Georgia, and the stakes were not only Cherokee property but Cherokee dreams as well.

Samuel Worcester and Elizur Butler bided their time in the Milledgeville Penitentiary, hoping for their imminent release. They were not out of touch with events outside their walls. Ross sent them copies of the *Phoenix,* and David Greene saw that Worcester got the latest medical journals along with the Boston *Recorder* and New York *Observer*. An item in the latter caught Worcester's eye and prompted him to send a letter of correction to the editor

"We notice in your paper," he wrote, "a statement . . . that we have been compelled to aid in the construction of the lottery wheels, by means of which the land and gold mines are distributed . . . we have the happiness to assure you . . . that we were not called upon for any assistance whatever in the construction of these wheels. We would add, in gratitude to the principal keeper of the Penitentiary, that, at some sacrifice of convenience, he studiously avoided calling upon us to assist in that work, from the apprehension that it would be a task ungrateful to our feelings."[4]

Nevertheless, the work went on, with the wheels delivered and the lottery inaugurated on the courthouse steps a hundred yards away. The Reverend J. B. Payne of Milledgeville, in ministerial frock coat and collar, lent an air of righteousness to the proceedings. Under the watchful eye of the district Methodist minister (just in case), the Reverend Payne gave the first ceremonial spin of the wheel that started, in mid-October 1832, one of the more lucrative games of chance in Southern history. A pasteboard ticket a little larger than a playing card entitled the lucky winners to 160 acres of farmland in Cherokee country or 40 acres of land believed to shelter gold.[5]

Georgia's honor, wrote Elijah Hicks in one of his early *Phoenix* editorials, was about to "be run through a sporting wheel to seize our lands . . ." It was, the editor asserted, "one of the darkest and most shameless moral crimes that has ever been consummated in Christendom . . . the national rights of the Cherokees are now trampled under foot . . . the lottery can never convey to Georgia a title; it can only be a forcible entry and illegal possession . . . will endanger further American institutions and plunge the general government into deeper and darker chaos."[6]

His grim predictions were at least delayed. Despite the presence of the watchful parsons, state commissioner Shadrach Bogan managed to shuffle the winning cards that cleared through his hands and see that they went to selected friends and relatives. The fraud was detected, Bogan went to jail, the misdirected tickets went back into the hopper, and the lottery began again—but not until the Cherokees had concluded their second Council held at the Tennessee Council grounds in October.

While there was hope that fall that Henry Clay might be elected in November and that, in consequence, Chicken Snake Jackson would be unable to "play any more fantastic tricks before high heaven after the fourth of March, 1833," the October Council assembled in an atmosphere of gloom. Heavy rains and swollen rivers delayed Ross's arrival from Head of Coosa until October 8. The chiefs and delegates sat beneath their blankets in the shelter of nearby oaks, smoked their long-stemmed pipes, and tried to muffle their impatience. Interminable waiting was no help to their morale.

Elisha Chester, a man not easily discouraged, was again a Washington emissary to the Council, back with essentially the same proposals as before. Go West while there is still time. Presenting another letter from Secretary Cass, he warned of the government's waning patience, not suggesting in so many words that the use of force was imminent but hoping the Cherokees would come to that conclusion. The Council found Cass's message "dry and unwelcome," and as for Chester, the *Phoenix* reported, in the words of Hicks, that "only Lumpkin could be less popular with the Cherokees."

As before, Chester's proposition was rejected by the Cherokee majority, who, he wrote to Jackson, "always followed the advice of Ross and others who did their thinking for them." But the debate on the subject of removal, festering like an infected wound, was painfully reopened. John Ridge, now an avowed opponent of Ross's policy of standing firm, advocated sending delegates to Washington to discuss a treaty of removal with the President. Ridge's support was small; the proposal was defeated.

Instead the Council resolved to send to the capital a delegation composed of Richard Taylor, councilman John (Fox) Baldridge, and Joseph Vann, who would take up their problems with Jackson and Cass. John Ross would accompany the group as counselor. Perhaps by then his archenemy Jackson would have been defeated at the polls. Whig candidate Henry Clay had persistently opposed the President's Indian policy since the passage of the Removal Bill in 1830. His election should reverse the flood of Cherokee misfortunes.

Jackson swamped Clay in November by a popular majority of more than two to one, with 217 electoral votes against Clay's 49. William Wirt, also a candidate (7 electoral votes) and still preparing to fight for Worcester's rights in the Supreme Court, saw the Cherokees' foe as all but invincible. "My opinion is," said Wirt, "that he may be President for life if he chooses." So—one door was firmly closed, one hope was gone.

Governor Lumpkin sought to shut out any hope the Cherokees might see in Georgia's attitude. He was jolted to learn from his advisers that many influential citizens of Georgia—he called them "enemies of the state"—advocated sympathy and justice for the Indians. Perhaps these, as well as men like Ross, were at the root of Cherokee resistance. In his annual message to the legislature on November 6 he lumped them with the Cherokees in his excoriation:

Notwithstanding the extraordinary liberality of the propositions submitted to the Cherokees, and the kind spirit in which they were presented, the enemies of the President and of Georgia have so far succeeded as to prevent any satisfactory arrangement or treaty with them; and their reply to those liberal propositions evinces a most arrogant and uncompromising spirit.[7]

He suggested no way to break that spirit. But he had some ways in mind.

Pemberton Square in Boston on December 25 was like a Dickensian Christmas illustration. Silhouetted wreaths hung in the windows of the Mission Rooms; the trees of the park were etched in white; snow muffled the chimes of Trinity Church as they pealed their messages of Peace on Earth. All was calm. All was bright.

But all was solemn in the Mission Rooms despite the festive greenery and candles. Only a few weeks before, in what the Boston *Advertiser* called "the darkest hour of our history," members of the American Board had protested Jackson's defiance of the Supreme Court and had called on the President to intervene in the case of the still imprisoned missionaries.

Jackson replied that he would not intercede with Georgia on the matter; it was a state affair; he would not even comment on the case. He saw fit to add, regarding the missionaries, "I cannot refrain from observing that here, as in most other Countries, they are by their injudicious Zeal (to give it no harsher name) too apt *to make themselves tremendous obnoxious* to those among whom they are located."[8]

Now the Board members were confronted with another letter, this one just received from the imprisoned Samuel Worcester. Worcester and Butler were caught in a dilemma. Since Wirt had brought another suit to the Supreme Court, to force Georgia to obey the earlier mandate and release the prisoners, Governor Lumpkin had tried to wriggle out of the predicament. Through ex-Governor Forsyth he let it be known to the prisoners that they had only to withdraw their suit and be immediately freed.

What should their decision be? Worcester inquired of the Board. Their influence in the Cherokee Nation might be lessened by accepting a pardon without bringing Georgia to her knees—if the latter could be done. On the other hand, they had won their initial case in court; and since Georgia was willing to release them if they stopped all further action was there very much to lose? Each side would give a little, gain a little. Also, there was the possibility that by persisting in their suit, Georgia would be forced to join the "nullifiers," notably South Carolina, thus precipitating civil war.

The Board had no trouble reaching a decision. It would be expedient, they wrote to Worcester, for the missionaries to withdraw their suit. Theirs would be an "honorable pardon." But there was a grave provision: "the Cherokees must be advised that hope had ended; they must remove."

It would take two weeks for Worcester to receive their answer; another two weeks before the red tape was unraveled and the missionaries were released. The unknowing Cherokees would meanwhile send a wild turkey, a quill of chestnuts, and assorted sun-dried fruits to brighten their Christmas in the penitentiary.

For the Nation at large this wholly Christian fete was not a bright occasion. Added to winter's normal hardships was a burden altogether new. Brother Clauder of the Moravian Mission at Spring Place was first to feel the weight of it.

About the same time that the Board of Foreign Missions pondered Worcester's letter, Brother Clauder heard a pounding on the mission door. It was snowing too in Georgia on that Christmas Eve; a wet snow, one that melted fast and stranded travelers in sudden mountain avalanches. This might be a stranger in distress. Brother Clauder put aside the sermon he was writing and opened the door for his unexpected visitor.

A stranger stood outside the door, accompanied by two companions. He introduced himself as representing the "fortunate drawer of this place" and handed Clauder a bill for $150. "You can pay your rent to me," he said.

The puzzled Clauder told him there was some mistake. This was the Moravian Mission built on property that, if it belonged to anybody, belonged to Mr. Joseph Vann, whose plantation manor could be seen some distance off.

No, said the stranger; this was Georgia property on which the Moravians had been allowed to live by courtesy of the state. Now that freeloading period was over. The place had passed by lottery to a new, legitimate owner who was anxious to collect his rent.

Moravians did not, as a rule, slam doors in people's faces. But Brother Clauder slammed the door.

A few days later a wagonload of household furniture stood outside the mission and the driver told Clauder he was indeed the new ticket-holding owner and had come to take possession. He had decided not to rent the place but to live in it himself. He was ready to move in at once.

Again Brother Clauder slammed the door.

It was no use. When the lottery winner returned he brought with him eighteen friends and relatives. They forcibly crowded out the missionary and his family and filled the rooms with furniture of their own. They were only the vanguard of invaders. Clauder's house was to become a tavern serving the incoming residents of a thriving new community in what was henceforth Murray County, Georgia.

Spring Place had been the progenitor of mission stations in the territory, and for thirty years a Christian beacon in the wilderness. Yet the little Moravian chapel would no longer echo with "All Hail the Power of Jesus' Name." Wrote Brother Clauder in memoriam:

To abandon this time-honored spot where the first convert from the Cherokee tribes was baptized in 1810; where first the feet of them that brought glad tidings of great joy rested in their travel . . . and where so many prayers and tears had been offered to God and so many tokens of his goodness witnessed—this was a consideration far more painful than any amount of unrighteousness inflicted upon us by the miserable wretches around us. But the Lord gave us enlargement.[9]

The land rush was on, more devastating than the depredations of the Pony Club. For these were quasi-legal owners, white citizens who came with winning tickets in their hands. They might be polite, and often were. But law was law, and the state had made them the new owners of whatever land, whatever farm or house, the lottery had awarded them. Though to the Cherokees it was legal thievery, there was no court of last resort they could appeal to.

"The beautiful and beloved country of the Cherokees," wrote Elijah Hicks in the *Phoenix* of January 19, 1833, "is now passing into the occupancy of the Georgians . . . settlers, and droves of land hunters, to which the Indians daily cry, and it is literally, 'Robery! Robery!'"

Not Boudinot's equal in spelling, punctuation, or clarity of language, the editor continued:

This crusade on our rights forms a new era in the history of the United States by which the Cherokees are denationalized, treaties destroyed, the legislation of the Congress to carry them into effect annulled, and the faith of the republic fled to the western wilds.[10]

Like some of Elijah's prose, it seemed as if anarchy had taken over. Men returned from their fields to find wives and children packing their belongings, and strangers in possession of their farms. Or they were presented with impossible bills for rent due on the homes that they had built and owned and which they would now be allowed to live in only if they henceforth leased the property from new American landlords.

It dawned like thunder on the Nation that the loss of their country was no longer a threat but becoming a reality. Hordes of white men, veterans, widows of veterans who had never owned more than the clothes on their backs, found themselves by grace of the lottery in possession of the choicest homes, the choicest plantations in the Nation. Where force was used to evict protesting families, the Georgia Guard looked the other way. If fraud and trickery were employed to deprive a Cherokee of his home, no Indian, by Georgia law, could testify against the culprits.

"The usual scenes which our afflicted people experience are dreadfully increased since your departure," John Ridge wrote to Ross in Washington on February 1833, "& they are robbed & whipped by the whites almost every day."[11]

Though Ridge and Ross were openly divided in their views, there was at this time no hostility between them. They were bound by a common goal: the good of the Nation. Ridge, in his letter, even cautioned the chief to be on guard against the continuing subversive operations of John Walker, Jr., who was believed to be working with the federal authorities to form a splinter group within the Nation.

"In this movement I attach no consequence so far as that individual is concerned," he wrote to Ross, "but it affords to my mind a clear view of the extent that Jackson will go to divide our Nation."[12]

But in cooperating with his chief to this extent, Ridge was not retreating from his own position. He urged Ross and his delegates collectively to keep an open mind on the subject of removal. Though acknowledging that "the discussion of this subject may be disagreeable to you," he continued:

But Sir, I have the right to address you as the Chief of the whole Cherokee Nation upon whom rests, under Heaven the highest responsibility—the well being of the whole people, and . . . I know you are capable of acting the part of the statesman in this trying crisis of our affairs. After we all know upon consultation in Council that we can't be a Nation here, I hope we shall attempt to establish somewhere else. *Where,* the wisdom of the Nation must try to find.[13]

Places other than the Arkansas Territory had, in fact, been variously considered, if indeed the Cherokees were forced to emigrate. British Columbia, for one, or Mexico; or Texas when and if that province became independent—and right now Sam Houston, the Cherokee Raven, was agitating for that independence and expected a break with Mexico at any moment. But these proposals seemed suspiciously like blackmail, at best taunts to the United States: "If you desert us and uproot us, we—perhaps followed by other great Indian tribes—shall pledge to a foreign government that same unstinted loyalty and service that we gave to the United States."

In Washington, Ross did not ignore John Ridge's counsel. Firm as he was in his own attitude against removal, he at least discussed the matter with both

Cass and Jackson. And he listened to Senator Frelinghuysen, who had championed the Cherokees' position some years earlier. The senator had learned of Worcester's acceptance of a pardon from the Georgia governor, and felt it spelled the end of meaningful resistance. Reluctantly he too concluded that removal was the only answer.

In February, Ross had several meetings with the President. It was some time since they had met alone, and face to face. Jackson was a little more gaunt, a little grayer, and suffering from the extraction of a bullet in his shoulder. Ross was a little stouter, with thinner hair, and lines of worry splaying the corners of his eyes. Both were battle-scarred, despite the difference in their ages—which established between them a sort of cautious camaraderie. Jackson extended his hand, Ross took it, and the two sat down to talk things over.

Wasting no time on amenities, Jackson bluntly made an offer of $2,500,000 for all Cherokee lands in the states of Georgia, Alabama, and Tennessee, plus equivalent acreage in the Arkansas, with his guarantee that their borders would be held inviolable in the West. When Ross remained silent, the President raised the ante to $3,000,000. Ross replied curtly that the gold mines alone were worth more than that, and asked the President, "If you cannot protect us in the East, how can we believe that you will protect us in the West?"

Ross returned with his delegates in April and called a special Council at Red Clay for early May. To this assembly he reported Jackson's offer of $3,000,000—they had heard about it through the grapevine anyway—and confessed that their mission to the President had ended in a stalemate.

He did have, however, one happy development to report. In their many interviews with Secretary Cass they had complained bitterly about Georgia's distribution of their lands by lottery. They had especially protested the highhanded methods of the white usurpers who seized their homes and property on the questionable legal pretense of a winning ticket. They suggested that these "fortunate drawers" be rewarded, if they had to be, by federal lands elsewhere; or that the winning tickets should be purchased by the government.

Now Ross was able to report to the Council on a letter just received from Elbert Herring, Commissioner of Indian Affairs. Apparently acting on Cass's orders, Herring informed the chief that federal troops would be sent "to the assailed parts of your country for the purpose of expelling and keeping out intruders." If the delegates had got nowhere on the matter of removal, they had seemingly checked the tragic consequences of the Georgia lottery.[14]

Then the bomb fell. John Ridge got up to speak. If he had shown consideration for Ross's views before, he did not now. First of all, he said, the chief had misconstrued Herring's letter. In referring to "the assailed parts of your country," Herring did not mean the Cherokee Nation as a whole. As early as April, Ridge had learned from Governor Lumpkin—with whom he was becoming suspiciously friendly—that troops would indeed be sent. But not to Cherokee lands in Georgia; only to Tennessee and North Carolina. So the depredations which the Georgia lottery imposed would not be checked.

Further, Ridge took the chief to task for not accepting Jackson's offer. It might have been the best deal that the Cherokees could get. Why was it dismissed so lightly? Then, according to Benjamin Currey, who made a point of spying on these Councils, Ridge "depicted, in an eloquent and impressive manner, the forlorn situation of the country." He argued "with great force" that the Nation should make a treaty of removal with the government, without "unnecessary delay."[15]

What had been simply a division of opinion in the General Council now became a battle between organized, opposing forces, with the lines more clearly drawn. Siding with Ridge were Elias Boudinot and Ross's nephew William Shorey Coodey; also of course John's father, Major Ridge, Boudinot's brother Stand Watie, and David Vann, plus a score of their adherents. These drafted a petition to be presented to the Council, demanding that Ross show cause why his policy of obstinate resistance to removal should not be retracted.

It was an open break; and tensions became too high for calm debate. Before things got out of hand a compromise was reached. The petition, the whole matter of removal, would be postponed until the annual October Council, when "an immense concourse of people" could be present. By then tempers would have had time to cool. But would they?

Samuel Worcester was back at New Echota, home again with the devoted Ann, the worshipful Sophia Sawyer, and the wide-eyed daughters Elizah and Sarah, who had grown like daisies in his absence. His and Butler's release from the penitentiary had been accompanied by much face-saving fanfare. Governor Lumpkin—now signing his documents "Commander in Chief of the Army and Navy of this State, and of the Militia thereof," apparently to impress the federal government at this time of threatened insurrection—announced that the missionaries had gained their freedom by appealing "to the magnanimity of the State."

In other words, the Supreme Court decision had had nothing to do with Worcester's pardon and release. The prisoners had surrendered to the power of the governor. Georgia, wrote Lumpkin, had not retreated from "the triumphant ground which the State finally occupies in relation to this subject . . . as has been sufficiently attested . . . especially in the recent overwhelming re-election of President Jackson, the known defender of the State throughout this controversy."[16]

Editor Elijah Hicks appropriately took the opposite view, writing in the *Phoenix* two weeks after the event: "The decision of the high court, touching the right of the Cherokees, is by no means weakened by the discharge of the missionaries from their confinement." It was up to the United States likewise to honor the decision and protect the Cherokees' rights "according to treaties." But Elijah's words had a hollow sound. Jackson had long since announced the stand of the United States. Little had been accomplished by the missionaries' martyrdom. They knew it, and what was sadly apparent to them, the Cherokees also knew it.

Looking around him, Worcester observed the sad signs of deterioration that had scarred the people in his absence like a grim disease. Their once unshakable faith—in their God, their institutions, and their government—was in danger of complete collapse. Of what use was it to tend their fields, repair their homes, and care for their livestock if all these were to be taken from them by the Georgia lottery? Sloth was not a Cherokee trait, but indifference and despair gave birth to sloth. Their spirit had grown slovenly; they had let down their guard; and the white man had moved in with bribe and bottle.

Miss Sophia Sawyer also saw the signs from the very doorstep of her school. "Whiskey has been brought to the playground and children invited to drink by men of our own color and country," she wrote to the Board in Boston. Her pupils had been sufficiently disciplined to resist temptation; but "as it respects the parents, there have been many intemperate, all our efforts have hitherto been fruitless. My very soul sickens with the promise of the drunkard, and as to the retailer, it seems a still more hopeless case."[17]

Under such conditions how could the missionaries, especially one in such a key position as Worcester, continue to work effectively for the redemption of the Nation? Though Boudinot was of course no longer with the *Phoenix,* Elijah Hicks offered the press facilities for publishing, in Cherokee, the Acts of the Apostles. But Boudinot was essential to this work—in fact, Worcester got $100 from Boston to keep him employed as translator of the Gospels—and Boudinot himself was in a delicate position.

Worcester's alliance with Boudinot had always been a ticklish association. A number of times David Greene, whose help in supplying the press and type entitled him to speak freely, warned Worcester that Boudinot's political views were often offensive to the Board of Foreign Missions. His attacks on the anti-Cherokee stand of Georgia and the President, for instance. "It is hardly worth while," wrote Greene to Worcester, "to tell an enemy how he may vex & injure you most effectively."[18]

Now that Boudinot had shifted his position and veered to the side of John Ridge in supporting Indian removal, perhaps he appeared less offensive to the Board, which itself had concluded that removal was the only viable solution. But the turnaround left Worcester on the horns of a dilemma. In a letter to Greene in mid-June 1833, he acknowledged this predicament. He noted that those Cherokees who favored a treaty were "quite a minority" and "there is much prejudice against them among the mass of the people. On account of my intimacy with Mr. Boudinot . . . some of the prejudice is directed against me."[19]

Two weeks before, he had gone to a nearby village to preach, taking Boudinot with him "to interpret and exhort." Despite advance announcements, only fourteen Cherokees attended, and these had come largely from curiosity. Worcester was told by Stand Watie that a rumor was circulating to the effect that he and Boudinot were linked in "some sinister design," that "Mr. Worcester was still under bond to Georgia, and would probably be glad to purchase his liberty by promoting the objects of the state."

Thus, Worcester reported to Greene, "the people were left to infer that the design of our meeting was to encourage emigration to Arkansas." It was this that had deterred any sizable crowd from attending.

Yet he and Boudinot had long been a team together, each essential to the other. Apart from matters of friendship and loyalty, they could not be divided —even though this alliance had cost the valued confidence of John Ross, to whom Worcester wore the stigma of a turncoat.

In a sense he was already in exile. He would go on with his work, preaching to smaller congregations and continuing his translations. But he was living and working on borrowed time. Before too long, he knew, as did the Board in Boston, that the missionaries would move West with the Cherokees. That much seemed inescapable. The only question was, when? Perhaps they should make the journey first, blaze the trail to that uncertain future, and have the spiritual fires burning when the Cherokees arrived.

The October Council met again at Red Clay, Tennessee. That state had resisted Georgia's plea that she extend her laws over the Cherokees within her boundaries. Alabama had made a gesture of following Georgia's action, but—in contrast to Corn Tassel's case—the judge ruled that the state had no authority to prosecute a Cherokee offender, even within Alabama's borders. The emergency capital at Red Clay thus remained immune to interference if not altogether free of Georgia spies and federal agents.

Benjamin F. Currey, the enrolling agent, was present at the Council as observer for Secretary Cass; and since the *Phoenix* had grown wary of reporting dissidence within the Council, Currey's accounts were often the only ones to reach the War Department. They were passed on by Cass to Wilson Lumpkin at the governor's request; so that while Red Clay remained a sanctuary from political harassment, it was also something of a goldfish bowl.

Picking up the threads left dangling from the August Council, John Ross wove them into a plea for unity. The will of the people should prevail, he said in his opening address, "and whatever measure is adopted by the majority for the public good [it is] the duty of the minority to yield and unite in support of the measure; this is the rule of order sanctioned by patriotism and virtue."[20]

While the prompting seemed directed at John Ridge and the pro-removal faction, Ridge was unimpressed. As President of the National Committee he could disagree with Ross with some impunity. He recommended that a delegation, hand-picked by the Council, be sent to Washington with the specific goal of making a treaty for removal, under the best terms possible for the Cherokees. He had made the same proposal just a year ago, and it had been defeated. It was defeated now. Instead, the Council voted to send to the capital "a Delegation in whose wisdom and integrity we can confide." It was composed of members of the anti-treaty party, becoming known as the National Party. Headed by John Ross, the group included Richard Taylor, Daniel McCoy, John Timson, and Hair Conrad, the last two being younger members of the General Council.

In drafting the procedure to be followed by the delegation—and John Ridge had a hand in these directions—it was clearly stated that the group would have no power to negotiate a treaty of whatever sort. Its responsibility would be to place "the subject of our difficulties" before Congress, "and if possible to draw from it a favorable Resolution for the relief of our affected Nation." An ill-defined target. But Governor Lumpkin was sufficiently alarmed to warn Secretary Cass that, since the deputation was not empowered to treat for removal, it was "wholly undeserving the courtesy and marked attention of the official Authorities in Washington."

The Ross delegation left for the capital the following month. And with their departure a strange event occurred.

Three A.M., November 13, 1833.

Stars fell on Alabama. They also fell on North Carolina, Tennessee, and Georgia—a shower of shooting lights and meteors the like of which had never before been witnessed, except perhaps by Tennessee veterans who had seen the British rockets at the Battle of New Orleans. "The world was literally striped with fire," wrote Elijah Hicks from New Echota, where the sky blazed with unearthly light.[21]

Surely this portended something for the Cherokees. The more ignorant mountain Indians ran to their medicine men for reassurance. The *Phoenix* advised its readers that "this profusion of lights" and its possible cause was a matter for astronomers, and let it go at that. Miss Sophia Sawyer encouraged her pupils to search for an explanation in the *Celestial Atlas* sent on her request by the American Board of Foreign Missions.

The star shower passed, or the world slipped out from under it. But a whisper of anxiety remained, like the scampering of feet of fleeing animals. Something was underfoot to make the earth uneasy and the branches seem to quiver. The Cherokees looked at one another as at passing strangers. The old feeling of mass trust and confidence was gone. Some sort of end was near, if only they could see what sort of end.

Near the Indian Agency on the Hiwassee River the stockades were going up. Cherokee residents of Hiwassee Old Town watched Benjamin Currey's troops cut down the hickories, split the trunks, and shape them into pointed staves. These, planted upright, formed a colony of twenty-eight oblong pens or barracks. Here the latest batch of voluntary émigrés would soon assemble for the journey West, and another portion of the lifeblood of the Nation would be drained away. Currey estimated that 1,200 Cherokees would be ready to embark in early 1834.

Either in resignation or in protest against Ross's handling of the Council, John and Major Ridge, along with Boudinot and Stand Watie, enrolled for emigration. This did not mean that they would leave at once or even soon; they were simply declaring their intentions. Ridge wrote to Governor Lumpkin of the action they had taken, and asked that their respective homes be immune from seizure by lottery winners until they actually left the country. Ridge for one would remain in the Nation until he was certain that his followers, those deciding to emigrate, were fairly treated by the agents, duly compensated for their properties, adequately provisioned for the journey West.

Others among the prospective émigrés were following curious courses of their own. Shortly after John Ross left for Washington his younger brother

Andrew followed him. As amoral and devious as John was ethical and upright, Andrew was heavily in debt and needed money. He may have felt some of the perverse antagonism that a man feels toward an older brother. In any event, he signed up for removal, went to work on Currey's payroll, and began rounding up recruits for the pro-treaty faction. In Washington his purpose was to counteract his brother's efforts by making a secret treaty of removal with the President.

Unlike John Ross, unlike the Ridges, Andrew had no standing in the General Council. He represented no one but himself. He did have the backing of such men as William Hicks, who had formed a splinter group of those resigned to emigrating but intent on getting for themselves the best terms possible. This was enough to get an audience with Jackson, who saw his tactics of divide and conquer working of their own accord.

Face to face with Andrew Ross, however, the President realized he was dealing with a lightweight. A deal made with Andrew would never be agreed to by the Cherokees. Nor would it stand up in the Senate. He suggested as tactfully as possible that the free-lance emissary go back home and return with some compatriots of more authority. Then they could talk business.

Andrew followed the advice and, returning to the Nation, persuaded Major Ridge and Elias Boudinot to accompany him back to Washington. The Ridge was not enthusiastic about Andrew's self-appointed mission. On the other hand, he and Boudinot were reluctant to leave Andrew on his own. Meanwhile, from the Arkansas came yet another delegation, appointed by Chief John Jolly. The Raven's foster father was concerned about how this threatened emigration from the East might affect his people in the West. They would need more land, more guarantees, more annuities, more protection from their hostile neighbors.

Were the problem not so serious, there was an element of farce in these assorted delegations scrambling for attention—all with conflicting goals, darting in and out of offices, avoiding one another. The Ridge took time to sit for a portrait by artist Charles Bird King. Hung later in the hall of the Bureau of Indian Affairs, it showed the venerable chieftain elegantly dressed in dark-blue satin-collared waistcoat, buff vest, wing collar, and bow tie, his stern bronze features crowned with an aureole of white curly hair.

This duty accomplished, The Ridge had some second thoughts on Andrew Ross. He and Boudinot concluded, as Jackson had, that Andrew was somewhat like a chicken with its head off, frantic for action but lacking in direction. They withdrew their support from his deputation, and returned to their respective homes. Jackson was left unhappily with Andrew and a few anonymous Indians on his hands. He was not averse to dealing with a minority, but was this minority worthy of his personal attention? He solved this problem—along with the problem of what to do with former Secretary Eaton since the latter's enforced retirement after the Peggy O'Neill affair—by appointing Eaton his special commissioner to make some sort of deal with Andrew Ross.

Parenthetically, and to dispense with Andrew, Eaton met with the group in his office, drafted and signed with them a treaty by which the Cherokee Nation ceded its eastern lands in exchange for territory in the West. The terms, explicit and reasonably generous, are not worth documenting. When the treaty reached the Senate for ratification it was rejected, as it should have been, for not having the sanction of the Nation as a whole.

If this comedy of errors accomplished nothing else, it prompted Ross's delegates to work more seriously toward a settlement. National unity was being eroded; Ross's authority, still strong, still backed by the majority of Cherokees, could not buck fate forever. The delegation met with Secretary Cass, and Ross presented several tentative proposals.

Supposing, said Ross, the Cherokees ceded a portion of their eastern lands to satisfy, in part, the claims of Georgia. Would the government guarantee them protection for the rest? No, said Cass, such a guarantee would clash with state authority. Then, supposing the Cherokees applied for citizenship to the various states within whose boundaries their territory rested. Would they be allowed to retain their homes and enjoy the rights of other United States citizens? No, said Cass, nothing would satisfy the government but total removal to the West.

With the door thus closed on further negotiation, John Ross prepared to leave the capital. Once again his mission had been fruitless; he would have nothing to tell his people that was reassuring. Though not deserving a hero's welcome, he wondered what sort of reception he would get when he returned to Head of Coosa.

"Rich Joe" Vann, had he been free to do so, could have told him. But Vann had all that he could handle—and a little more.

12

Death of the *Phoenix*

"RICH JOE" VANN, in the winter of 1834, had every reason to expect the worst. He had witnessed, not long before, the occupation of the Moravian Mission a short distance from the broad veranda of his home at Spring Place. As one who employed a white overseer for his vast estate, Vann was guilty of breaking Georgia's law against unlicensed aliens. As a member of Ross's party advocating Cherokee resistance to removal, Vann was automatically an enemy of Georgians. One way or another, by lottery or by outright confiscation, they would get his property.

Anticipating trouble, Vann had moved with his family into an upstairs section of the house and turned a guest room over to Spencer Riley, a former sheriff of the county. Riley's presence was something of a mystery. Was he there to protect the Vanns? Or was he there to protect his own contrived claim to the property? Vann himself found it better to keep his mouth shut. Like Ross, he believed in nonviolence and reliance on the law.

It was Colonel William Bishop of the Georgia Guard who arrived with the eviction notice. Bishop, it seemed, was anxious to secure the property for his brother Absalom, who accompanied him on this mission as a member of the Guard. Riley either was possessed with a sudden sense of right and wrong or concluded he would keep the Vann house for himself. He came to the head of the free-hanging stairs, shotgun in hand, and challenged Bishop to a duel.

Bishop refused, and the fight exploded in true western frontier style. According to Riley, "They fired upon me and fell back; I then fired too. Their shot slightly wounded me in my hand and arms, and immediately after, ten or twelve muskets were fired at me, but being protected by the stairs, the shot did not take effect . . . they aimed at the spot they supposed I was and shot the banisters to pieces."[1]

One of the Guard threw a firebrand onto the stairs to smoke the sheriff out. Riley threw it back and resumed the unequal battle, when "a rifle was fired by

CHEROKEE ALPHABET.

CHARACTERS AS ARRANGED BY THE INVENTOR.

R D W Ꮀ G Ꮼ Ꮤ Ᏸ Ᏼ Ꮅ Ꭹ Ᏺ Ᏻ Ꮾ Ᏸ Ᏸ Ꮢ Ꮂ Ꮇ Ꮪ Ꮳ ꮳ

Ꭳ W B Ꮼ Ꮥ Ꮽ Ꮂ Ꭶ Ꭺ Ꭻ Ꭻ Ꭹ Ꮄ Ꮂ Ꮐ Ꮹ Ꭷ Ꮜ Ꭴ Ꭲ Z Ꮓ

Ꭱ Ꭱ Ꮒ Ꮢ Ꮎ Ꮅ Ꮛ Ꭼ Ꭼ Ꮦ Ꮏ Ꮕ Ꭶ Ꮖ Ꮛ Ꭻ J Ꭼ Ꮿ Ꮂ Ꮎ Ꭶ

Ꮐ Ꭹ Ꮑ Ꭼ Ꮝ Ꮝ Ꭼ Ꭹ Ꭲ Ꭴ Ꮗ Ꮗ Ꮗ Ꮗ Ꮝ Ꮲ H Ꮜ Ꮄ Ꭷ Ꮫ

L Ꮏ Ꭴ Ꮷ Ꭴ Ꮛ

CHARACTERS SYSTEMATICALLY ARRANGED WITH THE SOUNDS.

D a	R e	T i	Ꮿ o	Ꮜ u	i v
Ꮟ ga Ꮒ ka	Ꮄ ge	Ꭹ gi	A go	J gu	E gv
Ꮂ ha	Ꮅ he	Ꭿ hi	Ꮅ ho	Ꮦ hu	Ꮁ hv
W la	Ꮣ le	Ꮅ li	Ꮎ lo	M lu	Ꮄ lv
Ꮢ ma	Ꮷ me	H mi	Ꮝ mo	Ꭹ mu	
Ꮎ na Ꮏ hna Ꮐ nah Ꮑ ne	Ꮒ ni	Z no	Ꮕ nu	Ꮚ nv	
Ꮖ qua	Ꮹ que	Ꮗ qui	Ꮘ quo	Ꮚ quu	Ꮛ quv
Ꮝ s Ꮜ sa	Ꮪ se	Ꮢ si	Ꮠ so	Ꮡ su	R sv
Ꮮ da W ta	Ꮫ de Ꮴ te	Ꮧ di Ꮨ tih	Ꭺ do	Ꮪ du	Ꮫ dv
Ꮬ dla Ꮭ tla	Ꮮ tle	Ꭷ tli	Ꮯ tlo	Ꮰ tlu	P tlv
Ꮳ tsa	Ꮴ tse	Ꮢ tsi	K tso	Ꮷ tsu	Ꮳ tsv
Ꮹ wa	Ꮺ we	Ꮻ wi	Ꮼ wo	Ꮽ wu	Ꮾ wv
Ꮿ ya	Ᏸ ye	Ᏹ yi	Ᏺ yo	Ᏻ yu	B yv

SOUNDS REPRESENTED BY VOWELS.

a	as	*a* in *father*,	or	short as	*a* in *rival*,
e	as	*a* in *hate*,	or	short as	*e* in *met*,
i	as	*i* in *pique*,	or	short as	*i* in *pit*,
o	as	*aw* in *law*,	or	short as	*o* in *not*,
u	as	*oo* in *fool*,	or	short as	*u* in *pull*,
v	as	*u* in *but* nasalized.			

CONSONANT SOUNDS.

g nearly as in English, but approaching to k. d nearly as in English, but approaching to t. h, k, l, m, n, q, s, t, w, y, as in English.

Syllables beginning with g, except Ꮝ, have sometimes the power of k; Ꭺ, Ꮝ, Ꮠ, are sometimes sounded to, tu, tv; and syllables written with tl, except Ꮭ, sometimes vary to dl.

The Cherokee alphabet invented by Sequoyah, with approximate sounds in English.

Print shop and office of the Cherokee Phoenix *at New Echota, Georgia.*
HISTORIC PRESERVATION SECTION, GEORGIA DEPARTMENT OF NATURAL RESOURCES

Interior of the print shop at New Echota, showing the desk at which Elias Boudinot worked and a portion of the type frames.
HISTORIC PRESERVATION SECTION, GEORGIA DEPARTMENT OF NATURAL RESOURCES

CWY JCAUOA.

CHEROKEE PHŒNIX.

PROTECTION

VOL. I. NEW ECHOTA, WEDNESDAY MAY 14, 1828. NO. 12.

EDITED BY ELIAS BOUDINOTT
PRINTED WEEKLY BY
ISAAC H. HARRIS,
FOR THE CHEROKEE NATION.

At $2 50 if paid in advance, $3 in six months, or $3 50 if paid at the end of the year.

To subscribers who can read only the Cherokee language the price will be $2.00 in advance, or $2,50 to be paid within the year.

Every subscription will be considered as continued unless subscribers give notice to the contrary before the commencement of a new year.

Any person procuring six subscribers, and becoming responsible for the payment, shall receive a seventh gratis.

Advertisements will be inserted at seventy-five cents per square for the first insertion, and thirty-seven and a half cents for each continuance; longer ones in proportion.

☞ All letters addressed to the Editor, post paid, will receive due attention.

AGENTS FOR THE CHEROKEE PHŒNIX.

The following persons are authorized to receive subscriptions and payments for the Cherokee Phœnix.

Henry Hill, Esq. Treasurer of the A. B. C. F. M. Boston, Mass.
George M. Tracy, Agent of the A. B. C. F. M. New York.
Rev. A. D. Eddy, Canandaigua, N. Y.
Pollard & Converse, Richmond, Va.
Rev. James Campbell, Beaufort, S. C.
Col. George Smith, Statesville, W. T.
Rev. Benney Roberts—Powal Me.
Mr. Thos. R. Gold, an itinerant Gentleman.

CHEROKEE LAWS.

[CONTINUED.]

New Town, Nov. 8 1825.

Resolved by the National Committee and Council, That the law authorizing the appointment of light horse companies, passed at Browns Town on the 11th day of September, 1808, be, and the same is hereby repealed, and that in lieu of light horse companies, a marshal, sheriff, deputy sheriff and two constables, shall be chosen & appointed for each district, in the following manner; to wit:

The marshals to be elected by the national Com. and the principal sheriffs to be elected by the people in their respective districts; and the two constables by the people within their particular bounds, for the term of two years. The marshals and sheriffs shall enter into bond and give two or more good and sufficient securities in a penal sum of not less than one thousand dollars. The sheriffs to appoint their own deputies, and for whose conduct they shall also be held responsible and bound. The constables shall enter into bond and give two good securities in the penal sum of two hundred dollars. The duties of the marshals and sheriffs shall be to make collections of all just debts, such as notes of hand, liquidated accounts and judgements, & to arrest horse thieves and other rogues and murderers for trial, according to law.

The duties of the constables shall be the same as that of the marshals and sheriffs, but they shall be confined within their respective bounds in exercising their official duties; and each of the above named officers are hereby authorized, when in pursuit of criminals, to summons as many men as may be necessary to arrest such criminals, and any person or persons refusing to obey, without any reasonable excuse, such summons, he or they shall forfeit and pay a fine of twenty-five dollars for every such offence: to be recoverable in the same way and manner as all other debts, and the fines so collected, shall be paid into the national treasury. The person or persons obeying such summons, upon presenting the officer's certificate before the national treasury, for the service so performed, shall be entitled to receive one dollar per day for the time so engaged from actual necessity. The constables, when executing their duties in arresting & conducting criminals to the place of trial, shall also be entitled to one dollar per day for the time actually engaged. Each marshal shall be entitled to receive forty dollars, and each principal sheriff shall be entitled to receive thirty dollars per annum, for their services from the public funds, in addition to their fees of eight per cent. for collections. The deputy sheriffs and constables shall also be entitled to receive eight per cent. for collections.

By order.
JNO. ROSS, Pres't N. Com.
MAJOR RIDGE, Speaker.
his
Approved—PATH ✕ KILLER.
mark.
A. M'COY, Clerk of N. Com.
E. BOUDINOTT, Clerk N. Council.

New Town, Nov. 9, 1825.

Resolved by the National Committee and Council, That all written wills, bearing the signature of the testator and signed by one or two respectable witnesses, and the same appearing to the satisfaction of the court of the district wherein the testator lived, or where most of his estate may be situated, that it is the last will & testament of the deceased such will and testament, shall be valid and binding to all intents and purposes.

Be it further resolved, That nothing shall be construed in the foregoing, so as to impair or destroy the validity of any will having no witnesses, which may be found among the valuable papers of the deceased, bearing his or her signature, which will and signature, shall be satisfactorily proved to be the hand writing of the deceased.

Be it further resolved, That nuncupative wills, where witnesses are called, and the testator, in the presence of two or three respectable persons, at his or her last sickness, make known his or her will, and one of the witnesses being a disinterested person, such nuncupative wills being committed to writing in ten days after the testators decease, and the same appearing to the satisfaction of the district court to be agreeable to the testators last will and testament, such wills shall also be valid and binding.

Be it further resolved, That where a person possessing property and dies intestate, and having a wife and children, the property of the deceased, shall be equally divided among his lawful and acknowledged children, allowing the widow a share with the children, after all just debts of the deceased shall have been paid by those obtaining letters of administration, agreeably to law, and in case the deceased leave a wife without children, then in that case, the widow shall be entitled to receive one fourth of the estate, after said estate shall have been freed from incumbrance of all just and lawful demands, and the residue of the estate to go to his nearest kin; and in case a woman claiming and having exclusive right to property, dies and leaves a husband and children, her property shall revert to her children and husband, in the same manner as above stated and provided for.

By order of the National Com.
JNO ROSS, Pres't N. Com.
MAJOR RIDGE, Speaker.
his
PATH ✕ KILLER.
mark.
CHARLES R. HICKS.
A. M'COY, Clerk N. Com.
E. BOUDINOTT, Clk. N. Council.

New Town, Nov. 10, 1825.

Resolved by the National Committee and Council, That any person or persons, whatsoever, who shall lay violent hands upon any female, by force, bly attempting to ravish her chastity contrary to her consent, abusing her person and committing a rape upon such female, he or they, so offending, upon conviction before any of the district or circuit judges, for the first offence, shall be punished with fifty lashes upon the bare back and the left ear cropped off close to the head; for the second offence, one hundred lashes and the other ear cut off; for the third offence, death.

Be it further resolved, That any woman or women, making evidence against any man, and falsely accusing him of having laid violent hands upon any woman, with intent of committing a rape upon her person, and sufficient proof having been adduced in any of the district or circuit judges, to refute the testimony of such woman or women, she or they so offending, shall be punished with twenty-five stripes upon her or their bare back, to be inflicted by any of the marshals, sheriffs or constables.

By order,
JOHN ROSS, Pres't N. Com.
MAJOR RIDGE, Speaker.
his
Approved—PATH ✕ KILLER.
mark.
CHARLES R. HICKS.
A. M'COY, Clerk N. Com.
E. BOUDINOTT, Clk. N. Coun.

New Town, Nov. 10, 1825.

Whereas, it has been represented to the general council, that much injury is sustained by the inhabitants living on the boundary lines, from citizens of the United States, feeding and keeping their stock of property on Cherokee lands, whereby horses, cattle, hogs &c. belonging to the citizens of this nation, are exposed to be taken off by such persons, trespassing; therefore.

Resolved by the National Committee and Council, That the circuit judges are hereby authorised and directed, to appoint an assistant ranger in their respective districts, which border on the boundary lines of the United States, whose residence shall be nearest to said boundary line, and whose duty it shall be, solely to pay strict attention to such trespassers herein complained of, & to forwarn the frontier inhabitants of the United States, in the adjoining counties, against placing, keeping and feeding their horses, cattle, hogs, sheep or goats on Cherokee lands; and to take up, post, and dispose of, all such property which may be found within their respective bounds, agreeably to the laws respecting estrays, and any citizen or citizens of the United States reclaiming and proving away any such property, and be unable to produce satisfactory proof, that he, she or they, did not wilfully place such property on Cherokee lands, to feed and graze thereon, the assistant ranger, in that case, is hereby authorised and required, to exact a fine of two dollars for every horse, gelding or mare, and one dollar for every head of black cattle, and twenty-five cents for every head of swine, sheep or goats, so proven away. Such fines shall be in addition to the fees allowed by law to the rangers for their posting, keeping and selling estrays; but in case sufficient proof can be adduced to shew that such property was not wilfully placed on Cherokee lands to feed or graze thereon, and that such property had merely strayed thereon unknown to the owner or owners; then in that case, the fine herein imposed, shall not be exacted; excepting the necessary expenses and fees allowed by law in such cases.

Be it further resolved, That the assistant ranger is hereby required to observe and pay strict attention to the same rules and regulations required of rangers by law, and who shall also be entitled to the same fees of eight per cent. on the amount collected for the fines herein imposed, the remainder for the benefit of the national treasury.

By order of the National Committee,
JNO. ROSS, Pres't N. Com.
MAJOR RIDGE, Speaker.
PATH ✕ KILLER.
A. M'COY, Clerk, N. Com.
ELIJAH HICKS, Clerk N. Council.

The front page of the Cherokee Phoenix *carried three columns of English text compared with two in Cherokee; Sequoyah's syllabary generally required less space to convey the same information.*

LIBRARY OF CONGRESS

Andrew Jackson, President of the United States from 1828 to 1836, put all his weight of office behind Indian removal to the West.

Dr. Elizur Butler, imprisoned with Samuel Worcester for his refusal to submit to Georgia's coercion of the missionaries.

The home of Major Ridge, a Cherokee landmark of unpretentious elegance, still stands near present-day Rome in Georgia.

Samuel Worcester's house at New Echota (here restored) was almost a duplicate of that built by Elias Boudinot, his neighbor in the Cherokee capital.

George Lowrey, Assistant to Principal Chief John Ross throughout much of the latter's lengthy term in office.

THOMAS GILCREASE INSTITUTE, TULSA, OKLAHOMA

Brown's Indian Queen Hotel, a popular Washington caravansary, was the usual headquarters of visiting Cherokees who came to the

Absalom Bishop; the ball struck my gun and split one part of it striking glancingly on my forehead . . . fragments of it wounding me on several other places on my face. Several more muskets were fired at me . . . wounding me severely . . ."

Riley's last-ditch stand was futile. Half alive, he was trundled off to jail, where he recovered from his wounds. Joseph Vann accepted the inevitable. He enrolled for emigration to the West, meanwhile settling his family in a dirt-floor cabin near Red Clay, Tennessee. Because of his wealth and influence he was able to get some compensation from the federal government for the confiscated property on his estate, but none whatever for the land—to which the Cherokees themselves, by tribal policy, laid no claim of private ownership.

It was the winter of the dispossessed. A hard time to be rendered homeless, and the worst of times to journey through snow in search of shelter. In February the Haweiss Mission and home of Elizur Butler fell to the winning ticket of a lucky drawer in the lottery; and Butler moved with Lucy and his children up to Brainerd to find temporary refuge. Later he would join the Vanns at Red Clay. The following month Samuel Worcester was ordered to surrender his home at New Echota to Colonel William Harden, "or whoever he may put forward to take possession of same." His superiors in Boston offered scant comfort with the advice that "you had better get along as well as you can, if you are driven from your home, till next fall, & then cross the Mississippi." The Worcesters, with yet another baby daughter, followed the Butlers up to Brainerd.[2]

One by one the houses fell like ripe plums to the hungry Georgians. John Martin, former Treasurer of the Nation, was turned out of his home in mid-winter to make room for the lucky winner of his property, while Richard Taylor was forced to pay $200 a month rent in order to live in his house until he could find a refuge elsewhere. Worcester's neighbor, Elijah Hicks, knew he was living on borrowed time. He had been hauled into court for libel, having charged in the *Phoenix* that invading Georgians were raping Cherokee women. Elijah had reason to wonder how long his newspaper would survive. Released from jail on $2,000 bail, Hicks made a small gesture of defiance. He moved his name from the masthead of the paper and put it up higher, in bold type directly underneath the title *Cherokee Phoenix*.

Neither Hicks nor his neighbors, however, survived the clean sweep of New Echota's proud homes. His own two-story mansion and the houses of Alexander McCoy and Assistant Chief George Lowrey passed into the hands of lucky drawers. Though the Cherokee Nation retained precarious independence, its capital had fallen to the enemy. Buildings not immediately habitable were torn down to make houses for incoming Georgians. And eventually, with America's penchant for vandalism, everything would go—wiped from the face of the earth. When, a century later, some worthy Georgians would raise funds to restore the ancient capital, they would find only scattered, half-buried stones to guide them.

The *Phoenix* made no mention that winter of the emigrants that partially filled the barracks at Haweiss, awaiting transportation to the West. Enrollment agent Currey had estimated he would have two thousand ready to leave after the first of the year, but revised the figure to twelve hundred, having encountered more difficulty than he had expected. A fleet of barges and keelboats had been lined up opposite the landing, and steamers had been reserved to tow the vessels on difficult sections of the journey.

It was the worst time of year for such an undertaking, with snow in the mountains and streams overflowing and the wagon trails almost impassable. On top of that came bad news from the West. Wrote one of Currey's assistants, "This is the third season that the cholera has scattered desolation & dismay over the Western waters and during its malignant influence no bodies of people have been able to move in any considerable numbers for any length of time in contact, upon the rivers with impunity."[3]

Though resigned to some delay, Currey sent his wagons through the territory to round up reluctant Cherokees and fill his promised quota. John Ross kept conscientious track of these activities for future reference. Simple bribery, paying an Indian to enroll, was the least of Currey's offensive measures. Of one incident, Ross wrote:

Atalah Anosta was prevailed upon to enroll when drunk, contrary to the wish and will of his wife and children. When the time arrived for him to leave for Arkansas, he absconded. A guard was sent after him by B. F. Currey, which arrested the woman and children, and brought them to the agency about dark, in a cold rain, shivering and hungry. They were detained under guard all night, and part of the next day, and until the woman agreed to enroll her name as an emigrant. The husband then came in, and he and his wife and their children were put on board a boat and taken to Arkansas. There they soon lost two or three of their children, and then returned on foot to the Cherokee Nation east of the Mississippi.[4]

Another Indian named Sconatachee was enrolled when drunk but refused to appear at Hiwassee, having gone to court and secured an injunction against Currey. The agent sent a wagon for him anyway, arrested Sconatachee, and hauled him to the stockades, leaving behind his wife and children, who had hidden in the woods. Another enrollee named Richard Cheek refused to appear at the agency, pleading a change of circumstances. His wife was arrested in his absence, put aboard one of the departing flatboats, and died en route to the Arkansas without again seeing or hearing from her husband.[5]

Men were beaten and threatened with death for refusing to enroll. Others were told that their homes were about to be confiscated. Still others were given whiskey to soften their resistance, finding, when they sobered up, that they and their families were already on the wagons. One Indian wife and mother, alone at the time, was told that her husband and children had already departed for Hiwassee. Discovering, when she went to join them, that this had been a lie, she was not permitted to return.

In reluctant charge of the evacuation at Hiwassee was a New England-born West Point graduate, Lieutenant Joseph W. Harris. Like the average Northerner, he had little knowledge of the Cherokees, but found himself sympathetic to their plight. Harris was pleased to note that the site of the evacuation camp, with its twenty-eight stockaded cabins built to hold forty persons each, had been "judiciously selected," being some distance from the "boisterous riot and revelry" of Hiwassee Old Town.

He had had to revise that judgment. Aware that many of the Indians had been paid for their abandoned property, white traders swooped down the river in "floating doggeries," peddling cider, applejack, and whiskey. The trading boats "became the nurseries & receptacles of idleness, drunkenness and vice . . . introducing shameful & bloody quarrels & drunken orgies into the camp." Why was not something done, Harris asked his diary, "to remove the source of so much mischief, and . . . purge these waters of lawless venders who daily and every hour in the day & night are openly demonstrating themselves to be a public nuisance?"[6]

There was yet another menace. Unused to living in tight confinement, unable to maintain the sanitary standards they were used to, and weakened by liquor and unaccustomed food, the Indians became an easy prey to illness. Measles broke out in camp, threatening the future of the expedition. Although by mid-March only 457 of the expected 1,200 had been rounded up—almost 800 of those enrolled had changed their minds—Currey decided against further waiting. It might lead to more trouble in camp, more desertions, a general impairment of the emigration program.

The flatboats were brought to the landing place for loading. Sorrowing friends and relatives thronged the bank to witness the embarkation, as Lieutenant Harris noted in his diary:

The parting scene was more moving than I was prepared for; when this hour of leave-taking arrived I saw many a manly cheek suffused with tears. Parents were turning with sick hearts from children who were about to seek other homes in a far off and stranger land; and brothers and sisters with heaving bosoms & brimful eyes were wringing each others hands for the last time.[7]

To allay the Indians' apprehension over the turbulent river and the fear of cholera farther west, Benjamin Currey agreed to accompany the expedition. He did so as far as the Ohio River. Then, in the confusion of shifting from flatboats to more substantial keelboats, he slipped away and returned to his duties at the agency.

It was not long before misfortunes overtook the party. Midway down the Tennessee a keelboat sank. All sixty-seven passengers were rescued but the remaining boats were overcrowded. As they entered the Mississippi a woman preparing dinner over a cookstove in the stern lost her footing and fell over the side. After a fruitless search in darkness she was given up as drowned. Harris forbade further cooking on the vessels' decks; the Indians would have to eat their dinners cold.

Arriving at the mouth of the Arkansas, the riverboat fleet found the water dangerously low. Some ninety barrels of salk pork and flour were jettisoned to lighten the keelboats, but the vessels still encountered snags and sandbars which brought the expedition to a total halt at Cadron Creek. Here a party went ashore to explore a possible land route to their destination but returned disheartened. They were walled in by a wilderness. All able-bodied men were put to work building a temporary camp.

Still miles from their goal, the emigrants' situation was becoming desperate. A dozen had died, most of them children, from the epidemic of measles that had traveled with them. To avoid contagion the Indians scattered and built their fires far removed from one another. While native whites refused to come to their aid, the more unscrupulous raided their camps and made off with what was left of their diminishing provisions.

Gravely concerned about his charges, Lieutenant Harris made his way to the town of Little Rock and persuaded the resident doctor, Jesse C. Roberts, to accompany him back to camp. Roberts was to be an unsung hero of the expedition. Arriving at night, he groped his way from group to huddled group, tending to the old and young, the frightened and the stricken. He helped check the spread of measles, but the weakened Indians fell prey to a more deadly scourge.

In mid-March six cases of cholera developed. On March 16 twelve died of the fever; the next day, seventeen; the day after, another seventeen. In four days fifty-one were dead and not enough coffins could be built to provide them with a decent burial. "In some cases," Harris noted in his diary, "we have been obliged to put two or even three bodies in one coffin . . ."

Harris himself came down with cholera, but he forced himself to continue working beside Dr. Roberts, suffering as much as the Indians he tended. Of these he wrote:

At one time I saw stretched around me and within a few feet of each other, eight of these afflicted creatures dead or dying. Yet no lamentations went up from the bereaved ones here. They were of the true Indian blood; they looked upon the departed ones with a manly sorrow & silently digged graves for their dead and as quietly they laid them out in their narrow beds . . . There is a dignity in their grief which is sublime; and which, poor and destitute, ignorant and unbefriended as they were, made me respect them.[8]

The story of the journey became one of tragic repetition. Exhausted from overwork, Dr. Roberts came down with cholera and was dead in twenty-four hours. Lieutenant Harris, himself barely half alive, was left to care for a party of women and children so debilitated that they could "scarcely crawl about." He managed somehow to engage sufficient wagons to haul his charges overland toward the Arkansas; but when the hired drivers saw the condition of their passengers, they fled in panic. The Cherokees climbed into the wagons and Harris mounted one of the horses—"although for a while I could scarcely keep my saddle"—and led the caravan laboriously toward the West.

The survivors would get there, by a miracle, and settle near the new Dwight Mission in eastern Oklahoma. But few were left with the strength or will to build a new life in a new land. Half of those who reached the West were dead within a year, which, including the mortalities en route, left only 190 of the 457 who had started out. Lieutenant Harris was relatively lucky. After being furloughed, he survived for three more years in his native New Hampshire before dying in Portsmouth in May 1837.

The catastrophic journey was a preview of the tragedy to come, something which Ridge and Ross, in different ways, were seeking to avert. News of the emigrants' misfortunes did not reach the East for some weeks. The removal-minded John Ridge tried to discountenance the reports as "gross exaggerations," insisting that the Western territory was indeed the Promised Land, although there might be some "discomforts" involved in getting there. But Elijah Hicks lashed out at the removal program in the *Phoenix,* headlining the initial government-supervised expedition as "The Tyrant's Masterpiece," and comparing the enrolling agents to "rooting swine" and barnyard predators.[9]

It was a Nation in desperate circumstances, riddled with distrust, to which the various delegates returned from Washington that spring. John Ross arrived at Head of Coosa in early April and was startled to find a stranger on his doorstep. The man presented himself as a lucky winner in the lottery who had come to take possession of the estate. He had allowed the chief's wife Quatie and the children to remain in two rooms of the mansion until Ross returned to take them elsewhere.

For the head of a Nation, accustomed to wealth and power, Ross showed extraordinary self-control. He was losing his handsome two-story home with its precious library, his barns and outbuildings, herds of cattle and sheep and extensively cultivated fields, and even the strutting peacocks which had added a touch of Old World grandeur to the sloping lawns. His lucrative ferry across the Coosa was in the hands of two more strangers bearing rifles.

But Ross had preached recourse to law as preferable under any circumstance to violence. Sooner or later such wrong must be righted if one kept the faith. He led his family on horseback up to Red Clay to be near the Council grounds and installed them in a one-room dirt-floor cabin built of logs.

He was shrewd enough not to be surprised that the homes of John and Major Ridge a mile or so upriver, as well as Elias Boudinot's house at New Echota, were still in the hands of their respective owners. In return for supporting Georgia's program for removal, John Ridge had insisted on their tenure, until the time their owners chose to leave. The Ridge's estate of 160 acres on the Oostanaula had already been won in the Georgia lottery, but the sexagenarian chief would not be evicted; Governor Lumpkin had instructed Benjamin Currey to "assure Boudinot, Ridge, and their friends of State protection under any circumstances."

Elijah Hicks had worried about his legendary bird, the *Phoenix,* fearing its extinction. Up to now it had not been seized or even interfered with by the state authorities, who showed a wise restraint in that respect. It had simply had the life squeezed out of it—by a surly postmaster who withheld its mail; by lack of funds from federal annuities now paid to individuals and not to the National Treasury; and by Elijah's own inability to cope.

Unable to create copy as Worcester and Boudinot had done, Hicks picked material from handy almanacs and filled his columns with such features as "A Father's Advice to His Daughter," "Cultivation of Peach Trees," "On the Constituent Parts of Water," and "The Benefit of Female Education." As a consequence, interest and readership declined. The Indians had weightier matters to think about. The *Cherokee Phoenix,* once the proud voice of the Nation, ended not with a bang but a whimper.

In the issue for May 31, 1834, Hicks told his readers that the paper was temporarily suspending publication, "say to the last of July, for the purpose of collecting funds." But the announcement had the ring of valedictory. The editor expressed his thanks to his readers who, with their prayers, had supported the *Phoenix* in its battle against "the most wicked policy that the wit of man could conceive, to expel the Cherokees from their beloved homes." The editor concluded:

To our Cherokee readers we would say, DON'T GIVE UP THE SHIP. Although our enemies are numerous we are still in the land of the living . . . and the JUDGE of all the earth will impart means for the salvation of our suffering Nation.[10]

There was need for such judicial guidance when John Ross called a meeting of the General Council at Red Clay in August. Cherokee thinking and Cherokee affairs were in a turmoil. Already rumors of Andrew Ross's abortive treaty had leaked back to the Nation, along with reports of Starr and Walker's presence in the capital. When Ross presented Andrew's treaty to the Council, not for confirmation but for condemnation, there were those who vowed that the culprits would not leave the Council grounds alive.

The Ridge himself had rejected Andrew's treaty before leaving Washington. But the fact that he had been with Andrew in the capital was enough to draw the Council's fire. Andrew was merely a blundering fool. The Ridge, on the other hand, was a man of honorable stature in the Nation—hence his had been the greater treachery.

Thomas Foreman, firebrand member of the Council from Amohee District, charged that while in Washington The Ridge had conspired "to do something against his country." As always, Benjamin Currey was present to take notes and report to Cass on what transpired. Foreman's speech, as translated from the Cherokee, was embellished with Indian imagery. Major Ridge had told the people to love their country and had stamped his foot for emphasis. Wherever he stamped, the land was crushed beneath his heel. He and his followers, not content with their wealth, were trying like vampires to suck from its veins the lifeblood of the Nation.[11]

When angry muttering and threats of assassination against Treaty Party members followed Foreman's diatribe, John Ridge rose in his father's defense. Major Ridge, said John, had seen his people "on the precipice of ruin. He told them of their danger. Did he tell the truth or not? Let every man look at our circumstances & judge for himself. Was a man to be denounced for his opinions?"

But The Ridge was well qualified to make his own defense. With some of the old-time fire his voice rang out above the assembly. He was not concerned with wealth and honor for himself. "His sun of existence was going down," he told his listeners. "He had only a short time left to live." So:

It may be that Foreman has better expectations & that he should in slandering men establish his fame among you. But I have no expectation that he will enjoy it long, for we have no government. It is entirely suppressed. Where are your laws! The seats of your judges are overturned. When I look upon you all, I hear you laugh at me. When harsh words are uttered by men who know better . . . I feel on your account oppressed with sorrow. I mourn over your calamity.[12]

It was a noble speech, but it came too late. Elijah Hicks rose to propose that the Ridges be impeached for "maintaining opinions and a policy to exterminate the Cherokee community . . ." The Council voted approval of the motion, but the National Committee, of which John Ridge was President, recommended a period for further deliberation and ordered that the accused appear before the October Council to answer the charges preferred against them.

Those who had vowed that indicated traitors would not leave the Council grounds alive were not appeased. For reasons of his own John Walker slipped out of the meeting early to return on horseback to North Carolina. James Foreman, cousin of the tempestuous Thomas, perched with his brother in a tree beside the trail that Walker was certain to follow. When the rider appeared James brought him down with a bullet between the eyes, and left his body where it fell as a grisly example to his fellow travelers.

The precipitous murder may have prevented further bloodshed. The Ridges and Boudinot were duly forewarned and took circuitous routes in returning to New Echota and Running Waters. David Vann was believed by Currey to be also marked for death, and there had been threats against the enrolling commissioner himself. Currey had the two suspected Foremans arrested on a charge of murder. But the crime had taken place in Tennessee, which, unlike Georgia, claimed no judicial authority over Cherokee affairs. The suspects were dismissed.

Daniel Butrick had donned spiritual armor and returned to Georgia, to take over the management of the mission at Carmel. It was a drastic reversal of position. Earlier he had written to a member of the American Board that "during the present distress it was my determination to devote one day a week to fasting and prayer, with special reference to the Cherokees, but in all other respects to appear indifferent with regard to their worldly prospects . . ." He "would not unnecessarily oppose the views of Georgia. It is not our right to judge. Missionaries are like any other citizen & subject to laws of states where they live."

He could remain indifferent no longer. Though believing that Cherokee affairs were "plunging thicker and thicker into darkness" and that "the United States, and the southern states in particular, are hastening to the brink of an awful precipice," he chose to become involved. "We may be removed at any time," he wrote to David Greene from Carmel, but "our strength is evidently to sit still." Ignoring Georgia's laws and the threat of the lottery, he would, like Sophia Sawyer at New Echota, carry on.[13]

Sophia and her school, however, had been under siege. A lucky lottery winner by the name of Burke showed up at the courthouse at New Echota and, showing her his cardboard ticket, told her he was taking over. As with the Georgia Guard who threatened her two black pupils, Sophia refused to be intimidated. The courthouse was her school; she would not give it up. Burke then, according to Samuel Worcester, "returned with a hammer and went about nailing up the door."

Sophia appealed for help to a local lawyer named Buchanan. Buchanan must have had much of her bristling spirit. Both he and his wife hurried to the courthouse to intercede in her behalf. What happened next was reported by Worcester in a letter from Brainerd to the Board in Boston:

Buchanan first expostulated, and then attempted forcibly to prevent the door from being shut, when Burke laid about his head with the hammer, and a violent scuffle ensued, in which Mrs. Buchanan took part with her husband, & also another lawyer by the name of Wiley; and a young clerk also threw a stone, which did no harm.

Burke, Buchanan, and Wiley came off with very bloody heads, & Mrs. Buchanan also received one stroke of the hammer. Burke was brought under, but yet was left in possession of the house. Now Buchanan has prosecuted Burke for assault and battery, and Burke, on his part, has brought an action against Miss Sawyer & all the four above named, for $5000 damages for housebreaking, assault & battery, & etc. The court comes on next week . . .[14]

Members of the American Board must have winced at this latest episode in Sophia's checkered career. But Worcester stood by her. Though admitting that "the conflict was a very unhappy occurrence," he told the Board: "Had I been present, I should have advised Miss S. by all means to leave the house; yet I suppose, before a judicial tribunal . . . she must be entirely acquitted. She took no part in the scuffle . . ."[15]

Predictably Sophia lost the suit and one more missionary outpost fell to the invaders. The courthouse became a grogshop and Miss Sophia was without a classroom. Always in her life, however, a white knight seemed to ride from nowhere to her aid. Samuel Worcester had been first to salvage her disoriented but impetuous career; but Worcester, of course, had left for Brainerd. Now it was John Ridge, gallant, handsome, personable, who came to Miss Sophia's rescue.

John proposed that she move her school to Running Waters, where one wing of the house would offer living quarters for her and a classroom for her pupils. Sophia saw nothing ticklish in the arrangement. True, at this time of bitter party politics she would seem to be aligning with the Ridges, and thus might antagonize the majority of the Cherokees. On the other hand, and more important, here was a chance to carry on the work which the missionaries had been sent to do. Did it matter greatly where the offer came from? The Board reluctantly acquiesced and Sophia reopened her school at Running Waters.

She had had some doubts at the beginning. Worcester had not too gently hinted that people "found her difficult," and Sophia herself acknowledged moon-oriented fits of nervousness and temperament. She confessed to Sarah Ridge that she was afraid, when "the fits" came over her, she might "speak and act *wrong*." Sarah had had her own problems of adjustment in the move from the Puritan Cornwall to Indian wilderness, and had overcome them. She assured Sophia they would work things out together.

The move to Running Waters was an immediate success. Her Cherokee pupils marveled at the polished floors and real glass windows. Harriet Boudinot came by day to teach the students music on the Ridges' new piano, and the sweet strains of "When Jesus Wept" brought tears to Miss Sophia's eyes. John Ridge brought the pupils gifts when he returned from Washington, including, once, a bonnet for her; and though she was grieved at John's lack of piety, Sophia could not help but love him.

Just as she had idolized Worcester during his courageous stand against emigration, so she now admired Ridge for his stand in favor of removal. She knew it was not a popular position; some parents took their children out of school rather than have them identified with Ridge's politics. But Sophia listened to her heart, and if it beat inconsistently she still believed it. Though John was sometimes impatient and brusque, she knew this was due to strain and worry. As it was—for John Ridge had reached a critical point of no return.

Not all encounters with the Georgia militia had dire consequences. One of Miss Sophia's pupils was Sally Ridge, John's sister and the Major's daughter. Sophia considered her "a young lady of superior talents . . . very interesting in her person & appearance," which suggests that she had more than ordinary charm and beauty. She was also an accomplished rider, and was noticed one morning seated in the saddle, trying to fix the bridle on her pony.

A young lieutenant named George Paschal, aide-de-camp of General Wool, now stationed at New Echota, came to her side to help, but the bridle slipped from the horse's head as he was trying to adjust it. Finding itself unfettered, the spirited animal took off at a runaway gallop and Sally, wrapping her arms around its neck, clung to the pony for thirteen miles, up hill and down dale, until she had mastered and gentled the animal and brought it safely back.

Witnessing that mad ride and its outcome, George Paschal lost his heart to the dark-eyed Indian maiden. From that moment on, Sally was destined not to ride through life alone.[16]

John Walker's assassination had done more harm than good to the Cherokees' struggle for survival. Not only were Cherokee Council members shocked by the act but the fact that Walker was related by marriage to former Indian

Agent Jonathan Meigs gave the incident nationwide publicity. President Jackson wrote to Currey on September 3, a few days after the murder:

I have just been advised that Walker has been shot and Ridge and other chiefs in favor of emigration and you as agent of the United States government threatened with death.

The Government of the United States has promised them protection. It will perform its obligations to a tittle. On the receipt of this letter, notify John Ross and his council that we will hold them answerable for every murder committed on the emigrating party.[17]

The outbreak of violence brought alarm to Georgia and to lottery-winning whites who had settled in the Nation. Howell Cobb, an aspiring young lawyer who in another quarter century would help lead Georgia's secession from the Union, headed a "Citizens Committee" of vigilantes. Believing that white Georgians were "in constant danger of assassination and other lawless violence," the Committee passed a resolution declaring that "for every citizen of the County killed by Cherokees, we will select three male Indians, out of the County of Cherokee, and put them to death as an atonement for the murder of such citizens."[18]

Governor Lumpkin, to his credit, discountenanced such summary executions "until the civil courts have had full opportunity to resolve the matter." But he did recommend "the immediate organization of volunteer companies through the new Counties . . . supplied with good arms and ammunition"; and he wrote an extraordinarily blunt letter to War Secretary Cass, concluding: "If you cannot control these Indians, through some agnecy, the authorities of Georgia will be under the painful necessity of exterminating the evil in the only practical way." Lumpkin did not specify what practical way he had in mind.[19]

But the most damaging result of Walker's murder was its evidence of the bitter division within the Nation. Washington would make the most of it, and so would Georgia. Attempts among the Cherokees to heal the breach were doomed by the firm belief of each side in the justice of its cause. In mid-September, prior to the autumn Council, John Ross appealed to Ridge by letter:

It is sincerely hoped that every honorable and patriotic man will under the existing state of things unite in exerting an influence among the people with the view of cultivating harmony among one another and to suppress as found practicable all causes tending to unnecessary excitement and evil. The general welfare of our much oppressed and suffering people requires it . . . and their peace and happiness demands it of us—and therefore every course calculated to produce strife among the people from partyism should be discarded.[20]

John Ridge, under threat of impeachment, was not inclined to greet this overture with warmth. But Ross and his followers took other conciliatory steps. At the October Council at Red Clay it was voted to drop the motion for impeachment of John and Major Ridge. The Ridges, however, were not that easily satisfied. They demanded a trial that would clear their name. Denied this, they walked out of the Council before its adjournment and, accompanied by Elias Boudinot, rode back to their respective homes.

There was only the sluggish Conasauga River to be left behind on leaving Tennessee. For all practical purposes, however, they had crossed the Rubicon.

At John Ridge's home at Running Waters on November 13, 1834, a more or less secret conclave was in progress. It was attended, among others, by Major Ridge, Elias Boudinot, and enrollment agent Benjamin Currey, who wrote to Governor Lumpkin on that date:

Sir—I am now at John Ridge's where a council is to be held on the 27 inst in order to organize a party favourably disposed to Cherokee removal. An election of chiefs in favor of transplanting the tribe will be held . . . and a delegation is to be appointed to go to the city—Washington—to memorialize Congress.[21]

So—division within the Cherokee Nation was no longer an affair of petty feuding. It was a political reality. "The party about to be organized will require money," Currey advised the governor. Hopefully the necessary funds would come from the War Department. This realized, "they desire me to say one season more will give them entire ascendancy over all opposition . . ."

The confidence implicit in the phrase "one season more" was not euphoric optimism. For behind this Treaty Party, which was formally organized ten days later, stood the United States government, the state of Georgia, and the silent blessing of North Carolina, Tennessee, and Alabama. Supporting John Ross and his National or Anti-Treaty Party was the loyalty of three fourths of a crippled Nation and the militant approbation of certain statesmen in the North—high-caliber men like Henry Clay whose voices were too distant to be heard.

It was the first serious challenge to Ross's authority and he knew it. Dissenting voices had opposed him in the past. Men like the Ridges, Boudinot, Jolly, Walker, Starr, and his brother Andrew had visited the capital in groups or separately to press their case as individuals. But an organized party with elected chiefs was something else again, a political machine with which the Jackson-Georgia axis might see fit to deal.

On November 27, 1834, the Treaty Party emerged from the Running Waters conference with John Ridge as its president or chief and Elias Boudinot and Alexander McCoy as his assistants. These three were appointed heads of a six-man delegation authorized to go to Washington that winter to confer with the President and Secretary Cass "in regard to the present condition and future prospects of the Cherokee people."

As a preliminary to this mission a memorial was drafted which was essentially a party platform. Signed by fifty-seven of those present, it was addressed to Congress, and John Ridge's fluent pen seemed evident in the wording. Possibly it was Ridge who recommended that the document be handed first to Representative Edward Everett—hitherto one of Ross's strong supporters—to be presented by him to Congress. If it was a subtle means of winning Everett over to the Treaty Party's side, it worked.

After reviewing the Cherokees' summary of the injustices that they had suffered—"in which views I fully concur"—Everett noted:

They express, however, the sorrowful conviction that it is impossible for them, in the present state of things, to retain their national existence, and to live in peace and comfort in their native region. They therefore have turned their eyes to the country west of the Mississippi, to which a considerable portion of their tribe have already emigrated; and they express the opinion that they are reduced to the alternative of following them to that region, or of sinking into a condition but little, if at all, better than slavery, in their present place of abode . . . In contemplating the subject of removal, they cast themselves on the liberality of Congress.[22]

Congress might not be as liberal as the appellants hoped. But to put one's fate in other hands is one way of inciting generosity. When the Treaty Party delegates reached Washington that winter, they would find a sympathetic audience.

They would find a sympathetic audience in Andrew Jackson, too. The protective tariff had been adjusted to South Carolina's satisfaction, and the threat of nullification had abated. The President could now give full support to Georgia's interests without compromising his position. Out West, Sam Houston, aided in part by his Cherokee brothers, was prying Texas from the arms of Mexico. When this was accomplished, and Texas made part of the United States, there would be a vast new area available for problem Indians.

In the West, too, Chief John Jolly had molded his people, the Old Settlers and more recent emigrants, into a viable community deserving of the title "Cherokee Nation West." Land-boundary problems and tribal disputes had been settled, six years earlier, by exchanging their Arkansas lands for seven million acres in Oklahoma Territory—*"a permanent home,"* read the treaty signed in Washington, "and one which shall, under the most solemn guarantee of the United States, be and remain theirs forever . . ."[23]

Most of the Arkansas Cherokees had moved to the new territory, establishing their capital and Council grounds at Tahlonteskee, named for the former chief, at the mouth of the Illinois River. The western missionaries had gone with them, setting up a new Dwight Mission near the north bank of the Arkansas. Should the Eastern Indians, selling their lands to the United States, join the Old Settlers in Oklahoma, they would bring with them not only extra manpower with which to strengthen the Western Nation, but additional annuities due them for the cession of their eastern territory.

All of these considerations, which seemed to favor emigration of the Eastern Indians, overlooked one ineradicable truth. To the Eastern Cherokees the West was still by tradition "the Darkening Land," tomb of the sun, where the shades of the dead found a final dwelling. Against its specious beckoning, they had only just begun to fight.

13

Dark Sun and
Devil's Horn

OLD MYTHS die hard. Among the less enlightened Cherokees some legends lingered with the strength of medieval superstitions. When the sun was blacked out, or eclipsed, it was because "the great frog up in the sky" was trying to swallow it. . . .

Everybody knows this . . . and in olden times whenever people saw the sun grow dark they would come together and fire guns and beat the drum, and in a little while this would frighten off the great frog and the sun would be all right again.[1]

None of the Cherokees fired guns or beat drums when the sun at high noon blackened over Georgia in December 1834. At the mission station in Carmel the horses whinnied and pawed the earth, dogs howled and birds grew silent, and invisible winds made a rushing, sighing sound through swaying pines. But those assembled for communion service listened quietly to Daniel Butrick's reasonable explanation of the dark phenomenon. There was no cause, he assured them, for alarm. At Running Waters the resourceful Miss Sophia Sawyer referred her pupils to E. H. Burnet's *Geography of the Heavens* to help allay their apprehension.

But a full eclipse had not occurred for many years in Georgia. Like the shower of stars the year before—even more so perhaps than during that strange phenomenon—the world seemed suddenly filled with the scampering feet of fleeing animals. Perhaps the invisible creatures were aware of some dark thing the Cherokees had missed.

In secret groups they sought out the old discountenanced medicine men but were given no satisfactory explanation beyond the fable of the great frog in the sky. They began to wonder with some trepidation if this eclipse was not an omen. The death of the sun at high noon, did that portend the dying of the Nation at its brightest hour? Butrick, looking back upon it some months later, might himself have cause to wonder.

When the eclipse was followed by the coldest winter within memory, with the snows deep on the mountains and the laurel branches split by ice, the feeling of impending doom seemed very real. The *Phoenix,* which had been the Cherokees' light in times of darkness, had flickered out like a sputtering candle reaching the bottom of its wick. In its place were only rumors and the fears that only rumors can instill. They knew that their divided chiefs were up in Washington engaged in bartering with Andrew Jackson, one group bargaining to save the Nation, the other to trade it out beneath their feet.

They had faith that John Ross and his party would prevail. They clung to that faith as to a life raft in a stormy sea. But sometimes one wondered, as one wondered about the muttered parables of the medicine men. Would the great frog—Andrew Jackson?—regurgitate the sun when he found it difficult to swallow?

Before the two rival Cherokee delegations, John Ross's Nationalists and the Treaty Party delegates headed by John Ridge and Boudinot, left the Nation for the capital, some attempt had been made to bring them together. Ross still believed that if the Cherokees united they could force a settlement for remaining in the East, perhaps by becoming citizens of the states in which they lived. The Ridge, wiser and older than any of them, cautioned against such a dream of integration. It might be all right for the mixed-breeds, he said, accustomed to the white man's ways. "But the body of the lower class, according to my forebodings, will be perpetually made drunk by the whites, cheated, oppressed, reduced to beggary, become miserable outcasts, and as a body dwindle to nothing." So the two factions went their separate ways, as far apart as ever.[2]

In Washington, Jackson astutely played one party against the other. He could not ignore the fact that Ross was Principal Chief and represented the majority of Cherokees; he treated John at first with courtesy and even cordiality. But any serious negotiations would be carried on with Ridge. Not by Jackson himself—the President would try to keep a posture of impartiality—but by his newly appointed commissioner, John F. Schermerhorn, "a sort of loose Dutch Presbyterian Minister" who had been brought to Jackson's attention by Vice-President Van Buren, whose ancestors also came from Holland.

Perhaps Schermerhorn's ecclesiastical background recommended him; the missionaries, Jackson acknowledged, obnoxious as they were, seemed to have influence among the Cherokees. But viewed from any angle the retired clergyman from Utica, New York, was an extraordinary choice. Large, flamboyant, with a bullhorn voice, he was described by the press as "a crafty and subtle individual, as able in some ways as the wily prelates who in by-gone centuries dictated the policies of kings and emperors." The shadow of Rasputin had not yet darkened the horizon over western Asia, but the reporter's definition seemed to conjure up his image.

One thing was evident: despite the cloth, Schermerhorn was not handicapped by any sense of moral obligation. During the first weeks of February he met with Ridge and Boudinot to draft what Ridge referred to as "a preliminary treaty." The terms Schermerhorn offered were not much better than those obtained a year before by Andrew Ross, and since rejected. The Cherokees were to cede their remaining territory in the East for a sum of $3,250,000 along with other monetary considerations and equivalent land grants in the West. Schermerhorn was playing his cards as close to the vest as a riverboat gambler.

Though the two rival delegations maintained little contact, John Ross, when he interviewed the President, was aware of what was going on behind his back. Once again he and Jackson faced each other like bare-knuckle fighters entering the ring, sparring, feinting, probing for one another's weaknesses. Ross threw a long list of grievances before the President like rabbit punches: broken promises, dishonored treaties. Jackson accused him of stalling. They were together to discuss a treaty, nothing else. Ross, knowing of Schermerhorn's terms with Ridge, then made a counter-proposal: $20,000,000 for all Cherokee lands in the East, plus equivalent territory in the West.

An outraged Jackson called it "Filibustering!"

Then submit the matter to the Senate, Ross suggested. Whatever amount the Senate offered, he and his delegates would consider.

Fair enough, said Jackson, and referred the matter to the Senate. The senators recommended a maximum payment of $5,000,000. Ross, dissatisfied with the amount, came back with yet another proposition. What would the Senate allow the Cherokees if they left the United States altogether and settled, say, in Mexico?

This seemingly bizarre alternative was not entirely a ploy on Ross's part. He had thought about it, and kept it to himself, for several years. A letter was on its way to Sr. de Costello y Lanza of the Mexican embassy asking what arrangements might be made with the Mexican government to secure the Cherokees "land sufficient for their accommodation—and also the enjoyment of equal rights and privileges of citizenship."[3]

Whatever de Costello answered would be academic now. Jackson would not even entertain the proposition and the interview was ended.

But the abortive negotiations had one salubrious effect, especially the Senate's recommendation of a $5,000,000 payment. It forced Schermerhorn to raise his offer to Ridge and Boudinot from $3,250,000 to $4,500,000 in cash and 800,000 additional acres in the West worth enough to bring the total value to the Senate's figure of $5,000,000.

Ridge considered the arrangement "very liberal in its terms," especially a $40,000 annuity that would provide for the schools which he and Boudinot considered vitally important to constructing a new Nation in the West. Gleefully he and Boudinot reported this triumph to the Nation before leaving Washington.

"Our proceedings," Boudinot wrote to his brother Stand Watie, "have finally so frightened Mr. Ross that he made several propositions lately all of which have been rejected . . . His intention is to get the money and hunt out a country for himself . . . I am sure the Cherokees, when they find out that they are to remove at all events, will not think of going to a Country of which they know nothing."[4]

Ten days later John Ridge addressed a letter to his father "& others" which showed an ever deeper hatred and hostility toward Ross. Complaining of "the hard struggle I had to make against John Ross & his party," he continued:

. . . we have succeeded to get a treaty made to be sent home for the ratification of the people . . . Ross has failed before the Senate, before the Secretary of War, & before the President. He tried hard to cheat you & his people, but he has been prevented. In a day or two he goes home, no doubt to tell lies.

The U. States will never have anything more to do with John Ross. Thus it becomes of selfish men.[5]

The Ridge-Schermerhorn treaty was provisionally signed in Washington on March 14 and five hundred copies, printed by Benjamin Currey, were brought home to the Nation for ratification by the people. Schermerhorn returned with Ridge and Boudinot to lubricate the operation.

There was marked contrast in the homecoming of Ross and Ridge—two men dedicated to the welfare of the Nation, both on a collision course. Ross returned virtually empty-handed, with little to offer his people but the promise of sweat, blood, and tears. John Ridge brought them an offer of more money than they had ever dreamed of, with side benefits besides—guaranteed territory in the West, annuities to support schools and even missions there, liberal compensation for the home improvements they would leave behind, and ample expenses for the journey West.

Yet while Ross returned a hero in the Nation's eyes, having stood up to Chicken Snake Jackson in the White House, Ridge was more than ever suspect. There were renewed threats and rumors of assassination. According to the reconstituted Blood Law, the Ridges and Boudinot deserved no better than death for their designed betrayal of the Nation. Only John Ross's outspoken insistence on peaceful procedure and respect for law restrained his more hot-headed followers from violence.

But intimidation of a curious sort could not be checked. Now around John Ridge's home at Running Waters shrouded figures, wearing blankets over their heads, stood in the nearby fringe of woods and watched the house like sentinels of doom. They made no threatening gestures. They shouted no abuses. They simply stood, silent and motionless, and stared.

Perhaps Miss Sophia's pupils wondered at this ring of sinister figures, but Sophia herself was more angered than alarmed. Why did they seek to persecute her benefactor and the Cherokees' savior who sought only to present the truth with honesty and courage? Samuel Worcester, himself a victim of persecution, would have understood her feelings. But Worcester had joined what some might call the soldiers of retreat.

Since the previous September, Worcester had decided on moving to the West, writing to David Greene, "I am in haste to get to the Arkansas, and would go this fall, but that Mr. Boudinot cannot, and I wish to lose as little time from translating as possible." His departure at whatever time, he noted, "will awaken considerable prejudice among the Cherokees, but indeed it is already awake, as my going is anticipated."[6]

As for Miss Sophia, who had apparently felt "compelled" to leave the Worcesters for other reasons than their moving to the West, Worcester wrote, "I am sorry to feel constrained to vindicate myself & Mrs. W. from insinuations that we often unkindly reminded her of the principles on which we invited her to remain with us. We never spoke of it except when we felt compelled to do so in self defense . . ."

What principles Sophia had violated was not explained. But one hears in the background Sophia's own, proverbial complaint: "What right have others to judge me? I am what I am!"

The Worcesters left Brainerd on April 8, 1835, traveling in a two-seated wagon with the children piled upon the baggage in the back. Samuel Worcester, though he disapproved of Ridge's provisional treaty as "morally wrong," was convinced the Cherokee cause was hopeless. They must start over again and rebuild the Nation in a new land.

"Towards the state of Georgia or her authorities," he wrote in one of his last apologias, "we are conscious of no vindictive feelings. It is our unceasing prayer that her transgressions and the transgressions of our countrymen be forgiven, and those judgments of heaven averted, which there is too much reason to fear."[7]

It would take more than seven weeks to reach Dwight Mission in Oklahoma Territory. They were obliged, Worcester wrote, "to make a circuitous route, through Kentucky, Illinois, & Missouri, to avoid swamps which at present are almost impassable for wagons." Ann suffered "bilious fever" from poor diet on the way. Their household goods which followed by water were lost when the steamboat sank. They were robbed in transit of the few possessions that they carried with them and arrived at their destination stripped of everything they owned.

Their misfortunes forced Worcester to think of the thousands who might shortly be compelled to make the journey on foot or horseback under the same, or worse, conditions. Among them, presumably, would be Elias Boudinot, his partner and translator, which would enable Worcester to continue his translations of the scriptures.

But Harriet Gold Boudinot would not accompany her husband, and Ann Worcester would miss the one woman who had shared her trials at Cornwall and buoyed her spirits at New Echota. Not long after the Worcesters said farewell to Brainerd, Harriet died, presumably from overwork and from sharing the constant political pressures which her husband was subjected to. On top of those pressures now, for Elias, was the task of bringing up five motherless children with no one to help. But Delight Sargent, still young, still unmarried, was on the staff at Brainerd. So perhaps . . .

That spring both parties girded for battle prior to the Council to be called in May, at which the treaty signed in Washington would be presented. At Red Clay and at Running Waters, respectively, the Ross and Ridge factions met to discuss their separate strategies. Meanwhile, Colonel William Bishop of the Georgia Guard, nominally allied with Ridge, had returned from a tour of the Cherokee territory undertaken "to ascertain the feelings and views of Those people in regard to the Treaty arrangement." Now he wrote to Governor Lumpkin:

. . . from my observations I am led to the conclusion that a large portion of the Ross Party will go against the propositions offered through Ridge. Some will, from force of circumstances, be driven from their Servile Love of Ross—but since his return amongst them they are much more Hostile to Ridge and his Party. An opinion is now prevailing amongst Them that Ross will yet be able to make a more advantageous arrangement with the President than the one proposed through Ridge.[8]

Lumpkin, now serving his second and last term as governor, was importuned from all sides. More than any other man in Georgia, any in the United States save Andrew Jackson, he stood in the public eye as a symbol of Indian subjection to the white man's wish. The crucial moment was at hand. What, came the insistent question, was he going to do about it?

Colonel Zachariah B. Hargrove, one of three prominent well-to-do land speculators who, the year before, had founded the city of Rome in Cherokee territory near The Ridge's mansion, was concerned about his investment. From his on-the-spot vantage point he warned the governor "that the prospect is at present gloomy of an acceptance of the treaty made by the Ridge party. Mr. Ross . . . is using the whole weight of his influence against it. His party, you are doubtless aware, has the ascendancy and unless something is done, all that has been attempted will be defeated . . . Ross has the most astonishing control over his party . . ."[9]

Colonel Bishop of the Georgia Guard saw specters of violence and assassination hovering over these divided, bitterly antagonistic factions. "I have no doubt," he wrote to Governor Lumpkin, "that Cherokees favorable to *Ridge* are in danger, and *Ridge himself* is in *eminent* danger. Many Threats are made against him. Those Intelligent Half Breeds are constantly Stating his will be another *McIntosh* case." Bishop offered to raise a vigilante band of "hardy mountaineers" to keep things under control. The governor cautioned him simply to keep an eye on Ross and his followers and arrest them at the first sign of violence toward the Treaty Party members.[10]

Yet another militia officer, Colonel William Harden, to whom the Georgia lottery had bequeathed the house of Samuel Worcester, had a similar concern— for his family's safety in their new abode, and for the safety of those he considered "friendly" Cherokees. "We earnestly believe," he wrote to Lumpkin, echoing the words of Bishop, "that John Ridge and his friends who negotiated the late treaty are in eminent danger of assassination by the Ross party." Harden recommended that the state authorities send armed troops to protect the Treaty Party Indians and the new white settlers in the Nation.[11]

By odd coincidence, Colonel Harden was at the moment entertaining a guest from New York, one John Howard Payne, who was on his way north from Florida. In fact, Payne, an actor, playwright, and itinerant journalist, was courting Harden's maiden daughter, Mary. Harden did not oppose the courtship. Payne seemed harmless enough, though eccentric in his views. Harden would, however, revise that estimation in the course of time.

Under the circumstances, the atmosphere was anything but congenial in the Council House when Schermerhorn, the last week in May, rose to introduce to the assembly the agreement signed in Washington in March. He prefaced his presentation with a message from Andrew Jackson urging acceptance of a treaty which had been drafted "with every consideration for their welfare." Benjamin Currey, present as observer, was annoyed to note that much irreverent snickering greeted this remark.

Even Schermerhorn's slick diplomacy and clerical appearance failed to overcome the general animosity. "The Reverend Agent," wrote a visitor to the Nation, "being of amorous turn had been detected tampering with some of the young Cherokee women, so that he came to be an object of detestation to the Indians who took every opportunity to affront him." The Cherokees gave the pious pastor an adhesive nickname which was passed around the hall with audible laughter and suggestive gestures—Skaynooyaunah, which in Cherokee means "Devil's Horn."

The Council's reaction was predictable. The assembly refused even to consider the Washington treaty and passed a resolution condemning the delegates who had, without authority, agreed to it. Letters were read from former Council members who had moved to Oklahoma "giving a most unhappy picture of the country and the condition of emigrants there—the faithlessness of the Govt. in fulfilling its pledges, &c . . . more lamentable accounts of death, delay of payments, consequent suffering, &c, &c."

A vote of confidence was passed, giving Ross "full powers to adjust all their difficulties in whatever way he might think most beneficial to the people." Then the Council turned to considerations of plans for the future, one of which was the revival of the *Phoenix,* to be published at Red Clay with Richard Fields, a senior councilman, as editor. It was resolved that Ross should send teamsters to New Echota to pick up the equipment.

Perhaps it was just as well, for him, that Samuel Worcester was on his way West. He more than any other had helped to hatch the fledgling *Phoenix;* he was not present to witness, from the windows of his nearby house, the robbing of the nest. For Bishop and the Georgia Guard got wind of the Council's intentions. A mounted detachment led by Boudinot's brother, Stand Watie, beat Ross's wagons to New Echota by a scant two hours.

The print shop was emptied of press and type and bindery. Elijah Hicks's home was raided and all papers relative to the *Phoenix* seized and confiscated. The press was hauled to Spring Place to be held in the custody of Stand Watie. Nothing was left that might enable the Cherokees to resurrect the *Phoenix* and regain their voice.

Ross strongly protested by letter to Schermerhorn and Currey against this "extraordinary seizure" of "property belonging to the Nation," and charged John Ridge with complicity in the "crime." Benjamin Currey gave him the courtesy of a fairly frank reply. First of all, Currey argued, the press had been originally purchased by Elias Boudinot with voluntary contributions from citizens of the United States (a partial truth) "for the general benefit of the Cherokee people, to convey to them the truth and correct intelligence on all subjects." He continued:

> In this manner it was conducted by Boudinot and [Watie] until 1832, when they were compelled by you and your partisans to give it up: because you would not permit them to conduct it in a fair, candid and impartial manner by giving both sides, those in favour of emigration and a Treaty and those opposed to it, an opportunity to express their views and sentiments . . . [instead] you gave the Press into the hands of your brother in law Elijah Hicks who was completely under your dictation; and it was prostituted to party politics among yourselves; misleading the common people and prejudicing their minds against . . . the measures of the government.[12]

Removing the slanted verbiage—"partisans," "dictation," "prostituted," and "prejudicing"—Currey's charges were sound. Ross had taken over the *Phoenix* and used it openly for anti-government attacks. But Ross's control had been majority control; Ross's opinions and attitudes were those of more than three fourths, even more than four fifths, of the Nation. True, he had subverted freedom of the press, a culpable offense by later standards. But that hardly justified the confiscation of the property and seizure of the premises.

Bishop explained the seizure as a necessary means of restoring the *Phoenix* to Elias Boudinot, its original editor, to be "conducted to the general satisfaction of the people." Plainly "the people" here meant Boudinot's people; one slanted editorial policy was to replace another.

As it turned out, not Bishop, nor Ridge, nor anyone else of the Treaty Party had serious intentions of reviving the *Phoenix*. Any newspaper, to succeed, must reflect the interests of its readers. They would hardly dare to take that chance. They never did.

So that battered bird, the *Phoenix,* which had started out so cockily in 1828, was caught and crushed, as was the Nation itself, between the inexorable pressures of opposing forces. Like its namesake, however, it was graced with immortality. Even before leaving Brainerd, Samuel Worcester had written to the American Board in Boston declaring that to continue their work in the West among the Cherokees the missionaries would need another press. A bigger one.

So promptly did the Board respond that the press was on its way by steamer the last week in August. John Wheeler, the printer, was also on his way to Dwight. So was John Candy, the apprentice. And as a member of the Treaty

Party the onetime editor Elias Boudinot could be expected to arrive in time. By early fall the press was producing copies of Sequoyah's alphabet and passages from the scriptures. Almost all the original newspaper staff was back together again; it seemed only a matter of time before that legendary bird, the *Phoenix,* would rise from its ashes to begin again the cycle of its life.

John Ridge was intelligent enough to realize that seizures of property belonging to the opposition only harmed his cause. Particularly when the homes of Treaty Party members—his own, and Boudinot's, and those of Stand Watie and others—were pointedly spared in Lumpkin's orders to the Georgia Guard. He cautioned the governor to watch his step. Enough hostility existed to warrant not arousing more.

Back at Running Waters after the Council had adjourned, he sent to Lumpkin a revealing letter which sheds light on his estimations of himself, his motives, and the situation in which he found himself. Also his conspiratorial *modus operandi*. "As a Cherokee who cherishes the most ardent devotion for the preservation of his people as a distinct community," he wrote, "I stand in a delicate situation, which requires of me the most cautious and prudent conduct." He continued:

To effect the great objects I have in contemplation, it is evidently necessary that I should retain all the influence I possess & to acquire as much more as possible. Purely for that consideration, relying as I do to posterity to award to my motives the tribute of Justice they deserve, I trust that the influence will not be endangered by exposing to the public this communication. *It is therefore confidential.*[13]

Outlining the merits, as he saw them, of the treaty signed in Washington, which "dispenses full & equal justice to all parties in the Nation and to every individual," and noting that "the President has assured me that he will stand by this treaty as the Ultimatum of the Government and no other shall be offered to the Cherokee people," he added:

But, Sir, the Ross party disbelieve it, & this party composed as it is of Halfbreed Nullifiers wish to change it to suit themselves—that they might prey upon the last avails of an oppressed race. They are, by means of falsehoods, in the field, valley & mountain opposing the ratification of it because, as I believe, it is a *just and honest one.*

When the Indians are urgent to receive the treaty they promise to make a better one . . . The object is procrastination—to out live Jackson's administration or to compel it to abandon the rights of the Indians into their own Keeping and management. Five millions of dollars, managed and disbursed by a few of the Halfbreed race & Georgia-Lawyers would be a speculation which even the Rothschilds of Europe would be glad to obtain.[14]

Was the mention of the Rothschilds a play on names? Certainly his repeated emphasis on the half-breeds constituting Ross's party, a new element in Ridge's venom, had almost racial overtones. Strange, that the eighth-breed Ross, who had cultivated the image of the full-blood, and the full-blood Ridge, who had adopted the mantle of the whites, should find their relative political positions so peculiarly reversed.

"In the meantime," Ridge told the governor, "you have a most important part to act." That was, to pursue and arrest "the *banded outlaws*" of the opposition; send the Georgia Guard under Colonel Bishop "to scour and range in their fastnesses & to search for them in their caves, and to suppress their secret meetings close to all night dances where the leaders of the Ross party usually meet with them for consultation . . .

"As to the accomplishment of the removal of our people there is no doubt. We are gaining upon the enemy gradually & surely . . . John Ross is unhorsed in Washington and you must unhorse him here."[15]

If Ridge had been shaken by the cool reception of his treaty in the Council, Schermerhorn was not. He had only just begun to fight. And he found a weakness in Ross's position which he pointed out to Ridge. Since elections had, by Georgia's interdiction, been suspended—none had been held since 1828—John Ross was no more head of the Nation than was Ridge himself. At least, one could look at it that way. In fact, the National Council which had disapproved the treaty was itself unconstitutional since all the members' terms had now expired. Ridge could call a Council of his own, which he might be better able to control.

It was a rash and revolutionary measure, but Ridge succumbed to Schermerhorn's persuasion. He called an unofficial Council at Running Waters in July, letting it be known that a vote would be taken on the distribution of government annuities—whether to individuals or the Treasury—as a drawing card. John Ross, however he felt about the matter, encouraged his followers to attend. He could not afford to give Ridge a free hand in any matter affecting the National interest.

On the third Monday in July the sloping lawns of Running Waters looked like a county fairgrounds, with hundreds and then thousands—men, women, and children—occupying every square yard with their tents and wagons despite an obtrusive rain. Benjamin Currey had ordered the Georgia Guard to stand by but was forced to admit that seldom if ever had "so great a number of persons of any color . . . met and preserved better order than was observed on this occasion." The Guard had no more serious job than entertaining the assembly with its fife-and-drum corps.

To Sophia Sawyer's delight, and the excitement of her pupils, the Ridges' mansion played host to many notables, Commissioner Schermerhorn outstanding among them, Benjamin Currey, and The Ridge himself arriving in a new coach imported from New York City with a team of horses handled by a liveried black driver. John Ross was invited to sleep in the house with other distinguished guests, but politely declined. He would camp with his people on the grounds outside.

During the night Schermerhorn had requested that a large platform be constructed, on which he could address the assembly from an appropriate height. But when Schermerhorn mounted the dais, John Ridge began to have some doubts about the federal commissioner. One of the purposes of the Council was to restore unity and to reach some agreement on a satisfactory treaty—preferably some version of the document brought back from Washington. But Schermerhorn tactlessly took the occasion to lash out at John Ross for opposing removal when nothing but removal could save his country. "Were the chiefs still disposed to delude their people, when ruin demanded entrance at the red man's door, and the heavy hand of oppression already rested upon his head?"

These were not words calculated to bring harmony to the assembly. Ross responded simply that he was "not disposed to quarrel with any man for an honest expression of opinion," while even John Ridge was impelled to say that if Ross and he had any difference of opinion, it resulted from "honest conviction" as to what manner "the Cherokee people could be preserved."[16]

Nothing could have saved the Council now. Schermerhorn proposed another meeting later that month when tempers had had time to cool. Ross suggested to Ridge that perhaps it would be better if the leaders of their separate factions got together for discussion at Red Clay—Cherokees only, no Schermerhorn, no Currey. Ridge agreed; but when the time came for the meeting Ross did not appear. A messenger informed Ridge that the chief was detained indefinitely by a bad case of diarrhea. All matters would have to await discussion at the annual October Council.

It was a hot tempestuous summer of suspense. Benjamin Currey wrote the Commissioner of Indian Affairs in Washington there were continued threats of violence in the Nation. And indeed four members of John Ridge's Treaty Party were killed, one beaten to death, one stabbed in sixteen places, two cut to shreds by knives. Ridge bitterly charged the crimes to Ross and his followers, who "tried hard to counteract the growth of our party by murders—it is dreadful to reflect on the amount of blood which has been shed by the savages on those who have only exercised the right of opinion."[17]

Ridge himself, however, had begun to regard Commissioner Schermerhorn as a dubious ally and to put more reliance for aid on Governor Lumpkin. Also, battle weariness among the Cherokees was bringing new adherents to his side; many were tired of fighting and wanted the issue settled one way or another— which was a somewhat different stance than Ross's posture of all-out resistance.

"I feel pleasure now to say that our cause prospers," Ridge recorded in late September 1835, "& I believe will result in the general cession of the Nation . . . John Ross and his party will try to *outlive* the administration of Genl. Jackson if they are not forced into the treaty, & it now depends upon the treaty party to take a bold and decided stand. We have gained so much now in Georgia & Alabama that we shall soon organize chiefs & a regular Council for those two states and close the treaty."[18]

But it all depended, Ridge added, on the outcome of the annual October Council. He was still relying on some sort of compromise with Ross, some version of a treaty that would be acceptable to both sides. To that end he himself had softened his position, was prepared to make concessions.

But not Schermerhorn. Deserted by Ridge, he was more than ever determined to push through the treaty he had made in Washington. It was the only way of saving face with his superiors. He suggested by letter to Jackson that subtle bribery might be used to gain approval for the pact; certain influential chiefs might be offered substantial sums for their homes if they enrolled for emigration. No deals, said the President. Then, proposed Schermerhorn, let him as commissioner "conclude a treaty with a part of the Nation and compel its acceptance by the rest." No, said Secretary Cass in behalf of the President, any pact with the government must be sanctioned by the Nation, without resort to trickery—for now.

Jackson, however, had once said of the intransigent Cherokees, "Build a fire under them . . ." Schermerhorn decided he would do just that and smoke them out. He sought support from the governors of Alabama and Tennessee. Most of Ross's influential followers were in Tennessee, as was Ross himself. If the two states adopted Georgia's tactic of forcible evictions, the Ross party would be driven into limbo, and Ross himself would have no place to hide.

The Commissioner got some cautious assent from Alabama's Governor C. C. Clay, but none whatever from William Carroll of Tennessee. Despite Carroll's close relations with Andrew Jackson in the Creek War, at the Battle of New Orleans, and in the Washington political arena, the Tennessee governor was not a rubber-stamp Jacksonian. He thought for himself and was beginning to have some doubts about this two-way pressure on the Cherokees. In fact, when the President suggested that he serve as co-commissioner with Schermerhorn, Carroll pointedly ignored the assignment.

There remained for purposes of intimidation only Colonel Bishop and the Georgia Guard, stationed in Camp Benton at Spring Place. Prompted by Ridge and now by Schermerhorn, the governor sent arms and ammunition up to Benton, and the Guard was ordered into action. There followed a series of arrests and detentions without pretext, perhaps the commonest form of political harassment. Elijah Hicks, former *Phoenix* editor, was taken into custody, and the venerable Chief White Path was jailed without charges. Councilmen James Martin, Thomas Taylor, Walter Adair, and James Trott were arrested as agents of John Ross.

Ross sought legal counsel for his imprisoned followers, and discovered that, apparently at Ridge's instigation, the firm of William Underwood had been bribed by the governor to forsake its Cherokee clients in favor of Georgia and the Treaty Party. Ross did, however, obtain the services of two Milledgeville attorneys, Richard and Samuel Rockwell, who worked for and achieved the prisoners' release.

But the persecutions did not stop there. Goaded by Benjamin Currey, the enrollment agents continued their strong-arm tactics. Cherokees in the outlying areas who refused to sign up for removal found their cattle stolen, their farms burned or seized, and in not a few cases they were beaten for "resisting a government agent."

United States officials, meanwhile, were acting as if the treaty signed in March was final; difficulties could be worked out as the year progressed. It was final so far as Andrew Jackson was concerned; it had been drafted by Cherokees with government approval, and signed by Cherokees. One way or another the Nation would accept it. Acting on this assumption, Secretary Cass ordered a census taken of the tribe as a first step in their organized removal.

No sooner had the census takers reached the Nation than Ross dispatched letters to the district chiefs. No one was to give the agents any information as to families and numbers—"thereby defeating the object of the Genl. Government," reported Colonel Nelson of the Guard, "and inflaming the minds of the Cherokees to an extent . . . not before witnessed in the Territory . . ."[19]

To Benjamin Currey, the two brothers John and Lewis Ross were the source of all his troubles. Lewis lived on a tract of land near the government agency in Tennessee and, according to Currey, spied on its activities with "implacable hatred" and sought "to paralyze every measure connected with the business of emigration." But John was the target of Currey's personal vendetta, and the chief's interference with the census was the final straw. On September 29 he took drastic action. He wrote to Governor Lumpkin urging that John Ross be arrested for his "manifold violation of state laws."[20]

No doubt Lumpkin gave the matter careful thought. The earlier arrests might have put some fear in Cherokee ranks; they had also crystallized resentment and resistance. He would have to think it over. . . .

Time was running out for the Cherokee Nation, but Ross refused to see it that way. The Principal Chief—and despite Ridge's efforts to dispossess him of that office, he was still Principal Chief in Cherokee eyes—had accepted the fact that some treaty would have to be consummated. Perhaps the Nation would move West. It was a harsh conclusion to face up to; but one thing might make it easier to take. If emigration was unavoidable (and he would go on fighting it) he would settle for removal on his own terms or the best terms he could get.

He had told his people on getting back from Washington: "Hold on, be united, and all will be well shortly." Unity was still his goal; and to this end he pocketed his pride and bent a little toward Ridge. In September he proposed a meeting of the rival factions, to iron out their difficulties and arrive at a united front before the autumn Council in October.

Presumably all was amicable; there are no minutes of that meeting. But Ridge's position at this point is hard to calculate. Only weeks before, he had branded Ross the enemy, an "outlaw" and a "Halfbreed Nullifier." Now he was sitting at the table with him, planning a common strategy. Did he, in truth, switch suddenly to Ross's side, and promise to hold out against the present treaty? Or was he going along for now, playing a waiting game, and lulling Ross into a soft sense of security?

The only clue is a letter he wrote to attorney William Underwood on September 7, at about the time of his meeting with John Ross. He mentions that the Washington treaty is about to be submitted to the Council; and he asks Underwood about legal protection for the rights and properties of those who enrolled for emigration. Nothing very indicative in this, except that Ridge makes no suggestion that the treaty might not be approved—although he was ostensibly allied with Ross for its rejection.

October descended on the highlands with an incandescent torch. Smoke plumed over the chestnut groves where the ground was being cleared of under-brush. The hills burst into flaming colors, and somnolent mists in the valleys looked like blue lakes from the mountaintops. Butrick was reminded of standing on one of those mountaintops with Chief Rising Fawn, a full-blood with the etched face of a Biblical prophet. As the ancient chief squinted his eyes to focus on the view, he expressed himself in one repeated word: "Glory! Glory! Glory!"

Plainly, thought Butrick, the Cherokee's love of his country was not love for a piece of real estate; and the Council that was meeting on the second Monday in October had a sacred duty to perform.

14

"Spare Our People!"

THE CHEROKEE case won many strange adherents, and none more unlikely than John Howard Payne, now forty-four and at a critical point in his eventful life. At the time when John Ross was beginning his political career as Principal Chief of the Cherokee Nation, Payne, one year his junior, was reaching a peak in his theatrical career—starring triumphantly in the London production of his own play, *Brutus, or the Fall of Tarquin*.

Since the age of fourteen the New York-born Payne had been a versatile and peripatetic prodigy. His successes as playwright, actor, publisher of a theatrical journal, took him to London, where he became the only American actor to achieve distinction on the English stage. For twenty years he was lionized in the London theater, and his *Maid of Milan* at Covent Garden introduced to the public his ballad "Home, Sweet Home," which did as much as anything to make him famous.

There had been ups and downs in his sensitive, inwardly lonely life. Among the down periods were some months spent in debtor's prison, from which he was rescued allegedly by Charles Lamb. There followed an unhappy love affair with Mary Wollstonecraft Shelley, the poet's widow—in which Payne's sometime drama collaborator, Washington Irving, provided a sort of counterpoint—after which he returned to America in 1832 somewhat at a loose end.

In America he abandoned the stage, with sixty original plays to his credit, and sought to establish a national journal, with international appeal, that would portray to the world "the character, manners, and institutions" of the United States. To this end in 1835 he traveled throughout the country—as far west as New Orleans and as far south as Florida—gathering pertinent material and soliciting subscriptions. Entering Georgia in August of that year, he "was induced by the descriptions I had heard of the beauty of its mountain region, to turn somewhat aside from my road in order to seek the upper part of the State."[1]

He knew nothing about the Cherokees and their embattled condition, having been abroad when the controversy gained national prominence. A chance encounter with Alexander S. Tennille, brother of Georgia's Secretary of State, led him to consider composing a history of the Cherokees for his projected journal. Other encounters probably encouraged this endeavor, among them a meeting with John and Sarah Ridge, through whom he met other members of the Treaty Party. Of these he wrote:

The other day I had a very interesting interview with the principal chiefs of that party—the conversation was brief, but very characteristic. I have passed a couple of days & got very well acquainted with Boudinot, a Cherokee educated at the North, who married a Gold . . . They are a very intelligent and amiable couple. I was delighted with my reception from the family.[2]

Payne might have remained under Boudinot's spell, for they found one another congenial and intelligent, but for another chance meeting with Colonel Samuel Rockwell, who had earlier done legal work for Ross. Rockwell gave him a letter of introduction to the Principal Chief, whose knowledge of Cherokee affairs, the colonel said, would be indispensable to the historian.

"Mr. Payne's object in visiting you," wrote Rockwell in his note to Ross, "is to obtain an insight into your national history & copies of such documents as you may have in your possession concerning the traditions of this oppressed People in order that if the race is to be extinguished, its history & that of its wrongs may be preserved."[3]

Ross may have winced at the suggestion that his race might be extinguished. But he received the visitor with "cordiality and unreserve" when on September 28 Payne arrived at Red Clay to find his host and hostess and their children living in "a log hut, of but one single room, and scarcely proof against the wind and rain." Payne had been told in Georgia that the Principal Chief was "selfish, sordid, and violent." In contrast he found him "mild, intelligent, and entirely unaffected." Ross gave him what documents he thought might be of interest, including the voluminous letters of Charles R. Hicks, and urged Payne to stay over for the October Council shortly to be held at Red Clay. The visitor readily assented.

In the ensuing interval Payne became thoroughly convinced of the justice of the Cherokee cause, and began preparing the first of a series of magazine articles that would present "their views and feelings." In an initial paper he mentioned the maraudings of the Georgia Guard. He spoke of the Guard's outward appearance as "more resembling banditti than soldiers" and alluded to "an Indian prisoner who had hanged himself while in their custody, through fear that they would murder him." He also began the draft of a proposed memorial to the American people, to be signed, he hoped, by the entire population of the Nation. He worked to have it finished by the time of the October Council.

Ross had assured Payne that this particular assembly, coming at a moment of crisis, would draw all the principal chiefs and head men of the Nation. More than a thousand came, in groups of thirty and forty, from every corner of the territory, some walking or riding hundreds of miles from Alabama, North Carolina, Georgia. All the great chiefs were there, including White Path, Going Snake, and George Lowrey of John Ross's faction. John Ridge and Elias Boudinot of the opposing Treaty Party appeared at Ross's invitation.

It was perhaps the most important Council meeting in the Nation's history and one, it appeared, at which the country's fate would be determined. It was a time, wrote Payne, when "the Cherokee Nation stands alone, moneyless, helpless, and almost hopeless; yet without a dream of yielding . . . I cannot imagine a spectacle of more moral grandeur than the assembly of such people, under such circumstances."

Though the delegates were to meet in the open-sided Council House at Red Clay, Ross's followers first rendezvoused at the nearby cabin of their chief, where Payne noted their arrival on the morning of October 11:

The woods echoed with the trampling of many feet: a long and orderly procession emerged from among the trees, the gorgeous autumnal tints of whose departing foliage seemed in sad harmony with the noble spirit now beaming in this departing race. Most of the train was on foot. There were a few aged men, and some few women, on horseback. The train halted at the humble gate of the principal chief: he stood ready to receive them.

Everything was noiseless. The party, entering, loosened the blankets which were loosely rolled and flung over their backs and hung them, with their tin cups and other paraphernalia attached, upon the fence. The chief approached them. They formed diagonally in two lines, and each, in silence, drew near to give his hand. Their dress was neat and picturesque: all wore turbans, except four or five with hats; many of them, tunics, with sashes; many long robes, and nearly all some drapery: so that they had the oriental air of old scripture pictures of patriarchal processions.

The salutations over, the old men remained near the chief, and the rest withdrew to various parts of the enclosure; some sitting Turk fashion against the trees, and others upon the fences, but with the eyes of all fixed upon their chief. They had walked sixty miles since yesterday, and had encamped last night in the woods. They sought their way to the council ground . . .[4]

Representing the United States and Georgia were Benjamin Currey, the enrolling agent, and Colonel Bishop of the Georgia Guard, though the Guard itself encamped discreetly a short distance off, south of the Tennessee-Georgia line. And Payne, arriving at the Council ground with Ross, was surprised to recognize an old acquaintance from his Union College days in New York: John F. Schermerhorn, commissioner for Andrew Jackson.

After exchanging pleasantries, Payne made it clear to Schermerhorn where his sympathies lay. The latter, deploring Payne's association with the anti-treaty sentiment, assured him, "Ross is unruly now, but he will soon be tame enough," adding, "I'll have a treaty within a week." Payne announced that he would later put his views in writing and said jocosely, "Don't complain if I use you rather rough." To which Schermerhorn replied, "No, but if you do, don't complain if I return the compliment."[5]

Elizur Butler came over from Brainerd to attend the Red Clay Council, and reported to David Greene that "Mr. Schermerhorn became very much excited against Mr. Ross" and that Schermerhorn presented the chief with a written charge that "Mr. Ross and the Council were usurpers, and destitute of all legal authority. Mr. Ross read a part of this communication to the large body of Cherokees who had assembled, when objections were made on the part of the Cherokees to its being finished. It was stated that enough had been read to show the tenor of the communication." Continued Butler:

I was often at the council ground and heard of no one who approved the above communication. Mr. S. was soon told that he could effect nothing by attempting to break Mr. Ross and the council; for if the people present were called on to elect a Principal Chief, there would be an overwhelming majority in favor of Mr. Ross. He immediately changed his measures and addressed himself to Ross as Principal Chief.[6]

What Schermerhorn had to say, however, was little more welcome than his accusations against Ross. The Cherokees had heard most of it before. The frock-coated pastor presented again the terms of the treaty drafted earlier that year, with only minor modifications and adjustments. These terms were: $3,250,000 to the Cherokee Nation for its land in the East, $150,000 to settle accumulated debts dating back to the War of 1812, a proportionate share of the millions of acres already guaranteed to Western Cherokees, and an added bonus of 800,000 acres to those moving West upon the treaty's ratification.

The proposition was put to a vote and overwhelmingly rejected. "More than a thousand people voted against the treaty," wrote Butler, "and none in favour." Among those voting "Nay" were members of the Treaty Party controlled by Ridge, Watie, and Boudinot. This sudden opposition from those who had formerly supported the agreement obviously took Schermerhorn by surprise. As if responding to a cue, he raised the capital offer to $5,000,000. Another vote was taken and the terms again rejected—though the voting was rather bizarrely conducted, according to John Ridge:

The question was asked, Are you willing to take five millions of dollars for your country? No, no, was the cry of the people. Some few of the better informed were placed in different positions to lead the way, and the Indians, without knowing the difference between 5,000 and five millions, said No! They did not understand.

The question was then put to the people: Would they consent to let a committee of selected representatives handle their affairs in Washington, with full power to do what they thought best? "The answer was Yes," recorded Ridge, who added:

They were then dismissed, and they scattered that very night. There was no deliberation . . . A vast majority . . . were of the opinion that they had rejected the propositions of the Government altogether, and had instructed their delegation to make no treaty, and consequently *had saved the land*. This was the result of a manifest equivocation and double dealing with an ignorant people.[7]

But the real question remained: If Ridge was so cynical about the method of voting and the result, why did he and his adherents vote with the majority? It is hard to clarify the Treaty Party's actions at this Council. Were they siding with Ross as a means of forcing better terms from Schermerhorn and Jackson? If so, once they had obtained better terms, why did they continue to reject the treaty? Time might reveal the strategies behind the contradictions, but Schermerhorn for now was stumped. He had no authority to negotiate on any other terms than those endorsed at Washington.

That being the case, the Council, before adjournment, voted to send a committee of ten to the capital to negotiate further with Cass and Jackson, the group including John and Lewis Ross, Elijah Hicks, Joseph Vann, John Martin, and James Brown. At the last moment John Ross, as elected leader of the delegation, appointed Ridge and Boudinot to the committee.

Ridge and Boudinot accepted. At long last the rift in their ranks that had mortally wounded the Cherokees and split the Nation into hostile camps was mended. Once again they could present to their opponents a united front.

Then the strange factors operating undercover in that Council worked again. Ridge and Boudinot were seen in conference with Schermerhorn—after which they withdrew their support from the National Party and resigned from the committee.

Boudinot gave as an explanation the illness of his wife. John Ridge offered no explanation; it would seem that he had other plans. So, in fact, did Schermerhorn—who in his report to Washington piously concluded, "the Lord is able to overrule all things for good."[8]

Returning with Ross to his cabin after the Council had adjourned, Payne completed his address for the Cherokee Nation, gathered up his papers, and prepared to head south into Georgia. But on Saturday evening, November 7, both suddenly heard "a loud barking of dogs, the quick tramp of galloping horses, then the rush of many feet." The door flew open and twenty-four members of the Georgia Guard burst in with bayonets fixed and pistols drawn.

"Gentlemen, you are under arrest," a sergeant told them.

Inquiring what the charges were, and on whose orders, Payne was struck across the mouth.

"You'll know that soon enough," the sergeant said, ordering his men to gather up the various documents and papers Payne had written or accumulated.

Mounting their horses and flanked by the Guard, the pair were escorted south through Georgia in a penetrating rain. No one spoke to the prisoners, but Captain Absalom Bishop, brother of the colonel, began humming "Home, Sweet Home."

"I wrote that song," said Payne in a move to foster communications.

"Oh, yeah?" said Absalom.[9]

After a twenty-four-mile ride they arrived at dawn at Camp Benton, the Spring Place quarters of the Georgia Guard, to be imprisoned in one of the windowless slave cabins on the Joseph Vann estate. Chained to a table in one corner, his arms tightly pinioned, was a prisoner who had been taken earlier, a son of Chief Going Snake against whom the charges appeared equally baseless. "Hanging from the rafters above," writes one historian of the event, "was the odoriferous decomposing corpse of a Cherokee who had been executed some weeks before." Payne, however, made no mention of this grisly detail.

How well John Ross had disciplined his followers was evident now in their restraint. As news of this supreme indignity spread from village to village, it would have been easy for the Cherokees to follow their outraged instincts, descend en masse upon Camp Benton and Spring Place, overcome the Guard by vastly superior numbers, and release their leader. But Ross had preached passive resistance and reliance on the law. Smoldering inwardly, they kept their rage in check.

Meanwhile the generally illiterate Guard pored over the papers seized in Ross's cabin. They concluded that Sequoyah's alphabet was some sort of foreign code, that manuscripts written in Cherokee were French, and that Payne was a northern Abolitionist—than which nothing was more heinous—intent on inciting the blacks and Indians against the southern whites. In an English version of Payne's writing they found his reference to the Georgia Guard as resembling "banditti." *That* they understood. "Banditti" was a favorite epithet of President Jackson in describing enemies of the United States.

To the self-possessed Ross, who believed that their predicament was due to Schermerhorn and Bishop, there was an obvious illegality in their arrest. That they were being detained for purely political reasons would gain no credence or admission in the Georgia courts. But they had been seized at Red Clay, over the Georgia line in Tennessee. Somehow the prisoners smuggled out word to Governor William Carroll in Nashville. Would the governor put up with such a flagrant violation of Tennessee soil and sovereignty?

No direct reply came from Carroll, though Georgia's Governor Schley, succeeding Lumpkin, got a verbal blast that all but blew his head off. And on Monday, November 16, Colonel Bishop arrived and gave orders for Ross to be set free. Losing no time in departing, Ross promised Payne to work for his release.

One dreary week later that release came. There were no explanations or apologies. He could hardly have expected any. Colonel Bishop lined up the Guard outside the prison, brought Payne out, pointed to the soldiers standing loosely at attention, and shouted in his bullhorn voice:

"That, Sir, is your banditti!"

Payne's unspoken thought was: Then I owe an apology to the banditti.

"Now, Sir!" roared Bishop, pointing to Payne's waiting horse, "cut out of Georgia! If you ever dare to show your face in these territories, I'll make you curse the day that you were born. Clear out of the state forever, and go to John Ross, God damn you!"[10]

Payne did—and it would be to Bishop's sorrow and to Georgia's shame. Returning to Tennessee, the playwright-author prepared an inflammatory account of his imprisonment and treatment by the Georgia Guard, which was published in early December in the Knoxville *Register*.

There were immediate repercussions. Tennessee was so indignant that volunteers offered to patrol the southern boundaries to keep the "Georgia ruffians" out. Even the *Georgia Journal* of Milledgeville castigated the Guard as "Governor Lumpkin's strong arm gang," and urged its dissolution, while ex-Governor Lumpkin—happy to be out of office—declared that the arrest had been a tactical mistake.

The general indignation was too much for Colonel Bishop. He resigned his commission and retired to civilian life. (There was one other little-known casualty of Payne's crusade in Georgia. Mary Harden, the colonel's daughter, had lost her heart to the cavalier writer. She would wait for forty years for him to renew their courtship—then die with a copy of "Home, Sweet Home" in her hands.)

Payne's most eloquent contribution to the Cherokee cause—his message *The Cherokee Nation to the People of the United States*—being less inflammatory, got less notice, though it cried for notice:

Friends—Listen! The voice of thousands and of thousands now speak to you in one voice. Listen! A Nation asks it of you—Listen! We bring you no angry words. We would touch your hearts; for we think your hearts are good; and, therefore, for your own sakes, as well as for ours, friends, we would have you listen!

He spoke of the Cherokee Nation as a small forest standing proudly in the path of a universal hurricane. "The wild tempest howls around, yet still it stands." He spoke of the Cherokees' inherent love of "the soil that gave us birth . . . We cling to it because it is our first love; we cling to it because it will be our last . . . there can be no better for us than what we have—for us, there can be none so good."

And he cited the warning that came from those Cherokees already induced to emigrate; those who had grieved and died in their western homes, "whose wail is on the night wind crying to their Eastern brethren: Beware! . . . Still we are told, 'Remove! Remove!'—for the eyes of avarice are on our lands."

And last of all, "We appeal to you as Ambassadors of the Living God." A Nation which had adopted Christianity in emulation of the white man surely deserved Christian treatment—charity, compassion—in return.

On this note, Payne closed his "talk" with a somewhat hyperbolic but poetic passage:

Friends! While we have spoken, the autumn has deepened and the glory has departed from the forest trees, and even now the withered and the many colored leaves are burning on the hills, and Winter approaches and they will be seen no more. But that Winter will be followed by Spring, and the fires will have made the earth more fertile, and in the Spring new leaves will come and the forest trees will smile again, and again will the world look beautiful. Friends, the leafless season of our fate is come upon us. If you forget us, the fires will have consumed the fallen leaves, will kill the trees too, and to our Winter there will succeed no Spring!

Our talk is over.[11]

John Ridge's shift to Ross's side during the October Council was one of calculated strategy, as he revealed in a letter written at the time to Governor Lumpkin: "A conference is now in session . . . to try to compromise and close the treaty but if it can't come to an agreement, the plan is to make a treaty in December." He added: "The Rev. Mr. Schermerhorn will . . . forward you such projects or laws as he deems will be useful on this subject. *My name must be reserved from the public eye.*"[12]

"The plan is to make a treaty in December." The words left little doubt about why Ridge and Boudinot had resigned from Ross's committee and refused to go to Washington. They had projects under way at home. And Ridge's insistence on anonymity suggests either a guilty conscience or a fear of retaliation, even assassination, if those projects became known.

With Ross out of the way, first arrested according to plan and now in Washington, the field was clear. Schermerhorn put the machinery in motion with his next move. By word of mouth and posters circulated in the Nation he announced that another Council would be held at New Echota in December. The purpose: to agree on an "acceptable" treaty that would take the place of that rejected by the Council.

Though Ross must have learned of this bit of chicanery in Washington, he chose to ignore it. He felt he could afford to. As Elizur Butler had written to David Greene after the October Council, "Mr. Ross seems rather to be gaining than losing influence among his people." The loyalty of the overwhelming majority of Cherokees was solidly behind him; they could be counted on to boycott any subversive effort in his absence.

Schermerhorn, too, was aware of these odds. To boost attendance at his December Council he promised free blankets and subsistence money for all who assembled at New Echota. More shrewdly, he warned that all who failed to attend would be counted as voting favorably on any motion, any treaty, presented at the Council.

Despite these inducements and threats, as Schermerhorn himself admitted, only from three to five hundred Cherokees—men, women, and children—arrived at New Echota on December 23, most of them drawn by the offer of free blankets. They comprised at best not more than 3 percent of the total population, and only eighty of the group were eligible voters. Among these eighty only Elias Boudinot, Stand Watie, and the Ridges were men of any standing in the Nation.

The sparse attendance was by no means representative. Plainly the vast majority of Cherokees were boycotting the assembly, possibly, as Boudinot believed, on word from Ross to stay away. An unwise move perhaps, considering Schermerhorn's tactic of counting all absentees as voting in the affirmative, willy-nilly. Once again the much-thumbed, shopworn treaty was presented to the gathering, prefaced by a speech from Schermerhorn—"in his usual style," said one of his hearers, "only a little more so"—and followed by a reading of the document by Currey.

At this point the Council had a diverting break. The roof of the Council House caught fire. Delegates rushed from the building, climbed the walls, and formed water-bucket relay lines to douse the blaze. Then all returned, resumed their seats and lit their pipes, and prepared to listen to what their leaders, especially The Ridge and Boudinot, might have to say.

It would be the last address The Ridge would make in public. He was sixty-five now, somewhat frailer, somewhat whiter, but his resonant voice retained its fire. If he had learned nothing else in his threescore years, he had learned to understand and arouse the emotions of his people. He told them:

I know we love the graves of our fathers, who have gone before to the happy hunting grounds of the Great Spirit—the eternal land, where the deer, the turkey and the buffalo will never give out. We can never forget these homes, I know, but an unbending, iron necessity tells us we must leave them. I would willingly die to preserve them, but any forcible effort to keep them will cost us our lands, our lives and the lives of our children. There is but one path of safety, one road to future existence as a Nation. The path is open before you. Make a treaty of cession. Give up these lands and go over beyond the great Father of Waters.[13]

The Council might well have ended there. What The Ridge said was all that needed saying. His was the voice of the prophet that no one present could dispute.

Boudinot, however, recalled another, more strident voice, that of Thomas Foreman, who had called The Ridge a traitor and demanded his impeachment. Of Foreman and his followers who had rejected the treaty at Red Clay, Boudinot told his audience:

. . . No, those braves are not here. Their places are vacant. Ross has induced them not to come. They are at their homes with the loud thunder. Ah! They will come again. I know I take my life in my hand as our fathers have also done. We will make and sign this treaty. Our friends can then cross the great river, but Tom Foreman and his people will put us across the dread river of death! We can die, but the Cherokee Nation will be saved.[14]

Boudinot's, too, was the voice of a prophet. He himself could not have known how clearly he foresaw the future.

There was no real debate on the issue before the Council. As Boudinot said, the treaty would be signed. Schermerhorn's problem was how to give the signatories a semblance of authority. By common agreement with Currey, the Ridges, and Boudinot, a committee of twenty was formed "to represent the Nation." With no one present to challenge this device, the Council adjourned and the Committee of Twenty repaired to the house of Elias Boudinot to draft a final, formal version of the compact.

The group worked far into the night, and Boudinot regretfully confessed to Harriet that liquid refreshments were resorted to from time to time. By midnight a reconstituted treaty was agreed to. It did not differ greatly from the terms rejected at the October Council. All Cherokee territory east of the Mississippi was ceded to the United States for $5,000,000 plus a joint interest in the Western lands already guaranteed to the preceding emigrants. The United States would recompense the departing Cherokees for their "improvements," would pay the cost of removal, and would provide for their subsistence for one year following their arrival in the West.

Some additional inducements were included, such as an extra tract of land in Kansas. And Ridge and Boudinot insisted that a limited number of Cherokees who chose to remain in North Carolina, Tennessee, or Alabama could do so provided that they qualified for citizenship in those respective states. Removal was to take place two years after the treaty was ratified by Congress and signed by the President of the United States.

Solemnly the committee lined up to put their names or marks on the final document. Last to do so was The Ridge—he who had so ardently defended his people's sovereignty through the years, who had driven the Georgians by force from Cherokee soil, and who had restored the death penalty for any who sold or ceded another foot of precious soil. More than any other he must have felt the dread significance of what he was about to do.

It was an agonizing moment for him as he put his mark at the bottom of the treaty. "I have signed my death warrant," he told those around him. He was right.[15]

To Secretary Cass the last week in December 1835, Schermerhorn wrote:

I have the extreme pleasure to announce to you that yesterday I concluded a treaty. Ross, after this treaty, is prostrate. The power of the Nation is taken from him as well as the money, and the treaty will give general satisfaction.

Cass sent the note over to the White House, where the President, in his cluttered study, was graciously playing host to John Ross and his delegation.

Up to that moment, so far as Jackson knew, Ross still represented four fifths —even nine tenths—of the Cherokees. Now, with this word from Schermerhorn, that did not seem to matter. Ross was suddenly dispensable. A treaty had been signed; Schermerhorn, Ridge, and Boudinot were at this very moment bringing it to Washington for Senate ratification.

The President curtly informed Ross of this *fait accompli* and showed him the White House door. There would be no need for further communication between them. There was nothing more to be discussed.

Schermerhorn, however, was self-deceived in stating that Ross was "prostrate" and that the agreement would give "general satisfaction." Of all the treaties negotiated with the Indians in the past, this was the most outrageous on the sorry record. Ross knew it. The Cherokees knew it. So did a surprising number of Americans, including members of both houses of the Congress.

Schermerhorn, Boudinot, and Ridge had barely reached the capital before a wave of protest swept the country. In Washington such notable stalwarts as

Daniel Webster, Henry Clay, Edward Everett, and David Crockett spearheaded opposition to the compact. Speeches in Congress on the subject, observed C. C. Royce, "were characterized by a depth and bitterness of feeling such as had never been exceeded even on the slavery question."[16]

The Cherokee Nation itself had lost its official voice with the suppression of the *Phoenix*. But it found an unexpected and outspoken champion in Major William M. Davis, whom Cass himself had appointed to supervise Cherokee emigration after the passage of Jackson's Removal Bill in 1830. Since that assignment Davis had remained at the Hiwassee Agency; he had had a chance to know the Indians a little better, and his sympathies had changed. Shortly after the turn of the year he wrote to Secretary Cass regarding the pact that Schermerhorn and Ridge had brought to Washington:

Sir: That paper . . . called a treaty, is no treaty at all, because not sanctioned by the great body of the Cherokee and made without their participation or assent. I solemnly declare to you that upon its reference to the Cherokee people it would be instantly rejected by nine-tenths of them. There was not present at the conclusion of the treaty more than one hundred Cherokee voters, although the weather was everything that could be desired . . .

No enumeration of them was made by Schermerhorn. The business of making the treaty was transacted with a committee appointed by the Indians present, so as not be expose their numbers. The power of attorney under which the committee acted was signed only by the president and secretary of the meeting, so as not to disclose their weakness . . .

Mr. Schermerhorn's apparent design was to conceal the real number present and to impose on the public and the government upon this point . . .

As to the delegates who had brought the pact to Washington with Schermerhorn, they "had no more authority to make a treaty than any other dozen Cherokee picked for the purpose." And the major concluded:

I now warn you and the President that if this paper of Schermerhorn's called a treaty is sent to the Senate and ratified you will bring trouble upon the government and eventually destroy this the Cherokee Nation. The Cherokee are peaceable, harmless people, but you may drive them to desperation, and this treaty cannot be carried into effect except by the strong arm of force.[17]

Despite the bitterly cold weather prevailing in northern Georgia, Second Chief Lowrey, acting as head of the Nation in John Ross's absence, called a special Council meeting at Red Clay in January to organize resistance to the treaty. Those unable to attend were later canvassed by delegates soliciting signatures to a protest or memorial, approved by the Council for submission to the government in Washington.

There were some who said that John Howard Payne had penned the memorial. Or possibly Ross, before or after his departure for the capital. In any event, it was a piece of literature to be enshrined in history. Declaring that the Treaty of New Echota was one in which the majority of Cherokees had had no part, it asserted: "In truth, our cause is your own. It is the cause of liberty and of justice. It is based upon your own principles, which we have learned from yourselves; for we have gloried to count your Washington and your Jefferson our teachers . . ."

Under those principles, under this tutelage, the Cherokees had carved from the wilderness a nation founded upon Christian virtues. And now,

. . . we speak to the representatives of a Christian country; the friends of justice; the patrons of the oppressed. . . . On your kindness, on your humanity, on your compassion, on your benevolence, we rest our hopes . . . On your sentence our fate is suspended . . . Spare our people! Spare the wreck of our prosperity![18]

Goliath was still in the White House with a year to go and already grooming Schermerhorn's compatriot, Martin Van Buren, to succeed him. From a distance he had watched proceedings in the Cherokee Nation with increasing satisfaction. It had taken too long, but things were happening. His Removal Bill, now more than five years old, had been beset by snags; but he had got rid of the Creeks, the Choctaws, and the Chickasaws. The Seminoles were causing some trouble in the swamps of Florida, but General Winfield Scott would flush them out—and when he did the President would sick him on the Cherokees.

For the Cherokees were still a thorn in his side if not a blight on his administration. In many quarters Jackson had been castigated for his treatment of them; and on top of that was the time and exasperating effort he had had to put forth to settle the fate of a bunch of Indians. He would like to believe, as Governor Lumpkin averred, that "John Ross is a mere pigmy" beside the images of Ridge and Boudinot. But he thought differently of the cocky chief impersonating David with his giant-killing slingshot. Ross could not be beaten; he must be circumvented somehow. The President would leave that up to Schermerhorn, the greatest circumventer of them all.

Future historians would portray Andrew Jackson as both charitable toward the Indians and diabolical toward them. Perhaps it depended on whether one went by deeds or words. In words, as Jackson prepared his second presidential message on Indian removal—his seventh address to Congress, to be presented on April 7, 1835—he proclaimed himself the savior of the aborigines. It would be his final statement on the subject, and the world had better believe him.

His program to promote the welfare of the Indians by their removal, Jackson would tell the Congress, "approaches its consummation. It was adopted on the most mature consideration of the condition of this race, and ought to be . . . prosecuted with as much vigor as a just regard to their circumstances will permit, and as fast as their consent can be obtained . . .

"It seems now to be an established fact they cannot live in contact with a civilized community and prosper. Ages of fruitless endeavor have at length brought us to a knowledge of this principle . . . no one can doubt the moral duty of the Government of the United States to protect and if possible to preserve and perpetuate the scattered remnants of this race which are left within our borders."

And the solution? The nirvana he foresaw for them out West. He made it sound like a real-estate promoter's dream. "Of its climate, fertility, and capacity to support an Indian population" it was worthy only of his highest praise. "Ample arrangements" had been made for the construction of schools, Council Houses, churches, mills, "dwellings for the chiefs." The Cherokees could live by agriculture or hunt buffalo, and this utopia was forever "secured and guaranteed to them" by the United States.[19]

Those were the words.

Nothing was said of past broken promises, dishonored treaties; of all the improvements in the East that the Cherokees would be abandoning. Of the violation of their rights, the indignities they had suffered and were still being subjected to in order to force their unwilling surrender. Of the misery and loss of life that had attended the first efforts of removal to the West. Only that hollow phrase "secured and guaranteed" by the United States. Were these the words? Were they to be believed?

Out in that mythical West, as Jackson spoke, an American artist named George Catlin was composing his own thoughts on the future of the red man. Like John Howard Payne, he had found a mission among the Indians; he was haunted by the noble, tragic faces that he painted—portraits that would long outlive their subjects. He saw in their eyes "the rapid declension of these people, which must sooner or later lead . . . to their extinction."

White Father, *spare our people!*

15

Phantom Treaty

ONCE AGAIN two rival Cherokee delegations were in Washington, both staying at the Indian Queen Hotel. Ross's group had arrived in January 1836 and had been the first to talk with Secretary Cass and Jackson. They had been told that their presence in the capital was a waste of time. There would be no further discussion of the treaty drafted at New Echota the previous December. It had been signed by Ridge and Schermerhorn's Committee of Twenty, who in Jackson's eyes did indeed, as they themselves asserted, represent the Nation.

The Ridge faction arrived at the Indian Queen in early February under the wing of Schermerhorn. Hearing of the snub that John Ross had received from Cass and Jackson, they tried again for a reconciliation. If they could get Ross's signature on the treaty it would overcome the obvious weakness of their position, the fact that they represented only one small segment of the Nation. Ross refused. He was busy interviewing sympathetic congressmen, stirring up opposition to the compact that would shortly be submitted to the Senate. Exasperated, Boudinot noted:

> Mr. Ross is using his influence to defeat the only measure that can give relief to his suffering people . . . He says he is doing the *will* of the people . . . they are opposed, and that is enough. The will of the people! . . . This has been the cry for the last five years, until that people have become a mere wreck of what they once were; all their institutions and improvements utterly destroyed; their energy enervated; their moral character debased, corrupted and ruined.[1]

The vitriolic editor went further, and directed a personal attack on Ross, to be later published as a pamphlet and circulated among the Congress—a move which Ross and many of his followers regarded as an act of treachery. In it, he accused the Principal Chief of placing the price he obtained for the ceded Nation above the welfare of the people. For as long as the Cherokees resisted removal, and remained exposed to the incursions of the white man, they approached "the last brink of destruction."

Look around you and see the progress that vice and immorality have already made! See the spread of intemperance and the wretchedness and misery it has already occasioned . . . you will find its cruel effects in the bloody tragedies that are frequently occurring—in the frequent convictions and executions for murders, and in the tears and groans of the widows and fatherless, rendered homeless and hungry by this vile curse of our race . . .

We are making a rapid tendency to a general immorality and debasement. What more evidence do we need, to prove this general tendency, than the slow but sure insinuation of the lower vices into our female population? Oh, it is heart rending to think of these things—but the world will know them—the world does know them, and we need not try to hide our shame.[2]

And what, in contrast to Ross's "prejudice and stupid obstinacy," did Boudinot propose? "My language has been, 'fly for your lives'—it is now the same. I would say to my countrymen, you among the rest, fly from the moral pestilence that will finally destroy our nation."

The pamphlet had little effect, other than further to alienate Boudinot from the great mass of Cherokees. Ross regarded the diatribe as "disgraceful and degrading" and sent a copy to John Howard Payne, but never dignified the charges with an answer. More depressing was a letter Payne received from Henry Clay that winter implying that his cause was hopeless. Payne forwarded the letter to Ross with the comment: "Alas, poor Indians, what rights can they assert against the State of Ga., backed by the tremendous power of Gen. Jackson."[3]

Possibly Ross foresaw defeat, or perhaps he was merely hedging his bets, for among the papers compiled in his hotel room that winter are innumerable drafts of what appear to be alternatives to the Treaty of New Echota, whether or not the latter was finally ratified. There is no evidence that he submitted any of the versions, nor is there any indication of which he finally preferred. But the amount of work represented by the different drafts indicates that he had far from given up on finding a solution to the crisis.

One version, selected at random, begins:

The Cherokee people being altogether opposed to treating on the basis of general removal. They are not willing to sell out their entire country for a gross sum of money. Therefore it is proposed in the spirit of reconciliation to meet the question and settle the existing Cherokee difficulties upon a principle of compromise. To wit—

Project 1.   Cede all lands in Georgia to U.S. for $1 an acre plus improvements evaluated by commissioners appointed by both sides. In Tennessee & Alabama 640 acres shall be allowed in fee simple [and] Cherokees shall be granted all the rights & privileges of Citizens on an equal footing with the white citizens of these respective states.

Project 2. On the other hand, should the U. S. Govt. refuse to treat on the basis herein before stated, and shall decline to grant any reservations to the Cherokee people and should insist upon a cession of the entire Cherokee Territory—

In the six or seven times he copied down these paragraphs Ross was never able to finish what he had in mind in Project 2. Perhaps the alternative was too forbidding to consider. He would wait and see how the Senate voted on ratification of the treaty in motion, and, as he wrote, pin his faith on the United States' intentions to reach "a fair & honorable settlement of Cherokee difficulties."[4]

Significantly, Ross rarely if ever used the term "Cherokee removal" in the various drafts of his unfinished memorials. "Removal" was a word that had no place in the vocabulary of his mind. There were only "difficulties" standing in the way of Cherokee aspirations, and difficulties could be settled.

Like Ross under sharp attack from Elias Boudinot, John Ridge also found himself on the defensive. He was aware that his group, and he particularly, were being criticized for false claims and pretensions; that he was charged with seeking to depose John Ross in order to win for himself the post of Principal Chief. Writing in the third person, a popular conceit suggesting objectivity, he presented his own defense:

John Ridge has not acted blindly, for he sees plainly that his people cannot hope to stand against the white man in their present situation. By removing to the West they may in time learn to hold their own with the white man. Let it not be said that John Ridge acted from motives of ambition, for he acted for what he believed to be the best interests of his people.[5]

Debate on the treaty when it reached the Congress was as bitter as that which had raged over Jackson's Indian Removal Bill. David Crockett of Jackson's state of Tennessee, John Calhoun of South Carolina, Frelinghuysen of New Jersey, Henry Storrs of New York, Sprague of Maine, joined in denunciation of the treaty. Daniel Webster pronounced the compact "a great wrong." Henry Clay declared that its execution would inflict a deep wound on the American character, and quoted the words of Thomas Jefferson: "Indeed I tremble that God is just and that His justice cannot sleep forever."

It was Representative Henry A. Wise of Virginia who made before the House the most eloquent plea for justice for the Cherokees. Citing the valor of John Ross, who had risked his life at Horseshoe Bend and with his comrades had sealed the victory for Andrew Jackson, Wise observed:

And now he is turned out of his dwelling by a Georgia Guard and his property all given over to others. This is the faith of a Christian nation! John Ross is known by many members of the House to be an honest, intelligent man worthy to sit in the councils of the nation, let alone the councils of an Indian tribe.[6]

Lest the Congress slight Ross's qualifications to speak for the Cherokee people, Wise made a barbed comparison. From the standpoint of intellect and moral honesty the Cherokee chief contrasted favorably with John Forsyth, former governor of Georgia, now sitting in the audience. Both men, Wise noted, were products of the same state, and the contrast was invidious so far as Forsyth was concerned.

The treaty came up for a vote on May 17. In their rooms at the Indian Queen the separate delegations nervously waited for the outcome. Ross had reason to be optimistic. According to his nephew William Shorey Coodey, present though not an official delegate, he believed the pact would be defeated, based on his interviews with leading senators. Hugh Lawson White of Tennessee had assured Ross it was in the bag.

White had succeeded Andrew Jackson in the Senate, and as chairman of the Committee on Indian Affairs had helped to push through the Removal Bill of 1830. But he had lately cooled toward the Chief Executive; had rejected an appointment to the Jackson cabinet; and had protested Georgia's arrogant arrest of Ross and Payne. He had since expressed himself as regarding the "Phantom Treaty" of New Echota a fraud.

When the ballot was counted in the Senate late that afternoon, Coodey rushed the word to Ross. The treaty had won by the exasperating margin of a single vote. At the last minute White had changed his mind. No one but White would ever know the reason why. His motive still remains a mystery.

The pact was to become effective two years hence, May 1838. In signing it, Jackson deleted only one provision—that which permitted certain Cherokees to remain if they qualified as citizens of Tennessee, North Carolina, or Alabama. He wanted no remnants of the tribe on eastern soil. As to the Cherokee memorial of protest drafted at the January Council and relayed from Lowrey to Ross to Jackson, the President regarded it as "impudent." He sent word through the Commissioner of Indian Affairs that he no longer recognized "the existence of any legal government in the Cherokee Nation East."[7]

Things moved fast in the wake of ratification. Two weeks later ex-Governor Lumpkin was back in the picture, gratified to share in an accomplishment that he had spent his political lifetime working for. Jackson appointed him and Governor William Carroll of Tennessee as co-commissioners to supervise execution of the treaty ("the two worst agents that could have been selected in all God's creation," wrote a congressman from Tennessee). Carroll barely acknowledged the appointment. He first pleaded illness as a reason for not joining Lumpkin; then, as the weeks went by, he simply failed to show up. This was all right with the former governor of Georgia. He preferred to work alone toward a goal that he regarded as peculiarly his own, and was pleased to get letters of congratulation on his appointment from John Ridge, Stand Watie, and Elias Boudinot—partisan leaders of the people he was planning to get rid of.

John Ross, to Lumpkin's gratification, had been theoretically "dethroned." But despite his calm acceptance of the Senate's vote, Ross was as unmoved and unmovable as ever. Immediately after news of ratification reached him, Ross wrote to Second Chief George Lowrey to advise his people to ignore the treaty. Whatever the United States had done, the Cherokee Nation knew the pact to be a fraud. It didn't exist; the Cherokees were to go about their business, plant their spring crops, mend their fences, look to their future as before.

Ross should have been aware by now that Bishop's network of agents was able to intercept his mail. They did, and passed the information on to Currey.

Returning to the Nation, Ross was greeted not as a deposed leader stripped of power by an act of Congress but as a man whose right to lead had been confirmed. He had not compromised the Nation. He had lost one battle, but he had not lost the war. With such a man, defeat could be no more than temporary. So long as Ross stood fast, the Nation would stand fast. As he had told them earlier, "Remain united and all will soon be right again."

The Council had voted him a horse, a fine black stallion with a silver-studded saddle, to be known as "the National Horse." And wherever he appeared, riding from town to town, the people gathered round their mounted chief to shake his hand, to wish him well, and to hear his reassurance that the Nation would endure.

Perhaps it was Ross's command to his people to ignore the treaty, as revealed in his intercepted mail, that aroused a sudden sense of panic among lottery-established settlers in the Nation. The Indians, it was rumored, were preparing to massacre the white usurpers in anger at the hated treaty (actually, there had been some unrelated trouble with the Creeks and Seminoles along the lower Chattahoochee River). Families huddled behind barricaded doors or hastily-built stockades, and called on their state governors for armed protection.

William Schley, Lumpkin's successor as governor of Georgia, responded by giving the Cherokee region a wide berth on his gubernatorial missions, for fear of being scalped. But he did alert the militia which had, in name alone, succeeded the notorious Georgia Guard. Brigadier General R. G. Dunlap in command of troops in East Tennessee was sent to patrol the territory, found the Indians going peacefully about their business, and decided they were more in need of protection than the whites.

Dunlap's conclusion was well founded. In counterpoint to the fears and alarms of the settled whites stood the plight of the Cherokees whose property was being overrun by greedy hordes of Georgians. With a treaty signed, the Cherokees were regarded as already ousted. Why wait for their departure before taking the pick of what they would have to abandon anyway? The usurpers stormed north like locusts, driving intimidated families from their homes, seizing their grain and livestock, sometimes exacting "rental fees" in return for letting them remain.

Where the earlier lucky drawers in the lottery had often behaved in civilized fashion, the present land-hungry rabble recognized no limits. Friendly, or pro-treaty, Cherokees were treated like the rest. The promises Lumpkin had made to Ridge that the Cherokees' rights would be respected up to the moment of their departure had vanished with the wind.

Even The Ridge's estate on the banks of the Oostanaula had been nibbled at by the invading Georgians. A man named Cox had appropriated a piece of his land across the river, and another named Garrett had tried to take possession of

his farm and ferry. Unable, as an Indian, to defend himself in court, The Ridge
was obliged to accept the situation, with rancor in his heart.

In the light of these and similar circumstances it was not surprising that
John Ridge showed symptoms of another change of mind. This was not the orderly transfer of land that he had bargained for. He agreed with his father,
Major Ridge, that they had been to some extent betrayed. On June 30, a little
more than five weeks after the ratification of the treaty, the two composed a letter of protest to Andrew Jackson, and this is part of what they said:

We come now to address you on the subject of our griefs and afflictions from the
acts of the white people. They have got our lands and now they are preparing to
fleece us of the money accruing from the treaty. We found our plantations taken either in whole or in part by the Georgians—suits instituted against us for back rents
for our own farms . . . Thus our funds will be filched from our people, and we
shall be compelled to leave our country as beggars in want.

Even the Georgia laws . . . are thrown aside . . . The lowest classes of the white
people are flogging the Cherokees with cowhides, hickories, and clubs. We are not
safe in our houses—our people are assailed by day and night by the rabble . . .
This barbarous treatment is not confined to men, but the women are stripped also
and whipped without law or mercy . . .

Send regular troops to protect us from these lawless assaults, and to protect our
people as they depart for the West. If it is not done, we shall carry off nothing but
the scars of the lash on our backs . . . we appeal to you for protection.[8]

Whether in direct response to this appeal, or to convince the Cherokees that
the treaty ratified in May was final and enforceable, Jackson dispatched General John Ellis Wool and 7,000 federal troops to occupy the Nation. Wool was
authorized to call for militia help as needed from adjoining states, and did so.
If the purpose of this force was to protect the interests of removal-minded
Cherokees, it was also, stated Jackson, "to overawe the Indians and frown
down opposition to the treaty." To prevent violence, Wool was to start by
disarming the supposedly vengeful-minded Cherokees.

As Wool discovered when he reached the Nation in July, the order was
superfluous. The Cherokees did not carry arms. As they had stated in one of
their many memorials to Congress, they had no military weapons or supplies.
The scalping knife and tomahawk had been buried for half a century. A few of
the older chiefs such as Junaluska remembered vividly fighting for the United
States in 1814 and seeing their brothers killed at Horseshoe Bend. But the
younger Cherokees had never known war, never learned to carry firearms,
never known combat fiercer than the ball-play.

General Wool, a career officer for twenty of his fifty-two years, was not an
indulgent sentimentalist—as he would prove by disciplined leadership in the
war with Mexico and later in the War between the States. He was strong for
authority and operated strictly by the book. He expected to confront bellig-
erence, and his initial attitude toward the Cherokees was: Stand up and fight
or shut up and listen. But instead he found them reasonable, courteous, and almost friendly. The only weapons he found were shotguns owned by many of

the farmers. These were obligingly surrendered to him, though the owners asked when they might expect to get them back; they were needed to protect the crops and livestock against predators.

Like Davis before him, Wool's manner softened to the Cherokees. He dropped the authoritarian stance, and began to find the circumstances of his job distasteful—"a heart-rending one," he wrote to Secretary Cass after only two months in the Nation, "and such a one as I would gladly get rid of as soon as circumstances permit." He viewed his whole objective in a different light:

> If I could, and I could not do them a greater kindness, I would remove every Indian tomorrow beyond the reach of the white men, who, like vultures, are watching, ready to pounce upon their prey and strip them of everything they have or expect from the government of the United States. Yes, sir, nineteen-twentieths, if not ninety-nine out of every hundred, will go penniless to the West.[9]

With the presence of federal troops and volunteer auxiliaries from Tennessee and Georgia, the rumors of rebellion, massacre, and assassination of Treaty Party advocates subsided. Commissioner Lumpkin worked with General Wool on plans for fortified detention camps and points of departure for the Indians to be evacuated. John Ross, ignoring these preparations, continued to hold Council meetings at Red Clay, where another memorial of protest was composed for Wool to give to President Jackson.

The acerbic President, failing in health, had had his fill of Cherokees. Sam Houston, Cherokee by adoption, was causing him some embarrassment by setting himself up as president of the new Republic of Texas. Jackson approved of Houston's buccaneering tactics; he had used them plenty of times himself. But now the Raven was showing Cherokee traits of independence and defiance. He was dictating terms to the President instead of the other way around.

And here was John Ross with another memorial of protest relayed via General Wool—as if the matter of removal were unsettled—along with a report from C. A. Harris, Commissioner of Indian Affairs in Washington, declaring that "Mr. Ross not only pronounces the Treaty a corrupt fraud, but has declared it *null and void*." Jackson waspishly reprimanded Wool for even submitting the Ross memorial, "a document odious and insulting to himself and to the people of the United States." He reminded Wool again that there was no longer a Cherokee Nation and hence no leader qualified to speak in its behalf.[10]

With his memorials shunted aside by the White House and the War Department, Ross resorted to the press to get his message to the public. He released what he headed "A Letter to a Gentleman of Philadelphia" (the gentleman, one J. R. Tyson, a Philadelphia lawyer with whom the chief had recently been corresponding). On Tyson's advice and with his help, the document was widely circulated and reprinted. In it Ross repeated the familiar charges of betrayal and fraud. But one point of interest was the praise he had for General Wool, who, said Ross, agreed on the impossibility of shaking the Cherokees' determination to remain where they were.[11]

Lumpkin, for one, was outraged by this seeming alliance between Ross and

Wool. Here was a veteran army officer, sent to the Nation for the express purpose of forcing the Cherokees into line and to "frown down opposition to the
treaty," consorting and agreeing with the enemy. The Commissioner made a
note to take the matter up with Jackson. Wool was a man to get rid of, by
whatever means.

From the West in midsummer of 1836, Samuel Worcester wrote to the
American Board of Foreign Missions:

> We have lately received the intelligence that Mr. Schermerhorn's treaty is ratified.
> I am sorry for it, because the whole transaction appears to me to have been morally
> wrong . . . I hope all will be over-ruled for the good of the Cherokees, though I
> have many fears . . .[12]

He himself had come to the West not merely because he concluded that removal was inevitable. He wanted to be in position early, have time to build his
spiritual ramparts and be ready to greet and aid the immigrants to follow.

But despite his and Butler's gallant battle in the Georgia penitentiary—
which had ended, alas, in surrender—the missionaries had lost caste with the
Cherokees. Once they had been warm friends and staunch supporters; now
they appeared to have sold out to the other side. They had broken the faith,
while praising the quality of faith so highly.

It was a tragic falling out. The alliance would be restored in time, and in the
West, but never with the same warmth that had once existed when they fought
the good fight side by side. The missionaries who now remained—men like
Evan Jones, Elizur Butler, and Daniel Butrick—seemed to operate as isolated
units rather than part of a great evangelical crusade. Their missions were out-
posts, not bricks in a mighty wall.

The estrangement had been due in part to Elias Boudinot, who as Worcester's partner in printing and distributing religious tracts was identified closely
with the missionaries. Now many of the latter had abandoned the fort and
Boudinot himself had done an about-face and was working for removal. They
were birds of a feather, the Treaty Party and the missionaries.

Boudinot made things worse by his attacks on Ross and by trying to defend
himself and Ridge. Replying to the charge that the "Phantom Treaty" of New
Echota had been engineered by a small minority, he wrote to the Georgia
press:

> If one hundred persons are ignorant of their true situation and are so completely
> blinded as not to see the destruction that awaits them, we can see strong reasons to
> justify the actions of a minority of fifty persons to do what the majority *would* do if
> they understood their condition, to save a *nation* from political thralldom and
> degradation.[13]

It was such words that made Boudinot, formerly so strong a champion of
Cherokee resistance, now a marked man in the Nation. It did not help matters

that Wilson Lumpkin held the same view, believing the average Cherokee incapable of thinking for himself. Even Daniel Butrick, who had vowed to remain silent on political issues, felt constrained to censure "traitors and rebels" in such a way that he plainly meant Boudinot and Ridge. Butrick particularly resented any inference that the Indian was inferior to the white man.

"Americans do not feel towards the Indians as they do towards other heathen nations," he protested to the Boston Board, "therefore reports of their wretchedness do not excite sympathy as they ought, but paralyze every exertion; thereby that old and cruel theory Indians are to be destroyed."[14]

Sophia Sawyer faced another troublesome decision. She had come to feel secure at Running Waters, with the school running smoothly and no trouble from the Georgia Guard since Mr. Ridge had signed the recent treaty. Now she was told she would have to move again. John explained that he had been elected chairman of a new Indian committee to implement the execution of the treaty, and had rented Boudinot's house at New Echota to be closer to the center of the Nation. Since Harriet's death Boudinot himself had found it hard to keep house for his children and was boarding elsewhere.

When John's duties with the committee had been fulfilled he would take his family to the West, and he hoped that Sophia would go with them or would join them there. Wherever they settled she could open up her school again. He would pay all expenses, supply whatever she needed—a building or classroom, books, equipment, teacher's salary.

Worcester had defined Sophia's character as "a strange compound of inconsistencies." Now her mind swung back and forth like the pendulum of the Ridges' Connecticut-manufactured clock. She could not bear to give up her school, though more and more she found herself exasperated at the "ceaseless inquiries" of her pupils. She could not bear to leave this country she had grown to love, though the National anxiety was telling on her. In short, she knew not what she wanted or where she stood or where precisely she belonged.

She asked John for a furlough and for time to think it over. John agreed. When the Ridges finally reached the West they would write to her and ask for her decision. If she wanted to join them, Ridge would send her travel money.

So it was that on a hot midsummer day of 1836 Sophia turned her back upon the sorely troubled Nation, where even now they were cutting timber to build stockades to house the emigrating Indians. She looked for the last time on the berry-laden meadows and the streams where she had frolicked with the children; and a little over ten weeks later found herself back in New Hampshire, where the quiet rolling hills, beginning to turn color, seemed light-years away from troubled Georgia.

Would she ever hear the singing voices and young laughter of the Cherokees again?

Some fifty miles distant from Sophia's home, another New Englander, groping for his future, had finished a short but revolutionary book on transcendentalism. It was Ralph Waldo Emerson's first step to fame. As philosopher, essayist, poet, and scholar, he would concern himself henceforth with "the divine sufficiency of the individual"—generally on a lofty, abstract plane. But he paused at this point, turned from philosophy to the mundane cause of human rights. His goal, the only political crusade of his life, was justice for the Cherokees. He studied and read about their plight. He thought about it. He could not keep silent long. . . .

As the year drew to its close the vast majority of Cherokees still showed no signs of emigrating. Following the precept of their leader, Ross, it was business as usual in the Nation, despite the presence of federal troops and Tennessee and Georgia volunteers. Benjamin Currey died in December; if he had not died of a serious illness, General Wool believed, he would have been shot by justice-minded Cherokees. Currey was replaced by General Nathaniel Smith of Tennessee, who, like William Carroll, seemed apathetic toward Indian removal.

With Carroll ignoring and finally resigning the office of co-commissioner with Wilson Lumpkin, another Tennessean named John Kennedy was assigned to take his place. Though Lumpkin was careful to credit Kennedy with sharing his burden, adding Kennedy's name to all reports to the War Department, the ex-governor appeared to ignore his partner and insist on plenary power for himself, which, he wrote, "was cheerfully granted by President Jackson."

What good, however, did it do him? Ross ignored him; even John Ridge was getting under his skin. As head of the Indian committee designed to help in the removal operation, Ridge was concerned that the emigrating Cherokees should get full value for what they left behind—homes, household furnishings, equipment, livestock. It was the committee's job to appraise these properties, and Ridge saw to it that the estimates were generous.

"While I shall never cease to bear witness to the honor and fidelity of Ridge and his party," Lumpkin wrote from his makeshift cabin office in Spring Place, "it costs me great care, watchfulness, and labor to prevent [them] from running into gross improprieties and extravagances."[15]

He cautioned Ridge to go easy on appraisal estimates, and especially to curb his tendency to entertain visiting Cherokees at government expense, regardless of what business brought them to New Echota. The battered and neglected town was beginning to look like a refugee camp, with scores, then hundreds, of clamoring Indians flocking to their former capital to present "despoliation claims" against the government, demanding payment for damages done to their property by federal troops and Georgian interlopers.

Worst of all, none seemed anxious to enroll for emigration or accept removal as a fact. Currey had told Lumpkin earlier that two thousand Cherokees would be ready to leave before the year was up. Now it appeared that none was ready. "With the procrastinations, disappointment, and near approach of winter," he complained, "I am wholly unable to say what number of Cherokees (if any) will be emigrated the present winter."[16]

He found his job "unpleasant and perplexing," as he wrote to Jackson. While John Ridge was becoming difficult, Ross could be said to be impossible.

"This man Ross, sir, and his mischievous efforts," Lumpkin told the President, "have brought more than enough evil upon his unfortunate race . . . in truth nineteen-twentieths of the Cherokees are too ignorant and depraved to entitle their opinions to any weight or consideration . . . They have been and are still governed by the opinions of their leading men."[17]

When Ross called an early Council for September 15, 1836, at Red Clay, Lumpkin advised Wool to keep an eye on the proceedings. The general himself, though not unsympathetic to the Principal Chief, felt any meeting in this overheated atmosphere was dangerous. He warned the War Department that "no good will come of it, and much evil may be anticipated," but he allowed the Council to convene. He stationed his troops nearby, and cautioned Ross that "the destinies of these people are in your hands." Stay in line, he told him; keep a tight control on things.

Elizur Butler came over from Brainerd to attend the Council, as he had done in the past, and sent to David Greene a summary of the proceedings. Concerning the "instrument purporting to be a Treaty made at New Echota," the General Council passed a resolution declaring that "the said instrument is null and void, and can never, in justice, be enforced upon our Nation. And we do hereby solemnly disdain and utterly reject said instrument in its principle and all its provisions."

It was also resolved, wrote Butler, that an eight-man delegation headed by John Ross should visit the Western Cherokees "to confer on the subject of their acting in concert with us in our efforts to procure the rescinding of said instrument . . ." The resolutions were approved and signed by more than two thousand adult Cherokees.

"Mr. Ross gave me leave to send this copy to the [Prudential] Committee," wrote Butler, *"but wished it to be considered confidential."*[18]

Ross knew he was being watched, with a view to obstructing his every move, and that he was subject to arrest on the slightest provocation. His plea to Butler that the Council's proceedings be kept confidential was, however, obviously futile. If Wool did not report to Lumpkin, the governor had his own spies keeping track of things.

And there was danger, Lumpkin saw, in Ross's visit to the West. If he got the cooperation of the Western Cherokees, he would have the treaty blocked at both ends of the trail. And he was likely to get the Westerners' support. For, as Lumpkin knew, there was growing dissatisfaction in the Western territories, grievous reports of conditions there and the misfortunes that had overtaken earlier emigrating parties. Moreover, those settling in the West had been promised that their lands would be immune from the encroachment of any other state or territory. Since that promise, Arkansas had become a state in June 1836 and once again the Indians were threatened by land speculators on their doorstep.

It was important that Ross be stopped before making an alliance with Chief Jolly of the Western Nation. It would seem, without documentation, that Lumpkin appealed for help to Andrew Jackson. In any event, only Jackson could have given Wool instructions to take steps that must have been distasteful to the general. On November 3, Wool posted "General Order No. 74" for all to read and ponder:

I am instructed by the President of the United States . . . to make known to Mr. John Ross, and all others whom it may concern, that it is his determination to have the late Treaty . . . "religiously fulfilled in all its parts, terms, and conditions, within the period prescribed," and that the President regards the proceedings of Mr. Ross and his associates in the late Council held at Red Clay, "as in direct contravention of the plighted faith of their people, and a repetition of them will be considered as indicative of a design to prevent the execution of the Treaty, even at the hazard of actual hostilities, and they will be promptly repressed."[19]

Predictably, Ross ignored the order, and started on his way. Lumpkin could think of no reason for detaining him. In a desperate move, he sent word to the Indian Agent Captain George Vashon in Oklahoma Territory, urging that Ross be arrested on arrival. The charge: violation of the Intercourse Act passed by Congress in 1834, which forbade unauthorized trespassing on Indian land. Since this, however, was a case of Cherokee visiting Cherokee, the application of the law appeared uncertain—but try anyway, suggested Lumpkin.

Ross got wind of the threat, but was becoming adept at avoiding arrest. He went directly to Fort Gibson, sought federal protection, and appeared at a Council called by Chief Jolly at Tahlonteskee, then the Western capital. Up until now East had been East and West had been West, and the twain had never truly met. But on December 8, 1836, the Council unanimously resolved that the Phantom Treaty of New Echota was "equally objectionable" to both branches of the Nation and that henceforth the Western delegates would cooperate with the Easterners to have the pact rescinded.

If nothing concrete or immediate came from Ross's mission it gave a boost to the resistance movement in the East and established a liaison between the two wings of the Nation that would hopefully endure. Ross brought back with him to Red Clay a young Cherokee named John Mooney, who for now would only study the situation but in time might be a factor in solidifying the East-West unity already in the making.

During Ross's absence, prolonged by severe winter weather which delayed the delegates' return for several months, the wheels of Indian emigration had begun to turn. Not, however, under force or government supervision. In January 1837 some six hundred Cherokees (Lumpkin estimated "seven or eight hundred") gathered at New Echota to form a vanguard of those headed for the West.

Towering among the group in influence and reputation was The Ridge, who as the third-richest man in the Nation—next to Joseph Vann and Ross— had received more than $24,000 for his relinquished property. He was now prepared to depart with this elect contingent, in a coach for himself and his family, a carriage for his servants, and a wagon for household belongings. At the last minute, however, The Ridge withdrew. He pleaded illness; but of seemingly greater influence was the fact that his daughter Sally had agreed to marry the importunate Lieutenant George Paschal. The Ridge wanted to be at home to give the bride away. He would join a later group embarking for the West.

There was no sign of sorrow or regret in this initial band of emigrants. They gathered in a setting of bright sun and pristine whiteness; even shabby and neglected New Echota gleamed like an enchanted city. Gaily caparisoned horses pawed the frozen ground, their breath like white plumes on the frosty air. The mounted chiefs, in skins and furs, headed the cavalcade; then the carriages carrying the muffled women with laughing children at their sides. Following came the wagons filled with household possessions; and trailing all, the herds of cattle prodded by excited slaves. It might have been a holiday excursion bound for a winter carnival.

For these were the willing emigrants, the wealthy Treaty Party followers. They had chosen to go ahead of the rest, under their own supervision. The committee had certified that they were qualified to do so, and allowed them extra money for expenses. "The good character, intelligence and standing of these persons," noted Lumpkin, "clearly entitle them to the privileges which they desire under the Treaty, and consequently could not be denied . . . Payments have already been made, to an amount exceeding one hundred thousand dollars . . ."[20]

Considering that the government had set aside $400,000 to satisfy Indian claims on abandoned property and to pay the cost of transportation to the West, $100,000, or a fourth of the total, seemed a disproportionate amount to allot to this small group. But Lumpkin, and presumably Nathaniel Smith as well, reasoned that these were influential, aristocratic Cherokees whom the common Indians looked up to. If people like these could be started on their way, seemingly content and well provisioned, the rest might be inclined to follow. It was worth the money paid to them.

"The policy of making prudent advances to the wealthy and intelligent," Lumpkin wrote to C. A. Harris, Commissioner of Indian Affairs in Washington, "has gone far to remove opposition to the treaty among the most influential."

The successful emigration of this token group was good publicity, giving the lie to the tales of suffering, disease, and death that had drifted back from earlier bands of emigrants. As the cavalcade passed through the populous centers on their overland route—through Tennessee, southern Illinois, Missouri, and northwestern Arkansas—the travelers gave the impression of being prosperous, civilized, well-mannered, as indeed they were.

So far so good. But these initial emigrants had comprised the wealthy, better-educated Cherokees, capable as individuals of handling their own affairs. The real test would come when the commissioners and Ridge's Indian committee had to start the next group off—under government supervision. Major Ridge, Stand Watie, and Boudinot were scheduled to go, but the rest of the contingent would comprise what Lumpkin called "the common Indians."

Already these "common Indians" were causing trouble. Lured to New

Echota on the promise of expense advances for the journey, they spent their payments on liquor to anesthetize the pain of waiting for the others to arrive. There was no joy, only a sense of desperation in their artificial revelry. And a cause to wonder, as one saw them reeling and hallooing on the grounds, if they could ever be sobered up again and started on their way.

Lumpkin complained to John Ridge, head of the Indian committee, since he regarded this unruly horde as Ridge's people, "recommended to us by you and your Committee as persons of ample prudence and capacity to manage their own affairs." And now:

It has been reported to us through various channels . . . that the effect of these payments has been to increase drunkenness, gambling and disorder among the Cherokee people. Indeed, Gen'l Smith, the Emigrating Agent, has sent us a message requesting that no further advances be made to the Cherokees, until the moment for their departure to the West.[21]

Another thorn in Lumpkin's side was General Wool. Wool's considerate and lenient attitude toward the Indians was, the commissioner felt, undermining his imperatives. "We are by no means singular in not being able to co-operate with Gen'l Wool, as it is well known here that he has constantly complained of every officer and agent of the Government here, since he entered this country, from the President down, who has had the misfortune to have to advise or instruct him in his operations."

The charge was not ill founded. Wool had performed his duties as he saw them, but he saw them differently from the commissioners and emigration agents, preferring persuasion to bribery and coercion. Earlier he had toured the mountainous region of North Carolina, where resistance remained strongest, and in February attended a winter Council at Red Clay, where he had a chance to speak with the Indians openly on the subject of removal. He found the Cherokees, as he reported to his Washington superiors, "a people almost universally opposed to the treaty and who maintain that they never made such a treaty." He observed:

So determined are they in their opposition that not one of all those who were present and voted at the council . . . however poor or destitute, would accept either rations or clothing from the United States lest they might compromise themselves in regard to the treaty.

These same people as well as those in the mountains of North Carolina, during the summer past, preferred living upon the roots and sap of trees rather than receive provisions from the United States, and thousands, as I have been informed, had no other food for weeks. Many have said they will die before they leave the country.[22]

March 4, 1837, was a warm and sunny day in Washington, a city already exhausted by pre-inaugural festivities. Standing among the thousands who lined Pennsylvania Avenue, John Ross watched the bare-headed President pass in his "Constitution" carriage with Martin Van Buren toward the Capitol. The crowd's applause seemed as much for the departing President as for the

President-elect; Jackson, though gaunt and cadaverous from recent illness, seemed physically to tower over his dapper diminutive successor.

At least, Ross must have thought, he had outlasted Andrew Jackson as the head of their respective nations. More important, the Cherokee Nation had outlived the one man most determined to destroy it. But how much longer could it hold on? Van Buren, Ross knew, was a Jackson man. Old Hickory's intransigent policy toward the Indians was in obedient hands.

Ross, back from the West with his delegates, wasted no time in asking for and getting an interview with the new Chief Executive. As Vice-President, Van Buren had been as unapproachable as Jackson; and his new Secretary of War, Joel Roberts Poinsett, was no improvement over Cass. Van Buren, however, received the delegates with noncommittal courtesy and listened to their arguments for abrogation of the treaty—the gist of which was that the treaty was invalid before the Senate ratified it—a phantom document composed by a minority. "We are not aware," said Ross, "that the Senate could make that valid which before was void."[23]

Van Buren had been cautioned by Lumpkin to be wary of the "subtle and sagacious" Ross, who was wrongly credited with "talents and wisdom he never possessed." The Cherokee chief, asserted Lumpkin, should be put in chains and banished from the country—perhaps sent to Haiti or placed "amongst the New England Abolitionists" where the trouble makers and the anarchists belonged.[24]

But Van Buren saw no harm in simply listening to the delegates, nodding his smooth-domed head in a manner that could mean agreement or dissent. Then he shunted the group onto Secretary Poinsett, who in time would be best known for the tropical red-leafed plant he introduced to America's Christmas flora. After several sessions and much deliberation, Poinsett gave Ross his answer, namely that "the President regarded himself as bound to carry into effect all the stipulations of the document in question, because it had been ratified according to the forms prescribed by the constitution . . ."[25]

Ross was used to running into dead ends; Van Buren and Poinsett presented yet another double-barreled one. But though he returned to Red Clay in April with little positive accomplished, he left in Washington a host of eloquent supporters for his cause. Congress had ratified the Treaty of New Echota, but still, surprisingly, many opposing congressmen continued to question its validity. The familiar names of Crockett, Calhoun, Frelinghuysen, Clay, and Webster were linked again to vigorous attacks upon the Phantom Treaty.

To Van Buren in the White House came a letter from an unknown Yankee in New England named Ralph Waldo Emerson. Emerson would in time have much to say on the condition of the human race, but none of his writing would burn with quite the same fierce fervor of his message to the President:

Sir, my communication respects the sinister rumors that fill this part of the country concerning the Cherokee people . . . Even in our distant state some good rumor of their worth and civility has arrived. We have learned with joy of their improvement in the social arts . . . And not withstanding the unaccountable apathy with which of late years the Indians have been sometimes abandoned to their enemies, it is the understanding of all humane persons in the Republic . . . that they shall be duly cared for; that they shall taste justice and love from all to whom we have delegated the office of dealing with them.

And now regarding that Treaty of 1835, "pretended to be made by an agent on the part of the United States, with some persons appearing on the part of the Cherokees [who] by no means represent the will of the Nation, and against which fifteen thousand six hundred and sixty-eight have protested. It now appears that the government of the United States choose to hold the Cherokees to this sham treaty, and are proceeding to execute the same."

Such a dereliction of all faith and virtue, such a denial of justice, and such deafness to screams for mercy were never heard of in times of peace and in the dealings of a nation with its own allies and wards, since the earth was made.

Sir, does this government think that the people of the United States are become savage and mad? From their minds are the sentiments of love and a good nature wiped clean out? The soul of man, the justice, the mercy that is that heart's heart in all men, from Maine to Georgia, does abhor this business . . .

There was more—in which the writer excoriated "a gloomy diffidence in the *moral* character of the Government." Concern over the financial panic in America that year, which so occupied the citizens and legislators, was but a "mote" in comparison with "so vast an outrage" about to be perpetrated on the Cherokees and on humanity. Would the government condone such action sure to recoil on the aggressor?

In screaming letters slanted across the paper, the Sage of Concord demanded:

"In the name of God, sir, we ask you if this be so . . ."[26]

16

The Drums of War

LITTLE HAD changed when Ross got back to his Tennessee cabin in early March 1837. The privileged six hundred who had left in January were reported safely on their way. But these, in Ross's mind, were the expendables, those who put personal advantage above principle. The Nation was well rid of them.

Of more significance was a second contingent, 446 in all, which had assembled at New Echota for removal under government supervision. While these too were "voluntaries," many of whom had enrolled for the sake of the "prudent advances" offered by the government, the group included some influential members of the Treaty Party. Elias Boudinot's brother Stand Watie was present, alone with his children, his wife having died in childbirth only weeks before. The Ridge had seen his daughter Sally married to George Paschal and now, though still not sound in health, was ready to make the trip with his wife Susanna.

One of the treaty terms provided that a government-employed physician should accompany each detachment on the journey West. In this instance two physicians traveled with the group, Dr. C. Lillybridge, attending to medical matters, and Dr. John S. Young, acting as "conducting agent." Young led his charges from New Echota to Ross's Landing on the Tennessee, where on March 3 they embarked aboard eleven waiting flatboats.

"It is mournful to see how reluctantly these people go away," wrote Brother H. G. Clauder, the Moravian missionary who himself had been driven from Spring Place into Tennessee. "Even the stoutest hearts melt into tears when they turn their faces towards the setting sun—& I am sure that this land will be bedewed with a Nation's tears—if not with their blood . . . Major Ridge is . . . said to be in a declining state, & it is doubted whether he will reach Arkansas."[1]

The open flatboats offered little shelter to The Ridge and the rest of the party, which included many children. March winds and bitterly cold nights exposed the Indians to nameless chills and fever, and Dr. Lillybridge found himself in bewildering demand. Coughs, colds, influenza, pleurisy developed, along with measles, diarrhea, and "gonorrhea among the younger men." Lillybridge "cupped" or bled them, dosed them with cathartics, pulled their aching teeth, and calmed their nerves with opiates.

At Gunter's Landing in Alabama a steamer waited to take the fleet in tow, and the ailing Ridge and his wife Susanna were given more comfortable accommodations aboard the larger vessel. Farther downriver, at Decatur, the entire party was transferred to open railroad cars to make a land detour around the unnavigable Muscle Shoals. Few of the Indians had ever seen a railroad train before and they regarded the fulminating locomotive with "inquisitive silence and gravity." From Decatur to Tuscumbia they sat on the floor of the cars, impassive, with eyes straight ahead, as if participating in some ritualistic test of fortitude. At Tuscumbia they were transferred again, this time to covered, more substantial keelboats towed by the steamer *Newark*.

Breaks in the journey became hazardous because of the grogshops in the river towns. Even before their departure liquor had become a problem, and Lillybridge added "whiskey colic" to his list of ailments. Befuddled by spirits smuggled aboard the boats, some of the Indians had second thoughts about the journey; home beckoned to them through an alcoholic haze. The doctor noted in his journal:

Alexander Brown an Indian six feet seven inches in height and tolerable well proportioned seized a canoe and for fear he should be interrupted before he got out of reach of the shore, paddled with all his strength. When the main current struck the canoe, he lost his balance, and fell; in endeavoring to recover, the canoe dipped so much water that she immediately sank; Brown however managed to turn her and get upon her bottom, in which condition he floated downstream 200 yards to a point of land.[2]

Brown's ultimate fate was not recorded, but it became a policy thereafter to tie up at islands rather than at the shore towns, to frustrate those who felt a sudden urge to slip away. Even so, liquor appeared miraculously, and Lillybridge's log included the almost daily entry "Good number of Indians drunk." From one passenger stricken with delirium tremens the doctor cupped two pounds of blood, leaving the patient weak but easier to handle.

One account of the journey states that in western Tennessee The Ridge and his party stopped off to visit Andrew Jackson at the Hermitage. This seems hard to credit since their river route came no closer than sixty miles from Nashville. Allegedly the group had detoured to have their horses shod, but if they had horses with them, would they have ridden so far inland? If the visit to Jackson did take place it would have been a memorable, almost historic, encounter—two battle-scarred warriors famed among their respective peoples but now relegated to the past, bound by memories of days when they campaigned against the Creeks together.

They had since been bitter enemies. But Jackson had one rare trait; he could not withhold admiration for a worthy foe. He would have seen in The Ridge the same qualities he saw in William Weatherford, the Creek chief who, after Horseshoe Bend, offered himself as hostage that his people might survive. The Ridge was making the same sort of sacrifice—giving up all that was most dear to him, leading his people to the Dark Land in the West, that the Cherokee Nation might survive.

As they entered the Mississippi River, Lillybridge recorded: "High winds from the South, with appearance of rain; during the night the boats ran afoul of a snag which caused considerable alarm among the Indians; one wheel was considerably damaged and the top of the keels burst in. No new cases of sickness further than common colds and Diarrhea. The wind renders it very difficult for the Indians to cook as their fires are on the top of the boats."

Turning into the Arkansas, the going was slower against the current. There was a "dank, muddy smell in the air," and both The Ridge and Susanna came down with troublesome coughs which called for Dr. Lillybridge's attention. Occasional groundings in the sluggish, shallow river with its myriad sandbars caused further delays, and it was not until March 27 that the flotilla reached Fort Smith, just short of the Oklahoma line. Here The Ridge and his party disembarked, for the Major had already chosen his future homesite some fifty miles north of the river.

Only a few stayed with the expedition till it reached Fort Coffee, the ultimate destination, farther up the river. For as The Ridge marched down the gangplank, proud of bearing, firm of step despite his illness, the Indians moved after him as if the earth had tilted. Unlike their chief, they had no chosen homesites, but they knew their Bible and heard the words "whither thou goest, I will go; and where thou lodgest, I will lodge." They followed him as the Hebrews followed Abraham to Canaan.

It was not until three months later, toward the end of June, that Brother Clauder, who had witnessed their departure, heard of the fulfillment of his fears. "From Arkansas," he wrote to a friend, "we have the intelligence, upon good authority, that the celebrated & well known Major Ridge departed this life since his arrival in his new home. He had been in a low state of health long before he left here & doubts were entertained whether he would live to see his new home; he survived however for a few weeks after his arrival."[3]

Brother Clauder's "good authority" was fortunately not as solid as the Major. By the date on the letter The Ridge was erecting his new home on Honey Creek in the northeastern corner of the Western Nation. It was rich and fertile prairie land, and while one army of servants cleared large fields for crops and pasture, another corps worked at felling the oaks and hickories and cutting the timber for the houses. "We had to undergo many privations in new country," wrote Susanna. "But we bore all under the belief that we had found a comfortable home for our children and grandchildren."[4]

"That portion of the execution of the Treaty confided us has been attended with many difficulties and embarrassments," Commissioner Lumpkin wrote to

President Van Buren late in June 1837, adding, however, that completion of the task appeared now as "a plain and easy duty."

Considering that little over a thousand Cherokees had left the Nation, and only those already predisposed to do so, there was little real cause for Lumpkin's optimism. He himself confessed as much, in his letter to Van Buren:

> In the meantime, Ross, who is the soul and spirit of all opposition to the Treaty . . . has returned home [from Washington] with increased weight of character . . . He, Ross, feels secure in the courtesy and respect which he receives from every officer of your administration, and the kind feelings entertained for him, in a special manner, by the Army agents. Sir, under this state of things, the Cherokees will not emigrate under this Treaty, except by force of arms, and when that is applied the result may be war. Nothing now can preserve the peace of the country and emigrate the Cherokees but such movements on the part of the Government as shall convince Ross and his adherents of the utter imbecility of their great *idol.*[5]

Plainly the President's cordial reception of John Ross at the White House, even though it led to nothing, was a source of chagrin to the commissioner. Plainly, too, he resented the friendly, accommodating attitude of United States troops and officers toward the Cherokees. "Nothing was done by the military which we advised to be done . . . the commander of the military forces being chagrined at the confidence placed in us by the President of the United States." Instead of harmony between the officers and the commissioners, wrote Lumpkin, there was only discord.[6]

He was indeed correct on that point. General Wool had undergone a radical change of sentiment. As recently as March 27, 1837, he had addressed a firm letter to the Cherokees noting that, for nearly a year, he had pledged himself to protect their rights provided they in turn complied with the terms of the New Echota Treaty. "You would not listen, but turned a deaf ear to my advice." This, the general warned them, "may lead to your utter ruin. The President, as well as the Congress, have decreed that you should remove from this country . . . Your fate is decided; and if you do not voluntarily go by the time fixed in the treaty, you will then be forced from this country by the soldiers of the United States."[7]

By midsummer, however, General Wool had had his fill of what he considered an unsavory assignment. He had been sent not only to urge Indian compliance with the treaty, but also to protect the Cherokees against unlawful seizures of their property, especially in Alabama, where white intruders, it was said, were "robbing and plundering the Indians, and exercising every species of oppression towards them." Taking his orders literally, he reversed this popular practice. Where land-hungry whites had taken possession of Cherokee farms and homesteads, Wool threw them out and reinstalled the rightful owners.

As if this diligence were not enough, Wool also cracked down on the sale of whiskey to the Indians, designed to befuddle their judgment and make them partners in their own destruction. This drew the wrath of the Alabama governor and legislature, who charged the general with having "usurped the powers of the civil tribunals, disturbed the peace of the community, and trampled upon the rights of the citizens."

The state authorities demanded of Secretary Poinsett that Wool, for these "outrages," be "investigated and condemned." Disgusted, the general himself asked to be relieved of his commission and, although a military board of inquiry later cleared him of all charges, he was replaced by Colonel William Lindsay as commander of United States troops in the Nation.[8]

Meanwhile, Tennessee volunteers under Brigadier General R. G. Dunlap had been halfheartedly building stockades at strategic points throughout the Nation for the reception of future Cherokee emigrants as these were assembled willingly or not. During the period Dunlap had had a chance to observe the Cherokees' stoic forbearance toward their persecutors.

Before the summer was over he, like General Wool, had had enough of this assignment. He had done what he could toward protecting the Indians from renegade Georgians; he could not protect them against the tidal wave of forces that would sweep them from the country. Addressing his troops, he told them their job was over—that he "would never dishonor the Tennessee arms by aiding to carry into execution at the point of a bayonet a treaty made by a lean minority against the will and authority of the Cherokee people." He marched them home, removing Tennessee from the ranks of state authorities pressing for forcible expulsion of the Cherokees.[9]

These military defections gave Joel Poinsett some food for thought. Hearing from Ross himself that the chief had called a General Council to be held at Red Clay in early August, Poinsett replied that he was sending a special agent, John Mason, Jr., to present to the assembly the government's stand on the question of removal. At the same time, the Secretary informed Ross that Colonel Lindsay of the United States Army and General Nathaniel Smith, successors to Wool and Currey respectively, would also be present with sufficient uniformed and armed "observers" to guarantee the deputy a hearing.

George W. Featherstonhaugh, English scientist and a Fellow of the Royal Society of London, had come to America to collect samples of native mineral deposits. Starting in the northwestern states, he had made his way south to Georgia and the Dahlonega gold fields, where he found himself in the summer of 1837.

Cherokee magic is too fanciful a word to apply to the quick empathy the Cherokees so often established with strangers. Featherstonhaugh had not been in the country many days before he found himself immersed in a consuming interest in the Indians—in their tribal customs, their dress, their food, and above all their speech and alphabet. Meeting by chance the ubiquitous Daniel Butrick, he was further inspired to learn all he could about these people. He put aside his rock collection, and began to study Sequoyah's alphabet, trying out his linguistic ability on every Indian he met.

He traveled about the country, taking notes for a book he would later write of his travels in America, and arrived at Red Clay, either by accident or by design, just at the time the August Council was convening. Welcomed by

Elijah Hicks, he was given a cabin with the American agent, Colonel Mason. The hut was one of many hastily built to accommodate visitors and delegates, the floor "strewed with nice dry pine leaves . . . two rude bedsteads, with pine branches as a substitute for beds, and some bed-clothes of a strange fashion, but which were tolerably clean."[10]

After he and Mason had been served a cup of tea, General Smith took the pair in tow and showed them around the Council grounds, of which the Englishman later wrote:

Nothing more Arcadian could be conceived than the picture which was presented; but the most impressive feature was an unceasing current of Cherokee Indians, men, women, youths, and children . . . moving about in every direction, and in the greatest order; and all preserving a grave and thoughtful demeanour imposed upon them by the singular position in which they were placed, and by the trying alternative now presented to them of delivering up their native country to their oppressors, or perishing in a vain resistance.[11]

"An observer could not but sympathize deeply with them," he noted. Having traveled through the lands of the Dakotas and the Shawnees and the Illinois Confederacy, he found the Cherokees "not to be confounded with the wild savages of the West, being decently dressed after the manner of white people, with shirts, trousers, shoes and stockings, whilst the half-breeds and their descendants conformed in every thing to the custom of the whites, spoke as good English as them, and differed from them only in a browner complexion, and in being less vicious and more sober. The pure bloods had red and blue cotton handkerchiefs folded on their heads in the manner of turbans, and some of these . . . wore also deer-skin leggings and embroidered hunting shirts . . ."[12]

Under the aegis of General Smith and later Colonel Lindsay, Featherstonhaugh met a number of the chiefs. He dined at the Red Clay cabin of John Ross and Quatie. "Neither our host nor his wife sat down to eat with us, the dinner, according to Cherokee custom, being considered to be provided for the guests . . . Mr. Lewis Ross, the brother of our host, presided, and Mr. [Edward] Gunter, a very intelligent and obliging half-breed, sat at the other end of the table. I sat on his right and obtained a great deal of information from him."[13]

Moving around the tents and tables of the Council grounds, the Englishman was introduced to the septuagenarian White Path, "remarkably cheerful and light of step," and to the ancient chief Going Snake, "a fine old man with a good deal of Indian dignity." Going Snake, he learned, had fought with Andrew Jackson at the Horseshoe. "Nothing appears to have stung the Cherokees more deeply," Featherstonhaugh observed of this encounter, "than the reflection that, after serving General Jackson so effectually, it should have been under his administration . . . that their independence had been broken down, and their territories appropriated without their consent."[14]

What most deeply impressed the visitor, however, was the conduct of the Council sessions. These opened and closed with religious services. There were readings from the scriptures by the Baptist missionary Evan Jones, translated into Cherokee by Jesse Bushyhead, who "rendered every passage with the most enthusiastic energy at the very top of his noble voice, and marked every sentence with one of his deep-toned, sonorous *uh-hunhgs,* that came from him like the lower note from a bassoon." Daniel Butrick of Brainerd delivered the sermons that Bushyhead "linkested" line by line. Cherokee language hymnals were distributed to the assembly and the treetops seemed to sway with song.

"I certainly never saw any congregation engaged more apparently in sincere devotion," wrote Featherstonhaugh, adding:

This spectacle insensibly led me into reflection upon the opinion which is so generally entertained of its being impossible to civilize the Indians in our sense of the word. Here is a remarkable instance which seems to furnish a conclusive answer to skepticism on this point. A whole Indian nation abandons the pagan practices of their ancestors, adopts the Christian religion, uses books printed in their own language, submits to the government of their elders, builds houses and temples of worship, relies upon agriculture for their support, and produces men of great ability to rule over them, and to whom they give a willing obedience. Are not these the great principles of civilization? They are driven from their religious and social state then, not because they cannot be civilized, but because a pseudo set of civilized beings, who are too strong for them, want their possessions![15]

The high point of the convention was to be the "talk" by agent Mason, postponed for several days by drenching rain. When the downpour refused to ease, Ross ordered the ceremonies to continue. The chief conducted Mason and the English visitor, along with General Smith and Colonel Lindsay, to a stand erected near the Council House around which two thousand Cherokees waited, composed and attentive, in the rain. It was an all-male audience, the women and children keeping to the shelter of their tents.

Mason's address was a combination of saccharine seduction and barbed warning. "The President is very powerful but his power is guided by justice, and his first wish is for the safety and happiness of the Cherokees . . . The President loves you . . . He has not forgotten that when the Country has been plunged in war, the Cherokee warrior has poured out the full tide of his heart's blood for the sake of the white man." The President had in mind only the Cherokees' own good in urging them to seek a new home in the West. So: "Listen not to those who tell you to oppose the benevolent design of the government. They speak with a forked tongue, and their bad advice would lead to inevitable ruin."[16]

It was evident, noted Featherstonhaugh, that the talk made little impression on the Cherokees. "It was full of friendly profession towards the Nation . . . but there was a passage in it which showed the United States Government were determined to enforce the treaty which the minority had made with the Government, and even insinuated that resistance to it was factious. This gave offense, and even Mr. Ross objected to it."[17]

The Council as a whole objected to it, and appointed another deputation to carry their protest to the capital. Led by John Ross, the delegates included Richard Taylor, James Brown, Samuel and Edward Gunter, Elijah Hicks, Situwakee, and White Path. They would not wait for the usual October Council; there was nothing more to be discussed; the delegates would leave for Washington at once.

Mason was talking to a wall of stone, and knew it. At the conclusion of the Council he was forced to admit that "opposition to the treaty was unanimous and irreconcilable, the Cherokees declaring that it could not bind them because they did not make it, that it was the work of a few unauthorized individuals and that the Nation was not a party to it." He reported later to Secretary Poinsett that, despite the suspension of elections in the Nation, John Ross was still regarded as their Principal Chief with "influence unbounded and unquestioned," and that:

> The whole Nation of eighteen thousand persons is with him, the few—about three hundred—who made the treaty having left the country, with the exception of a small number of prominent individuals—as Ridge, Boudinot, and others—who remained to assist in carrying it into execution. It is evident, therefore, that Ross and his party are in fact the Cherokee Nation . . . I believe that the mass of the Nation, particularly the mountain Indians, will stand or fall with Ross . . .[18]

The small number of prominent individuals to whom Mason referred left for the West by carriage in late September. The group comprised the last of those who had signed or assented to the treaty, including John Ridge, and his wife and children, John's sister Sally and her new groom, George Paschal, and Elias Boudinot, who a few weeks before had married Delight Sargent, the dedicated teacher at the Brainerd Mission. The mission itself was now abandoned; but its work would be continued in the West under the veteran aegis of William Chamberlin and Samuel Worcester, already settled in their Oklahoma homes.

For John Ridge, despite his espousal of the treaty, it was not easy to "bid an everlasting farewell to the land of my birth." He could not, as he wrote to Wilson Lumpkin, "be an indifferent spectator," and added:

> In the history of the Nation, if there is a page assigned to my name *and that of our house,* I know not what will be said. Foul misrepresentations have been made by our opponents as to our motives, and we have passed thro' the ordeal of awakened prejudices of the ignorant portion of our people. If we have merits to be seen and adjudged we leave them to the consideration of an enlightened world and to our God.[19]

In closing, he thanked the two commissioners, Lumpkin and Kennedy, for their labors and for "the humanity which you have manifested for my people."

Lumpkin promptly replied in an equally warm vein. He commended Ridge for his "lofty efforts and sacrifice made in the face of death and the most determined opposition" and noted that his fortitude had saved "your people from certain impending ruin and destruction . . . May the God of our fathers prosper your way!"[20]

Though sincere in these sentiments of goodwill, Lumpkin must have been relieved to see the last of Ridge, who had served his purpose and was now dispensable. In fact, in recent months, John had shown more spunk than Lumpkin had anticipated. He had demanded and got the best possible settlement for his people with respect to indemnities, removal expenses, and land guarantees in the West. And he had fought as ardently as Ross for the rights and protection of those Cherokees he numbered as his followers.

Still, the departure of Ridge's group, the last but one of the contingents that would leave in 1837, represented progress of a sort. Lumpkin was prompted to write to Commissioner Harris in Washington that "we are now busily engaged in setting up all the affairs of such Cherokees as have determined to emigrate this fall, and if you were here to witness the bustle and business now going on, you would be ready to conclude that the spirit of emigration among the Cherokees was such as to remove all doubts of their yielding . . . without further trouble."[21]

Without further trouble for Lumpkin, perhaps, whose term as commissioner was coming to a close. But for the 365 Cherokees assembled at the Indian Agency on the Hiwassee in mid-October the trail ahead was fraught with little else. The wagons carried their household furnishings, the aged, and the very young. The rest would trudge the thousand or more miles on foot, except for the very few who were wealthy enough to own their ponies. Starting on October 14 and heading northwest through Tennessee, they averaged from twelve to sixteen miles a day.

It took two days to cross the Mississippi, hampered by high winds, and once across the river fever and dysentery struck the band. Sixty fell ill in the next few days; and soon there was scarcely room in the wagons for the sick to lie. Autumn rains turned the Missouri bottomlands into quagmires, and one by one the wagons became mired, lost a wheel, or suffered a broken axle. The accompanying physician, G. S. Townsend, stopped the train and herded his charges into an abandoned schoolhouse, where four of the emigrants died—one of them the son of Corn Tassel, whose father had been hanged during the Cherokees' first battle with the state of Georgia.

After ten days of uneasy rest the cavalcade moved on. The entries in the written record kept by B. B. Cannon, conductor of the expedition, became grim: "Buried Nancy Bigbear's grandchild" . . . "buried Elleges wife and Chas. Timberlake's son" . . . "Buried Goddard's grandchild" . . . "Buried Rainfrog's daughter" . . . "Buried Alsey Timberlake, Daughter of Chas. Timberlake." And finally, under the date of December 28, 1837: "halted at Mr. Beans in the Cherokee Nation West."[22]

Having crossed the border into Cherokee territory, the band refused to go further. They would remain where they found themselves and care for their sick, try to recover their health, and take stock of what possessions remained to them from abandoned wagons, punishing rains, and cargoes jettisoned. So far, fifteen of the group had died, or one out of twenty—not an unenviable record, had they been able to foresee the future.

By the end of 1837, the last full year before the treaty deadline, fewer than two thousand Cherokees had emigrated to the West. The remainder, some sixteen thousand persons, the solid mass of the Nation, was still firmly at the side of Ross and dedicated to resistance. Commissioner Lumpkin was preparing to close his log-cabin office at New Echota, having finished his term of duty, and because of Ross he had made only a token beginning in the task he had undertaken with such high resolve.

He vented his frustration in a letter dated September 24 to a Colonel John H. ——— (last name indecipherable), presumably an officer with Colonel Lindsay's troops, who had shown an all too prevalent sympathy for the unsubmissive Cherokees:

> The Treaty, Sir, should be executed faithfully, to sustain the honor of the country, and to promote the best interest of the Cherokee people. And to secure this object no person should have been charged with any official responsibility in its execution who is *a Ross man*—who joins Ross in denouncing the Treaty as a corrupt fraud practiced upon the Cherokee people.
>
> At a time like this, no person should be subsisting on the government, in this country, whose feelings and views coincide with this man Ross . . . Ross should be distinctly informed that the Treaty will be executed at all hazards; and he should not be permitted longer to encourage the delusive hopes of the ignorant Indians that, through his mighty influence, the Treaty will yet be abrogated, or modified.[23]

So far, in Lumpkin's estimation, the United States troops had merely wasted their time in building fortifications for their own and the Cherokees' protection. "A silly business!" The need was for "good soldiers, well armed, under proper commanders. With proper forecast and preparation, no war can possibly arise here that might not be terminated in four weeks. With one thousand militia volunteers, raised in Georgia, I can drive every Cherokee Indian in the Nation to Arkansas, without the loss of a man . . ."[24]

The drums of war! Had Lumpkin stayed on as commissioner they might have sounded—for time was running out, and force seemed the only quick solution to the problem. But a month later Lumpkin was in Washington as elected senator from Georgia. From the floor of the Senate he would continue to battle John Ross, whom he regarded as "the last lingering hope of the Cherokees."

From Honey Creek in Oklahoma that December, John Ridge wrote to Commissioner Kennedy that he had found his father and mother "and all my friends" in good health, and that this corner of the Western Nation was "superior to any country I ever saw in the U.S. . . . is populating very fast and in a few years it will be the garden spot of the United States . . . The Cherokees have settled here almost together in consequence of their being introduced in this quarter by the agents. Honey Creek . . . and all the region about is large enough for the whole Nation. Perfect friendship and contentedness prevail all over this land."[25]

John and his party had arrived in late November, traveling the overland route through Tennessee, Kentucky, southern Illinois, and across the Mississippi to Missouri. At Honey Creek, Ridge set about building a new home, "a good double log house," adjoining 150 acres of rolling prairie. He began clearing the fields for crops and purchasing livestock. In partnership with his father, he opened a general store at Honey Creek, employing George Paschal as clerk, and set his sights on becoming a prosperous merchant-farmer.

But there was one thing missing in this new life. Before leaving the East he had written to Sophia Sawyer, sending her 150 dollars and urging her to join his party before it left or to meet the expedition at some place of rendezvous like Nashville. Not only would Sarah welcome Sophia's help in caring for their six exuberant children, but John was eager to discuss and implement plans for a new school in the Western Nation, "for which we have an ample budget."

In Rindge, New Hampshire, Miss Sophia had been torn between assorted impulses. She had started a book to be entitled *Lights and Shades of Indian Character,* based on her thirteen years among the Cherokees; had enjoyed some stimulating visits to Philadelphia, New York, and Washington; and had done some teaching among black children which recalled her experience with Sam and Peter at New Echota.

But, as with John, something was lacking in her life. She missed the Ridges, who had been her refuge in a time of storm. She missed the Boudinots, though Harriet of course was gone and Delight Sargent was looking after Elias' five children. Most of all she missed the Cherokees, among whom her life had seemed fulfilled. She still had the 150 dollars John had sent her, secreted among balsam sachets in a bureau drawer. At year's end she packed her portmanteau, wrote the Board of Foreign Missions of her intentions, and embarked aboard a ship for New Orleans.

Shipboard life to an ex-New England schoolmarm was a revelation in itself. While she might close her mind to the loud profanity of westbound gamblers, she wondered if these were the kind of white men whom the Cherokees would have to deal with in the West. If so, was the transplantation such a wonderful solution to their problems as the Ridges had maintained?

There was cause for reassurance when she reached Dwight Mission and John brought her by carriage to Honey Creek. For John had spared no pains in making good his promise. Only a short distance from his home he was building a two-story schoolhouse, the ground floor for classrooms, the upstairs for Sophia and selected boarders. She would have a companion in Sarah Ridge, a woman she found of "moral courage." And happiest development of all, John Ridge was leaning "in favor of the Christian religion"—though Sophia feared "it may be difficult for a man of his habits and temperament to retain."

In short, as she wrote to David Greene in Boston, "our family is nearer what it should be now than it ever has been since I was connected with it"—and in her "family" she included the twenty or so Cherokee pupils flocking to her classes. Hers would be one of the first Christian schools in the Western Nation. Miss Sophia was a pioneer. In spirit, it was what she always had been.[26]

Coming up to Honey Creek from Dwight, where John had met her, the carriage passed through the little village of Park Hill, christened by Samuel Worcester a few months before and now the home of Elias Boudinot as well. Since coming West, Worcester had lost no time in setting up his press, whose appearance from Boston had almost been timed with his arrival. With Chief John Jolly's skeptical approval he established himself and the press at Union, an abandoned mission on the banks of the Grand River, a tributary of the Arkansas. John Wheeler came West as printer and John Candy served as translator until Elias Boudinot should join them.

Worcester had promised Chief Jolly to "stand aloof from all political affairs of the Nation, & devote his time & talents to the preparation & publication of Cherokee books, & to efforts for the literary, moral, & religious instruction of the people." Within this framework the production of the press, in Cherokee, had been prodigious—a *Hymn Book* and *Select Passages of Scripture,* each in editions of five hundred, copies of Sequoyah's alphabet, religious calendars, and an immensely successful *Cherokee Almanac,* which Worcester hoped to publish regularly.

Reception of his religious tracts encountered only one snag, and that concerned the illustrations, reproduced from cuts from Boston. These showed the saints and other holy figures wearing halos. The literal-minded Western Indians were unable to accept the Messenger's explanation for this "radiance around the head" and regarded it as a derogatory "blemish." John Wheeler chiseled the halos from the cuts, and the saints became acceptable.

Union was only a temporary stand. It was on the west side of the river; most of the Cherokees lived between the east bank and the Arkansas-Missouri border. With the permission of the Board, Worcester in late 1836 moved his press to a central location on the Illinois, due east of Union, of which an Oklahoma resident-historian wrote:

The site of the new mission was beautiful indeed. The Illinois was clear and picturesque; the prairie grass carpeted the rolling ground; trees grew in abundance to serve for lumber and for shade; the house stood on an elevation that promised healthfulness and a fine view. "Park Hill" suggested itself as a suitable name for such a place . . . For the rest of his life, Samuel Worcester was to know no other home.[27]

At the time of Sophia Sawyer's arrival in the West, Park Hill had already become a center of the Nation with, besides the press, a church, post office, a medical dispensary attached to Dr. Worcester's home, and a general store whose stock was limited at first to an overabundance of New Orleans molasses. A modest beginning for a city set on a hill, whose light, however, would not long be hid.

Elias Boudinot arrived at Park Hill in the late fall of 1837, at the time of the Ridges' emigration to the West. He and Delight commenced at once to build a home there, and he and Worcester were teamed again in the operations of the mission press. But what should have been, in all respects, a promising reunion was darkened by the shadow which had followed Elias from the East. Even among the Western settlers the members of the Treaty Party bore the mark of Cain. They had sold out their brothers at New Echota; they were, so to speak, on parole.

It was not long before Samuel Worcester was forced to write to a member of the Foreign Mission Board that "the greatest trial we have at present is in relation to my translator, Mr. Boudinot." Shortly after the first of the year 1838 he had received a letter from John Smith, President of the National Council of the Western Cherokees, reading:

Sir: the National Council has been informed that Mr. Boudinot is to be your translator. It is understood by the Council that his name is very unpopular, & that his services as printer to you, or his name upon the Books you print, will cause very unpleasant feelings to exist among the Cherokee people. The National Council therefore respectfully requests you not to use his services, or use his name in your Printings, in order that nothing unpleasant may occur . . .[28]

As Worcester explained to the American Board, it was Boudinot's "extreme anxiety to save his people [that] led him to unite with a small minority in the Nation in forming a treaty with the United States: an act, in my view, entirely unjustifiable, yet, in his case, dictated by good motives." Arguing on this basis, he was able to get permission from Chief John Jolly to keep Boudinot on his staff until the National Council could decide more firmly the fate of the former editor of the *Phoenix*.

"What will then be done," wrote Worcester, "I know not. It is *possible* that the Council will be so offended with me as to pass an order for my removal from the nation." On a sad note the Messenger concluded: "I do not know that the cause of religion has made much sensible progress among the Cherokees since we crossed the Mississippi."[29]

It was a commentary that applied to other areas besides religion. Now that the Eastern Nation, heartland of the Cherokees, seemed destined for removal to the West, what did the future really hold? Worcester may have been reminded of the ancient myth that the land of the setting sun, where earth and sky meet, is "the Darkening, or twilight Place." Was the West to mark the twilight of the Cherokees?

George Rockingham Gilmer at the start of 1838, back in office as governor of Georgia, took up the battle for removal of the Cherokees with the same fierce resolve that Governor Lumpkin had displayed two years before. In the interval between their two administrations, Governor William Schley had had it easy. During the years 1836 and 1837 two thousand Indians had gone West, mostly voluntarily, mostly under government supervision. There had been little force applied, and little violence. Any unpleasantness involved, such as death, disease, and heartbreak, took place on the trail—at a convenient distance from the Nation.

But those who had gone were the Treaty Party members and their followers. The great resisting heart of the Nation still remained—and seemed intent upon remaining. This was the situation Gilmer had inherited, and along with it the governor had inherited Lumpkin's fierce antipathy for Ross. But for Ross, Lumpkin told the Senate, the whole happy prospect of Indian removal would have been accomplished long ago. Now May 1838, the Treaty deadline, was approaching, and John Ross's party stood as firm as ever.

"I would earnestly request any readers of these pages," Lumpkin wrote some years later, "who may entertain a doubt of the extraordinary advantages secured to the Cherokees by the provisions of this Treaty, to read and consider . . . that it was the most liberal, honest, and just treaty ever before, or since, negotiated with any Indian people."

He praised those "wisest and best men of the Cherokee people"—the Ridges, Boudinot, Starr, Watie, Fields, the Rogerses—who had seen the light and led their people to the Promised Land, and condemned "Ross and his assassins," who opposed and continued to oppose the validity of the Treaty. The Ridge-Boudinot faction had remained in the Nation to aid their people in preparing for removal,

. . . while Ross, and a few of his selected favorites, were, from year to year, regularly spending as much of their time at Washington as though they had been members of Congress, feasting and enjoying high life, in the circles of their political partisans, and, at the close of Congress, visiting our great Northern cities, and thus spending the annuities of the Cherokee people in luxury, high life, and lordly ease.[30]

At that particular moment, it so happened, John Ross was in Washington but not indulging in a life of lordly ease. John Howard Payne had joined him there at Ross's request; in fact, Ross was paying his expenses in the capital. Samuel Morse was also in town—"showing his telegraph with great success," wrote Payne—and tended to steal attention from the Indian-removal issue. It was Payne's purpose, however, and his purpose in Washington, to flood the Washington press with anti-administration letters and help Ross and his associates with yet another memorial to Congress.

So far, the Ross delegation had been denied interviews with either the President or Secretary Poinsett, the latter writing to him that the Treaty of New Echota "is considered by the President to be a law of the land which the Constitution requires him to execute, and therefore no negotiations can be opened or proposition entertained upon the basis you propose." The Secretary of War concluded:

The Department regrets to perceive a settled purpose on your part to involve your people in the difficulties and to expose them to the sufferings which will inevitably follow their opposition to the treaty. It is well informed that you have held out to them false hopes which have led them to refuse to emigrate on the season of the

year best suited for their comfortable removal. This is very much to be regretted
. . . and all that now remains for me to say . . . is, that it is expected the Cherokee
Indians will remove from the States at the period fixed by the treaty of December
1835.[31]

The words had the final sound of doom. But back in the Cherokee Nation,
where in Ross's absence Assistant Chief Lowrey presided over the Council, a
petition had been prepared which differed markedly from previous protests. It
was not to represent the attitude of Ross's party only, but of every living Cherokee. Already runners had been dispatched to all corners of the Nation with
copies of the *Memorial of the Cherokee People to the People of the United*
States. They had gathered the signatures or marks of thousands of Indians—
men, women, and children—to be affixed to the document before its presentation to the American Congress.

By this instrument the conflict and its resolution would be taken out of the
hands of the generals and politicians, and placed squarely in the hands of the
citizens of the United States vis-à-vis the Cherokees themselves. Acting as free
individuals in free democracies, they could not fail to reach a just conclusion.
Or could they?

17

A Sudden Gleam
of Bayonets

It HAD BEEN snowing in North Carolina and Virginia, with deep drifts in the southern Appalachians. Yet Lewis Hilderbrand, like a courier bearing important wartime intelligence, had chosen to ride the six hundred miles plus to Washington City rather than take the uncertain water route from Georgia. Reaching Fuller's Hotel on March 10, 1838, in a state of exhaustion, he warded off sleep long enough to dispatch a note and document addressed to Mr. John Ross, Principal Chief of the Cherokee Nation:

Sir: At 2 o'clock this morning I arrived in Washington, deputed by our people to place in your hands the accompanying protest, signed by fifteen thousand six hundred and sixty-five of them, which they desire their delegation to present as soon as possible to Congress, in the name of the Cherokee Nation.[1]

The document itself was not long; but the signatures, some identified by no more than a mark beside the name written by a surrogate, covered more than a hundred pages—a curious jumble of English lettering and Sequoyah's spiny characters. It took Ross's delegation two days to recopy the text to present in tidy order to the Congress. Perhaps the text contained nothing new, for there was nothing new, really, to be said. But it constituted the Cherokees' last word as a Nation in their battle for survival. It deserved more attention than either Congress or the American Republic would accord it.

After a preamble restating the previous arguments the Nation's representatives had, from time to time, presented, it noted that the President "has formally declined all intercourse with Mr. Ross in relation to the treaty" and so "the cup of hope is dashed from our lips, our prospects are dark with horror and our hearts are filled with bitterness. Agonized with these emotions, language fails; our tongues falter as we approach the bar of your august assemblies before whom we again beg leave humbly to present our grievances." And it went on, in part:

What have we done to merit such severe treatment? What is our crime? Have we invaded anyone's rights? Have we violated any article of our numerous treaties? Have we, in any manner, acted in bad faith? We are not even charged with any such thing.[2]

What they had been charged with, protested the memorial, was allowing themselves to be "duped and deluded" by their chiefs—meaning the very delegation now in Washington. This was alleged to be "a dangerous error," for the chiefs were their "worst enemies." Yet, was it a dangerous error to believe that the United States would never knowingly sanction "a transaction originated in treachery," would enforce the Treaty of New Echota "by violence and oppression? . . . Is it a crime to confide in our chiefs, the men of our choice, whom we have tried and found faithful?" The Cherokees' true enemies were those who had drawn up and signed, without authority, the "ill-omened compact" in the first place.

For adhering to the principles on which your great empire is founded, and which has advanced to its present elevation and glory, are we to be despoiled of all we hold dear on earth? Are we to be hunted through the mountains, like wild beasts, and our women, our children, our aged, our sick, to be dragged from their homes like culprits and packed on board loathsome boats, for transportation to a sickly clime?

Already are we thronged with armed men; forts, camps, and military posts of every grade already occupy our whole country. With us, it is a season of alarm and apprehension. We acknowledge the power of the United States; we acknowledge our own feebleness. Our only fortress is the justice of our cause. Our only appeal on earth is to your tribunal. To you, then, we . . . do solemnly and earnestly protest against that spurious instrument . . . Our minds remain unaltered. We never can assent to that compact; nor can we believe that the United States are bound, in honor or in justice, to execute on us its degrading and ruinous provisions.

There were only two more paragraphs—one declaring that "if we fail to transmit to our sons the freedom we have derived from our fathers, it must not be an act of suicide, it must not be with our own consent." The other concluded:

With trembling solicitude and anxiety, we most humbly and respectfully ask, will you hear us? Will you extend to us your powerful protection? Will you shield us from the horrors of the threatened storm? Will you sustain the hopes we have rested on the public faith, the honor, the justice, of your mighty empire?[3]

It took less than a month for John Ross and his delegates to receive an answer to those questions—not a long time for a document to pass through Congress. On April 9, 1838, the title page of the memorial was stamped with the notation "Laid on table," a euphemism meaning generally to be disregarded.

Those who sought to discredit the Cherokee appeal charged that the nearly sixteen thousand signatories represented more than the entire adult population of the Nation. Mothers had signed for babes in arms; fathers had put their son's mark after names of those not old enough to understand the content. John Ross himself would probably have so admitted. For the Cherokees put a high premium on youth. Who more than the young had a right to endorse a document that strove to guarantee their freedom and survival in maturity?

Ross had comforting contact with the deserving young, in letters he received throughout that gloomy winter in the capital. Two of his nephews, William and Robert Ross, were studying Greek and Latin at Lawrenceville School in New Jersey with the hope of entering Princeton in another year or two. His niece, Araminda Ann, was at the Lawrenceville Female Academy, not getting the high marks of her cousins but, as she proudly boasted, learning to skate as well as her Yankee classmates.

The boys offered a refreshing contrast to the teen-age norm of midcentury America. They complained only of insufficient privacy to study properly; and they were vitally interested in the welfare of their people, proud of being Indians and not conforming to the pattern of their peers. William signed his letters in Sequoyah's characters, pronounced *ka wat lee os, tat gat eh,* "Peace, peace to the Cherokees!" while Robert urged his uncle, "Please to write *my name in Indian* the next time you write."[4]

Araminda Ann asked her "beloved uncle" for the length of his foot, "for I am going to work for you a pair of slippers." During her knitting, it appeared, she too was concerned with the problems and the future of her people in the South. And was not above giving Uncle John advice. "If I were in your place I would show the President the way to treat the Indians—If he does not listen, he ought to suffer for it. Please send the *width* of your foot also."[5]

Other messages arrived at Brown's Indian Queen Hotel from Cherokee supporters, ranging from quacks and cranks to somber clergymen. Among Ross's surviving papers for the month of March is a letter from O. S. Fowler, "Practical Phrenologist" of Chestnut Street in Philadelphia. Addressing Ross as "one whose phrenological developments I once had the pleasure of describing," Dr. Fowler proposed a method of gaining instant sympathy for the Indians— namely, "by procuring plaster of Paris busts, easily secured, I should have tangible proof to show the world, that your race is a *highly intellectual* & moral one & thus exert a powerful interest in your favor."[6]

Ross and his delegates, however, adhered to a more practical approach. Even before the People's Memorial was tabled, they drafted another presentation of their own, less emotional, appealing more to the pecuniary concerns of the federal government. They suggested that a "new arrangement" be arrived at, to replace the Treaty of New Echota, on the grounds that it would be far less costly to remove the Cherokees by a treaty acceptable to both sides than by force.

To Governor Gilmer in Milledgeville this strategy was simply stalling. Perhaps it was. The deadline of May 23 was closing in. The whole Nation appeared to be marking time, unaware that such a date existed on the calendar. One of Gilmer's agents, Samuel Tate, had traveled up and down the territory "in a kind of zigzag" and found the Cherokees repairing their cabins, plowing their fields, planting their corn as always "as though there was not the least prospect of early removal."

Tate appended to his report to Gilmer the provocative note that the Indians "dance all night," and suggested that federal troops be sent to quell their untimely exuberance. "I assure you," he added, with curious deduction, "the Indians could ruin the whole country if they were to try."[7]

Gilmer took the matter up with John Ross, who, according to Senator Lumpkin in Washington, was gadding about with his partisan associates in Congress. Why, Gilmer demanded of the chief, was he not home with his people, awakening them to the reality of imminent removal, helping them to settle their affairs and make their preparations for the journey West?

His letter of March 9, 1838, seemingly written in a fit of spleen, was blunt and tactless. The President had declined to receive any further propositions from the Cherokees; their memorial to Congress had been rejected; only a fool, suggested Gilmer, could fail to see that "all hope of success in your efforts must be at an end." Warming to the subject he continued:

The law of necessity, or, if you please, the harsh and unyielding will of superior power, has determined that the portion of the Cherokees remaining in this State, must remove to the country provided for them in the West. How will you meet this necessity, against which you can no longer contend? Will you bend to the blast to rise with renewed energies when it passes away, or by resisting sink beneath its force?

Admitting that "the Cherokees are not preparing to emigrate; that they are yet hoping that you and the other chiefs will obtain a modification of the treaty, so as to permit them to remain where they are," the Governor continued:

It requires no strong invention to imagine the suffering and distress which must be inflicted upon your people, if hunted up by an undisciplined soldiery, and forced from their homes. You, at least, stand in no need of the description. Your people are looking to you to direct them in this their greatest difficulty. You can save them from the evils that threaten them, by persuading them to unite with their friends in the West, before the time arrives when, by the terms of the treaty, force can be used.[8]

Ross answered somewhat curtly four weeks later, April 6, defending his presence in Washington as "a post assigned me by the Cherokees . . . They expect me to superintend their interests here at the seat of the United States Government, as the source from which their weal or woe must emanate . . ." As for the rest of Gilmer's plaint, "I can see no necessity whatever for any collision between your citizens and the Cherokees . . ."

Nor could he foresee "the remotest pretext for employing force. It is my wish to settle all difficulties by amicable treaty, and on perfectly reasonable terms." He warned of the "inevitable danger which must result from the employment of an uncalled-for army. Should blood be spilt, therefore, which I trust can never be the case, the blame can never rest on us."[9]

Gilmer did not wait for Ross's reply before informing Secretary Joel Poinsett of "the loss of all hope of obtaining the cooperation of Ross. I am convinced that I was mistaken in my endeavor to make him an instrument for doing good." He urged on Poinsett "the importance of concentrating in the Cherokee country, in as short a time as possible, the whole of the United States army . . . Ross's refusal to return home after the conclusive action of both Houses of Congress on his memorial, renders it certain that force must be used in removing his people."

Gilmer had shot his bolt, for now. He left it up to Senator Lumpkin in Washington to continue the quashing action against Ross. Though he and Lumpkin as political opponents cherished no love for one another, they agreed on their opinion of "the assassin Ross." But Ross had the shell of a June bug; even stepped on, he would move toward his goal. He hammered on President Van Buren as he had pestered Andrew Jackson; and Van Buren lacked Old Hickory's hardness. As the May deadline approached he succumbed to Ross's rational request for time.

Two more years, Van Buren said—postponing the removal date to May 1840.

Only twice in his life, wrote Governor Gilmer, had he fully lost his temper. He did not specify the first time; but Van Buren's concession to Ross, as reported to Gilmer by the War Department, was the second. He protested vehemently to Poinsett and at greater length to William C. Dawson, head of the Georgia bloc in Congress. His patience, and Georgia's patience, was exhausted. His people could no longer be restrained from claiming Cherokee lands that rightfully belonged to them. He would call out the militia if he had to.

To Dawson, he laid it on the line. "We have two thousand men in the field under General [Charles] Floyd, not one of whom will obey any order to set at defiance the sovereignty of the State. If the United States troops shall attempt to resist our laws, they will be required . . . to leave the State . . . If the President refuses [to remove the Indians at once], the consequences must be upon his head."[10]

In short, in defiance of the United States, in defiance of federal troops in the Nation—even in defiance of the Pact of 1802, which specified that Indian removal should be "peacable"—Gilmer was prepared to expel the Cherokees by force.

If this led to civil war, so be it.

It was a beautiful spring, wrote William Cotter, a Georgia settler in the Nation. "There was no cold weather after the first of March . . . The buds burst into leaves and blossoms; the woods were green and gay and merry with the singing birds. The Indians started to work in their fields earlier than before . . . Fence corners and hedgerows were cleaned out. The ground well plowed and the corn planted, soon to be knee high and growing nicely." The approach of the appointed day for their removal, Cotter noted, "found the Indians at work in their houses and in their fields."[11]

General Nathaniel Smith, removal agent, found no consolation in the singing birds and knee-high corn. Only a fraction of the Cherokees had been transported West. The great heart of the Nation, more than sixteen thousand souls, remained—and intended to remain. Smith had approached the problem conscientiously. Aware that suffering and tragedy had attended some of the earlier emigrating parties, he tried to improve the mode of transportation. At the Tellico Agency on the Tennessee he assembled an impressive fleet of keelboats, constructed by the government and designed to ensure a fair amount of comfort and protection.

"These boats," wrote one of the Cherokee family of Foremans, "were 130 feet in length, with a house one hundred feet long, twenty wide, two stories high, 'banistered' around the top. They were made with partitions on each floor, making four rooms fifty by twenty feet furnished with windows. They were provided with stoves inside and five hearths on top of each boat for cooking."[12]

The fleet could carry a thousand or more Cherokees on the initial lap of their journey West and then return for more, getting rid of the whole bunch by December. But only three hundred showed up, apprehensively, by late March. They had heard of the outbreak of cholera on the rivers, the danger from rapids and wrecks, the many who had been buried on the banks. Fifty deserted before the remaining Indians were ready to embark on April 5, clambering aboard a keelboat towed by the steamer *Smelter*.

As they reached the Ohio, severe waves alarmed the passengers, who, fearing the craft was sinking, swarmed aboard the *Smelter*. Nothing could persuade them to return. The keelboat was cast adrift and the overloaded steamer got as far as the Arkansas, where its increased draft threatened it with grounding. Lieutenant Edward Deas, government conductor, shifted his charges to a steamer of lighter draft, which consumed a week in trying to get past several shallows. Finally, disgusted, Deas put the Indians ashore, hired wagons and oxen, and took them the rest of the way by land.

It was not a disastrous trip, a little more than three weeks on the way, and two dead from hardship and exposure. If it pointed up some of the hazards of water transportation, there was really no other choice. Smith had ordered the keelboats, banisters, stoves, and all; he would have to use them.

Martin Van Buren changed his mind.

The combined pressure of Wilson Lumpkin's bloc in Congress and Governor Gilmer's vocal outrage at the President's proposed two-year extension for removal of the Cherokees, broke down his tenuous resolve. The removal, he reluctantly decided, would go on as scheduled, starting May 23, 1838. Some compromises had been suggested—one, that the whole operation be turned over to John Ross's supervision since these were essentially his people. Ross himself turned the proposition down. He would not be instrumental in executing an abhorrent treaty.

Since it was now apparent that only armed might could dispel the Cherokees, the President and Poinsett planned accordingly. In early April 1838 Van Buren appointed General Winfield Scott to command the military operations in the Nation aimed at Cherokee removal. The six-foot-four Virginian, fifty-two years old, was amply qualified. He had come up against Indians in the War of 1812, the Black Hawk War of 1832, and the campaign against the Seminoles of Florida in 1836. His penchant for military pageantry which gained him the sobriquet of "Old Fuss and Feathers" was no encumbrance. Martial showmanship was something that the Indians could understand.

Hearing of Scott's appointment, John Ross, still in Washington, wasted no time in calling on the general. He came to ask no special favors, only to make clear the Cherokees' position—why they refused to yield, the justice on their side. Scott was impressed with the soft-spoken Indian chief; they got along well. Both had faced a onetime foe in Andrew Jackson. Earlier, in 1817, when the quick-triggered Jackson challenged the Virginian to a duel, Scott turned his back on the Hero of New Orleans. Criticized for this, Scott later sent a message offering to meet Old Hickory anytime at any place. They met. They shook hands. That was it. Jackson subsequently sent Scott to South Carolina to help pacify the nullifiers.

If, however, Scott and Ross came to any understanding, it was one whose subtle influence would be apparent later.

Scott arrived in the Cherokee Nation in early May and established headquarters at New Echota, using the Council House as barracks for his troops. Under his command were seven thousand United States regulars and volunteers including a regiment each of infantry, cavalry, and artillery. Should this force prove inadequate, he was authorized to call on the governors of adjoining states for four thousand additional militia.

No request was needed by the governor of Georgia. Gilmer not only sent troops to New Echota under General Floyd; he sent advice. He recommended that Scott's combined forces start at the Chattahoochee River on the southern border of the Nation, and fan out to the north, "taking the whole of the scattering Indians in abreast before the army." This would force the Cherokees up to the Tennessee River, the initial artery for transportation to the West. It would also drive them steadily away from Georgia, where the fear of vengeance and retaliation haunted the white community.[13]

Scott began more methodically by establishing three districts in the Nation, east, west, and central, and erecting more than a dozen forts or collection camps at strategic points throughout the territory. The Indians would be brought first to these concentration camps, then relayed to points of departure, notably the Cherokee Agency on the Hiwassee, Ross's Landing on the Tennessee, and Gunter's Landing in Alabama, where the river swung abruptly to the west.

On May 10 at the Cherokee Agency the general issued his first proclamation to the Cherokees. His words were not harsh, but they were firm. He warned the Indians that their emigration must begin at once, and that "before another moon passes every Cherokee man, woman, and child must be in motion to join his brethren in the far West . . ." He assured them that "you will be received in kindness by officers selected for the purpose. You will receive food for all, and clothing for the destitute, at either of those places [of departure], and thence at your ease, and in comfort, be transported to your new homes according to the terms of the Treaty."

In a less conciliatory tone, he warned:

My troops already occupy many positions . . . and thousands and thousands are approaching from every quarter to render resistance and escape alike hopeless . . . Will you, then, by resistance compel us to resort to arms . . . or will you by flight seek to hide yourselves in mountains and forests and thus oblige us to hunt you down?[14]

Defiance, the general reminded the Cherokees, resistance by force, would lead only to needless bloodshed and perhaps to general war.

Hearing these words, the Cherokees were puzzled. War was something they had long since put behind them. They had already been disarmed by General Wool, who had taken the fowling pieces needed to protect their herds. To many, especially the more illiterate, the presence of uniformed soldiers in the Nation could mean only one thing. The United States had sent troops to protect them from the Georgians.

Then, like the swift incursions of the Raven Mocker, there came the reign of terror. From the jagged-walled stockades the troops fanned out across the Nation, invading every hamlet, every cabin, rooting out the inhabitants at bayonet point. The Cherokees hardly had time to realize what was happening as they were prodded like so many sheep toward the concentration camps, threatened with knives and pistols, beaten with rifle butts if they resisted.

One who gathered a firsthand account of their ordeal "from the lips of the actors in the tragedy" was Indian ethnologist James Mooney, who felt that the Cherokees' story "may well exceed in weight of grief and pathos any other passage in American history." In his words:

Families at dinner were startled by the sudden gleam of bayonets in the doorway and rose up to be driven with blows and oaths along the weary miles of trail that led to the stockade. Men were seized in their fields or going along the road, women were taken from their wheels and children from their play. In many cases, on turning for one last look as they crossed the ridge, they saw their homes in flames, fired by the lawless rabble that followed on the heels of the soldiers to loot and pillage.[15]

Serving as an interpreter with General Scott's infantry was Private John G. Burnett, who unwillingly witnessed what he called "the execution of the most brutal order in the history of American warfare." The tactics were, in fact, precisely those of warfare. The soldiers were ordered to ambush their victims in the fields or silently surround their cabins and pounce upon them unawares. One ancient patriarch, thus surprised, requested a moment's time in which he asked his children and grandchildren to kneel with him and pray. The embarrassed troops leaned on their arms as the group recited the Lord's Prayer in Cherokee—after which the old man led his family into exile.[16]

Not many were given time to collect even their most precious personal belongings. Private Burnett, inspecting a cabin cleared of its occupants by the invading troops, found a beautifully fashioned rocking horse apparently created by the father for his children. He thought of taking it apart to be shipped home as a souvenir. Then he discovered that the horse had been painstakingly carved from a single piece of hickory and could not be dismantled. He left it, gently rocking, in the cabin.

Perhaps because of his satisfactory meeting with John Ross in Washington, and the mutual respect it generated, Scott cautioned his troops against brutality. "The Cherokees," he told them, "by the advances they have made in Christianity and civilization, are by far the most interesting tribe of Indians in the territorial interests of the United States." However, he added, "it is understood that about four fifths are opposed or have become averse to distant emigration."

The situation called for tact, forbearance, even courtesy:

Considering the number and temper of the mass to be removed . . . it will readily occur that simple indiscretions—acts of harshness and cruelty on the part of our troops, may lead . . . in the end, to a general war and carnage—a result, in the case of these particular Indians, utterly abhorrent to the generous sympathies of the whole American people.

Every possible kindness . . . must, therefore, be shown by the troops, and if, in the ranks, a despicable individual should be found, capable of inflicting a wanton injury or insult on any Cherokee man, woman or child, it is hereby made the special duty of the nearest good officer or man, instantly to interpose, and to seize and consign the guilty wretch to the severest penalty of the laws.[17]

While *Niles' Register* in Baltimore, a generally faithful monitor of Indian events, reported that "in most cases the humane injunctions of the commanding general were disregarded," it is fair to assume that many of the more atrocious acts of persecution were performed by the horde of vagabonds and stragglers who follow in every army's wake, taking advantage of the doomed civilians, looting and plundering at will, snatching up Indian possessions that were still warm from their owners' hands. Recorded Mooney:

So keen were these outlaws on the scent that in some instances they were driving off the cattle and other stock of the Indians almost before the soldiers had fairly started their owners in the other direction. Systematic hunts were made by the same men for Indian graves, to rob them of the silver pendants and other valuables deposited with the dead. A Georgia volunteer, afterward a colonel in the Confederate service, said: "I fought through the civil war and have seen men shot to pieces and slaughtered by thousands, but the Cherokee removal was the cruelest work I ever knew."[18]

In his General Orders issued at the beginning of the roundup Scott had advised his troops to "get possession of the women and children first, or first capture the men," and the other members of a group or family would follow. Children, seized while playing away from home, were used as hostages to bring the parents in; and although the general justified this blackmail as a means of keeping families together, children were often lost in the ensuing panic, husbands and wives remained apart.

Indifference and impatience, rather than practiced cruelty, were the causes of much of the suffering. The sick, General Scott had ordered, were to be left behind with one or more of their people in attendance, while the rest of the family could be removed. "Infants, superannuated persons, lunatics and women in a helpless condition, will all, in the removal, require particular attention, which the brave and humane will seek to adapt to the necessities of the several cases."

But the troops had no time for special cases calling for particular attention. Old people and those too ill to walk were, of necessity, left behind without attendance, to live or not as fate decreed. Those who fell by the wayside were left to die; it was a humane group of guards indeed who paused long enough to give the dead a decent burial. The bewildered Cherokees were driven like cattle into the stockades, and those who tried to escape, men, women, or children, were given fifty lashes on their bare backs to discourage further such attempts.

When a frightened Cherokee lad fled from the troops, a soldier ordered him to halt. The boy kept on running, and the soldier brought him down with a bullet through the back. Only then was it learned that the youth was deaf and had not heard the order. One minor Cherokee chief named Sawnee went to extreme lengths to make certain of escape. He asked his family to seal him up in a prepared tomb in a Georgia mountainside. He would die and his corpse would remain in the mountains that he loved.

In the Valley Town district of North Carolina, beautiful, rugged, isolated, the Baptist missionary Evan Jones wept for the suffering of his people. "Multitudes," he wrote, "were allowed no time to take anything with them, except the clothes they had on. Well-furnished houses were left a prey to plunderers who, like hungry wolves, follow in the train of the captors. These wretches rifle the houses, strip the helpless unoffending owners of all they have on earth."[19]

The soldiers were helpless to control these scavengers, who, if they went through the motions of paying an Indian for his abandoned property, cheated him outrageously. The head of a household, noted Mooney, "in a state of distressing agitation, his weeping wife almost frantic with terror," was in no condition to bargain for his rights. His home and its furnishings, his barns, crops, implements, and cattle were signed away for a pittance he might never see.

The plight of the weeping women, for this was the start of a long time of weeping, moved Evan Jones himself to tears. Women among the Cherokees were treated with traditional respect, on a level once reserved for warriors. But now, recorded the Reverend Jones, "females who have been habituated to comforts and comparative affluence, are driven on foot before the bayonets of brutal men. Their feelings are mortified by vulgar and profane vociferation. It is a painful sight."

Not all the Cherokees submitted passively to capture. In Evan Jones's country, the wild region of Valley Town, resistance was often stubborn and effective, but with aftermaths of tragedy. From here came one of the legendary heroes of the Cherokees, whose story, so often retold and with so many variations, is sometimes hard to separate from myth. The man's name was Tsali, an old man now, living in Valley Town the day the soldiers came.[20]

According to one version, Tsali, his wife and brother, his three sons and their families were taken by surprise and marched at bayonet point toward the Indian Agency on the Hiwassee River. When Tsali's wife paused to care for the needs of her baby, one of the guards whipped her and prodded her with his bayonet, to force her on her way. This so enraged the husband that he consulted in Cherokee with the others in his group; they would take the risk, overcome the guards by force, and make a break for freedom.

In the surprise attack on the soldiers, one guard was killed and the rest wounded or subdued. Tsali and his relatives fled to the mountains and hid out in a cave in the Great Smokies. His successful evasion was reported to the other Indians by grapevine and soon the mountain Cherokees by dozens, then by hundreds, joined him in the hideout, living off roots and berries on the border of starvation.

General Scott was baffled by the situation. He had not the troops to track down Indians in that impervious and secret region. Nor was he certain that he wanted to. But if Tsali's freedom went unchallenged, a fateful example would be set for other Cherokees. Scott enlisted the services of William Thomas, a white trader who had lived for twenty years among the North Carolina Indians and had their confidence. Thomas was given a message to the leader of the fugitives. If Tsali and his family would surrender themselves to military justice, the rest of the Cherokees in the mountains could remain free.

That Tsali agreed to the deal was a foregone conclusion; what more could honor ask? He and his brother and sons came down from the mountains and gave themselves up. Tsali's youngest boy, Wasidana, was spared; the others were executed. According to Wasidana, they were shot by a firing squad of Cherokee prisoners, compelled to the act as a means of impressing on the Indians the hopelessness of their position.

Tsali's martyrdom, however, marked not a hopeless end but a beginning. The three hundred fugitives remaining free became the forebears of some five thousand Cherokees living today in the North Carolina mountains, legatees of the once proudest Nation in the red man's history. And Tsali's story survives, close to the scene of its original enactment, in the annual presentation of a Cherokee drama entitled "Unto These Hills."

The summer was well advanced when Ross returned with his delegates from Washington. Though Van Buren had reneged on his promise of two more years for Cherokee removal, and Ross's memorials of protest had been tabled by the Congress, the chief himself had not diminished in the Nation's eyes. While Governor Gilmer gloated that "Mr. Van Buren's schemes are blown sky high," he complained in the same breath of "the power and subtlety of Mr. Van Buren and John Ross"—suspecting some sort of understanding or conspiracy between them. To a degree he was right. Ross had won the President's confidence; more important, he still retained the confidence of the Cherokee people.

But Ross himself was shocked at what he saw on his return—a country of ghost towns, littered and derelict, as if stripped by a plague of locusts. Vagabonds prowled around that devastated landscape, picking at the piles of rubbish, collecting the remains of ravaged crops, poking through abandoned cabins. Had he possessed the power to divine the future, Ross could have foreseen the same tragedy repeated a quarter century later, as dispossessed Georgians returned to their shattered homes in the wake of General Sherman's armies.

For the Cherokees, all sixteen thousand of them, had been rounded up—not in the three weeks General Scott had scheduled, but close enough to that goal. The dragnet that had started on May 26, 1838, was completed on June 20; and which was worse, the manner of their capture or the mode of their detention, would be difficult to say. By the third week of June the stockades were packed with Indian humanity, bewildered children, brokenhearted wives and mothers, stunned warriors, ancient and resigned chiefs.

They were never meant to endure confinement, to live in close quarters without adequate food and sanitation. And above all, without the simple possessions they needed to retain their dignity and comfort. General Scott himself confessed to "the distress caused the emigrants by the want of their bedding, cooking utensils, clothes and ponies," and added, "I much regret also the loss of their property consequent upon the hurry of capture and removal." But Scott felt that the Indians themselves were to blame for trusting too completely on John Ross to save them. John Ridge naturally held the same view and spread it among disgruntled emigrants arriving in the West.

But whoever or whatever was to blame, the horror of the concentration camps was another blot on the dreary annals of America's mistreatment of the Indians. The stockades themselves were built of split logs, sharpened, and positioned upright to form the four walls of a sixteen-foot-high square. They were open at the top, but the prisoners were allowed to build crude shelters as protection from the sun and rain. The food was standard army prison fare, salt pork and flour, adequate but far removed from the beef and garden vegetables and fruits the Indians were used to.

Evan Jones, the Baptist preacher of Valley Town, may not have deserved the army's charge of "meddling" and "interfering," but he could no more keep aloof from the Cherokees' plight than could the other remaining missionaries. At Camp Hetzel in Tennessee on June 16, the Reverend noted in his diary that "the Cherokees are nearly all prisoners. They have been dragged from their houses and encamped at the forts and military places all over the Nation."

As a result of this disruption and the seizure of their property, "many of the Cherokees who, a few days ago, were in comfortable circumstances, are now the victims of abject poverty." Of Camp Hetzel, the Reverend Evans observed:

Our brother [Jesse] Bushyhead and his family, Rev. Stephen Foreman, native missionary of the American Board and Speaker of the National Council, and several men of character and respectability, with their families, are here prisoners. It is due to justice to say that, at this station (and I learn that the same is true of some others) the officer in command treats his prisoners with great respect and indulgence. But fault lies somewhere. They are prisoners, without a crime to justify the fact.[21]

Similarly at Fort Butler, also in Tennessee, a number of missionary workers were imprisoned and strove to bolster the morale within the camp. They were allowed to build shelters for worship, and as Evan Jones noted, "never relaxed their evangelical labors. They held church meetings . . . and one Sabbath, June 17, by permission of the officer in command, went down to the river and baptized five males and five females. They were guarded to the river and back. Some whites present affirm it to have been the most solemn and impressive religious service they ever witnessed."

Brainerd Mission—empty now of scholars, teachers, and most of its staff—provided a point of refuge for a few escaping Indians. Perhaps it was natural that they should turn to what had once been a beacon of hope in the Tennessee wilderness. And, in a desultory fashion, the Mission Journal was still maintained. It is hard to tell from handwritten manuscripts just who the faithful author was, but Daniel Butrick and Elizur Butler were both present from time to time at the otherwise abandoned mission. Perhaps they took turns as the keeper of the records.

In any event, the writer reports for the second week in June:

Five Cherokee families have fled to this neighborhood from Georgia where they are not safe for one day. They have made camp in the woods, that is, they have put up four posts and a roof, and here they live with their cattle and horses, dogs, chickens and cats, with their household goods they brought with them. They are in a thicket, and only the fires at night, the cries of their children, the howling of the dogs, or the cackle of the hens show us where they are.

June 12. In the morning a company of soldiers came here, and seized all the Indians camped around us. They drove them forth without distinction, among them

an old woman of more than 80 years. The poor folk were just about to eat breakfast, but that made no difference; they had to leave at once, and in order to pack
they cut open their feather beds and emptied the feathers into the brush, and then
in their fright they had to leave much behind them.

And another entry, at another time:

. . . we were disturbed by the arrival of a company of soldiers with 200 poor prisoners, Indians, soaked through by the rain, whom they drove through the Chickamauga River before them like cattle . . . It was pitiful to see the poor folks, many
old and sick, many little children, many with heavy packs on their backs, and all
utterly exhausted. In the confusion some had left behind their children, who chanced
not to be at home; other children had run away from their parents in terror.[22]

Visiting Spring Place and the two hundred Indians confined there, the writer
of the day is surely Daniel Butrick, for he speaks in Butrick fashion of the former Moravian Mission "now become the place where Satan sits upon his
throne, and where the air seems full of evil spirits . . ." By then, June was
coming to a close, and Butrick was blissfully unaware of evil clouds on the horizon. What he was witnessing at this point, what the Cherokees were going
through, was only a harbinger of the ordeal still to come.

18

As Makes the
Angels Weep!

I T W A S still early summer, only the sixth of June, but unseasonably warm and dry. Pressed nose to stern against the riverbank at Ross's Landing, the six double-decked barges rested with their keels almost aground. The hundred-ton tow ship stood a little way offshore, keeping up a head of steam, wary of being trapped by the subsiding water level.

Lieutenant Edward Deas, who had seen the Tennessee at flood stage three months earlier, was worried. His native New England waterways were more predictable. He wondered how much longer the river would be navigable. Long enough, he hoped, to carry this initial batch of reluctant emigrants on the first lap of their journey West. Otherwise the party would have to travel overland, a murderous alternative in summer drought and heat.

Since the roundup of the Cherokees had started four weeks earlier, General Scott estimated that only 200 had escaped the dragnet. He must, however, have discounted the several hundred freed by Tsali's sacrifice and still in the North Carolina mountains. Penned in the stockades were approximately 15,000 Cherokees, though the estimates varied, some placing the figure as high as 17,000, including blacks, miscellaneous whites, and servants. Of the total, some 2,800 to 3,000 were scheduled for immediate evacuation, to depart from Ross's Landing in three roughly equal groups which would follow one another in close succession. The first contingent, with Lieutenant Deas as conductor, would get under way that morning of June 6.

The numbers of the emigrating parties were a constant riddle. In trying to keep track of the groups the conductors had little cooperation from the Cherokees themselves. The Indians would not respond to roll calls. They would not line up and be counted. They would not reveal the names and numbers of their families. Trying to keep track as they surged aboard the boats was like trying to count heads in a moving crowd. Once they were aboard the boats the reigning confusion made it impossible to get an accurate tally free of omissions or duplication.

Deas estimated about 800 in his group, the first of the three contingents forced aboard the boats by the escorting soldiers. But the mood of the Indians was ugly; they were still bitter about the method of their capture and the crowded condition on the barges; Deas would never be certain of their numbers.

Little Jay Bird of Rising Fawn's district, who had witnessed the secreting of the family gold before abandoning their home, professed to be among this initial group. But Jay Bird's recollections, as recorded some years later, seem distorted by time and a child's imagination:

We went to the stockade early on the morning on which we had been told to report. Here for the first time in my life I saw the white soldiers, each in uniform and carrying a long rifle with bayonet attached. We walked into the stockade, and the heavy gate closed behind us. We were now prisoners of the hated white man. Inside the stockade all the Indians were being treated like cattle. Some were so old they could scarcely walk around and some of the babies and small children, already sick, were crying pitifully. Some of the Indians, mostly the very old, had been brought in on stretchers from their sick beds.[1]

From the stockade, Jay Bird recalled, they were packed in army wagons and transported to Ross's Landing, "where we joined all the other Indians, about ten thousand in number. About half the Indians were loaded into several steamboats, including my father, mother, and me." At this point Jay Bird's inventive imagination got the better of fact:

Just after we started down the river the boat behind the one we were on was completely demolished when one of the steam boilers blew up. Over three hundred Indians were killed instantly, as well as an uncounted number of Negro slaves belonging to the Indians.[2]

There is no record, official or otherwise, of such a catastrophe—which would certainly have appeared in the conductor's log. Lieutenant Deas's own careful report notes only that the expedition got under way at noon without significant incident. The flatboats were lashed together, three on each side of the steamer, and the flotilla moved downstream at a cautious five miles an hour.

Dangerous rapids awaited them ahead, known in order as the Suck, the Boiling Pot, the Skillet, and the Frying Pan. The first of these, Lieutenant Deas noted in his log, was the most difficult. "The river here becomes very narrow and swift and the banks on either side are rocky and steep, it being the point at which the stream passes thro' a gorge in the mountains."[3]

At this point began a delicate reshuffling of the flatboats, with the steamer escorting two at a time through the danger zone. The steamboat, Deas recorded, "with one Flat on each side passed through, the most of the people on board, but after getting thro' the most rapid water, it was found impossible to keep her in the channel, and in consequence was thrown upon the north Bank with some violence but luckily none of the people were injured although one of the Flats was a good deal smashed. The other four boats came thro' two by two and the party was encamped before dark as it was too late in the day to reach the rapids in the daylight."[4]

The next day the balance of the rapids was negotiated without incident and on June 9 the flotilla reached Decatur. From here they would travel by railroad to Tuscumbia, bypassing the unnavigable section of the river. Thirty-two cars pulled by double locomotives were able to carry only half the group, excluding the guards, whom Deas dismissed to relieve the overcrowding. The other half remained at Decatur until the cars and locomotive could return for them.

Any form of waiting was disastrous on a trip like this. Whiskey peddlers at Decatur zeroed in on the stranded group, "much drunkenness resulting, and over one hundred of the emigrants escaped." When the railroad train came back for the rest of the group, those stranded at Tuscumbia succumbed to the same contingencies, the euphoria of alcohol, the opportunity for flight. When the entire party was reassembled above Waterloo and loaded aboard two double-decked keelboats escorted by the steamer *Vesper,* Lieutenant Deas found one of the keelboats superfluous and ordered it left behind. He estimated that his original party of 800 had been reduced to 489.

From that point on Deas kept his reduced fleet moving day and night, stopping only for wood, and permitting no time ashore for the disgruntled passengers. This continued till the cutoff from the Mississippi to the Arkansas, after which too many sandbars and shallows prevented navigation after dark, and the Indians camped by night on the riverbanks. Though destined for Fort Gibson, most of the emigrants never got that far. Reaching Sallisaw Creek in Cherokee Territory West, the travelers were hailed by their comrades on land and, tossing their baggage ashore, promptly disembarked. They would settle wherever these brethren had settled.

With understanding kindness Deas let them go, recording that he "issued a sufficient quantity of Cotton Domestic to the Indians for Tents to protect them from the weather. I have done so in consideration of their destitute condition, as they were for the most part separated from their homes in Georgia without having the means or time to prepare for camping and it was also the opinion of the Physician of the Party that the health of these people would suffer if not provided with some protection from the weather."

Lieutenant Deas had cause for self-congratulation. Not a single Indian had died en route, though none knew what happened to those who disappeared. Right behind this initial contingent, however, the second group of emigrants was faring badly. According to the company's conductor, Lieutenant R. H. K. Whiteley, they numbered about 875—but he was never certain. They refused to line up to receive the clothing and provisions offered them, nor, wrote the lieutenant, "would they be mustered, as all attempts to obtain their names were without success."

Eight flatboats lashed together in pairs were conducted by the steamer *George Guess* through the rapids, during which Whiteley recorded in his journal "One death (a child) and one birth." Before reaching the railroad cutoff at Decatur twenty-five Indians escaped from nighttime shore encampments and before boarding the railroad an aged woman died and a man was killed when he tried to retrieve his hat from beneath the train. Reaching Tuscumbia, they shifted from train to river craft again, and the steamer *Smelter* towed the company in a single keelboat.

Another child died as they reached the Ohio, and three more as they reached the junction of the Mississippi and the Arkansas. Though the *Smelter* was replaced by a steamer of lighter draft, the flotilla was grounded a short distance above Little Rock. Whiteley scoured the countryside to obtain enough wagons to carry the children and the hundred or more Indians too sick to walk, and the party set out on the long overland route through Arkansas to Oklahoma. According to Grant Foreman, dean of Indian historians, who chronicled this tragic period:

The weather was extremely hot, a drought had prevailed for months, water was scarce, suffocating clouds of dust stirred up by oxen and wagons, and the rough and rocky roads, made the condition of the sick occupants of the wagons miserable indeed. Three, four, and five deaths occurred each day. To avoid the heat the marches were started before sunrise and ended at noon. Before the end of the month there were between two and three hundred ill.[5]

Worse was to come when on August 1 the party was forced to camp at Lee's Creek, just short of Indian Territory. Lieutenant Whiteley recorded in his journal: "Did not move this day, the party requiring rest and being more than one half sick; notwithstanding every effort used, it was impossible to prevent their eating quantities of green peaches and corn—consequently the flux raged among them and carried off some days as high as six and seven."

Green peaches and corn could not alone have caused the dreadful mortality among them. Hardship, exposure, fatigue, and lack of adequate water took a heavy toll. By the time they had reached the Cherokee Nation West, only 602 of the original 875 remained, seventy having died in three weeks and the rest simply disappearing.

The tragic hegira was a preview of events to come, a bitter foretaste of what the Cherokees later called *nunna-da-ul-tsun-yi,* or "the trail on which they cried." Perhaps John Howard Payne, still waging a running campaign for justice for the Cherokees, visualized the mournful picture from a distance. In one of his documents on Cherokee removal, slightly misquoting Shakespeare, he closed with the lines:

> Frail man, frail man,
> Drest in a little brief authority
> Plays such fantastic tricks before high Heaven
> As makes the angels weep![6]

On June 17 Scott discharged the volunteer troops used in rounding up the Indians; their job was done; and General Charles Floyd of the Georgia militia wrote gloatingly to Governor Gilmer from New Echota:

Sir: I have the pleasure to inform your excellency that I am now fully convinced there is not an Indian within the limits of my command, except a few in my possession, who will be sent to Ross's Landing tomorrow. My scouting parties have scoured the whole country without seeing an Indian, or late Indian signs. If there are any stragglers in Georgia, they must be . . . near the Tennessee and North Carolina line; but none can escape the vigilance of our troops. Georgia is ultimately in possession of her rights in the Cherokee country.[7]

Gilmer wasted no time getting the message to the Georgia legislature, assuring them they would no longer be harassed by the perplexing Cherokees, "that our citizens are at last in the quiet possession of all their lands, and the State the undisputed sovereign over all her territory." He felt a personal pride in the achievement, in having overcome "the power and subtlety of Mr. Van Buren and John Ross . . ."[8]

It was true that the Cherokees were at long last out of Georgia. But they were still in the East, most of them in two of the three departure zones, at Ross's Landing and the Indian Agency on the Hiwassee, the latter a vast stockaded area containing perhaps ten thousand captive Indians. On the same day that Scott discharged the volunteers the last of the three initial contingents, estimated at 1,070 in number, started the westward trek from Ross's Landing. They were seen as "in a destitute condition, with very little clothing," but following the pattern of pride observed by previous emigrants, they refused to accept clothes or blankets from the emigration agents.

By now the summer's drought was serious. Throughout the entire South the wells were drying up, drinking water was becoming scarce, crops were threatened with failure, and the waterways were shrinking. The upper Tennessee River, as the agents had feared, was no longer navigable; and the third band of emigrants was forced to travel by wagon and on foot to Waterloo, 160 miles distant in western Alabama, before being able to board the flatboats. Five died in the arduous overland trek, four children and one adult; they were buried on the roadside and the caravan trudged on.

But news of the tragedy and of conditions in the country, where drought was aggravating sickness in the fever season, prompted Assistant Chief George Lowrey, while Ross was still in Washington, to seek relief. A five-man committee headed by Lowrey and including Ross's brother Lewis, Hair Conrad, Thomas Foreman, and Chief Going Snake petitioned General Scott to postpone further emigration until conditions bettered in the fall. Scott on June 19 agreed, advancing the removal deadline to September 1. The Cherokees had been rounded up; Georgia was off his back; further disasters among the emigrating Indians would only hamper future operations.

But what of the third contingent already on the march to Waterloo to board the boats, bound for the land of drought and fever? Lowrey's committee addressed a moving petition to Nathaniel Smith, Superintendent of Indian Emigration, which said in part:

Spare their lives; expose them not to the killing effects of that strange climate, under the disadvantages of the present inauspicious season, without a house or shelter to cover them from above, or any kind of furniture to raise them from the bare ground, on which they may spread their blankets and lay their languid limbs, when fallen prostrate under the influence of disease.[9]

The petition pointed out that the "cries of humanity," including those of physicians in the South, were sympathetic to their appeal. It requested that the third contingent be halted where its members were, to settle in encampments and await the September exodus or, better yet, be returned to their former stockade at the agency. Smith denied the application. But he did have the conscience to journey west to see what could be done about the emigrants en route. By the time he reached Alabama he found a hundred of the party had already escaped. The rest, having learned of General Scott's postponement of emigration till the fall, repeated the plea that they be permitted to return. Smith noted for the record:

As they would have traveled over 120 miles, their health improving and they well provided with transportation and subsistence, I determined they should go on and so informed them. Shortly after which about 300 of them, threw a part of their baggage out of the waggons, took it and broke for the woods and many of the balance refused to put their baggage into the waggons, or go any further and shewed much ill nature.[10]

Many of them, wrote Smith, told the agents in charge that all whites were "liars and bad men"; they were going back to fight for John Ross. Whereupon Smith instructed the army officer in charge to call for citizen volunteers to make certain that the mutinous party boarded the boats at Waterloo. "As very many of this party," Smith recorded, "were about naked, barefoot and suffering from fatigue," they were offered clothing, tents, and shoes. He should have known the pattern by now. The Indians refused; their pride would not submit to patronage.

Smith accompanied the expedition as far as Little Rock, recording wholesale desertions on the way—seventy-six in a single night—until only 722 of the original 1,070 remained. West of Little Rock the low waters of the Arkansas made the river impassable for deep-draft vessels, and the Indians awaited the arrival of the light steamboat *Tecumseh* to take them further. Smith left the expedition, predicting that when this last of three contingents reached the West, about a third of the emigrating Indians would have died, escaped, or remained unaccounted for. His estimate proved close to right.

On July 13, 1838, John Ross returned from Washington to find the Cherokee Nation abandoned and lifeless. Empty cabins stood looted and neglected. Crops withered in the fields. Untended cattle wandered through the forests and stray pigs rooted through decayed fruit in the orchards. New Echota alone remained sluggishly alive, for the onetime capital was now an army camp where the soldiers, with the roundup ended, had little to do but await Scott's orders to remove them to the North.

The Cherokees themselves, roughly 14,000 of them now, were penned in the stockades. The largest captive community, numbering 3,000, was at the Indian Agency, with 2,500 more at Ross's Landing. The rest were scattered among inland forts, about a thousand to a camp. Conditions presaged those at Georgia's Civil War stockade at Andersonville in a quarter century to come. Though the captives were able to build some shelters from the merciless sun, the lack of adequate sanitation, the stagnant water, unfamiliar and irregular meals lowered resistance and fostered disease.

The Indians were dying like flies, or so it was rumored and published in the northern press. Though the stories were exaggerated, epidemics of pleurisy, measles, whooping cough, and "intermittent fever" swept through the concentration camps. While General Scott denied the reports, asserting that "there is no more sickness amongst the Indians than might ordinarily take place amongst any other people under the same circumstances," and that "good physicians and medicine" were provided, at least one physician proved to be a dentist and the rest were overworked army doctors with little interest in and less knowledge of the red man's needs.

Cherokee babies born in captivity were given scant chances of survival. Mothers pleaded for permission to hunt outside the stockades for wild fruits and berries and especially for medicinal herbs for their ailing children. The guards, perhaps understandably, refused to turn them loose.

To the concerned and observant missionaries still in Tennessee, this was indeed the pestilence that walked in the night. Dr. Butler reported seventeen deaths in one camp in a week, from what he branded "putrid dysentery." He later recorded that two thousand died that summer in the concentration camps, though other estimates put the figure at considerably less. Daniel Butrick noted in his journal that the Cherokees' enforced captivity was "a most expensive and painful way of putting these poor people to death." It would have been more merciful, he cynically observed, to have executed every Indian over sixty years of age.[11]

To Butrick the plague that hovered over the encampments was as much a sickness of the soul as of the body. Where liquor was smuggled into the stockades the Cherokees sought release in alcoholic coma or in sometimes fatal brawling. Young Cherokee girls, Butrick sadly noted, became victims not only of the bottle but of the seductive lures of guardian soldiers who took them for brief solitary outings in surrounding underbrush.

The missionaries and the native converts did what they could to salvage souls in the removal forts. At Camp Hetzel that summer Evan Jones noted in his diary that "these prisoners of *Christians*, are now all hands busy, some cutting and some carrying posts, and plates and rafters—some digging holes for posts, and some preparing seats for a temporary place of preaching . . ." The Baptist convert Jesse Bushyhead and Stephen Foreman, also a convert, held regular services in the stockade, and the army officers to their credit made no attempt to interfere.

Working against these efforts were rumors arriving daily from the West, which seemed to indicate that something was rotten in the Promised Land beyond the Mississippi. Wrote the Reverend Cephas Washburn from Dwight Mission on July 31: "Among the recent immigrants there has been much sickness, and in some neighborhoods the mortality has been great." In one locality, Washburn reported, fourteen died within three weeks, and the Indians were direly in need of medical aid. Illness and death were reported among each group arriving from the East.[12]

Bad planning was at the root of much of the tragedy. Summer was the worst time of year for travel between East and West, and extreme drought added to the hazards. Had they gone earlier—or later—things might have been different. But timing, in Cherokee eyes, was not the author of their misery. That they should be forced to emigrate at all was the source of this catastrophe.

Puzzling to the missionaries, who regarded the delay in emigration as disastrous for the Indians, was the fact that none of these victimized people blamed John Ross for their predicament. Had they rejected his leadership earlier and agreed to voluntary emigration, they might now be free in the West instead of suffering and dying in the concentration camps.[13]

Yet such a thought never, apparently, occurred to them. Though Ross had promised that by rejecting the Treaty of New Echota they would ultimately triumph, they had been defeated and humiliated. Yet that was not considered due to Ross's failure to make good his promise; it was due to Boudinot, the Ridges, and the rest of the Treaty Party now in exile. These were the men who had betrayed them, on whom the white heat of their hatred remained focused.

Ross himself, on his return, quickly applied himself to bettering conditions in the concentration camps. His earlier talks with General Scott in Washington gave him considerable leverage in this direction. Incensed at what he found in visiting the stockades, he appointed a committee of three to make regular inspections of the camps, report on the needs of the prisoners—whether for food, or clothing, or medical aid—after which he applied to Scott and Smith for relief. Among other measures he demanded that all grogshops around the camps be closed by the Army and that liquor smuggling be suppressed.

In Ross's estimation the whole early stages of removal had been bungled, largely through ignorance and indifference to the red man's welfare. He proposed to Scott that subsequent emigration starting in September be conducted by the Cherokees themselves, somewhat on the honor system. Using government funds provided by treaty, they would organize their own detachments, arrange for the necessary means of transportation, lead and police the emigrating groups in transit.

With surprising alacrity Scott granted the request, informing the War Department he had done so and giving them no chance to approve or disapprove. Presumably Secretary Poinsett was glad to get the Cherokee problem off his shoulders by any convenient means and this was one of them. It was a concession that had not been granted to the Creeks or Chickasaws, the Choctaws or the Seminoles, but these had not presented as much resistance nor had their removal aroused such a tide of public sympathy.

Scott warned Ross, however, that the Cherokee National Council would hereafter be held responsible for the conduct of the people throughout the balance of the summer as well as during transit to the West. The mere fact that Scott and the War Department acknowledged the continued existence of the Council, considered extinct by Georgia, was a concession in itself. The fact, too, that Ross was recognized as active Chief, when he had been ignored as such at the signing of the treaty, was a belated, sadly hollow victory for Ross.

Early in August the Council convened on the grounds of the Aquohee District camp a few miles south of the Hiwassee River, where many of the Nation's leaders were interned. It was a curious, skeleton assembly held under curious circumstances. Officially the Cherokees were no longer prisoners; they were free under their own recognizance. But their freedom was relative. Stripped of their property, they had no homes remaining to them—only the stockades.

As an uprooted people they clung to traditions as their only anchor. They took pains to restate those traditions as a means of self-perpetuation. Wherever they went and settled, whatever happened to them, the Cherokee Nation and its constitution, as conceived in 1827, must survive. To this end they passed a resolution stating in part:

WHEREAS the title of the Cherokee people to their lands is the most ancient, pure, and absolute known to man . . .

And WHEREAS the natural, political and moral relations existing among the citizens of the Cherokee Nation toward each other and toward the body politic, cannot in reason and justice be dissolved by the expulsion of the Nation from its territory by the power of the United States Government.

Resolved by the National Committee and Council and people of the Cherokee Nation, in General Council assembled, that the inherent sovereignty of the Cherokee Nation, together with the Constitution, laws and usages of the same, are, and by the authority aforesaid, hereby declared to be in full force . . . and shall continue so to be in perpetuity subject to such modification as the general welfare may render expedient.[14]

Turning to the matter of impending emigration, a management committee was chosen, consisting of Ross, Elijah Hicks, Richard Taylor, Edward Gunter, White Path, and Situwakee. Chief Ross was given the additional title of "Superintendent of Cherokee Removal and Subsistence," thus boldly replacing the government-appointed superintendent Nathaniel Smith. Among Ross's responsibilities would be the securing of federal funds to finance the operation, and Ross named his brother Lewis to handle the contracts for rations and provisions.

Plans were made for the Cherokees to start West in September in thirteen parties of roughly a thousand each. Whenever and wherever possible, they would travel by land, having had enough unfortunate experiences with river transportation. Each detachment would have its own conductors and its own

Light Horse police force; if army officers went along they would travel as observers, nothing more. The Indians would purchase cattle to be taken with them as a source of beef; other provisions would be picked up at appointed depots on the way.

On this basis Ross made his cost analysis and submitted to General Scott an estimate of sixty dollars a head for Cherokee removal, a figure that would bring the total cost to more than three quarters of a million dollars, or roughly double what Congress had estimated eight years earlier. Included in the sixteen cents per person per day for rations were such "useless luxuries" (in War Department eyes) as sugar, coffee, and soap, the latter "an item which we deem indispensable."

Scott approved the budget, knowing that objections would be raised in Washington. He winced at the addition of soap to the daily rations, but informed the committee in a carefully worded letter, "As the Cherokee people are exclusively interested in costs as well as the comforts in the removal, I do not feel myself at liberty to withhold my sanction. The estimate therefore of emigration costs submitted to me . . . with the small addition of soap is hereby approved."[15]

With this matter settled, Ross and his committee worked on indemnities due to the Cherokees for their abandoned property. All were invited to present their claims to be relayed to United States authorities for settlement before departure. Demands for compensation ranged from the sublime to the submarginal. Wealthy Cherokees billed the government for handsome mansions, elegant house furnishings, fine silverware, rare libraries, and blooded horses. At the opposite end of the spectrum was a typical list submitted by one Cherokee housewife recording the loss of "six ducks, a plaid cloak, a feather bed, a turkey gobbler, a set of china, two blowguns, a fiddle, garden tools, an umbrella, a coffee pot, and a plow."[16]

The sum total of these claims approximated the estimated cost of removal. A reluctant Congress would try to get its money back through the sale of the Cherokees' abandoned lands.

While the War Department and Congress might go along with this arrangement for self-supervised removal, an angry howl of protest came from Ross's arch-foe, Andrew Jackson. To the retired Indian fighter in the Hermitage, the Cherokee chief appeared to be having a last word in their ten-year battle, when he should have been long since dead and buried. Hearing from Nathaniel Smith that Ross was now back in command of Cherokee affairs, Old Hickory vented his wrath in a letter dated August 23 to Felix Grundy, United States Attorney General.

Writing that "I am so feeble I can scarcely wield my pen," but nonetheless "excited" by the subject, the former President declared:

The contract with Ross must be arrested, or you may rely upon it, the expense and other evils will shake the popularity of the Administration to its center. What madness and folly to have anything to do with Ross when the agent was proceeding well with the removal on the principles of economy that would have saved at least 100 per cent from what the contract with Ross will cost.

I have only time to add as the mail waits that the contract with Ross *must be arrested,* and General Smith left to supervise the removal . . . Why is it that the scamp Ross is not banished from the notice of the administration?[17]

Ross had his own answer to Old Hickory's complaint. He was being given a free hand because he had the confidence of both the Cherokees and General Scott. Despite the charges of the Treaty Party that he was a political opportunist working for personal aggrandizement, he had put the welfare of the Cherokees above any personal consideration. "If they did not know all this," he declared while still in Washington, "I should not so long have possessed the confidence with which they have honored me and which I prize more than all wealth or praise."[18]

As for General Scott's support, that officer confessed that since Ross had taken over, things had moved more smoothly. There was a "unanimity of feeling" among the Cherokees and "an almost universal cheerfulness since the date of the new arrangement." Scott himself cooperated with the chief and his committee in collecting equipment for the journey—645 wagons, 5,000 horses and oxen, and standby vessels for river transportation for the seriously ill. Lewis Ross arranged with contractors to supply the necessary food, fodder, and clothing at selected depots on the mapped-out route.

Morale among the Cherokees improved through the balance of the summer, despite their apprehension of the future. They were no longer under martial law, but could camp where they pleased, wander over the hills for a last look at their country, gather wild fruits and berries, drink from mountain springs. And in the former Council House at Red Clay, as they were aware, Chief Ross was carefully packing the Nation's precious records, dating back more than thirty years—their resolutions, their written laws, their sacred constitution—to be taken with them on the journey West.

They might be leaving their ancestral lands, as they had vowed that they would never do. But they were going as a Nation—not as dispossessed individuals—and taking their heritage with them. That made all the difference.

September came but not the expected autumn rains. Drought still held the country in a dusty and relentless grip. Ross applied to Scott for another postponement of the departure date. Scott agreed, admitting that any party of more than a hundred, starting out under such conditions, would be shortly stranded by lack of water and sufficient fodder for the horses. The streams were too low for the mills to grind the necessary flour to take with them, crop failures made provisions difficult to get. October 1 was set as the new departure date.

The delay increased the cost to the War Department for subsistence of the idle Indians. Poinsett protested that already the estimated figure was double the original congressional appropriation. Ross pointed out that subsistence payments were part of the contract; there was no provision for an act of God.

Late in September, after days of cloudless blazing skies, thunderheads crossed the Smokies bringing blessed rain to Tennessee and Georgia. The mountains and valleys came alive with chattering streams, the rivers rose, the mill wheels turned. In twos and fours and then in bands of hundreds the Cherokees swarmed into Rattlesnake Springs two miles below the Indian Agency, the assembly point for their departure.

One group remained apart from the rest, the proud pariahs, some seven hundred Treaty Party members who had not yet emigrated. They refused to submit to Ross's supervision; they would travel on their own, under the direction of Lieutenant Edward Deas. Since these had been supporters of the federal government in its efforts to remove the Cherokees, they were rewarded with special dispensations, principally increased allowances for transportation and subsistence. They could travel in style and comfort, with their own horses, carriages, and many with their slaves. Much of their baggage was shipped by river in advance of their departure.

Despite these advantages their progress was slow, averaging ten to twelve miles a day, due, according to Deas, to "obstructions in the road over which we have passed." But they suffered no misfortunes apart from oxen who sickened and died from eating poisonous weeds. Having started out in early October, they reached the Indian Territory on January 7, after an uneventful journey of a little less than three months.

Rattlesnake Springs on October 1 resembled a vast army camp, with tents, wagons, horses, and oxen spread over an area of ten square miles. The morning campfires sputtered in the rain, the smell of cooking mingled with the woodsmoke, children played under and around the shelter of the wagons. There was excitement in the air as the Cherokees made a last check of equipment and supplies, pored over maps and charted their projected course. Though they would move in thirteen separate groups, they would travel closely on one another's heels, the advance contingents sending back advice and information to the party in its wake.

The first contingent, numbering 1,103 Cherokees, would start that day under the supervision of John Benge and Assistant Chief George Lowrey. The wagons and horses were lined up on the trail, making a caravan a quarter of a mile long. Solemn-faced Cherokees gathered about the wagons, saying last words of encouragement to one another. Children shouted to departing friends. The Light Horse guards listened to the orders of their supervisors, then took their positions flanking the long cavalcade.

John Ross would not delay their start with ceremony. But he stood on a wagon to lead the little army in a final prayer. With bowed heads the Cherokees moved their lips in rhythm to the words. Among them was Chief Going Snake, an old man now with white hair, seated on his favorite pony, waiting for the prayer to end and the bugle call to sound for their departure.

Ross's nephew William Shorey Coodey, in the ranks as contractor for this first contingent, saw over Going Snake's shoulder a spiral cloud rising in the west. In an otherwise empty sky this struck young Coodey as a strange phenomenon. Then, even more inexplicably, thunder sounded from the mountains

Stand Watie, brother of Elias Boudinot and nephew of The Ridge.
WESTERN HISTORY COLLECTION, UNIVERSITY OF OKLAHOMA LIBRARY

Wilson Lumpkin, governor of Georgia from 1831 to 1835, dedicated much of his career to removing the Cherokees from Georgia's soil.

Martin Van Buren, succeeding Jackson to the presidency, continued and furthered Jackson's program of Indian removal, completed for the Cherokees in 1839.

PHOTO BY BRADY, LIBRARY OF CONGRESS

General Winfield Scott was placed in charge of Cherokee removal during the turbulent years of 1838 and 1839.

*John Howard Payne, actor, journalist, and author of "Home, Sweet Home,"
was jailed for his defense of the Cherokees.*

Federal troops round up Cherokee emigrants for removal to the West; scene reenacted in Cherokee pageant "Unto These Hills," at Cherokee, North Carolina.

Cherokee martyr Tsali and his sons surrender to Major W. M. Davis of the U.S. Army; scene re-created in the Cherokee drama "Unto These Hills," at Cherokee, North Carolina.

"The Trail of Tears" as depicted in a painting by Robert Lindneux. Some four thousand Cherokees, almost a quarter of those surviving in the East, died during their roundup and journey to the West.

FROM THE ORIGINAL OIL PAINTING AT WOOLAROC MUSEUM, BARTLESVILLE, OKLAHOMA

Burial on "The Trail of Tears," as depicted in a painting by the Indian artist Ecbobawk in 1957.

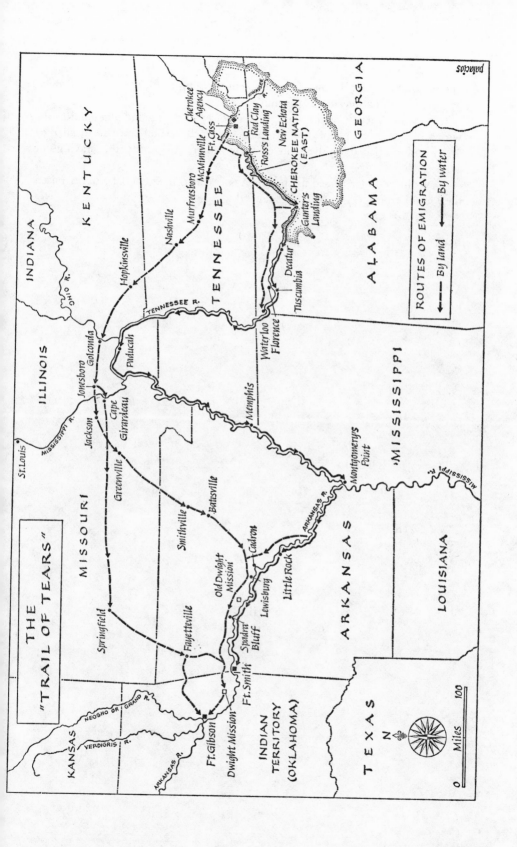

like the beat of giant drums—for a moment seeming to fill the sky and drowning out the intonations of the praying Cherokees.

It was an omen, Coodey thought, "a voice of divine indignation for the wrong of my poor unhappy countrymen, driven by brutal force from all they loved and cherished in the land of their fathers, to gratify the cravings of avarice."[19]

Then the thunder passed as suddenly as it had come. The Cherokees raised their heads from prayer. A bugle sounded.

19

The Trail of Tears

THIS WAS the beginning. Or the end, should one prefer to call it that. Appropriately the forest dressed in autumn colors and a blue veil draped the mountains. The scent of woodsmoke lingered in the air from smoldering ·shelters that would no longer be needed. The errant cloud had disappeared, and the thunder had retreated to wherever thunder goes.

It was something for the Indians to carry with them, this last picture of the land they loved, bright in the noonday sun that seemed to radiate a greater warmth this time of year. Young William Coodey would remember the scene and the day, October 1, 1838, writing later to John Howard Payne:

At noon all was in readiness for moving, the teams were stretched out in a line along the road through a heavy forest, groups of persons formed about each wagon, others shaking the hand of some sick friend or relative who would be left behind. The temporary camp covered with boards and some of bark that for three summer months had been their only shelter and home, were crackling and falling under a blazing flame; the day was bright and beautiful, but a gloomy thoughtfulness was depicted in the lineaments of every face. In all the bustle of preparation there was a silence and stillness of the voice that betrayed the sadness of the heart.[1]

On the last note of the bugle the caravan moved off. "It was like the march of an Army," wrote James Mooney, "regiment after regiment, the wagons in the center, the officers along the line and the horsemen on the flanks and at the rear." Each detachment had its Light Horse guard of ten or more mounted braves to keep the column in order, its own contractor responsible for provisioning the army on its line of march, its own physician chosen in advance by Ross. Only the aged, sick, and very young rode in the wagons, whose space was needed principally for blankets, cooking utensils, and fodder for the horses; the rest, including some mothers with babes in arms and women with stout packs on their backs, trudged behind the wagons.[2]

The column crossed the Hiwassee River a few miles upstream, proceeding north. All thirteen parties would follow the same route: northwest through Tennessee by way of Murfreesboro and Nashville, on through Kentucky and across the southern tip of Illinois, then either westward through Springfield, Missouri, or southwest through Arkansas, depending on conditions and the weather. While their departures from Rattlesnake Springs were staggered several days apart, and the time span for the journey set at eighty days, the speed of each contingent fluctuated. As time went on they would overlap, some catching up with the company ahead, others falling behind to join the party following.

Three days after Lowrey's band left Rattlesnake Springs the second contingent, headed by Elijah Hicks, followed in its wake. At the head of the column rode White Path, leaving behind more than threescore years of memories. Though failing in health, he refused accommodation in the wagons. That was not for one who had led the famed rebellion of 1828 and of whom it was written, "It may be truly said that his history is the history of the Nation."[3]

Throughout October nine contingents were scheduled to leave from Rattlesnake Springs in regular succession, with four to follow in November. The conductors of each were expected to send back, down the broken line of caravans, reports of progress made and conditions to anticipate. Elijah Hicks was the first to comply, writing from Nashville on October 16 that his company was suffering sorely from lack of clothing, and it was feared that "scores of them must inevitably fall the victims of disease and death before reaching the far place of their destination. Indeed, when they passed through Nashville, 40 or 50 were on the sick list, and four or five were afterward buried near the city."

A week later the column reached the Cumberland River, south of the Kentucky border, having passed en route the slower-moving party led by Lowrey. After twenty-one days on the road and two hundred miles of travel through strange country over unfamiliar trails, a sense of despair at their exile seemed to overtake the group. Hicks reported from Port Royal that "the people are very loath to go on, and unusually slow in preparing for starting each morning. I am not surprised at this because they are moving, not from choice, to an unknown region not desired by them. I am disposed to make full allowance for their unhappy movement."[4]

There were problems with some of his people. One of his Light Horse had taken to the bottle, to the point that he not only was too drunk to be of service but had finally to be dragged along the trail in chains. And Hicks reported with sorrow that "White Path has been in the last stages of sickness for many days and has to be hauled & is helpless who cannot last but a few days."

It took but a few days for White Path to succumb to sickness, old age, and the hardships of the trail. He was buried beside the trail near Hopkinsville, Kentucky. A slab of wood, painted to resemble marble, was placed over the grave, and a pole erected with a white flag at the top to mark the place of burial for future travelers. White Path's grave became a shrine for the passing Cherokees, a place to pause and pray for one of whom all nature rose to say, There was a man!

Not a few of the conductors were missionaries or Cherokee converts from the missions. The sonorous-voiced Jesse Bushyhead, formerly imprisoned at Camp Hetzel, headed the contingent following Elijah Hicks, while the Baptist minister Evan Jones led the next column in the broken line. Their Christian fortitude was sorely taxed. Bushyhead wrote to Ross in late October, "We have a large number of sick and very many extremely aged and infirm persons in our detachment that must of necessity be conveyed in waggons." This meant delay since the wagons no longer had room for fodder needed for the horses. There was further delay when the hungry animals fell ill from eating poison ivy.

To the almost universal afflictions of fatigue and illness was added, in some cases, a strange form of highway piracy. Large landowners sometimes charged the Indians a toll for passing through their property. Evan Jones reported paying forty dollars to a collector in Tennessee, based on seventy-five cents a wagon, fifteen cents a horse. The rate remained reasonably constant as they moved west. "On the Cumberland Mountains," Jones wrote, "they fleeced us 73 cents a wagon and 12½ cents a horse without the least abatement or thanks."[5]

By the time a number of the caravans had passed through Nashville the wagon road they faithfully followed became a badly rutted obstacle course, cut to pieces by innumerable hooves. The wagons pitched and jolted, increasing the anguish of the ailing passengers. Frequent stops were called to enable the doctors to attend their patients. Further delays occurred when heavy rains transformed the roads into red ribbons of morass.

Needless to say, no friendly calls were made at Andrew Jackson's Hermitage in Nashville; none of these Cherokees had named their offspring for the former President as Ridge had done. Besides, on this tenth anniversary of his election to the White House, Old Hickory's health was rumored as poor, "with hearing failing, right eye nearly useless, and memory uncertain . . ." In addition, he was having financial troubles—all misfortunes which the Cherokees might like to aggravate.

Nevertheless, there were a few encounters, as the Indians passed through Jackson country, with local veterans of the general's Indian campaigns. Chief Junaluska had mellowed a bit since the days when he bewailed not shooting Old Chicken Snake when he had the chance. Yet the bitterness lingered on. Accosted by one of Jackson's former veterans who asked the chief if he remembered him from years when they had fought together, Junaluska lowered his head in some embarrassment. Yes, he recognized the man. And he remembered only too well.

"My life and the lives of my people were then at stake for you and your country," he said. "I then thought Jackson was my friend. But neither Jackson nor your country do us justice now."[6]

On November 4, 1838, the last save one of the wagon trains prepared to start out for the West. Its conductor, George Hicks, brother of Elijah, penned a farewell note to Ross:

We are now about to take our final leave and kind farewell to our native land, the country that the great spirit gave our Fathers; we are on the even of leaving the country that gave us birth . . . it is with sorrow that we are forced by the authority of the white man to quit the scenes of our childhood . . . we bid a final farewell to it and all we hold dear. From the little trial we have made in the start to move, we know that it is a laborious undertaking, but with firm resolution we think we will be able to accomplish it, if the white citizens will permit us.[7]

The provisional "if" had a disquieting sound. From those of the first to those of the last departing groups, the Cherokees realized that the white man's avarice was ever present, robbing them of their rights in the East, robbing them on their journey West. Back in the Nation, all but emptied of its Cherokee inhabitants, Ross was struggling with the matter of indemnities still due to the emigrants, which was one reason he had stayed behind.

Among the messages he received from the detachments moving West was one from Jesse Bushyhead, who reported having "a distressing time with the discontents." These had not received the compensations due them for possessions left behind—homes, barns, mills, farm and household equipment, crops and cattle. They refused to go farther, believing that in their absence measures were being taken—possibly fraudulent claims invented—to cheat them of their property.

If they were not being actually cheated, the matter of indemnities was in a muddle. The federal government had appointed two commissioners to settle all Cherokee claims before removal. One of these, predictably, was Wilson Lumpkin, who had been so deeply involved in Cherokee affairs from the beginning. It was a complicated task, admittedly, which Lumpkin offered as a reason for delay. Against the claims of the Cherokees were counter-claims presented by the whites—such as back rent due on Cherokee homes from Indians who had refused to yield those homes when lottery winners had arrived to claim them.

One thing, however, made it easier for the commissioners. The Cherokees had gone. They had passed the point of no return. Only white claimants remained to argue their side of the case. As Bushyhead's people feared, many fraudulent claims were upheld because no Indians were present to contest them.

Lumpkin and his co-commissioner, John Kennedy, to do them credit, made an honest effort to adjust the difficulties. Not all the Indians were fully recompensed for property left behind or stolen. But many received more than token payments. There was a natural inclination to give better treatment to supporters of the Treaty. Thus The Ridge, wealthiest of the Treaty Party emigrants, received from the government for his property on the Oostanaula $24,127, a substantial sum for the times.

By way of contrast, Sawnee Vann, a treaty opponent and cousin of "Rich Joe" Vann, received only $1,250 for the extensive holdings listed in his affidavit. Possibly Sawnee's minute recording of every penny due him aroused some irritation in the War Department. In his tabulation were "3 large troughs full of soap, $10" and "8 Bee Hives, $15," along with $62.50 worth of bacon stolen or consumed by federal soldiers. Vann also charged the Army with having seized and sold three of his horses worth a hundred dollars each. He claimed $355 for the loss, seemingly tacking on a little extra in punitive revenge. Most of his claims, warranted or not, were disallowed.[8]

Not only were the Indians being shortchanged in the East, but they were victimized along the road. Prices for provisions, if they were forced to buy them on the way, were doubled, tripled, sometimes increased as much as ninefold, by the farmers and merchants on their route. The cost of services such as ferry crossings was similarly inflated. At times a white man would accost the leader of a caravan, demanding a fee; he had, he said, buried a dead Indian that they had left behind and deserved some payment for his work.

Some predatory whites pursued them on their journey West. George Hicks, who had written to Ross that he hoped to overcome all difficulties, "if the white citizens will permit us," added:

But since we have been on our march many of us have been stopped and our horses taken from our Teams for the payment of unjust & past Demands. Yet the government says you must go, and its citizens say you must pay me, and if the debtor has not the means, the property of his next friend is levied . . . our property has been stolen and robbed from us by white men and no means given us to pay our debts.[9]

They had thought, on taking to the road, to leave white avarice behind. But they were too vulnerable in their innocence. The opportunists followed, like vultures picking at a corpse, presenting false claims by which to deprive the travelers of their horses or oxen, their wagons, even silver if they carried any. "They rob us in open daylight," Bushyhead complained; "they know that we are in a defenseless situation."

The Light Horse guards could not protect them, having no federal authority. The United States soldiers sometimes riding as observers with the emigrating parties were also without authority to intervene. Among these, however, Private Burnett, who accompanied George Hicks's detachment, at least showed outrage at mistreatment of the Indians. Seeing a brutal government-hired teamster named Ben McDonald using his whip on an aged Cherokee "to hasten him into the wagon," Burnett lost his sense of detachment.

"The sight of that old and nearly blind creature quivering under the lashes of a bull whip was too much for me," he wrote. "I attempted to stop McDonald and . . . He lashed me across the face, the wire tip on his whip cutting a bad gash on my cheek."[10]

Burnett drew a small hunting hatchet that he carried in his belt and, he recorded, "McDonald was carried unconscious from the scene." Though the incident was reported to Burnett's commanding officer, the private was never disciplined. As to the offending teamster, Burnett noted that "after a lapse of fifteen years he finally recovered."

As the great chain of Indians and wagons stretched through Kentucky into Illinois, some of its links as much as three miles long, it was overtaken by one who identified and signed himself "A Native of Maine, Traveling in the Western Country." The Down Easter rode with the Cherokees long enough to record his impressions and send them for publication in a northern journal. He noted, regarding the procession:

The sick and feeble were carried in waggons—about as comfortable as a New England ox cart with a covering over it—a great many ride on horseback and multitudes go on foot—even aged females, apparently ready to drop into the grave, were traveling with heavy burdens attached to the back—on the sometimes frozen ground, and sometimes muddy streets, with no covering for their feet except what nature had given them . . . We learned from the inhabitants on the road where the Indians passed, they buried fourteen or fifteen at every stopping place . . .[11]

The Indians "were suffering extremely from the fatigue of the journey," pausing only for roadside religious services on Sundays. In their countenances, the New Englander observed, "some carry a downcast dejected look bordering on despair; others a wild frantic appearance as if about to burst the chains of nature and pounce like a tiger upon their enemies." Still others submitted to grief and resignation, such as a mother clinging tightly to her stricken infant:

. . . she could only carry her dying child in her arms a few miles farther, and then she must stop in a stranger-land and consign her much loved babe to the cold ground, and that too without pomp or ceremony, and pass on with the multitude . . . I turned from the sight with feelings which language cannot express and "wept like childhood then."[12]

The ordeal was over first for Elijah Hicks's contingent, which arrived in Indian Territory on the fourth of January 1839. Of about 1,100 who had left the East in early October, some 950 were still with the party, the rest either dead or missing. The casualty figure of roughly 14 percent would compare favorably with that compiled for the emigration movement as a whole. For in the north, midwinter was building a relentless barrier of ice and snow across the path of the westward-moving columns.

The Old Settlers in the West—chiefly those who had crossed the Mississippi between 1818 and 1828 but including many still living who had traveled West in 1808—regarded the first trickle of arriving immigrants with sympathy but caution. The time gap, short as it was, had made them an unknown quantity. In contrast, the Treaty Party members had already been accepted. Despite the unsavory shadow of betrayal that hung over them (for in the West as in the East the ceding of Cherokee lands was a capital offense), they had caused no friction. They had paid obeisance to the Western government, had assented to its laws, and had showed no political ambitions.

The Eastern missionaries, such as Samuel Worcester, had also done their best to fit into the Western pattern. Worcester's connection with Boudinot had not enhanced his reputation, but the Messenger stood loyally by his collaborator, and Chief John Jolly had supported him. But apart from the press, the missionary movement had not prospered in the West, with a consequent decline in education. Dwight Mission still maintained an elementary school, and Sequoyah taught the Cherokee alphabet in his home at Skin Bayou. Beyond that, learning was not being actively promoted.

In fact, Cherokee life in the West had taken on a different cast from that which had existed in the Eastern Nation. Though the economy was primarily agrarian, as in the East, there was less emphasis on the so-called civilized arts and trades. There were a few industries, a gristmill, a sawmill or two, but in general the Old Settlers were grangers and cattlemen, with a man's wealth measured by the number of beeves and hogs or the acres of wheat that he controlled. Western life was frontier life, casual and irresponsible, with gambling, horse breeding, and racing the principal diversions.

Government, too, had retrogressed to the status of a loose confederacy such as that existing at the turn of the century in the East. There was no written constitution and few written laws. The territory was divided into four departments with locally elected judges and officials and with Light Horse units to keep order. A General Council met two times a year at Tahlonteskee near the junction of the Arkansas and Illinois, but no one took government or politics very seriously.

Though General Matthew Arbuckle, commandant at Fort Gibson on the western border of the Nation, professed to keep hands off Cherokee affairs—leaving these up to the Cherokee Agent Montfort Stokes—Fort Gibson was more a symbol of authority than the Cherokees' crudely built Council House at Tahlonteskee. And Arbuckle himself, Virginia-born and Jacksonian in character, was too aggressive not to throw his weight around. He regarded himself as protector of the Western Cherokees, especially of their status quo, and let his attitude be known.

The Treaty Party emigrants, when these arrived, stood high in the commandant's favor. They had promoted, and cooperated with, the government's program for removal to the West. Arbuckle made them welcome, and accepted Ridge's warning that the soon-to-arrive John Ross might be a troublemaker. Already there were predictions of a rift between the established settlers and the incoming horde of exiles. Arbuckle warned the governors of Arkansas and Missouri to protect their borders with armed militia, and alerted his own garrison to be ready for possible violence in the Western Nation.

Arbuckle's attitude, and the uneasy division between the Old Settlers and the Treaty Party emigrants, did not create a receptive climate for those already in transit from the East. These newcomers might present a problem at the fall elections, seeking, by numerical superiority, to put their own men into office. To avoid such a monopoly of the ballot, a Council was called to elect new officers ahead of schedule. John Brown was chosen Principal Chief of the Western Cherokees, with John Looney and John Rogers as assistants.

The West waited uneasily through the early weeks of 1839. The Easterners were on their way. Though they were blood brothers all, time and geography had a way of playing tricks.

Following December blizzards, January brought a bitter cold wave to the central states. The wagon trains crossed the Ohio River near the mouth of the Cumberland and found themselves trapped in the southern tip of Illinois. The Mississippi was clogged with ice, not solid enough to cross the surface but too thick for boats to pass. As the early arrivals pitched tents along the banks and searched for firewood, later detachments joined them at the bottleneck.

Evan Jones's company was first at the site, and as the contingents of Bushyhead and Stephen Foreman camped beside them he wrote to Ross that "I am sorry to say that both their detachments have not been able to cross. I am afraid that with all the cares that can be exercised with the various detachments, there will be an immense amount of suffering, and loss of life attending the removal. Great numbers of the old, the young, and the infirm will inevitably be sacrificed."[13]

Bushyhead recorded that his party "was detained by the ice in the Mississippi for a month," a month that was the frigid nadir of their journey. James Mooney later interviewed the survivors of that ordeal and "found that the lapse of over half a century had not sufficed to wipe out the memory of the miseries of that halt beside the frozen river, with hundreds of sick and dying penned up in wagons or stretched upon the ground, with only a blanket overhead to keep out the January blast."[14]

Lewis Ross, in charge of provisioning the caravans, was with one of the five detachments stranded at the Mississippi. He rode with an aide to St. Louis to purchase blankets and clothing for the campers. Fortunately Lewis shared in the family wealth, for government subsidies, promised to the emigrants, had not been paid. He was able to borrow money on his personal securities, and out of this sum purchased 520 pairs of brogans and a supply of mackinaws and army blankets. It was a small amount for the roughly five thousand stranded Indians, but it would take care of the more needy cases.

A crossing of the Mississippi was finally made by ferry near Cape Girardeau, and with the river at last behind them the caravans moved on across Missouri, following a northerly course by way of Springfield, having heard that game was unavailable along the more direct route further south.

The bitter cold persisted. Evan Jones recorded on December 30: "We have now been on our road to Arkansas seventy-five days, and have traveled five hundred and twenty-nine miles. We are still nearly three hundred miles short of our destination . . . It has been exceedingly cold . . . those thinly clad very uncomfortable . . . we have, since the cold set in so severely, sent on a company every morning, to make fires along the road at short intervals. This [has been] a great alleviation to the sufferings of the people."[15]

The trek across Missouri in the dead of winter, from Cape Girardeau to Springfield, was the hardest portion of their journey. Dr. W. I. I. Morrow, with one of the five groups that crossed the Mississippi as a unit when the ice permitted, saw the country as an arctic desert stretching in the clear air to illimitable distances. The last week of February it rained steadily, the rain changing to snow on February 27. When four Indians died of sickness and exposure, Morrow tried to find shelter for his charges among the scattered homesteads that they passed.

More often than not he was brusquely turned aside, noting in his diary for March 3, "Sunday, very cold—Jas. Harrison, a mean man—will not let any persons connected with the emigration stay on his property." It was an understandable reaction among isolated farmers on the fringes of the Great Plains. An army of ragged Indians, some of them stricken by possibly contagious illness, distraught, sullen, unable to pay for favors offered, did not give the appearance of desirable guests.

But there were a few light intervals in that dreariest of journeys. A farmer named Wilson opened his barn to the Indians, letting them sleep in the hayloft and in vacant stalls, while Wilson's father-in-law, "an eccentric fellow," brought them baskets full of eggs. He also brought them a singular diversion. "Mr. S. made his dog sing, talk, dance, etc.," Morrow noted in his diary. The performing dog made such a happy impression on the Indians, wrote Morrow, that "the young girls and boys talked and laughed all night."[16]

But in general there was not much talk or laughter in this last stage of the journey. A full-blood Cherokee recorded of the long haul through Missouri: "Womens cry and make sad wails. Children cry and many men cry, and all look sad when friends die, but they say nothing and just put heads down and keep on go towards West. Many days pass and people die very much."

Later, the Cherokee's father collapsed in the snow, too weak to move. Transferred to the wagons, he lived for only another day and then was buried by the trail. Within a week the wife and mother succumbed to exposure. "She speak no more; we bury her and go on." Subsequently the Cherokee's brothers and sisters went to join their parents. The grief-stricken man remembered:

One each day, and all are gone . . . Looks like maybe all be dead before we get to new Indian country, but always we keep marching on . . . People sometimes say I look like I never smile, never laugh in lifetime.[17]

When the last of the scheduled contingents had departed, John Ross prepared to leave the Nation. He applied to Captain John Page of the Army for provisions for his family—"thirty-one persons and eighteen horses and oxen." His final group would number 228, including friends as well as relatives. Thomas Clark, one of his contractors stranded with the Indians at the Mississippi, had written that Ross's presence was needed to "dispell the gloom and settle the doubts" of the disheartened emigrants. "You are the master workman and it is your peculiar province to come see and determine which I hope you will do."[18]

John's wife Quatie was not well; she had never been well since they had been driven from their home at Head of Coosa. But she dutifully mounted a wagon with her brood of children and the party left for Cumberland Gap in mid-November. It was preceded by Peter Hilderbrand's company of 1,800 emigrants, which stretched for several miles along the wagon road; and in time the two units merged and moved together as far as the Kentucky bank of the Ohio River.

Here it became plain to John that the overland journey was too rigorous for Quatie. She said little but her silence proclaimed much. The party had suffered the afflictions that had struck the others—excessive cold, fatigue, and malnutrition, which led in turn to fever, colds, pneumonia, and tuberculosis. John hired the little riverboat *Victoria* and loaded his family aboard the ship. The steamer was powerful enough to buck the Mississippi ice and turned into the Arkansas River the last week in January, reaching Little Rock on February 1, 1839.

It was at Little Rock that Quatie died one midnight of pneumonia. She had, it was reported, exposed herself to the cold by giving her blanket to a sick child, who as a consequence recovered. John waited till daylight to carry her body ashore for burial in a shallow grave hacked from the frozen soil. Then he gave the order for the ship to move on.

It was not until almost a century later that a patriotic citizens group erected a headstone over the grave, with the simple inscription:

QUATIE

Indian Wife of John Ross, Chief of the Cherokee Tribe,
Died in Little Rock, Arkansas, February 1, 1839

The ashes of their abandoned fires were still smoking, and the Cherokees still plodding through the sleet and snow, when Martin Van Buren eulogized their exile from the East. It was December 1838 when he informed the Congress: "It affords me sincere pleasure to be able to apprise you of the entire removal of the Cherokee Nation of Indians to their new homes west of the Mississippi. The measures authorized by Congress . . . have had the happiest effects, and they have emigrated without any apparent reluctance . . ."[19]

(At about the time the President was speaking, Private Burnett, with Hilderbrand's emigrants in Kentucky, was recording his impressions: "Many of these helpless people did not have blankets and many of them had been driven from their homes barefooted. They had to sleep in the wagons and on the ground without fire. And I have known as many as twenty-two of them to die in one night of pneumonia due to ill treatment, cold, and exposure."[20])

Supporting his message, the President read to Congress Joel Poinsett's euphoric statements on Cherokee emigration. "The generous and enlightened policy toward the Indians," the Secretary wrote, "was ably and judiciously carried into effect . . . with promptness and praiseworthy humanity . . . they had been treated with kind and grateful feelings . . . not only without violence, but with very proper regard for the interests of the people."[21]

("When I read the President's Message," Private Burnett wrote, "I wished he could have been there that day in Kentucky with myself . . . Many of the aged Indians were suffering extremely from the fatigue of the journey and the ill health consequent upon it . . . several were then quite ill, and one aged man we were informed was then in the last struggles of death."[22])

The Commissioner of Indian Affairs added his glowing tribute to the Indians' removal:

The case of the Cherokees is a striking example of the liberality of the Government in all its branches . . . A retrospect of the last eight months in reference to this numerous and more than ordinarily enlightened tribe cannot fail to be refreshing to well constituted minds . . . If our acts have been generous, they have not been less wise and politic . . . Good feeling has been preserved, and we have quietly and gently transported 18,000 friends to the west bank of the Mississippi.[23]

(And in Tennessee, Kentucky, southern Illinois, Missouri, the graves with their wooden markers stretched from the Appalachians to the Arkansas. "The trail of the exiles was a trail of death," recorded Private Burnett; and the *Arkansas Gazette* in late December reported of the westering Cherokees, "They have the measles and whooping cough among them and there is an average of four deaths per day."[24])

To the smug satisfaction and complacency of government executives were added some protesting voices. They would increase in time to hurricane proportions, expressing stormy outrage but unable to reverse the past. Only four days after the President's message to Congress the Washington *National Intelligencer,* perhaps the best informed on Indian affairs, published its editorial reply:

Before we can claim for our Government the credit for having dealt "justly" with Indians throughout, we must sponge from the tablet of memory . . . the refusal to fulfill our treaty stipulations with the Cherokees for ten years, and the final enforcement of a treaty to which they never assented, and which never could have been carried into execution but by an armed force which it was in vain for them to contend against.[25]

They began arriving in full force in January–February 1839. Most entered Indian Territory from the northwestern corner of Arkansas, branching out at Fayetteville toward Fort Gibson or Fort Smith—the latter being the principal terminus. After Elijah Hicks's contingent reached the fort, Hair Conrad's party joined them there on January 7, and three days later George Lowrey's group arrived. Three more contingents reached the West in February and the rest in March, with Peter Hilderbrand's and Ross's party arriving at the fort together on March 25 and 26.

They were a weary, footsore, decimated army as they pitched their tents and spread their camps along the valley of the Illinois. They applied at once for subsistence rations as promised them by the government contractors. The rations issued were branded by John Ross as "poor and unhealthy," the meat rancid and the flour and cereal riddled with weevils. But it would do for now, as they rested and regained their strength and prepared to look for homesites in the Western Nation.

Looking over that sprawling bivouac, it would have been impossible to take a census of their numbers. In fact, it would be years before any vital statistics of their journey would be adequately tabulated. And these would be inconclusive estimates. There were too many duplications, too many missing figures.

They had been roughly three months on the trail, some more, some less. There had been births along the way, and many deaths. And scores remained unaccounted for. Somewhere along the line these phantom figures disappeared. To die or to build a new life in the wilderness? Or to find their way back to the Eastern Nation? Who could tell?

It was chancy to try to make a tabulation of the casualties from the incomplete reports of the conductors. But using one group of figures, and identifying each contingent by the name of its leader, the list might look like this:

Elijah Hicks: 114 missing, 34 dead
Hair Conrad: 204 missing
Evan Jones: 217 missing, 71 dead
Jesse Bushyhead: 52 missing, 38 dead
James Brown: 142 missing
Stephen Foreman: 62 missing, 57 dead
Choowalooka: 180 missing
George Lowrey: 97 missing
David Colton: 651 survivors
George Hicks: 79 missing
Richard Taylor: 85 missing, 55 dead
John Drew: 12 missing
Peter Hilderbrand: 464 missing, some believed picked up by other units

The less than two thousand casualties gave an incomplete and inconclusive picture. The true scope of the tragic hegira—the cost in lives and human misery and heartbreak—would never be defined. Government sources would, of course, gloss over the reality. But in time some figures came to be accepted.

During the roundup in early June and their subsequent imprisonment awaiting emigration, some 2,500 Cherokees had died of illness, malnutrition, exposure, and in certain cases brutal treatment. Of the 16,500 who left the Nation with the wagon trains, 1,500 were buried on the way—forming a chain of graves from the Appalachians to the Arkansas along what history would call "the Trail of Tears."

Four thousand Cherokee dead. Almost a quarter of the tribe wiped out.

Elizur Butler, who wrote as early as June 1838, "I feel as if I have been in the midst of death," put the figure higher: 4,600 since that fateful spring began. Butler saw, too, another curious facet of the tragedy. Returning to Red Clay in March 1839 to pick up Lucy and pack their joint possessions for shipment to the West, he expected to find the old Cherokee Nation inhabited by whites; the great mansions of the chiefs refurbished by new owners; the farms and plantations being worked by Georgia squires and their slaves.

Instead, he found the Nation as quiet and empty as a tomb. The whites had

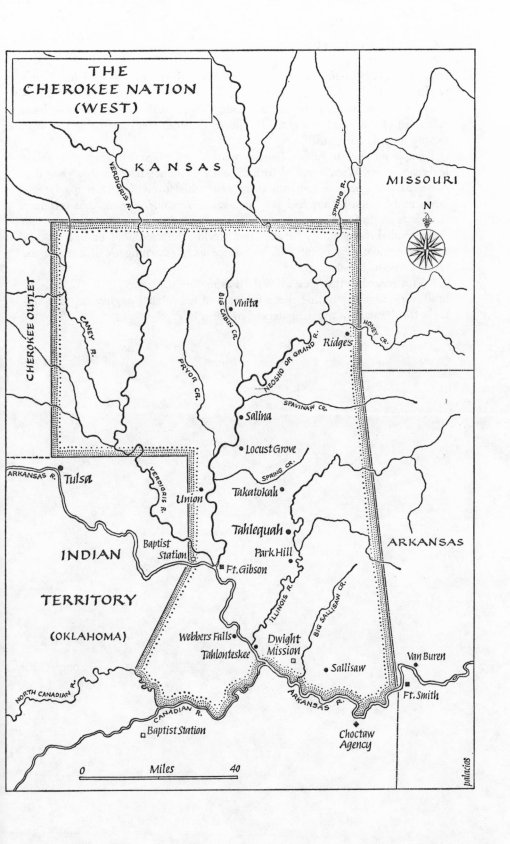

come and gone—many of them moving West themselves to find out if the world beyond the Mississippi was in truth the Promised Land, as the Cherokees had been assured. If he knew his Wordsworth he might have been reminded of the lines: "Dear God! The very houses seem asleep; and all that mighty heart is lying still!"

It made no sense to Elizur. Starting with his imprisonment in 1831, nothing had made sense. Why, he asked with a feeling of shame, had the Georgians dispossessed the Cherokees, driven them from this lovely land, occupied their farms and homes, if they had not intended to remain? For this hot certainty there was no dusty answer.

Suspended momentarily between two worlds, the moribund Eastern Nation and the strange new country he and Lucy were returning to, Butler felt an empty sense of hopelessness.

"With regard to the West all is dark as midnight," he recorded. "O that my head were waters and mine eyes a fountain of tears that I might weep day and night for the slain of the daughters of my people."[26]

20

Rebirth of a Nation

To the Old Settlers who had arrived between 1808 and 1828 and those who had followed in smaller groups, they seemed like an invading army. Up and down the pleasant spring-fed valley of the Illinois they pitched their tents and raised their rustic shelters, began clearing land and cutting timber for more lasting homes. They had been decimated by the cruel trek from the East; many were still ill, some were dying. But they turned to the tasks of survival with grim determination.

There was a marked difference in the state of these "Late Emigrants," as they were called, and the Treaty Party emigrants who had preceded them. The latter, by complying with government procedure, had been well compensated for their properties abandoned in the East. They had had time and funds to settle comfortably between Park Hill and Honey Creek. The Late Emigrants reached the West in a destitute condition, without even household utensils, much less farm equipment, with which to build anew. All sixteen thousand of them had to start from scratch.

Rebecca Neugin, Cherokee, was only six when she reached the West. Her most vivid memory of that journey into exile was of the pet duck she could not bear to leave behind. She had hugged it so closely on the loveless journey that it died in her arms and was buried on the trail. Now Rebecca and her family found themselves beginning life anew with none of the tools they sorely needed. They were obliged to make primitive bowls and pots of clay with which to cook and eat their meals. "We also," remembered Rebecca, "made wooden spoons, and for a number of years after we arrived we had to use these crude utensils."[1]

"We had no shoes," recalled Rebecca, "and those that wore anything wore moccasins made out of deer hide. Many went bare headed, but when it was cold they made things out of coonskins and other kinds of hides to cover their heads." Rebecca, even at that early age, was obliged to learn to spin and weave the garments that they wore, and to make dyes out of bark and indigo. After almost four decades of progress in the arts of civilized living, the Eastern Cherokees turned to the primitive methods of their ancestors for survival.

The War Department had guaranteed them subsistence for a year. But the government contractors, Glascow and Harrison, could not overlook this chance for easy profit. They delivered nearly worthless cattle to the Indians, "some so poor that they could hardly stand." Hungry families were obliged to sign receipts for inferior corn and flour, unwholesome or unpalatable meat, doled out in short measure. Even the officers at Fort Gibson, wrote Major Ethan Allen Hitchcock, were disturbed by the "outrages practiced on the Indians."

John Ross was quick to protest to General Arbuckle against these "abominable impositions" and the failure of the government to meet its obligations. Arbuckle passed the protest on to Hitchcock for investigation. Hitchcock found the protest warranted, and sent his report to War Secretary Poinsett. The War Secretary sent it to the Treasury Department, where an official therein advised that Hitchcock's affidavit be conveniently shelved. "It is not to be exhibited to anyone; nor are its contents to be made known."[2]

Frustrated, Ross took matters into his own hands. Declaring the provisions supplied by Glascow and Harrison "unfit for human consumption" and the meat, especially, "poor and unhealthy," he drew on the dwindling funds supplied by Winfield Scott for emigration and hired a private contractor to furnish his people not only with food but a limited amount of building materials. They would make it on their own, without benefit of government aid administered through Fort Gibson.

To General Arbuckle, commander of the fort, Ross's actions branded him a troublemaker. He was ready to believe the rumors circulated by the Treaty Party that the new arrivals were largely composed of drunkards, thieves, and vagrants. He kept a tight surveillance over Ross's home, which the latter had built at Park Hill, across the creek from Samuel Worcester's residence and mission.

Most apprehensive about the Late Emigrants, however, was the Ridge-Boudinot faction of the Treaty Party. They saw Ross's presence as a threat to take over the Western community in which they had so comfortably settled. Ridge warned Arbuckle that John Ross's home, as well as the Illinois Camp Ground, was a breeding place for conspiracy and revolution. If Ross did not regain his political power by peaceful means, he would resort to violence against the existing order, not to mention violence against Treaty Party members who had fought him in the East.

Arbuckle sent Captain George McCall to the neighborhood to size things up. McCall reported, doubtless to Arbuckle's disappointment, that the late settlers were engaged in no more than "building houses, clearing and fencing land, and planting," and that the only meetings at Ross's house were concerned with preventing the sale of whiskey to the Indians.

The recriminations passing back and forth, the reawakening of old prejudices and suspicions, created a tense climate in the Nation. From John Ridge's home at Honey Creek, Sophia Sawyer, whose antennae were keenly tuned to Cherokee wavelengths, wrote to David Greene in May: "The critical situation of the Nation I cannot communicate. It is such a time of excitement and I am always getting into trouble . . . The atmosphere of the old nation in its most disturbed state, compared to this, was like the peaceful lake to the boisterous ocean." Daniel Butrick noted of the troubled Cherokees that "they are the same dear people as always," but the prospect of their future gave him cause for weeping.[3]

The Old Settlers did not altogether share the Treaty Party's fear of Ross. They were willing to see how things worked out—and meanwhile responded to Ross's suggestion that a General Council be held to welcome and "extend the hand of friendship" to the new arrivals. All parties in the Nation were summoned to convene at Takatokah, or "Double Springs," on June 3, 1839.

Six thousand Indians assembled at the site a few miles north of Park Hill, and spent the first week in getting acquainted or reacquainted with the Easterners. Ridge and Boudinot made a brief appearance, but withdrew when they sensed the hostility of the new arrivals. "Speeches were made on both sides," wrote observer Cephas Washburn of Dwight Mission, "congratulating each other that they were now united as one nation, after having been separated for so long, & expressive of the hope that nothing would ever again occur to divide them."[4]

Chief Brown directed his opening speech to the new arrivals. "We cordially receive you as brothers," he told them. "The whole land is before you. You may freely go wherever you choose and select any place for settlement which may please you." The Late Emigrants would be allowed to vote in future elections, and would be eligible for any public office in the Nation.[5]

However, Brown added, "it is expected that you will all be subject to our government and laws until they shall be constitutionally altered or repealed . . ." With this proviso in the open, the chief invited the newcomers to present any questions or desires concerning their future in the West.[6]

Ross's response to this invitation was quick, specific, and unexpected. He and George Lowrey handed to the chiefs a set of written resolutions calling, in effect, for the immediate formation of "a new government West of the River Mississippi." An equal number of Eastern and Western Cherokees would form a joint committee to draft an updated constitution and code of laws to be approved by the General Council for submission to the people.

The Western chiefs were taken by surprise. They reminded Ross that they already had a firmly established government, under officers elected earlier that year. With this meeting of welcome, unity was an accomplished fact. All that was expected of the new arrivals was that they conform to the existing laws and institutions.

Ross and Lowrey urged that their proposal be submitted to a referendum of the people. Brown, Rogers, and Looney told them that the chiefs represented the people; there was no need for a public mandate. Wherewith Brown huffily dissolved the conference. Unity had been professed in garnished words, but nothing productive of unity had been accomplished.

At this point Sequoyah, who had done more for the Cherokees perhaps than any single individual, made an effort at restoring harmony. Before all but a portion of the delegates could leave the Council grounds, he teamed with Jesse Bushyhead as Eastern representative to propose that, when tempers had cooled, a further discussion in Council take place at the Illinois Camp Ground on July 1. The purpose: "That the desired Union be speedily formed, and a system of Government matured and established applicable to our present Condition and providing equally for the peace and Security of the whole people." The measure was approved by the assembly and the Council finally adjourned.[7]

That was Friday, June 21. Throughout that emotional week it was rumored that Ridge and Boudinot, before their withdrawal, had been seen conferring with the Western chiefs, allegedly urging them to reject John Ross's call for unity. True or not, according to Treaty Party leader John A. Bell, these suspicions "caused a sudden breaking forth of long-smouldering resentment—an ebullition of rage at the supposed intrigue," such as had preceded Doublehead's murder by The Ridge for his 1807 acts of treason.[8]

Twenty-four hours later, following hasty clandestine meetings, the pent-up passion for revenge exploded.

It might have been a coven of the Raven Mockers, those batlike creatures who swooped down upon the sick and snatched the lingering spirit from their bodies. Except that these were of human form, several hundred of them, mounted or on foot, all grimly silent as they listened in the darkness to instructions from their leader. Some wore masks, others had black neckerchiefs to be raised above their faces. All carried knives, rifles, pistols, hatchets.

It was a matter of minutes to select, by drawing numbers from a hat, the necessary executioners. These formed in three groups and rode off on their separate missions while the rest of the conclave disappeared as silently as they had come. It was midnight of June 22, just one day after the Takatokah Council had disbanded.

Before dawn the fury of long months of suffering found a target. In his home at Honey Creek, John Ridge was dragged from his bed by three masked intruders, hauled to the yard, where the rest of the party waited, and, with Sarah and her children watching, was stabbed twenty-five times by the invaders. Then his throat was cut, and the assailants ritualistically stamped upon the body and departed.

John remained alive long enough to be carried back to die in his bed, "the blood oozing through his winding sheet and falling drop by drop on the floor." To John's son Rollin, and surely to Sarah and the other children witnessing their father's death, it was "a scene of agony . . . which might make one regret the human race had ever been created. It has darkened my mind with an eternal shadow." By John's side, "with hands clasped and in speechless agony," was New England-born Sarah Northrup, "she who had given him her heart in the days of her youth and beauty, left the home of her parents and followed the husband of her choice to a wild and distant land."[9]

John's father, Major Ridge, was that morning on his way to Van Buren in western Arkansas, predictably following the Line Road running north and south along the border. A courier was dispatched from Honey Creek to inform the Major of John's assassination and warn him of possible further violence. He found The Ridge lying on the highway, apparently ambushed from surrounding underbrush, with five bullets in the head and body. The runner returned to tell Sarah of another murder in the family.

At Park Hill, Elias Boudinot was directing carpenters at the new home he was building. Four men he did not recognize approached him to say that they had come for medical supplies from Dr. Worcester. Could he intervene with the missionary in their behalf? Boudinot turned and started toward Worcester's house, when one of the strangers plunged a knife into his back. As he fell, screaming, another hacked at his head with a tomahawk, cleaving his skull in seven places. Both Delight Sargent and Samuel Worcester, summoned by the victim's cries, reached the scene in seconds, but Boudinot's eyes were already glazed in death.

"The murderers ran a short distance into the woods, joined a company of armed men on horseback, and made their escape," wrote Worcester to David Greene. "He [Boudinot] had fallen a victim . . . to his honest zeal for the preservation of his people. In his own view he risked his life to save his people from ruin, and he realized his fears." To Worcester the tragedy was an irremediable loss. "They have cut off my right hand," he said.[10]

News of the murders spread with the wind across the Western Nation. John Ross heard it, along with a warning that his own life would pay for the atrocities. He promptly dispatched a message to the commander at Fort Gibson, advising Arbuckle of Elias Boudinot's assassination and adding that a messenger, lately arrived, had urged him "to leave home for safety, saying that Stand Watie had determined on raising a company of men for the purpose of coming forthwith to take my life."

Why I am to be murdered without guilt for any crime I cannot conceive. Therefore with all due respect . . . I trust you will deem it expedient forthwith to interpose and prevent the effusion of innocent blood by exercising your authority in order that an unbiased investigation may be had in the matter.[11]

Arbuckle needed no investigation. He was convinced that the murders, if not directed by Ross himself, were the work of Ross's followers—a logical conclusion. He was also led to believe that Ross was harboring the killers. If this was so, he warned the chief, he would send troops at once to take the culprits into custody; and whether the charge were true or not, he recommended that Ross appear at Fort Gibson to discuss the matter.

Ross rejected the summons to Fort Gibson, aware of his probable arrest if he should do so. He also declined to meet with Western leaders summoned to the fort to consider means of preventing further violence. The murders, he now insisted, were an internal affair, to be settled by the Cherokees themselves without the military presence of Fort Gibson and the general. As to his own safety from retaliation, his home was surrounded by several hundred of his followers on whom he could depend.

A week later, on June 29, Arbuckle wrote to Ross and his associates charging that a band of his followers was ranging through the country intent on more executions "of a political nature." He charged further that Ross's attempts to establish a new government were the roots of this convulsion. "We believe," he wrote, "that two Governments cannot exist in the Cherokee Nation, without producing a Civil War, and are of the opinion that the Government that existed before the arrival of the Late Emigrants, should continue . . ."[12]

Ross replied that he sought only unity and harmony within the Nation, but that "our just and reasonable overtures" had been "unconditionally rejected by our Western brothers, and our communications treated with contempt." He would not allow his people to forgo their rights, or his chiefs to be stripped of power. While he sought "to stay the hand of violence," no individual could shoulder "the burden of Controlling public feeling, and stopping the effusion of Cherokee blood."[13]

Once again Arbuckle sounded the alarm, urging the neighboring states to call out their militias, requisitioning additional muskets, bayonets, and ammunition for his own Fort Gibson garrison. More sensibly, he urged that the General Council proposed for July 1 be postponed, in view of the explosive situation. This was rejected by both Ross and Sequoyah, and the conference went on as planned.

Some two thousand Cherokees gathered at the Illinois Camp Ground in the gentle valley running south from Park Hill. Most of the Western chiefs refused to attend, calling a counter-convention of their own at Tahlonteskee, farther to the south. But many individual Westerners were present, including, of course, Sequoyah, who served as pro tem "President of the Western Cherokees," with George Lowrey acting as President of the Eastern delegation.

Sequoyah's first act was to try to persuade the three Western chiefs, Brown, Looney, and Rogers, to join them, composing a message in Cherokee:

We, the old settlers, are here in council with the late emigrants, and we want you to come up without delay, that we may talk matters over like friends and brothers. These people are here in great multitudes, and they are perfectly friendly towards us. They have said, over and over again that they will be glad to see you and we have full confidence that they will receive you in all friendship. There is no drinking here to disturb the peace . . . and we have no doubt but we can have all things amicably and satisfactorily settled.[14]

Sequoyah's simple appeal brought Chief John Looney to the convention, though Brown and Rogers, and Boudinot's brother Stand Watie, now heading the Treaty Party, stayed disdainfully away. On July 12 a milestone was reached with the drafting and acceptance of an Act of Union, written by William Shorey Coodey and reading in part:

WHEREAS our Fathers have existed, as a separate and distinct Nation, in the possession and exercise of the essential and appropriate attributes of sovereignty, from a period extending into antiquity, beyond the records and memory of man:

AND WHEREAS these attributes, with the rights and franchises which they involve, remain still in full force and virtue . . . it has become essential to the general welfare that a union should be formed, and a system of government matured, adapted to [our] present condition, and providing equally for the protection of each individual in the enjoyment of his rights:

THEREFORE we, the people composing the Eastern and Western Cherokee Nation, in National Convention assembled . . . do hereby solemnly and mutally agree to form ourselves into one body politic under the style and title of the Cherokee Nation.[15]

A further paragraph resolved that rights to all lands east and west of the Mississippi, claimed by the two branches of the Cherokees, were henceforth vested in the Western Nation, "as constituted by this union." The act was signed by George Lowrey and Sequoyah and by fifteen of the Eastern delegates, sixteen of the Westerners.

Thus, one could hopefully believe, the Cherokee Nation was officially reborn, and a foundation laid for the same swift progress that had been realized in the East. Following the Illinois Camp Ground convention, a Council was called for September 6 for the purpose of holding national elections. The chosen site was five miles north of Park Hill, near the center of the Nation which would henceforth be the capital. Since the name of the former capital, New Echota, brought to mind the tragedies and sorrows of the late lost battles in the East, it was christened Tahlequah, after the Cherokee spelling of the former Indian Agency Tellico in Tennessee.

The Council sat till October 10, during which time it drafted a new constitution modeled after that adopted in the East in 1827. John Ross was elected Principal Chief and David Vann, a Westerner, Assistant Chief. The territory was redivided into eight departments, each with its local Council House and Light Horse unit. The Supreme Court was revived. District judges and high court judges were appointed from both Eastern and Western Cherokees.

Two days into these proceedings, Ross addressed the assembly:

Our Convention on the present occasion forms one of the most important events in the history of our Nation. And when we take a retrospective view of the many trials which it has been our hard fate to encounter, and see how we have escaped the dangers which impended over us, we should feel grateful for the dispensation of Mercy which Providence has so graciously bestowed upon us.[16]

He outlined what would be the national policy and goals: "To live in peace with the Indian Nations around us," to cultivate "friendly relations with the government and citizens of the United States," and for all past injuries suffered at the hands of state or federal governments "we should peaceably seek, and patiently await, redress from the scales of justice upheld by the United States." Turning to the vital matter of internal schisms and disharmony, he added:

"And from the extraordinary circumstances attending the expulsion of our Nation from the land of our Fathers . . . questions of controversy have arisen of the greatest magnitude, which should be adjusted as speedily as possible."[17]

They were brave words. The goals and hopes of the Cherokees were clear—they always had been. If only the trail had been a little clearer.

It would be heartening if, after the Act of Union, the Cherokee Nation had been truly reborn and had marched as neighboring Kansas had beneath its state motto, "Ad Astra per Aspera," to the stars through adversity. It was not to be that simple. Van Buren refused to recognize the reconstituted government, disdained to meet with Ross's representatives when they visited the capital in 1840. Instead, he conferred his blessing on the more or less discredited government of Stand Watie, John Bell, and William Rogers. When Ross refused to yield his legitimate power, Arbuckle briefly put the Nation under martial law.

There followed six troubled years of controversy and division. Ross kept his hold on the government, enjoying continued popularity along with the confidence of his majority. Even Andrew Jackson's final thrust against his old-time foe failed to have effect. "Lay the tyrant low," he wrote to John Bell and Stand Watie in October 1839, "free you and your party from the murderous schemes of John Ross." Six years later the durable Old Hickory himself was dead; Ross remained in office for another two decades.[18]

President John Tyler, following William Henry Harrison's brief term in office, adopted a friendlier attitude toward Ross's government. "You may assure your people," he told the chief in 1841, "that not justice merely shall be done them, but a liberal and generous policy will be adopted toward them." The Cherokees would be granted full indemnity for all wrongs suffered under previous administrations. Stable political relations would be maintained between the United States and Indian governments, with the result that, for the Cherokees, "a new sun will have dawned upon them."[19]

But the new sun shed a fragile light. Dissension continued to rend the Nation; more than thirty political assassinations in succeeding years kept near civil war alive. By early 1846, the situation had so deteriorated that President James Knox Polk and the Bureau of Indian Affairs were ready to recognize a permanent division of the Western Nation, the Old Settlers and the Treaty Party holding one area, the Late Emigrants governing the rest, with inviolable borders circumventing each.

Ross and George Lowrey, acting together, forestalled this fatal dissolution of the Nation. In a last-minute herculean effort they were able to bring representatives of all three factions to Washington in the summer of 1846. There, on August 6, a treaty was signed with the United States which, in fact, was a treaty of unity between the separate parties in the Nation. It secured at long last the $5,000,000 due the Cherokees for land ceded in the East, and at the same time decreed that the Western territory belonged indivisibly to all the Cherokees. While it did not declare the majority government the only government, it accomplished that effect; and according to one account, "after the treaty was signed, Stand Watie and John Ross shook hands."[20]

There followed twenty years of relative peace, progress, and prosperity until the War between the States dismembered the Nation once again. But the Cherokees, from one point of view at any rate, never fully regained their stride, never quite recovered the drive that had carried them to former greatness in the East. Perhaps they had suffered too greatly from attrition; had buried their future with the past; had lost too much along the Trail of Tears.

Sophia Sawyer put her finger on the ebbing pulse. After John Ridge's murder she had fled with Sarah and the remaining Ridges to Fayetteville, Arkansas. "I thought that if I could escape eternally from the Cherokees, I would go where I might not hear of their suffering and degradation." In Fayetteville she had opened a small girls' school to make ends meet, but she returned to visit the Nation in January 1840.

She found the people huddled in untidy huts, dispirited, disorganized, mourning their exile and those buried on the Trail of Tears, enveloped by self-pity and resentment of the past. These were not the Cherokees that she remembered. "We have all wept enough!" she told them briskly. "Go to work and build houses and cultivate your land. Talk no more about little huts with wood chimneys but let your houses be such as will make suitable homes, such as will tell to all around, *We are helping ourselves!*"[21]

Her former co-worker Elizur Butler stumbled on an answer which might best have been directed to Sophia's spirited advice. "For whom do I build here?" an old man asked of Butler. "I had three sons. One died in General Scott's camp. One died on the trail. The third died here. For whom do I build my house?"[22]

Butler hoped that religion might revive their spirit as it had once inspired them to reach for stars. But the missions were declining in influence; church congregations were divided; the Late Emigrants would not share a bench with Treaty Party converts. Even the irrepressible Daniel Butrick had written submissively to Ross in September 1839, asking only that he be allowed to remain "in this sickly country. I . . . cannot hope to be of any sort of service hereafter, yet we hope to teach school a part of the year . . . we wish to live near some Cherokee citizens of whom we may purchase our annual supplies . . ."[23]

Samuel Worcester remained a pillar of the muted missionary movement in the West. He had lost his translator and editor, Elias Boudinot; his printer, John Wheeler, fled the country following the Treaty Party murders; yet in 1844 he was able to see the *Phoenix* rise from its ashes, at least in counterpart. William Ross, the chief's son, now a graduate of Princeton, edited the first edition of the *Cherokee Advocate,* printed like its predecessor in both English and Sequoyah's alphabet. With its appearance, almost as if he had fulfilled a mission, Samuel Worcester died and was buried at Park Hill beside his wife Ann, earlier deceased.

There were not many left of that valiant New England band who had done so much for the distant Cherokees, borne with them so much trial and suffering. Daniel Butrick died at Dwight Mission in 1851 after more than forty years of service to the Indians. Elizur Butler was cruelly dropped by the American Board of Foreign Missions as a measure of economy, and he and Lucy spent their declining years as boardinghouse keepers in Van Buren, Arkansas. Delight Sargent took Elias Boudinot's children back to Connecticut, where they remained, hopefully unaware of the tragic circumstances of their mother's marriage, when a whole New England town had persecuted the young bride.

And Sophia Sawyer? Her name would always carry a question mark. Severed from the American Board, she continued to operate her school at Fayetteville, apparently making more money in buying up silver dollars, and trading them for paper currency, than she made in teaching. By 1848 her letters spoke of being in declining health. And then suddenly—silence. If Miss Sophia died, as presumably she did, she went for once quietly, without protesting, in speech or writing, the injustices of her removal.

Sam Houston, honorary citizen of the Cherokee Nation, won another distinction. The Raven became, for two divided terms, president of the new Republic of Texas. That was reason enough for some Old Settlers, during the time of dissension, to migrate south and settle in what would soon become the Lone Star State.

Many had crossed the Red River earlier, even before 1828, when Jackson launched the threat of Indian removal. They had hoped, with the remnants of other tribes, to set up an Indian nation beyond the reach of the United States. Houston had granted them patents for land, and they organized a government and Council headed by Chief Bowl, "War Lord of the Texas Cherokees." Between the Raven's separate terms, however, President Mirabeau Lamar had made things hot for the Indians, driving some of the Cherokees back across the river, forcing others into Mexico.

Sequoyah, now over seventy and more lame than ever, was a man possessed by curiosity. It was that which had led him to solve the riddle of the white man's writing and create his own syllabary. Now he was steeped in a semi-secret mission: to discover what had happened to the Cherokees in Mexico. In the summer of 1842, provisioned by Lewis Ross, he set out in search of a possible lost tribe below the Rio Grande. His companions returned without him, and soon word reached the Nation that Sequoyah had died somewhere along the trail. The details would remain a mystery.[24]

Education, slow to develop in the Western Nation, was not impeded by Sequoyah's death. His syllabary was alive in a growing number of schools, and he himself was immortalized by the giant conifers named for him in Sequoia National Park in California. The old dream of a National Academy was partially fulfilled by the establishment of a Male and Female Seminary at Park Hill, which, with the press and the bilingual *Cherokee Advocate,* made that community "the Athens of the Nation."

Tahlequah, too, grew from a sleepy Indian village to a bustling, year-round capital. A new Supreme Court Building and new Council House added stature to the town; streets were laid out and handsome residences built; and merchants prospered during the Gold Rush of 1849, when hordes of prospectors stopped to stock up for provisions on their way to California.

John Ross's National Party remained in power, and Ross himself found a second wife in an eighteen-year-old beauty from Delaware named Mary Stapler. He constructed for his bride a handsome two-story house named Rose Cottage, which became the showplace of Park Hill. With its rose-lined driveways, many outbuildings, stables, orchards, and slave-worked fields, Rose Cottage rivaled in splendor Ross's old estate at Head of Coosa.

At long last the Western Nation appeared to have caught up with the progress and stability of its earlier Eastern prototype. In 1857 Ross reported to the Council:

I visited in person during the past summer, the different districts to inform myself of the general condition of the country. The evidence of progress by the Cherokee people furnished by the tour was of the most cheering kind, and contrasts favorably with their condition of fifty years ago.

Well cultivated farms, which have yielded abundant crops of grain . . . well filled public schools, large and orderly assemblies, and quiet neighborhoods, which were seen in all the districts, showed marked improvement, and furnish a sure indication of the susceptibility of all classes among the Cherokee people for thorough civilization.[25]

A census taken two years later showed a population of 21,000 Cherokees and 4,000 slaves living in the Nation. In agricultural wealth they surpassed, by manifold numbers, the figures quoted by Elias Boudinot in 1826—with 240,000 head of cattle, 20,000 horses and mules, double the number of sheep, and twice as many acres under cultivation. There were thirty public schools, about the equivalent of those in the former Eastern Nation, but with a difference: almost all the teachers were Cherokees.

Thus they had arrived at, and in some respects overtopped, the plateau reached in that peak year of 1827, when the constitution was adopted. It was a point from which, Ross told the people, they would climb to even greater heights, to "discharge the debt we owe to posterity." No threats hung over the Nation as in that earlier time; no Andrew Jackson in the White House; no Georgia legislature passing acts for their oppression.

The Georgia legislature was, however, engaged in matters equally portentous, debating a bill for raising a million dollars to arm the state in preparation for secession.

When the War between the States broke out in 1860–61, the Cherokee Nation was again divided, along old factional lines. The Treaty Party, many of them owning slaves, sided with the South. Stand Watie raised a mounted regiment, of which he was elected colonel, to fight for the Confederacy, as did John Drew—both lured by Southern promises to fulfill the obligations to the Cherokees which the federal government had neglected. In time some two thousand Cherokees would fight for the Confederacy in the West.

For the Nation as a whole, however, Ross advocated strict neutrality, and threatened to shoot any who raised the Stars and Bars in Tahlequah. The Cherokees had made a treaty with the United States and they would honor it.

"Our duty," he told his people, "is to stand by our rights, allow no interference in our internal affairs . . . and rely on the Union for protection."[26]

But positioned between Bleeding Kansas and Confederate Texas, they found neutrality a hard position to maintain. It became more difficult still with early Confederate victories in the West, where Stand Watie became a military hero and Missouri wavered between North and South.

The pressure at last became too great, weighted by political considerations if not questions of survival. Should the Confederacy triumph, Stand Watie would return with greater power and Cherokee unity, so recently established, would again be undermined. On October 7, 1861, Ross signed a treaty of alliance with the South. "In time of war," he asserted, "we must fight together. As Brothers live, as Brothers die!" The Confederate flag waved over the capitol at Tahlequah, and once again, it was reported, Ross shook hands with Stand Watie.[27]

It was the first time Ross had wavered in loyalty, and it was fatal. For in 1862 the pendulum began to swing the other way. In July of that year Union forces, directed by General James G. Blunt, invaded Indian territory and Ross was made a prisoner of war. Stand Watie, as he had feared, assumed the role of Principal Chief in Ross's absence, governing an occupied country from the field, and rising to the rank of brigadier general in the Southern military hierarchy.

Taken in custody to Philadelphia, Ross was paroled on Blunt's advice to President Lincoln that the chief had acted under Rebel coercion and through a misunderstanding of the Union's aims. When, later in Washington, Ross met Lincoln face to face the President assured him that the Confederate alliance would not be held against the Cherokees in future relations with the United States.

Despite such assurances, the Nation was left in destitution by the war, as was most of the defeated South. Years afterward, a visiting Cherokee told a group of Athens businessmen, "When Sherman marched to the sea, you Georgians got a taste of what your ancestors gave the Cherokees in 1838, and I'm bound to say it served you right." By then, most Georgians agreed. In a sense they had cleansed the escutcheon, and had fought an oppressive, overwhelming foe as valiantly as had the Cherokees. The two were even.

John Ross was nearing the end of the trail. He was seventy-six, had served his people for more than half a century, and been their Principal Chief for nearly forty years. He was failing in health, yet he assured the new Commissioner of Indian Affairs with whom he was engaged in verbal battle, "I am still John Ross, the same John Ross of former years. Unchanged! No cause to change!"[28]

He had not changed. In his negotiations with Commissioner Dennis Cooley he skillfully swung federal support from Watie's government to that of his own party, which remained in power through the balance of the century. Appropriately, he was engaged in negotiating yet another treaty with the United States, this one dissolving the Confederate alliance and launching a new era in American-Indian relations, when he died on August 1, 1866, in Washington.

Ross's death, followed five years later by the death of Stand Watie, softened the feud which had troubled the Cherokees for three decades. Something like unity was observed as the Nation struggled to recover from the ravages of war and occupation. By the Treaty of 1866 they ceded more land, agreed to free their slaves, yielded railway rights across the Nation—the latter shattering their territorial integrity. Their misalliance with the Lost Cause made for a long and hard road back, across a land described as "one vast scene of desolation where only chimney monuments mark the sites of once happy homes."[29]

The Cherokee Nation endured, of course. It had risen from adversity before, and was still sovereign and independent. But America itself was racing westward, and an Indian nation in the path of Manifest Destiny was an anachronism. The Long Horns were coming up from Texas; the grangers were coming from the East; the railroads sliced across the prairies. Again the white man looked with hungry eyes on Indian territory. In an old familiar pattern, tract after tract of Cherokee land was sold under pressure to the government or citizens of the United States, with the Cherokee Strip overwhelmed by the Cimarron land rush of 1893.

All geographic entity vanished when, by agreement with the federal government, titles to Indian lands in the West passed from tribal ownership to individual possession, a first step toward statehood for the Western territories. Statehood would mean citizenship, and that at least had been one of Ross's goals before removal. When Oklahoma Territory applied for admission to the Union, the Cherokees asked that the state be named Sequoyah, for their most illustrious tribesman. But again the white man had the final say. In 1907 the Nation was absorbed by the new state of Oklahoma—and ceased to exist as an independent political unit.

The Cherokees would survive, and many of them prosper, as American citizens with a noble past. They would achieve distinction as lawyers, statesmen, doctors, writers, and industrialists—even as entertainers, with Will Rogers boasting to packed Broadway theaters that his Cherokee ancestors had not arrived on the *Mayflower*, "but they met the boat." They had already met the challenges of the white man's world; they would go on doing so. But not in the triumphant way that seemed so near when viewed from the splendid heights of 1827.

They survived, as well, in their ancestral homeland in the East. In time some 5,000 Cherokees occupied 5,500 acres of North Carolina reserved for them within the Qualla Indian Boundary. Many were descendants of the martyred Tsali, who through his sacrifice had escaped from federal troops in the dragnet of 1838. Others, in unknown numbers—bearing such family names as Going Home—had returned from the West during the dark years of dissension that had followed their removal.

They lived in primitive unpainted cabins in the mountains, the men engaging in farming and animal husbandry, the women making basketry and beaded belts and weaving fabrics so exquisite that they found display at the Crystal Palace in New York. They maintained their own tribal government with a Council elected from the seven clans. But if the old traditions, the Green Corn

Dance and Going to the River, survived at all, they existed in memory alone. Even Sequoyah's magical alphabet lingered only in the memory of their elders. Perhaps some of these, from the mountaintops, looked across the misty valleys of their ancient kingdom and sensed what Chief Rising Fawn had meant when he whispered the words, both prophetic and nostalgic, "Glory . . . glory . . . glory!"

NOTES

CHAPTER 1. THE GLORY AND THE DREAM

1. An account of the Battle of the Horseshoe appears in the *Cherokee Phoenix* for September 10, 1831 (Library of Congress microfilm, National Archives, Records of the States of the United States, GA, NC, reel 1a). In an earlier issue, March 19, 1831, John Ridge sought to resolve the question of who conceived the surprise cross-river attack upon the Creeks, giving the credit to his father, Major Ridge. Other published accounts of the engagement appear in James, *Life of Andrew Jackson*, pp. 170, 171; Wilkins, *Cherokee Tragedy*, pp. 74–78; McKenney and Hall, *Indian Tribes*, Vol. I, pp. 98, 99; James, *The Raven*, pp. 32–35; Mooney, *Myths of the Cherokee*, pp. 92–97. Coffee's report to Jackson, here quoted, appears in Mooney, op. cit., p. 94.

2. Jackson's report to Governor William Blount of Tennessee, March 31, 1814; quoted in Mooney, op. cit., p. 95.

3. Meigs's report to Secretary of War, May 5, 1814; Jackson Papers, Library of Congress.

4. Letter of William Fyffe to his brother John, February 1, 1761; Gilcrease Institute archives, Tulsa, Oklahoma.

5. Grace Steele Woodward, *The Cherokees*, p. 66. Mrs. Woodward cites Carolyn T. Foreman's *Indians Abroad* as giving the fullest available account of this bizarre hegira to the British court.

6. Mooney, op. cit., p. 36.

7. The complete text of the Treaty of Hopewell (Senate Document No. 452, 57th Congress, 1st Session) is reprinted in Guttmann, *States' Rights and Indian Removal*, pp. 12–16.

8. Mooney, op. cit., pp. 489, 490

9. Quoted in Royce, *The Cherokee Nation of Indians*, p. 160.

10. Essential acts incorporated in the Treaty of Holson are recorded in Guttmann, op. cit., pp. 16, 17.

11. Quotations in this paragraph from Woodward, op. cit., pp. 116, 117.

(Publications referred to are listed in the Bibliography.)

CHAPTER 2.   "THE PRINCIPAL PEOPLE"

1. Wade, *Cry of the Eagle,* pp. 63, 64. While Jay Bird includes no dates in the written recollections of his youth, he was born in 1825 and one might rightfully assume that he was a lad of, say, eight or ten when he learned from his elders about his racial origins.

2. Mooney, *Myths of the Cherokee,* pp. 185–87. Mooney gives fifty-eight different spellings of the name Cherokee, along with forty-four other names applied to the tribe—the latter appearing to have different, though not defined, meanings; e.g., Alleghans, presumably "people of the Allegheny Mountains."

3. Bartram, *Travels,* pp. 483–85. Some of the accompanying comments on the Cherokees' appearance also come from Bartram, as well as from William Fyffe's letters, Gilcrease Institute archives, and from Woodward's *The Cherokees,* pp. 36, 37.

4. The remarkable story of Nancy Ward is best presented in Mooney, op. cit., pp. 203, 204. Her warning to the Americans, p. 47.

5. Many of the Cherokee animal legends became the basis of Joel Chandler Harris's "Uncle Remus" stories, notably the race between the tortoise and the hare in which the tortoise announces, in true Cherokee tradition, "I know I cannot beat a hare, but I can try."

6. Mooney, op. cit., p. 82.

7. *Letters of Benjamin Hawkins, 1796–1806,* p. 23.

8. Mooney, op. cit., p. 83.

9. Sam Houston's life with the Cherokees is sympathetically portrayed in James's *The Raven;* the events in this chapter are discussed on pp. 4–23.

10. Thomas Jefferson's address to the chiefs of the Cherokees in Washington, January 10, 1806. Recorded in Vogel, *This Country Was Ours,* pp. 83, 84.

CHAPTER 3.   THIS LAST LITTLE

1. Quoted in Malone, *Cherokees of the Old South,* p. 66.

2. Ibid., p. 69.

3. Ibid., p. 93.

4. Payne Papers, Vol. II, Ayer Collection, Newberry Library, Chicago, typescript p. 46. Further details of James Vann's murder are given in Wade, *Cry of the Eagle,* pp. 4–6.

5. Woodward, *The Cherokees,* p. 125.

6. Malone, op. cit., p. 95.

7. Woodward, op. cit., p. 126.

8. Glenn Tucker, *Tecumseh* (Indianapolis: Bobbs-Merrill, 1956), pp. 82, 83.

9. National Archives RG 75, Records of the Cherokee Agency in Tennessee.

10. McKenney and Hall, *Indian Tribes,* Vol. I, p. 386.

11. Ross Papers, Gilcrease Institute archives, Tulsa, Oklahoma, transcript of conversation between Madison and Lowrey, February 22, 1816.

12. Jackson's address to the Council quoted in Eaton, *John Ross and the Cherokee Indians,* p. 30.

13. Foreman, *Sequoyah,* p. 6. In addition to the numbered reference, Foreman also gives an account of this early emigration to the West.

CHAPTER 4. THE LIGHT OF ATHENS

1. Woodward, *The Cherokees,* p. 127.

2. Much of the material in this chapter derives from the Mission Papers in the archives of Houghton Library, Harvard University, especially those documents covering the year 1817.

3. Ibid.

4. Butrick's Journal, Mission Papers, loc. cit. Butrick often omitted dates and the entries in his journal are hard to place in precise chronological context. Butrick kept two journals, one recording day-to-day events, the other containing his more secret thoughts and no doubt not intended for any eyes but his.

5. Among Butrick's papers, undated; Mission Papers, loc. cit.

6. Brainerd Journal entry for July 4, 1817; Mission Papers, loc. cit.

7. Walker, *Torchlights to the Cherokees,* p. 36. Except for the Mission Papers in the Houghton Library, Walker gives perhaps the best available account of Brainerd Mission, its staff, its converts and pupils. Also Starkey, *The Cherokee Nation,* pp. 29–42.

8. Ibid., pp. 95–97.

9. Edward Starr's *A History of Cornwall, Connecticut* gives an authoritative account of the founding and operation of the school, along with a list of the Cherokee students attending. Much of the material in this chapter comes from this source, especially pages 136–44, 154–57, 276–77. Also from Gabriel, *Elias Boudinot, Cherokee, and His America,* Ch. 5.

10. A detailed account of this courtship and controversial marriage appears in Starr, op. cit., pp. 155, 156, and Chamberlain, *The Foreign Mission School,* pp. 7–15.

11. For more details on Elias and Harriet's marital ordeal, see Starr, op. cit., pp. 277–79, and Chamberlain, op. cit., pp. 16–19.

12. Foreman's *Sequoyah* gives a comprehensive picture of the inventor's life and his development of the syllabary. The particulars described here come largely from pp. 20–27.

13. Tracy, *A History of the American Board,* pp. 147, 148.

14. Quoted in Mooney, *Myths of the Cherokee,* pp. 219, 220. In these pages Mooney also gives an analysis of the syllabary.

CHAPTER 5. "WHAT HATH GOD WROUGHT!"

1. The medal was finally delivered by Charles Vann to Sequoyah's home in Arkansas in January 1832. It was described by John Howard Payne as "made of silver to the value of Twenty Dollars. One side was thus inscribed: 'Presented to George Gist by the General Council of the Cherokee Nation, for his ingenuity in The Invention of the Cherokee Alphabet, 1825.' Under the inscription were two pipes crossed and an abridgment of the above on the reverse of the medal encircled a head meant to represent George Gist himself." Grant, *Sequoyah,* p. 8.

2. Walker, *Torchlights to the Cherokees,* pp. 114, 115. In his presentation of the structure of the government Walker lists by name all members of the National Committee and all members of the National Council by the districts from which they were elected.

3. Cherokee Delegation to the Secretary of War, February 11, 1824; files of the Bureau of Indian Affairs, II, 47. Also quoted in Cotterill, *The Southern Indians,* p. 218.

4. Memorial of the Cherokee Chiefs to the United States Commissioners, January 20, 1823; Ross Papers, Gilcrease Institute.

5. McIntosh to Ross, October 21, 1823; Ross Papers, loc. cit.

6. Quoted in Woodward, *The Cherokees,* p. 148.

7. Ross and Lowrey to Gales and Seaton, April 20, 1824; Ross Papers, loc. cit.

8. Walker, op. cit., p. 252.

9. Butrick's Journal, undated, and letter to Evarts, May 9, 1824; Mission Papers, Houghton Library, Harvard University.

10. Sawyer to Evarts, August 21, 1824; Mission Papers, loc. cit.

11. Chamberlin's Diary, October 25, 26, 1824; Mission Papers, loc. cit.

12. Ridge to the Boston *Recorder,* March 12, 1825.

13. Quoted in Wilkins, *Cherokee Tragedy,* p. 186.

14. Ibid.

15. Bass, *Cherokee Messenger,* p. 77.

CHAPTER 6. RISE OF THE *PHOENIX*

1. Bass, *Cherokee Messenger,* p. 34. The first two chapters of this dutiful biography of Samuel Worcester offer abundant material on his early life, his marriage, and the couple's introduction to the mission work at Brainerd.

2. Ibid., p. 50.

3. Worcester to Evarts, January 8, 1827; Mission Papers, Houghton Library, Harvard University.

4. Quoted in Woodward, *The Cherokees*, pp. 152, 153.

5. *Georgia Journal*, May 22, 1827.

6. Starr, *History of the Cherokee Indians*, pp. 55, 56.

7. *Cherokee Phoenix*, February 28, 1828; Boudinot reprinted parts of Worcester's prospectus in this second edition of the *Phoenix*, in addition to the subscription terms hereafter noted.

8. Quoted in Bass, op. cit., pp. 78, 79.

9. Both versions of this verse are given in Garrett, *Atlanta and Environs*, Vol. I, p. 62.

10. Acts of the Georgia General Assembly, 1827, p. 249; Georgia Department of Archives and History.

11. Jackson, *A Century of Dishonor*, p. 272.

12. *Cherokee Phoenix*, February 21, 1828.

13. Ibid., March 6, 1828.

14. Gabriel, *Elias Boudinot, Cherokee, and His America*, p. 113.

15. Sawyer to Evarts, July 25, 1828, and February 11, 1829; Mission Papers, loc. cit.

CHAPTER 7.   DAVID AND GOLIATH

1. Mooney, *Myths of the Cherokee*, p. 163.

2. *Cherokee Phoenix*, April 17, 1828.

3. Quoted in Duckett, *John Forsyth, Political Tactician*, pp. 114–15.

4. Proclamation printed in the *Cherokee Phoenix*, July 2, 1828.

5. *Cherokee Phoenix*, May 6, 1828.

6. Ibid., May 1, 1830.

7. Mooney, *Myths of the Cherokee*, p. 97. Actually, Junaluska was credited with saving Jackson's life during the Creek campaign, when a hostile Red Stick sneaked into Jackson's tent and tried to stab the general but was restrained by Junaluska's timely intervention. The incident is reenacted every summer in the Cherokee pageant "Unto These Hills," produced at Cherokee, North Carolina.

8. Ibid., p. 221. Extracts from the act, as passed by the Georgia legislature, are also given in the *Fifth Annual Report*, Bureau of American Ethnology, p. 260.

9. Fleischmann, *Cherokee Removal*, p. 20.

10. *Cherokee Phoenix*, October 16, 1830. Eaton's involvement with Peggy O'Neill, which split Jackson's cabinet and scandalized the capital as much as a later-date

Watergate, is told in Peggy's autobiography published by Scribner's in 1932, and more objectively in Queena Pollack's *Peggy Eaton* (New York: Minton, Balch & Co., 1931).

11. *Cherokee Phoenix*, October 14, 1829.

12. Bass, *Cherokee Messenger*, p. 129.

13. Ibid.

14. *Cherokee Phoenix*, February 11, 1829.

15. Benjamin Gold to Hezekiah Gold, December 8, 1829; reprinted in Gabriel, *Elias Boudinot, Cherokee, and His America*, pp. 115–19.

16. Greene's letter to Worcester, 1829 (no further date indicated); Mission Papers, Houghton Library, Harvard University.

17. Sawyer to Evarts, undated; Mission Papers, loc. cit.

18. Quotations from "Georgia's Forgotten Industry: Gold Mining," *Georgia Historical Quarterly*, Vol. XIX, June 1935; and Mooney, op. cit., p. 220.

19. *Cherokee Phoenix*, October 28, 1829.

20. Ibid.

21. Jackson's message to Congress, December 8, 1829, appears in Filler and Guttmann, *The Removal of the Cherokee Nation*, pp. 14–17.

22. Ibid. Georgia's act of December 19, 1829, is given on pp. 18–21.

23. The "William Penn" letters began appearing in the *Phoenix* on September 16, 1829, and were continued almost every week thereafter, reprinted from exchange copies of the Washington *National Intelligencer*.

24. Ibid.

25. Worcester to Greene, April, 29, 1830; Mission Papers, loc. cit.

26. James, *The Raven*, p. 127.

27. Ibid., p. 129.

CHAPTER 8. CIRCUMSTANCES LONG DREADED

1. *Cherokee Phoenix*, February 10, 1830.

2. Cotterhill, *The Southern Indians*, pp. 238–39.

3. Frelinghuysen's speech of April 9, 1830, was reprinted in its entirety in the *Phoenix*, starting with the issue of June 3, 1830.

4. Quoted in Vogel, *This Country Was Ours*, p. 111. Jeremiah Evarts edited and published a collection *Speeches on the Passage of the Bill for the Removal of the Indians*, published in 1830.

5. Quoted in Starkey, *The Cherokee Nation*, p. 123.

6. The essence of Lumpkin's speech appears in Guttmann, *States' Rights and Indian Removal,* pp. 50–55.

7. McKenney to Eaton, July 21, 1829; Bureau of Indian Affairs, Letters Received. McKenney's switch to Jackson's side and his efforts to foster Indian removal are described in Horan, *The McKenney-Hall Portrait Gallery of American Indians,* Ch. 13.

8. Butler to Evarts, September 1830; Mission Papers, Houghton Library, Harvard University.

9. Quoted in Gabriel, *Elias Boudinot, Cherokee, and His America,* p. 126.

10. *Cherokee Phoenix,* May 29, 1830.

11. Evarts to Ross, date illegible; Ross Papers, Gilcrease Institute archives, Tulsa, Oklahoma.

12. Quoted in Woodward, *The Cherokees,* pp. 161–62.

13. Foreman, *Indian Removal,* p. 231.

14. The entire Cherokee memorial was published in *Niles' Weekly Register,* Baltimore, August 21, 1830.

15. Evarts to Ross, undated letter presumably written in mid-July 1830; Ross Papers, loc. cit.

16. *Cherokee Phoenix,* October 20, 1830.

17. Jackson's second message to Congress, December 6, 1830, is reprinted in Filler and Guttmann, *The Removal of the Cherokee Nation,* pp. 49–52.

18. Lumpkin to Jackson, January 3, 1831; Georgia Governors' Letter Book, Department of Archives and History, Atlanta.

19. *Cherokee Phoenix,* January 15, 1831, quoting from the New York *Observer.*

20. Gold, *Historical Records of the Town of Cornwall,* p. 350.

21. Wirt to Ross, November 15, 1830; Ross Papers, loc. cit.

CHAPTER 9.   A NEW SPECIES OF COURAGE

1. The Resolution and Statement of the Missionaries was printed in full in the *Cherokee Phoenix,* January 1, 1831, along with an account of the meeting and a list of those present.

2. Prudential Committee's Memorial published in the *Cherokee Phoenix,* March 26, 1831.

3. Marshall's decision, along with dissenting opinions, is given in Filler and Guttmann, *The Removal of the Cherokee Nation,* pp. 61ff. This extract from p. 61.

4. Ibid., p. 65.

5. Ibid., p. 63.

6. Starkey, *The Cherokee Nation,* p. 156.

7. *Cherokee Phoenix,* July 16, 1831.

8. Ibid., April 30, 1831.

9. The arrest of the missionaries was described at length by Worcester in a letter to the *Cherokee Phoenix* appearing in the issue of July 20, 1831. Worcester's letter was dated July 11, and was written from the jail at Camp Gilmer, Georgia.

10. Conversation as reported by Ridge to Boudinot and printed in the *Cherokee Phoenix,* May 21, 1831.

11. Ibid.

12. Gilmer to Worcester, May 10, 1831; Georgia Governors' Letter Book, Department of Archives and History, Atlanta.

13. Worcester's reply to Gilmer was printed in the *Cherokee Phoenix,* July 12, 1831.

14. Bass, *Cherokee Messenger,* p. 140.

15. Ibid., p. 141.

16. This continued account of the roundup of the missionaries derives from Worcester's letter published in the *Cherokee Phoenix,* July 20, 1831.

17. Worcester to Boudinot, September 19, 1831. Letter published in the *Cherokee Phoenix,* October 7.

18. Bass, op. cit., p. 149.

19. Ibid., p. 150.

20. Starkey, op. cit., p. 145.

21. Ibid., pp. 163–64.

CHAPTER 10.   "WE ARE DISTRESSED . . . DISTRESSED!"

1. *Cherokee Phoenix,* August 12, 1831. Also, Malone, *Cherokees of the Old South,* p. 177.

2. Ibid.

3. Ibid.

4. Butrick's Journal for January 1832, Mission Papers, Houghton Library, Harvard University.

5. *Cherokee Phoenix,* March 24, 1832. The incident is described also in Starkey, *The Cherokee Nation,* pp. 175–77.

6. Cass to Currey, September 1, 1831; Georgia Department of Archives and History, Atlanta.

7. The assassination attempt was recorded in the *Cherokee Phoenix,* January 21, 1832.

8. Wilkins, *Cherokee Tragedy,* p. 225.

9. Reprinted in the *Cherokee Phoenix*, March 3, 1832.

10. *Cherokee Phoenix*, March 24, 1832.

11. Quoted in Dale and Litton, *Cherokee Cavaliers*, p. 6.

12. Ibid., p. 8.

13. Famous as Jackson's statement is, it is impossible to document. Though often quoted, no traceable source is given.

14. Foreman, *Indian Removal*, p. 245.

15. Dale and Litton, op. cit., p. 10.

16. *Cherokee Phoenix*, July 14, 1832.

17. Ibid.

18. Jackson, *Correspondence*, Vol. IV, p. 430.

19. Quoted by Gilmer, *First Settlers of Upper Georgia*, pp. 262–63.

20. Transcript of Ross's speech, misdated "Head of Coosa, August 9, 1833," in Georgia Department of Archives and History, Atlanta.

21. Taylor, Vann, and the National Committee to Cass from Red Clay, August 6, 1833; Georgia Department of Archives and History.

22. Sophia tells of her journey through the Valley Town district in a letter to David Greene dated August 9, 1832; Mission Papers, loc. cit.

23. Ibid.

CHAPTER 11.   A HOUSE DIVIDED

1. *Cherokee Phoenix*, August 11, 1832. It was a common custom, when Cherokees corresponded on affairs of state, to submit their letters for publication in the *Phoenix* to gain a wider audience. A review of the contention that blistered the pages of the *Phoenix* at this time is presented also in Malone, *Cherokees of the Old South*, pp. 167–70.

2. Quoted in Starkey, *The Cherokee Nation*, pp. 191–92.

3. Ross's letter was published in the *Cherokee Phoenix* for August 11, 1832, along with Boudinot's statement of resignation.

4. *Cherokee Phoenix*, December 1832. The Principal Keeper of the penitentiary, one Charles C. Mills, appears to have treated the missionaries with considerable kindness and compassion, judging from Worcester's prison correspondence.

5. The operation of the lottery is described in Smith's *The Cherokee Land Lottery*, along with the names and properties acquired by the "lucky drawers." The *Cherokee Phoenix* for November 11, 1832, also gave an account of the operation of the lottery.

6. Starkey, op. cit., p. 214.

7. Lumpkin's message to the legislature, November 6, 1832, was reprinted in full in *Niles' Register*, Baltimore, November 24, and is presented in extract in Guttmann, *States' Rights and Indian Removal*, pp. 77–79.

8. *Cherokee Phoenix*, October 27, 1832.

9. Gabriel, *Elias Boudinot, Cherokee, and His America*, pp. 141–42.

10. *Cherokee Phoenix*, January 9, 1833.

11. Ross Papers for February 1833; Gilcrease Institute archives, Tulsa, Oklahoma.

12. Ibid., Ridge to Ross, February 2, 1833.

13. Ibid.

14. *Cherokee Phoenix*, August 10 and September 21, 1833.

15. Wilkins, *Cherokee Tragedy*, p. 245.

16. *Cherokee Phoenix*, January 26, 1833.

17. Sophia Sawyer to David Greene, December 24, 1833; Mission Papers, Houghton Library, Harvard University.

18. Bass, *Cherokee Messenger*, p. 165.

19. Worcester to Greene, June 15, 1833; Mission Papers, loc. cit.

20. *Cherokee Phoenix*, November 23, 1833.

21. Ibid., December 7, 1833.

CHAPTER 12. DEATH OF THE *PHOENIX*

1. The battle for the Vann home is related in Perkerson, *White Columns in Georgia*, Ch. 19.

2. Greene to Worcester, January 7, 1834; Mission Papers, Houghton Library, Harvard University. Also Walker, *Torchlights to the Cherokees*, p. 45; Bass, *Cherokee Messenger*, pp. 175–76.

3. Foreman, *Indian Removal*, p. 252.

4. Memorial of protest, June 22, 1836; Ross Papers, Gilcrease Institute archives, Tulsa, Oklahoma. Reprinted in *Chronicles of American Indian Protest*, pp. 126–27.

5. Ibid.

6. Journal of Lieutenant J. W. Harris, quoted in Foreman, *Indian Removal*, p. 253.

7. Ibid., p. 254.

8. Ibid., p. 258.

9. *Cherokee Phoenix*, March 29, 1834.

10. *Cherokee Phoenix*, May 31, 1834.

11. Currey's report to Cass quoted in Wilkins, *Cherokee Tragedy*, p. 252.

12. Wilkins, op. cit., p. 253.

13. Butrick to Greene, March 5, 1835; Mission Papers, loc. cit.

14. Worcester to the American Board, September 16, 1834; Mission Papers, loc. cit.

15. Ibid.

16. Wilkins, *Cherokee Tragedy,* p. 289.

17. Jackson to Currey, September 3, 1834; Georgia Department of Archives and History, Atlanta.

18. Lumpkin, *The Removal of the Cherokee Indians from Georgia,* Vol. I, p. 276.

19. Lumpkin to Cass, February 5, 1834; Georgia Governors' Letter Book, Department of Archives and History, Atlanta.

20. Ross to Ridge, September 12, 1834; Ross Papers, loc. cit.

21. Currey to Lumpkin, November 13, 1834; Georgia Governors' Letter Book, loc. cit.

22. Quoted in Wilkins, op. cit., p. 256.

23. Mooney, *Myths of the Cherokee,* p. 139.

CHAPTER 13.   DARK SUN AND DEVIL'S HORN

1. Mooney, *Myths of the Cherokee,* p. 257.

2. Ridge's statement to Worcester recorded in the *Cherokee Phoenix,* March 24, 1832.

3. Ross to Costello y Lanza, March 22, 1835; Ross Papers, Gilcrease Institute archives, Tulsa, Oklahoma.

4. Boudinot to Stand Watie, February 28, 1835; quoted in Dale and Litton, *Cherokee Cavaliers,* p. 11.

5. John Ridge to Major Ridge, March 10, 1835; quoted in Dale and Litton, op. cit., p. 13.

6. Worcester to Greene, letter number 237, Mission Papers, Houghton Library, Harvard University.

7. *Cherokee Phoenix,* July 27 and August 3, 1833.

8. Bishop to Lumpkin, May 5, 1835; Georgia Department of Archives and History, Atlanta.

9. Hargrave to Lumpkin, April 22, 1835; Georgia Department of Archives and History.

10. Bishop to Lumpkin, March 15, 1835; Lumpkin's restraining letter to Bishop, June 13, 1835; Georgia Department of Archives and History.

11. Harden to Lumpkin, May 14, 1835; Georgia Department of Archives and History.

12. Currey to Ross, September 9, 1835; Georgia Department of Archives and History.

13. Ridge to Lumpkin, May 18, 1835; Georgia Department of Archives and History.

14. Ibid.

15. Ibid.

16. Wilkins, *Cherokee Tragedy*, p. 264.

17. Ibid., p. 268.

18. Quoted in *John Howard Payne to His Countrymen*, p. 7.

19. Nelson to Lumpkin, July 7, 1835; Georgia Department of Archives and History.

20. Currey to Lumpkin, September 29, 1835; Georgia Department of Archives and History.

CHAPTER 14. "SPARE OUR PEOPLE!"

1. *John Howard Payne to His Countrymen*, p. 14. This account by Payne of his arrival in Georgia, and events hereafter described, was first published in the Knoxville *Register* and subsequently widely reprinted in the eastern seaboard states.

2. Wilkins, *Cherokee Tragedy*, p. 272.

3. Rockwell to Ross, September 24, 1835; Ross Papers, Gilcrease Institute archives, Tulsa, Oklahoma.

4. Foreman, *Indian Removal*, p. 267.

5. Payne, op. cit., p. 18.

6. Butler to Greene, October 27, 1835; Mission Papers, Houghton Library, Harvard University.

7. Wilkins, op. cit., p. 271.

8. Bass, *Cherokee Messenger*, p. 170.

9. Payne, op. cit., pp. 18–21.

10. Ibid., pp. 38–39.

11. Payne's draft of the memorial appears in Payne, op. cit., pp. 49–61.

12. John Ridge to Lumpkin, dated only "1835"; Georgia Department of Archives and History, Atlanta.

13. Wilkins, op. cit., p. 277.

14. Ibid.

15. Starkey, *The Cherokee Nation*, p. 267.

16. Royce, *The Cherokee Nation of Indians*, p. 282.

17. Ibid., pp. 285ff.

18. These extracts from the memorial appear in Starkey, op. cit., pp. 270–71.

19. Quoted from Vogel, *This Country Was Ours*, pp. 134–35.

CHAPTER 15.   PHANTOM TREATY

1. Quoted in Wilkins, *Cherokee Tragedy*, p. 280.

2. Gabriel, *Elias Boudinot, Cherokee, and His America*, p. 163.

3. Payne to Ross, January 15, 1836; Ross Papers, Gilcrease Institute archives, Tulsa, Oklahoma.

4. These fragmentary extracts, generally undated but under the general heading of 1836, are found in the Ross Papers, loc. cit.

5. Wilkins, op. cit., p. 281.

6. Eaton, *John Ross and the Cherokee Indians*, p. 108.

7. Fleischmann, *The Cherokee Removal*, p. 34.

8. Wilkins, op. cit., pp. 282–83.

9. Mooney, *Myths of the Cherokee*, p. 127.

10. Harris to Jackson, December 10, 1836; Georgia Department of Archives and History, Atlanta. Fleischmann, op. cit., p. 40.

11. Ross's letter was written specifically for publication, probably at Tyson's suggestion. Lengthy and detailed, it narrates the history of the Cherokees in the first third of the century, presenting the Indian side of the controversy on removal. In December 1837, Tyson undertook to publish the document, 500 copies, in pamphlet form, in Philadelphia. Its text appears in *Chronicles of American Indian Protest*, pp. 132–51.

12. Bass, *Cherokee Messenger*, p. 198.

13. From the pamphlet issued by Elias Boudinot in justification of the Treaty of New Echota and his personal endorsement of it. The text was reprinted in, among other publications, the Washington *National Intelligencer*, May 22, 1838.

14. Butrick's Journal, undated; Mission Papers, Houghton Library, Harvard University.

15. Lumpkin, *The Removal of the Cherokee Indians from Georgia*, Vol. II, p. 85.

16. Currey to Lumpkin, November 4, 1836; Georgia Governors' Letter Book, Department of Archives and History, Atlanta.

17. Lumpkin to Jackson, September 24, 1836; Georgia Governors' Letter Book, loc. cit.

18. Butler to Greene, September 26, 1836; Mission Papers, loc. cit.

19. Original printed order in Georgia Department of Archives and History.

20. Lumpkin, op. cit., Vol. II, p. 94.

21. Ibid., p. 97.

22. Foreman, *Indian Removal*, p. 271.

23. *Chronicles of American Indian Protest*, pp. 145, 148.

24. Eaton, op. cit., p. 107.

25. *Chronicles of American Indian Protest*, pp. 146–47.

26. Emerson's letter to Van Buren is reprinted in its entirety in Filler and Gutt-mann, *The Removal of the Cherokee Nation*, pp. 94–97.

CHAPTER 16.   THE DRUMS OF WAR

1. Wilkins, *Cherokee Tragedy*, p. 290.

2. Lillybridge's journal is quoted extensively in Foreman, *Indian Removal*, pp. 273–78.

3. Wilkins, op. cit., p. 294 fn.

4. Ibid.

5. Letter to Van Buren, dated June 19, 1837; Lumpkin, *The Removal of the Cherokee Indians from Georgia*, Vol. II, p. 115.

6. Ibid.

7. Transcript dated "New Echota, Ga., March 22d, 1837"; Ross Papers, Gilcrease Institute archives, Tulsa, Oklahoma.

8. Fleischmann, *Cherokee Removal*, p. 42.

9. Mooney, *Myths of the Cherokee*, p. 128.

10. Love, *The Rambler in Georgia*, p. 124.

11. Ibid., p. 125.

12. Ibid.

13. Ibid., p. 129.

14. Ibid., p. 127.

15. Ibid., p. 126.

16. A transcript of Mason's saccharine "talk" is in the Ross Papers, 1837, loc. cit.

17. Featherstonhaugh, op. cit., p. 132.

18. Mooney, op. cit., p. 128.

19. John Ridge to Lumpkin and Kennedy, September 22, 1837; quoted in Wilkins, op. cit., p. 295.

20. Ibid.

21. Lumpkin, op. cit., Vol. II, p. 141.

22. Cannon's diary quoted in Foreman, op. cit., pp. 282–83.

23. The letter headed "The cabins, New Echota, September 24, 1837," is reprinted in Lumpkin, op. cit., Vol. II, p. 144.

24. Ibid.

25. Wilkins, op. cit., pp. 297–98.

26. Ibid., pp. 300–3.

27. Bass, *Cherokee Messenger*, p. 206.

28. Smith to Worcester, January 11, 1838; Collections of the Gilcrease Institute. Smith was averse not only to Boudinot but to Worcester and his associates as well. He enclosed a memorial drafted by the Council of the Western Nation which, among other things, sought to correct certain clauses in the Treaty of New Echota and "particularly to protest against Missionarys [sic] coming to this Nation."

29. Bass, op. cit., p. 219.

30. Lumpkin, op. cit., Vol. I, p. 191.

31. Poinsett to Ross delegation, December 27, 1837; Ross Papers, loc. cit.

CHAPTER 17.   A SUDDEN GLEAM OF BAYONETS

1. Hilderbrand to Ross, March 10, 1838; Ross Papers, Gilcrease Institute archives, Tulsa, Oklahoma.

2. Memorial in Indian Documents, Vol. IV, No. 11, on microfilm, University of Oklahoma Library.

3. Ibid.

4. William's letter dated November 28, 1837, and Robert's letter dated March 16, 1838; Ross Papers, loc. cit.

5. Araminda's letters dated January 11 and February 7, 1838; Ross Papers, loc. cit.

6. Fowler to Ross, March 28, 1838; Ross Papers, loc. cit.

7. In *Cherokee Indian Letters, Talks, and Treaties;* Georgia Department of Archives and History, Atlanta.

8. Letter reprinted in Gilmer, *First Settlers of Upper Georgia*, pp. 417–18.

9. Ibid., p. 419.

10. Ibid., p. 423.

11. William J. Cotter, *My Autobiography* (Nashville, 1917), pp. 38–39.

12. Foreman, *Indian Removal*, p. 284. Foreman goes on to describe the fate of the expedition as digested here.

13. The ex-governor's detailed instructions to Scott on how best to expedite the expulsion of the Cherokees are given in Lumpkin, *The Removal of the Cherokee Indians from Georgia*, Vol. II, pp. 227–30.

14. Scott's proclamation, May 10, 1838; Ross Papers, loc. cit.

15. Mooney, *Myths of the Cherokee,* p. 130.

16. Ibid.

17. Scott's order to his troops, May 17, 1838; Ross Papers, loc. cit.

18. Mooney, op. cit., p. 130. The Georgia volunteer whom Mooney mentions was Private John G. Burnett, 2nd Regiment, Mounted Infantry, who half a century later wrote his own account of the Cherokee removal, which was recently published in pamphlet form by the S. B. Newman Printing Co., Knoxville, no copyright date.

19. Foreman, op. cit., p. 288.

20. As mentioned, Tsali's story has been told in many versions: in Mooney, op. cit., pp. 131, 157, 158; Starkey, *The Cherokee Nation,* pp. 326–28; and McCullar's *Georgia,* pp. 470–71—to name a few. The Indian writer Denton R. Bedford has recently (1972) published a close-to-truth novel about Tsali's martyrdom, published by the Indian Historian Press of San Francisco. Every summer at Cherokee, North Carolina, on the border of the Qualla Reservation, the legend is reenacted in an outdoor pageant entitled "Unto These Hills," the receipts from which have sent many young contemporary Cherokees to college.

21. Foreman, op. cit., p. 289.

22. All quotations are from the Mission Journal, Mission Papers, Houghton Library, Harvard University.

CHAPTER 18.   AS MAKES THE ANGELS WEEP!

1. Wade, *Cry of the Eagle,* p. 71.

2. Ibid.

3. Deas's Journal, from which these quotations come, is in the Office of Indian Affairs, Washington, D.C., File D 225.

4. Ibid.

5. Foreman, *Indian Removal,* p. 295.

6. *John Howard Payne to His Countrymen,* p. 39.

7. Foreman, op. cit., p. 296.

8. Gilmer, *First Settlers of Upper Georgia,* p. 431.

9. Foreman, op. cit., p. 297.

10. Ibid.

11. Butrick's Journal, Mission Papers, Houghton Library, Harvard University.

12. *Missionary Herald,* Vol. XXXIV, p. 445.

13. Boudinot, perhaps expectedly, held this opinion, writing at about this time: "The whole catastrophe . . . might have been averted if Mr. Ross . . . had un-

folded to his confiding people the sure termination of these things. They might now have been a happy and prosperous community . . . But, no sir, he had dragged an ignorant train, wrought upon by nearsighted prejudice and stupid obstinacy, to the last brink of destruction."

14. Draft of resolution in Ross Papers for August 1838; Gilcrease Institute archives, Tulsa, Oklahoma.

15. Ross Papers, loc. cit. Correspondence between Ross and Smith, August 2 and August 24, 1838.

16. From compensation claims in *Cherokee Indian Letters, Talks, and Treaties;* Georgia Department of Archives and History, Atlanta.

17. Woodward, *The Cherokees,* p. 211.

18. Eaton, *John Ross and the Cherokee Indians,* p. 120.

19. Coodey to John Howard Payne, August 13, 1840; Payne Papers, Vol. VI, Ayer Collection, Newberry Library, Chicago.

CHAPTER 19. THE TRAIL OF TEARS

1. Coodey to John Howard Payne, August 13, 1840; Payne Papers, Vol. VI, Newberry Library, Chicago.

2. Foreman, *Indian Removal,* p. 302.

3. Mooney, *Myths of the Cherokee,* p. 114.

4. Foreman, op. cit., p. 303.

5. Ibid., p. 304.

6. Chief Junaluska's sayings are in the collections of the Sondley Library at Asheville, North Carolina. We learn from these that he appears to have changed his mind about Jackson, even after his forced removal to the West, saying: "My fate is a hard one; and harder because I have always been a friend to the President . . . I know that Jackson is a brave man."

7. Foreman, op. cit., p. 305.

8. Individual claims are in *Cherokee Indian Letters, Talks, and Treaties;* Georgia Department of Archives and History, Atlanta.

9. Foreman, op. cit., p. 305.

10. Burnett's original manuscript, chronicling his experience during the removal, is in the Indian Museum, Cherokee, North Carolina.

11. Quoted in Foreman, op. cit., p. 306.

12. Ibid., p. 307.

13. Ibid., p. 309.

14. Mooney, *Myths of the Cherokee,* p. 133.

15. Foreman, op. cit., p. 309.

16. The "Diary of Dr. W. I. I. Morrow, 1839" is in the archives of the Oklahoma Historical Society, Oklahoma City.

17. The unidentified Cherokee's experience is recorded in the *Daily Oklahoman,* April 7, 1929.

18. Clark to Ross from "Mouth of the Ohio, Illinois," December 28, 1838; Ross Papers, Gilcrease Institute archives, Tulsa, Oklahoma.

19. Quoted in Fleischmann, *The Cherokee Removal,* p. 65.

20. Manuscript of Private John G. Burnett, Indian Museum, Cherokee, North Carolina.

21. Fleischmann, op. cit., pp. 65–66.

22. Burnett manuscript, loc. cit.

23. Fleischmann, op. cit., p. 73.

24. Burnett manuscript, loc. cit., and *Arkansas Gazette,* December 20, 1838.

25. Washington *National Intelligencer,* December 8, 1838.

26. Butler, Mission Papers, Houghton Library, Harvard University.

CHAPTER 20.   REBIRTH OF A NATION

1. Quoted in the New York *Observer,* November 10, 1838.

2. This exchange of comment and protest concerning provisions is in the Ross Papers, Gilcrease Institute archives, Tulsa, Oklahoma. As in most cases of cover-up, the spokesman for the Treasury Department is not identified.

3. Sophia Sawyer to David Greene, December 27, 1838, and Butrick's Journal; Mission Papers, Houghton Library, Harvard Unviersity.

4. Washburn to Greene, August 12, 1839; Mission Papers, loc. cit.

5. Ibid.

6. Ibid.

7. Ibid.

8. *Cherokee Advocate,* March 5, 1846.

9. Wilkins, *Cherokee Tragedy,* pp. 322–23.

10. Worcester's account of Boudinot's murder is given in Bass, *Cherokee Messenger,* pp. 255–56.

11. Ross to Arbuckle, June 22, 1839, Ross Papers, loc. cit.

12. Arbuckle to Ross, June 29, 1839; Ross Papers, loc. cit.

13. Ross to Arbuckle, June 30, 1839; Ross Papers, loc. cit.

14. Foreman, *Sequoyah*, p. 34.

15. *Constitution and Laws of the Cherokee Nation*, pp. 16–17.

16. Transcript of Ross's address at Tahlequah, September 12, 1839; Ross Papers, loc. cit.

17. Ibid.

18. Jackson's letter, written from the Hermitage in Nashville and dated October 5, 1839, is quoted in Dale and Litton, *Cherokee Cavaliers*, p. 17.

19. Woodward, *The Cherokees*, p. 235.

20. Ibid., pp. 236–37.

21. Sophia Sawyer to David Greene, January 6, 1840; Mission Papers, loc. cit.

22. Butler's comments on morale in the West, in Mission Papers, loc. cit.

23. Butrick to Ross, September 20, 1839; Ross Papers, loc. cit.

24. Grant Foreman describes at length the circumstances of Sequoyah's death in his *Sequoyah*, pp. 48–67.

25. Ross's report to the Council on October 5, 1857, is quoted in Foreman, *The Five Civilized Tribes*, p. 415.

26. Ross's address to the Council, October 4, 1860; Ross Papers, loc. cit.

27. Ross's message to the Council, July 2, 1861; Ross Papers, loc. cit.

28. Quoted by Daniel Ross in letter to W. P. Ross, April 3, 1866; Ross Papers, loc. cit.

29. Dale and Litton, *Cherokee Cavaliers*, p. 234.

SELECTED BIBLIOGRAPHY

Adair, James. *History of the American Indians.* London: E. & C. Dilly, 1775.

Allen, Ivan. *The Cherokee Nation.* Atlanta: Privately published, 1959.

Barrows, William. *The Indian's Side of the Indian Question.* Boston: Lothrop, 1888.

Bartram, William. *Travels.* Philadelphia: James & Johnson, 1791.

Bass, Althea. *Cherokee Messenger.* Norman: University of Oklahoma Press, 1936.

Bedford, Denton R. *Tsali.* San Francisco: Indian Historian Press, 1972.

Brainerd Mission Journal in manuscript, 1817–38. Mission Papers, Houghton Library, Harvard University.

Brown, Dee. "The Trail of Tears." *American History Illustrated,* Vol. VII, No. 3 (June 1972).

Brown, John P. *Old Frontiers.* Kingsport, Tenn.: Southern Publishers, Inc., 1938.

Buell, Augustus C. *History of Andrew Jackson.* 2 vols.; New York, Scribner, 1904.

Burt, Jesse, and Ferguson, R. B. *The Removal of the Cherokee Indians from Georgia.* Nashville: Abington Press, 1973.

Butrick, Daniel. Journal in manuscript, undated, Mission Papers, Houghton Library, Harvard University.

Carselowey, James Manford. *Cherokee Old Timers.* Adair, Okla.: Privately published, 1972.

Caton, J. L. *The Eastern Cherokees.* Knoxville: Privately printed, 1937.

Chamberlain, Paul H. *The Foreign Mission School.* Cornwall Historical Society Bulletins, Vol. I, No. 3 (1968).

Cherokee Indian Letters, Talks, and Treaties, 1786–1838 (in three parts). W.P.A. project No. 4341, Georgia Department of Archives and History, Atlanta.

Cherokee Phoenix. February 21, 1828 to May 31, 1834. National Archives, Records of the States of the United States, microfilm, reels 1a and 1b.

Chronicles of American Indian Protest. Greenwich, Conn.: Fawcett, 1971.

Coleman, Kenneth. *Georgia History in Outline.* Athens: University of Georgia Press, 1960.

Constitution and Laws of the Cherokee Nation. Tahlequah, Cherokee Nation West, 1852.

Corkran, David H. *Cherokee Frontier: Conflict and Survival.* Norman: University of Oklahoma Press, 1962.

Cotterill, R. S. *The Southern Indians.* Norman: University of Oklahoma Press, 1954.

Coulter, E. Merton. *Auraria: The Story of a Georgia Gold Mining Town.* Athens: University of Georgia Press, 1956.

Dale, Edward E., and Litton, Gaston. *Cherokee Cavaliers.* Norman: University of Oklahoma Press, 1939.

Downey, Fairfax. *Indian Wars of the United States Army, 1776–1865.* Garden City, N.Y.: Doubleday, 1963.

Duckett, Alvin L. *John Forsyth, Political Tactician.* Athens: University of Georgia Press, 1962.

Eaton, Rachel C. *John Ross and the Cherokee Indians.* Menasha, Wisc.: Bantam Publishing Co., 1914.

Elliott, Charles W. *Winfield Scott: The Soldier and the Man.* New York: Macmillan, 1937.

Engelman, Fred L. *The Peace of Christmas Eve.* New York: Harcourt, Brace & World, 1960.

Evarts, Jeremiah. *Speeches on the Passage of the Bill for the Removal of the Indians.* Boston: Perkins & Marvin, 1830.

Featherstonhaugh, George. *A Canoe Voyage up the Minnay Sotor.* London: R. Bentley, 1848.

Filler, L., and Guttmann, A. *The Removal of the Cherokee Nation.* Lexington, Mass.: Heath, 1962.

Fleischmann, Glen. *The Cherokee Removal, 1838.* New York: Franklin Watts, 1971.

Foreman, Carolyn T. *Indians Abroad.* Norman: University of Oklahoma Press, 1936.

Foreman, Grant. *Indian Removal.* New ed.; Norman: University of Oklahoma Press, 1953.

——. *Sequoyah.* Norman: University of Oklahoma Press, 1938.

——. *The Five Civilized Tribes.* Norman: University of Oklahoma Press, 1934.

——. "The Great Human Cattle Drive." *Daily Oklahoman* (Oklahoma City), April 18, 1837.

Gabriel, Ralph Henry. *Elias Boudinot, Cherokee, and His America.* Norman: University of Oklahoma Press, 1941.

Gaines, W. Craig. "The Cherokee Nation in the Civil War." *Loyal Legion Historical Journal,* Vol. XXX, No. 2 (February 1974).

Garland, Hamlin. *The Book of the American Indian.* New York: Harper, 1923.

Garrett, Franklin M. *Atlanta and Environs.* Vol. I. Athens: University of Georgia Press, 1954.

Gilbert, William H., Jr. *The Eastern Cherokees.* Washington, D.C.: Bureau of American Ethnology, Bulletin No. 133, 1943.

Gilmer, George R. *First Settlers of Upper Georgia.* Americus, Ga.: Americus Book Co., 1926.

Gold, Theodore S. *Historical Records of the Town of Cornwall.* Hartford: Case, Lockwood & Brainard, 1904.

Guttmann, Allen. *States' Rights and Indian Removal: The Cherokee Nation v. the State of Georgia.* Lexington, Mass.: Heath, 1965.

Harmon, George D. *Sixty Years of Indian Affairs: Political, Economic, and Diplomatic, 1789–1850.* Chapel Hill: University of North Carolina Press, 1941.

Hawkins, Benjamin. *Letters, 1798–1806.* Collections of the Georgia Historical Society, Vol. IX. Savannah, 1916.

Hicks, Elijah. Journal for the year 1837. Manuscript in possession of Sequoyah Historical Society, Claremore, Oklahoma.

Horan, James D. *The McKenney-Hall Portrait Gallery of American Indians.* New York: Crown, 1972.

Jackson, Andrew. *Correspondence of Andrew Jackson.* John Spencer Basset, ed. 6 vols., Washington: Carnegie Institution, 1927.

Jackson, Helen Hunt. *A Century of Dishonor.* New York: Harper, 1966.

James, Marquis. *A Life of Andrew Jackson.* New York: Bobbs-Merrill, 1938.

——. *The Raven: A Biography of Sam Houston.* New York: Bobbs-Merill, 1929.

Josephy, Alvin M., ed. *The Book of American Indians.* New York: American Heritage, 1961.

Kilpatrick, J. F., and Kilpatrick, A. G. *New Echota Letters.* Dallas: Southern Methodist University Press, 1968.

—— and ——. *The Shadow of Sequoyah.* Norman: University of Oklahoma Press, 1965.

Klein, Bernard, and Icolari, Daniel, eds. *Reference Encyclopedia of the American Indian.* New York: B. Klein, 1967.

Klephart, Horace. *The Cherokees of the Smoky Mountains.* Ithaca, N.Y.: Privately published, 1936.

Lane, Mills. *The Rambler in Georgia.* Savannah: Beehive Press, 1973.

Laws of the Cherokee Nation, adopted by the Council at various periods, published at the *Cherokee Advocate* office, Tahlequah, Cherokee Nation West, 1852.

Leech, Margaret. *Reveille in Washington.* New York: Harper, 1941.

Lumpkin, Wilson. *The Removal of the Cherokee Indians from Georgia.* 2 vols.; Savannah: Privately published, 1907.

Malone, Henry T. *Cherokees of the Old South.* Athens: University of Georgia Press, 1956.

McCullar, Bernice. *Georgia.* Montgomery, Ala.: Viewpoint Publications, 1968.

McKenney, Thomas L. *Sketches of Travels among the Northern and Southern Indians.* New York: Burgess, 1854.

—— and Hall, James. *Indian Tribes of North America.* 3 vols.; Edinburgh: John Grant, 1933.

McNickle, D'Arcy. *They Came Here First.* Philadelphia: Lippincott, 1949.

Memorial of the Cherokee People to Congress, submitted March 12, 1838. Indian Documents, Vol. IV, Document 11, microfilm, University of Oklahoma Library.

Mitchell, S. Augustus. *Traveler's Guide through the United States.* Philadelphia: Thomas, Cowperthwait Co., 1835.

Mooney, James. *Myths of the Cherokee.* Washington, D.C.: Bureau of American Ethnology, *Nineteenth Annual Report,* 1897–98. Facsimile reprint: Nashville: Charles Elder, 1972.

Morison, S., and Commager, H. S. *The Growth of the American Republic.* Vol. I. New York: Oxford, 1962.

Nammack, Georgiana C. *Fraud, Politics, and the Dispossession of the Indians.* Norman: University of Oklahoma Press, 1969.

National Intelligencer (Washington), June 13, 1835 to May 15, 1837. Library of Congress, microfilm, reels 54, 55, 56.

Niles' Weekly Register (Baltimore), selected issues between 1827 and 1838.

Overmyer, Grace. *America's First Hamlet.* New York: New York University Press, 1957.

Parker, Thomas Valentine. *The Cherokee Indians.* New York: Grafton Press, 1907.

Parris, John. *The Cherokee Story.* Asheville, N.C.: Stephens Press, 1950.

Payne, J. H. *John Howard Payne to His Countrymen.* Athens: University of Georgia Libraries, Miscellaneous Publication No. 2, 1961.

Perkerson, Medora Field. *White Columns in Georgia.* New York: Crown, 1952.

Phillips, Ulrich B. *Georgia and State Rights.* Washington, D.C.: U. S. Government Printing Office, 1902.

Pound, Merritt B. *Benjamin Hawkins—Indian Agent*. Athens: University of Georgia Press, 1951.

Rand, James H. *The North Carolina Indians*. Chapel Hill: University of North Carolina Press, 1913.

Rights, Douglas L. *The American Indian in North Carolina*. Winston-Salem: Blair, 1971.

Ross, Mrs. W. P. *The Life and Times of Hon. Wm. P. Ross of the Cherokee Nation*. Fort Smith, Ark.: Weldon & Williams, 1893.

Royce, Charles C. *The Cherokee Nation of Indians*. Washington, D.C.: Bureau of American Ethnology, *Fifth Annual Report*, 1887.

Ruskin, Gertrude M. *John Ross, Chief of an Eagle Race*. Decatur, Ga.: Privately printed, 1963.

Sharpe, J., ed. *The Cherokees Past and Present*. Cherokee, N.C.: Cherokee Publications, 1970.

Shepard, Edward M. *Martin Van Buren*. Boston: Houghton Mifflin, 1888.

Smith, James F. *The Cherokee Land Lottery*. New York: Harper, 1838.

Starkey, Marion. *The Cherokee Nation*. New York: Knopf, 1946.

Starr, Edward G. *History of Cornwall, Connecticut*. New Haven: Tuttle, Morehouse & Taylor, 1926.

Starr, Emmett. *Old Cherokee Families*. Norman: University of Oklahoma Foundation, 1968.

——. *History of the Cherokee Indians*. Oklahoma City: Warden, 1921.

Strong, William E. *The Story of the American Board*. Boston: Pilgrim Press, 1910.

Swanton, John R. *The Indian Tribes of North America*. Washington, D.C.: Bureau of American Ethnology, Bulletin No. 145, 1953.

——. *The Indians of the Southeastern United States*. Washington, D.C.: Bureau of American Ethnology, Bulletin No. 137, 1946.

——. *Early History of the Creek Indians and Their Neighbors*. Washington, D.C.: Bureau of American Ethnology, Bulletin No. 73, 1922.

Terrell, John Upton. *American Indian Almanac*. New York: World, 1971.

Tracy, Joseph. *A History of the American Board of Commissioners for Foreign Missions*. Worcester, Mass.: Spooner & Howland, 1840.

Underwood, Tom B. *The Story of the Cherokee People*. Knoxville: S. B. Newman Co., 1961.

Van Every, Dale. *Disinherited: The Lost Birthright of the American Indian*. New York: Morrow, 1966.

Vogel, Virgil J. *This Country Was Ours*. New York: Harper, 1972.

Wade, Forest C. *Cry of the Eagle*. Cumming, Ga.: Privately printed, 1969.

Walker, Robert Sparks. *Torchlights to the Cherokees*. New York: Macmillan, 1931.

Wardell, Morris J. *A Political History of the Cherokee Nation, 1838–1907*. Norman: University of Oklahoma Press, 1938.

Webb, Walter Prescott. *The Great Plains*. New York: Grosset & Dunlap, 1957.

Wilburn, H. C. *Chief Junaluska*. Asheville, N.C.: Stephens Press, 1951.

Wilkins, Thurman. *Cherokee Tragedy*. New York: Macmillan, 1970.

Wissler, Clark. *Indian Cavalcade*. New York: Sheridan House, 1938.

Woodward, Grace Steele. *The Cherokees*. Norman: University of Oklahoma Press, 1963.

Wooten, John Morgan. *Red Clay in History*. Cleveland, Tenn.: Privately printed, 1935.

Wright, Marcus J. *General Scott*. New York: Appleton, 1894.

Index